Lecture Notes in Computer Science   9893

Commenced Publication in 1973
Founding and Former Series Editors:
Gerhard Goos, Juris Hartmanis, and Jan van Leeuwen

Ladjel Bellatreche · Óscar Pastor
Jesús M. Almendros Jiménez
Yamine Aït-Ameur (Eds.)

Model and Data Engineering

6th International Conference, MEDI 2016
Almería, Spain, September 21–23, 2016
Proceedings

 Springer

Editors
Ladjel Bellatreche
LIAS/ISAE-ENSMA
Futuroscope Chasseneuil
France

Óscar Pastor
Department of Information Systems
 and Computation
Universitat Politècnica de València
Valencia
Spain

Jesús M. Almendros Jiménez
University of Almería
Almería
Spain

Yamine Aït-Ameur
IRIT/ENSEIHT
Toulouse
France

ISSN 0302-9743   ISSN 1611-3349   (electronic)
Lecture Notes in Computer Science
ISBN 978-3-319-45546-4   ISBN 978-3-319-45547-1   (eBook)
DOI 10.1007/978-3-319-45547-1

Library of Congress Control Number: 2016949099

LNCS Sublibrary: SL2 – Programming and Software Engineering

Printed on acid-free paper

This Springer imprint is published by Springer Nature
The registered company is Springer International Publishing AG Switzerland

Preface

In 2016, the 6th international conference on Model and Data Engineering (MEDI 2016) took place in Aguadulce, Almería, Spain, during September 21–23. The main objective of the conference is to bridge the gap between model engineering and data engineering and to allow researchers to discuss recent trends in the field. It follows the success of previous conferences held in Óbidos (Portugal, 2011), Poitiers (France, 2012), Armantea (Italy, 2013), Larnaca (Cyprus 2014), and Rhodes (Greece 2015).

MEDI 2016 received 62 submissions covering both model and data engineering activities. These papers focus on a wide spectrum of topics, covering fundamental contributions, applications and tool developments, and improvements. Each paper was reviewed by at least three reviewers and the Program Committee accepted 17 long papers and 10 short papers leading to an attractive scientific program.

For this year's event, two internationally recognized researchers were invited to give a talk. Schahram Dustdar from TU Wien, Austria gave a talk entitled "Towards Cyber-Physical-Social Systems - Towards a New Paradigm for Elastic Distributed Systems" reporting the progress achieved with distributed systems, and Ulrich Frank from Universität Duisburg-Essen, Germany gave a talk entitled "Multi-Perspective Enterprise Modelling and Future Enterprise Systems" reporting the progress achieved with enterprise modelling. We would like to thank the two invited speakers for their contributions to the success of MEDI 2016.

MEDI 2016 would not have succeeded without the deep investment and involvement of the Program Committee members and the external reviewers, who contributed to reviewing (more than 186 reviews) and selecting the best contributions. This event would not exist if authors and contributors did not submit their proposals. We address our thanks to every person, reviewer, author, Program Committee member, and organization committee member involved in the success of MEDI 2016.

The Easy Chair system was set up for the management of MEDI 2016, supporting submission, review, and volume preparation processes. It proved to be a powerful framework.

Finally, MEDI 2016 received the support of several sponsors, among them: the Department of Informatics of the University of Almeria, ISAE-ENSMA, and the LIAS laboratory. Many thanks for their support.

September 2016

Ladjel Bellatreche
Oscar Pastor
Jesús Manuel Almendros Jiménez
Yamine Aït Ameur

Organization

Program Committee

Alberto Abello	Universitat Politècnica de Catalunya, Bracelona, Spain
Yamine Ait-Ameur	IRIT/INPT-ENSEEIHT, Toulouse, France
Idir Ait-Sadoune	LRI - CentraleSupélec, Gif Sur Yvette, France
Joao Araujo	Universidade Nova de Lisboa, Lisbon, Portugal
Kamel Barkaoui	Cedric- Le Cnam, Paris, France
Ladjel Bellatreche	LIAS/ISAE-ENSMA, Poitiers, France
Alberto Belussi	University of Verona, Verona, Italy
Boualem Benatallah	University of New South Wales, Sydney, Australia
Sidi-Mohamed Benslimane	University of Sidi Bel Abbes, Sidi Belabes, Algeria
Jorge Bernardino	ISEC - Polytechnic Institute of Coimbra, Coimbra, Portugal
Matthew Bolton	University at Buffalo, State University of New York, USA
Alexander Borusan	TU Berlin/Fraunhofer FOKUS, Berlin, Germany
Omar Boussaid	ERIC Laboratory, University Louis Lumière, Lyon, France
Narhimene Boustia	Saad Dahlab University of Blida, Blida, Algeria
Sebastian Bress	TU Dortmund University, Dortmund, Germany
Nieves Brisaboa	Universidade da Coruña, Corunna, Spain
Francesco Buccafurri	DIIES - Università Mediterranea di Reggio Calabria, Italy
Rafael Caballero	Complutense University of Madrid, Madrid, Spain
Barbara Catania	DIBRIS-University of Genoa, Genoa, Italy
Damianos Chatziantoniou	Athens University of Economics and Business, Athens, Greece
Antonio Corral	University of Almeria, Almeria, Spain
Alain Crolotte	Teradata Corporation, USA
Alfredo Cuzzocrea	University of Trieste, Trieste, Italy
Florian Daniel	Politecnico di Milano, Milan, Italy
Alex Dellis	University of Athens, Athens, Greece
Rémi Delmas	ONERA, Centre de Toulouse, Toulouse, France
Nikolaos Dimokas	The Centre for Research & Technology Hellas - CERTH, Greece
George Evangelidis	University of Macedonia, Thessaloniki, Greece
Anastasios Gounaris	University of Macedonia, Thessaloniki, Greece
Emmanuel Grolleau	LIAS, ISAE-ENSMA, Poitiers, France
Brahim Hamid	IRIT- University of Toulouse, Toulouse, France
Mike Hinchey	Lero-the Irish Software Engineering Research Centre, Limerick, Ireland

Patrick Hung	University of Ontario Institute of Technology, Oshawa, Canada
Akram Idani	Laboratoire d'Informatique de Grenoble, Genoble, France
Luis Iribarne	University of Almería, Almería, Spain
Mirjana Ivanovic	University of Novi Sad, Serbia
Nadjet Kamel	University of Sétif, Sétif, Algeria
Dimitrios Katsaros	University of Thessaly, Volos, Greece
Selma Khouri	Ecole nationale Supérieure d'Informatique (ESI), Algiers, Algeria
Admantios Koumpis	University of Passau, Passau, Germany
Regine Laleau	Université Paris-Est Créteil, Créteil, France
Yves Ledru	Laboratoire d'Informatique de Grenoble, Grenoble, France
Carson Leung	University of Manitoba, Winnipeg, Canada
Zhiming Liu	Southwest University, Chongqing, China
Pericles Locoupoulos	The University of Manchester, Manchester, UK
Sofian Maabout	LaBRI, University of Bordeaux, Bordeaux, France
Dominique Mery	Université de Lorraine - LORIA, Nancy, France
Tadeusz Morzy	Poznan University, Poznan, Poland
Samir Ouchani	University of Luxembourg, Luxembourg
Meriem Ouederni	IRIT/INP Toulouse/ENSEEIHT, Toulouse, France
Yassine Ouhammou	LIAS/ENSMA, Poitiers, France
George Pallis	University of Cyprus, Cyprus
Ignacio Panach	Universitat de València, Valencia, Spain
Marc Pantel	IRIT/INPT, Université de Toulouse, Toulouse, France
Apostolos Papadopoulos	Aristotle University of Thessaloniki, Thessaloniki, Greece
George-Angelos Papadopoulos	University of Cyprus, Cyprus
Oscar Pastor-Lopez	Universitat Politècnica de València, Valencia, Spain
Jaroslav Pokorny	Charles University in Prague, Prague, Czech Republic
Elvinia Riccobene	University of Milan, Milan, Italy
Oscar Romero	Universitat Politècnica de Catalunya, Bracelona, Spain
Antonio Ruiz	University of Seville, Seville, Spain
Dimitris Sacharidis	TU Wien, Vienna, Austria
Houari Sahraoui	DIRO, Université de Montréal, Montréal, Canada
Klaus-Dieter Schewe	Software Competence Center Hagenberg, Hagenberg, Austria
Timos Sellis	RMIT, Melbourne, Australia
Neeraj Singh	INPT-ENSEEIHT/IRIT, University of Toulouse, Toulouse, France
Spyros Sioutas	Ionian University, Corfu, Greece
Tomás Skopal	Charles University in Prague, Prague, Czech Republic
Manolis Terrovitis	Institute for the Management of Information Systems, RC Athena, Athens, Greece
Riccardo Torlone	Roma Tre University, Italy
Ismail-Hakki Toroslu	Middle East Technical University Ankara, Turkey
Goce Trajcevski	Northwestern University, Evanston, Illinois, USA

Invited Papers

Towards Cyber-Physical-Social Systems - Towards a New Paradigm for Elastic Distributed Systems

Schahram Dustdar

Distributed Systems Group, TU Wien,
Argentinierstrasse 8/184-1, 1040, Vienna, Austria
dustdar@dsg.tuwien.ac.at

Emerging elastic systems are made of compositions of complex building blocks made of People, Processes, and Things. They span whole business processes, sometimes even go across organizations. They capture, manage, and adapt to the needs of all involved actors. However, elasticity brings challenges in the design and management of software, the involved human organizations, and business processes. In this talk I will address today's challenges in combining People, Processes, and Things to build complex elastic systems.

Keywords: Complex systems · Elasticity · Business processes · People · Things

Multi-Perspective Enterprise Modelling and Future Enterprise Systems

Ulrich Frank

University of Duisburg-Essen, Germany
ulrich.frank@uni-due.de

The realization of efficient business information systems requires the joint analysis and design of the software system and the corresponding action system. The complexity of both, software system and action system, recommends developing appropriate abstractions. Co-designing information system and action system requires involving people with different professional backgrounds and different agendas. Enterprise models address this need by integrating models of software systems with models of surrounding action systems. In his talk, Ulrich Frank will elucidate that in times of the digital transformation enterprise models play a crucial role for developing and implementing competitive business models. To illustrate this claim he will present the conceptual foundation and languages of Multi-Perspective Enterprise Modelling (MEMO), a method for enterprise modelling which has been developed in his group over the last twenty years. In addition, he will outline his current research on multilevel language architectures that enable a common representation of models and code. Thus, they provide the foundation of a new kind of self-referential enterprise systems that integrate enterprise software systems not only with models of themselves, but also with models of the context they operate in.

Keywords: Enterprise modelling · Conceptual foundation · Information system co-design

Contents

Towards OntoUML for Software Engineering: Transformation of Anti-rigid Sortal Types into Relational Databases

Zdeněk Rybola$^{(\boxtimes)}$ and Robert Pergl

Faculty of Information Technology, Czech Technical University in Prague,
Thákurova 9, 16000 Praha 6, Czech Republic
{zdenek.rybola,robert.pergl}@fit.cvut.cz

Abstract. OntoUML is an ontologically well-founded conceptual modelling language that distinguishes various types of classifiers and relations providing precise meaning to the modelled entities. Efforts arise to incorporate OntoUML into the Model-Driven Development approach as a conceptual modelling language for the PIM of application data. In our previous research, we outlined our approach to the transformation of an OntoUML PIM into an ISM of a relational database. In a parallel paper, we discuss the details of the transformation of Rigid Sortal Types, while this paper is focused on the transformation of Anti-rigid Sortal Types.

1 Introduction

Software engineering is a demanding discipline that deals with complex systems [1]. The goal of software engineering is to ensure high quality software implementation of these complex systems. To achieve this, various software development approaches have been developed.

Model-Driven Development (MDD) is a very popular approach in the recent years. It is a software development approach where the model is elevated to stand as the key artefact if the development process [2]. The software is described using various types of models specifying various aspects of the system ranging from the requirements, functions and data of the system to the architecture, design and deployment. Transformations between the individual models and the code are used to construct the final system.

The most usual part of the MDD approach used in the practice is the process of *forward engineering*: transformations of more abstract models into more specific ones. The most common use-case of such process is the development of conceptual data models and their transformation into source codes or database scripts.

To achieve a high-quality software system, high-quality expressive models are necessary to define the requirements for the system [1]. To use such models in the

This research was partially supported by grant by Student Grant Competition No. SGS16/120/OHK3/1T/18.

L. Bellatreche et al. (Eds.): MEDI 2016, LNCS 9893, pp. 1–15, 2016.
DOI: 10.1007/978-3-319-45547-1_1

Model-Driven Development approach, the model should define all requirements and all constraints of the system. Moreover, it should hold that more specific models persist the constraints defined in the more abstract models [3].

In 2005, OntoUML was formulated as a graphical modelling language for developing ontologically well-founded conceptual models [3]. It uses various types of entities and relations to distinguish their ontological meaning and semantics in the domain of interest, which increases the quality and precision of the models.

As OntoUML is domain-agnostic, it may be used for any domain and therefore, it can be used also for modelling the conceptual data models. In our research, we use OntoUML for modelling the PIM of the application data. On the other hand, as relational databases represent a very common type of data storage, we focus on the transformation into an ISM of a relational database. However, as OntoUML uses various types of entities and relations in the PIM, the transformation needs to deal with these aspects.

In our approach, we divide the transformation into three consecutive steps:

1. Transformation of an OntoUML PIM into a UML PIM including all the aspects defined by the OntoUML constructs.
2. Transformation of the UML PIM with the additional constraints into a PSM of a relational database including the required additional constraints.
3. Transformation of the PSM with the additional constraints into the ISM to define the constructs in the database to hold the data and maintain the constraints.

In the prequel paper [4], we outlined our approach to the transformation of OntoUML PIM into an ISM of a relational database. In the parallel paper [5], we discuss the details of the transformation of OntoUML Rigid Sortal types. This paper presents the parallel research focused on the transformation of OntoUML Anti-rigid Sortal types (Roles and Phases).

2   Background and Related Work

2.1   Used Methods

Model-Driven Development (MDD) is a software development approach where models are elaborated to define various aspects of the system on various levels of abstraction – ranging from CIM, to PIM, to PSM, to ISM – and transformations are used to construct other models or to generate the source code of the system [2, 6–8].

Unified Modeling Language (UML) [9,10] is a popular modelling language for creating and maintaining variety of models using diagrams and additional components [8]. In context of the data modelling, UML Class Diagram is the notation mostly used to define conceptual models of application data.

Object Constraint Language (OCL) [6,11] is a specification language that is part of the UML standard. In our approach, we use OCL invariants to define additional constraints derived from various OntoUML universal types.

2.2 OntoUML

OntoUML is a conceptual modelling language focused on building ontologically well-founded models. It was formulated in Guizzardi's PhD Thesis [3] as a lightweight extension of UML based on UML profiles.

The language is based on *Unified Foundational Ontology* (UFO), which is based on the cognitive science and modal logic and related mathematical foundations such as sets and relations. Thanks to this fact, it provides expressive and precise constructs for modellers to capture the domain of interest.

Being domain-agnostic, we believe that it may be suitable for conceptual modelling of application data in the context of MDD as it allows to create more expressive and precise conceptual models. These models can be transformed into its realization as a database schema containing additional constraints to maintain the constraints defined by the OntoUML universal types used in the conceptual model.

The following description of the OntoUML and UFO aspects is based on the Guizzardi's theses [3].

Universals and Individuals. UFO distinguishes two types of things. *Universals* are general classifiers of various objects and they are represented as classes in OntoUML (e.g. Person). They express the fact that we perceive an object *to be* the universal (e.g. Mark is a Person). *Individuals*, on the other hand, are the individual objects instantiating the universals (e.g. Mark, Dan, Kate).

Identity Principle. According to UFO, each individual always has a unique immutable identity, that serves to distinguish the individuals from each other. It is determined at the time the individual comes to existence, based on the *identity principle* of a universal the individual is instance of. Various universals use different identity principles (e.g. a Person is something else than a University); different individuals of the same universal have different identities (e.g. Mark is not Kate even when both are Persons).

Certain types of universals provide the identity principle to their instances – they are called *Sortal universals* – while other types of universals do not provide the identity principle – they are called *Non-Sortal universals*. In this paper, we discuss only the transformation of the Sortal types of universals, as they form the basis of models.

Rigidity. UFO and OntoUML are built on the notion of *worlds* coming from Modal Logic – various configurations of the individuals in various circumstances and contexts of time and space. *Rigidity* is a meta-property of the universals which defines the fact if the extension of a universal (i.e. the set of all instances of the universal) is world invariant [12]. UFO distinguishes *rigid universals* (their instances cannot cease being their instances without ceasing to exist), *anti-rigid universals* (their instances on some world are not their instances in some other world) and *semi-rigid universals* (they contain both rigid and anti-rigid instances in their extensions).

In this paper, we discuss the details of the transformation of Anti-rigid Sortal universals into the relational databases.

Generalization and Specialization. In UML, the generalization relation is used to define the relation between more abstract classifier – superclass – and more specific classifier – subclass; the subclass inherits the features of the superclass. In UFO and OntoUML, the generalization relation defines the inheritance of the *identity principle*; the identity principle is shared by the superclass and the subclasses. Therefore, an instance of the subclass is automatically also an instance of the superclass.

Moreover, the relation is rigid in UML – when an instance of the superclass is also an instance of the subclass, it cannot cease to be so without losing its identity – while in OntoUML, the relation may be anti-rigid: a single individual may be an instance of both the superclass and subclass in one world and it may be an instance of only the superclass in another world.

Kinds and Subkinds. The backbone of an OntoUML model is created by Kinds. *Kind* is a Rigid Sortal type of universals that defines the identity principle for its instances. *Subkind* is a Rigid Sortal universal type that does not define its own identity principle, but it inherits it from its *identity ancestor* (a Kind or another Subkind) and provides the inherited principle to its instances. In OntoUML, the Kind and Subkind universals are depicted as classes with the ≪*Kind*≫ and ≪*Subkind*≫ stereotypes, respectively. Example of a Kind is a Person with its Subkinds Man and Woman.

More details about the Kinds and Subkinds can be found in the parallel paper [5].

Roles. *Role* is an Anti-rigid Sortal universal type. It is used to define certain facts and properties of individuals when they are related to some other individuals – i.e. they play a role in the context defined by their relation to the other individual. As the Role universals are anti-rigid, the individuals can change their instantiation of the Role universal depending on the world.

A Role universal does not define its own identity principle but it inherits it through the generalization relation from another universal defining it – so called *identity bearer*. In fact, the generalization relation defines the required identity principle of individuals who may be instances of the Role. The generalization relations of Role universals do not form generalization sets as each Role represents a different relation and an individual (with a single identity) may play many different roles.

Furthermore, the Role universals are *relational-dependent*: for each Role universal there must be a mandatory relation to another universal – so called *relationship truthmaker* – so that all instances of the Role universal are related to some instances of the other universal.

In OntoUML, a Role universal is depicted by a class with the ≪*Role*≫ stereotype and a generalization relation to its identity bearer. Example of a Role universal may be a Student, which is a role of a Person when attending a University.

Phases. *Phase* is another Anti-rigid Sortal universal type. It is used to express various states of instances of a universal. These states may vary in properties or meaning, defining various stages in the history of the individual. As the Phase universals are anti-rigid, the individuals may change the phase they are an instance of.

The Phase universals do not define their own identity principle but they inherit it from another universal – identity bearer – through a generalization relation. This relation – similarly to the Roles – defines the required identity of the individuals that may be instances of the Phase.

Phase universals always form {complete, disjoint} generalization sets – so called *phase partitions* Due to the *completeness*, each instance of the ancestral universal must always be an instance of one of the phases in the phase partition, as well.

In OntoUML, a Phase universal is depicted as a class with the ≪*Phase*≫ stereotype and a generalization relation to its identity bearer which forms the Phase partition. Examples of Phase universals may be Child and Adult phases of a Person.

Other Universal Types. UFO and OntoUML define several other universal types such as Relator, Mixin, Quantity et al. However, they are out of scope of this paper.

3   Running Example

Our approach to the transformation of the Anti-rigid Sortal universal types from an OntoUML PIM into an ISM of a relational database is illustrated on a running example shown in Fig. 1. The model shows an excerpt of the domain of an automotive company. The company represented by the kind Company uses various vehicles as their company vehicles. This is expressed by the role Company vehicle of the general concept of vehicles – represented by the kind Vehicle – related to the company.

As a single vehicle can be registered as a company vehicle only in a single company, the maximal multiplicity of the company in relation to a company vehicle is equal to 1. On the other hand, a vehicle is perceived to be a company vehicle only when it is related to a company, therefore the minimal multiplicity of the relation is 1.

For the purposes of using the vehicles, it is important to distinguish between available vehicles and vehicles in maintenance represented by the

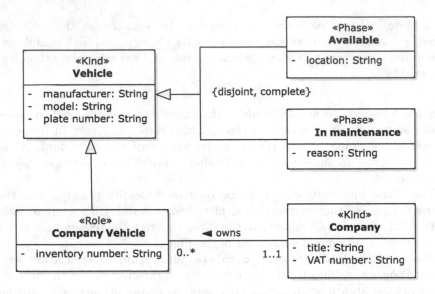

Fig. 1. OntoUML PIM of company vehicles

phases `Available` and `In maintenance`, respectively. For the available vehicles, their location is tracked, while for vehicles in maintenance, the malfunction is described.

4 Our Approach

Our approach to transformation of a PIM in OntoUML into its realization in a relational database consists of three steps which are discussed in the following sections:

1. Subsection 4.1 discusses the transformation of an OntoUML PIM into a UML PIM with additional constraints,
2. Subsection 4.2 discusses the transformation of the UML PIM into a PSM for relational database including the additional constraints,
3. Subsection 4.3 discusses the transformation of the PSM and the additional constraints into an ISM of the relational database.

Although we may formulate a direct transformation from OntoUML into ISM of the relational database, the transformation via an auxiliary UML model enables to leverage all the available knowledge (e.g. [13,14]) and tools for transformation of a UML PIM into database models such as Enterprise Architect[1]. Also, various optimizations and refactoring may be applied to the models in each step depending on the domain – e.g. phase classes without attributes may

---

[1] http://www.sparxsystems.com.au/products/ea/.

be transformed into a simple enumeration value in its identity bearer. However, these optimizations are not discussed here.

In the approach presented here, we assume the situation where all attributes of the model classes have multiplicities [1..1] as it is the most common and complicated case. In Sect. 5, we discuss how the situation changes for different multiplicity values.

4.1   Transformation of OntoUML PIM into UML PIM

This phase of the transformation deals with the transformation of various types of universals in an OntoUML model into a pure UML model while preserving all the semantics defined by the universal types.

As various OntoUML universal types define different semantics, they are also transformed in a different manner. We use OCL to define the additional constraints required to preserve the semantics derived from the OntoUML constructs. The basic principles of the transformation were discussed in [4]. In this paper, we discuss only the transformation of Anti-rigid Sortal types (Roles and Phases) and their variants.

Kinds and Subkinds. As discussed in [5], the Kinds and Subkinds from the OntoUML PIM are transformed into standard UML classes in the UML PIM. As the generalization relation between the Subkinds and their identity bearer is rigid, also the generalization sets are transformed into standard generalization sets in the UML PIM.

Roles. The Role universals from the OntoUML PIM may be transformed into standard UML classes in the UML PIM, as well. However, the generalization relation of a Role universal to its identity bearer in OntoUML is anti-rigid – an instance of the identity bearer may be or not be instance of the role depending on the world. Because in UML the relation is rigid, it can not be used for realization of the relation from the OntoUML PIM. Instead, the relation must be transformed into an association with the is a meaning to enable the instance of the identity bearer to change its relation to an instance of the Role. This association has always the following strictly defined multiplicities:

– The identity bearer's class's multiplicity is 1..1, as in fact this binds the identity of the role instance.
– The role's class's multiplicity is 0..1 as the object's role is optional.

The relation to the relationship truthmaker can be taken to the UML PIM unchanged from the OntoUML PIM, as it is a standard association between two classifiers.

The applied transformation for the Role in the running example is shown in Fig. 2.

Fig. 2. UML PIM of the role of a company vehicle

Phases. Similar to the Role universals, the Phase universals from the OntoUML PIM can be transformed into standard UML classes in the UML PIM. Also, similar to the Roles, the anti-rigid generalization relation to the identity bearer from the OntoUML PIM must be transformed into an association in the UML PIM. However, as the Phases form the phase partition, they must be treated together.

There are two general ways to realize the phase partition in the UML PIM discussed in the following paragraphs.

Abstract Phase. The whole phase partition may be transformed into a generalization set of an abstract phase class as shown in Fig. 3. Then, the anti-rigid relation between the identity bearer and its phase is realized by the association between the identity bearer's class and the abstract phase's class. The multiplicity of this association is 1..1 at both ends, as the phase instance cannot exist on its own – it does not have own identity – and each instance of the identity bearer must be in some phase – the partition is complete. The disjoint property is kept by the generalization set of the phases in the UML model.

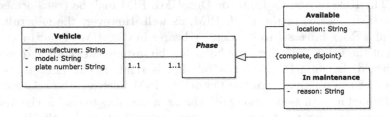

Fig. 3. UML PIM of the phases of a vehicle realized by an abstract phase

Exclusive Associations. The phase partition may also be transformed into a set of associations between the identity bearer's class and the classes of the individual phases as shown in Fig. 4. Such associations would have multiplicity 1..1 at the identity bearer's end, while the other ends would have multiplicities 0..1, as the instance of the identity bearer can be only in one phase. However, to maintain the exclusivity defined by the {complete, disjoint} phase partition, a special constraint must be defined. Such constraint can be defined as shown in Algorithm 1.

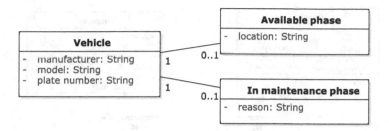

Fig. 4. UML PIM of the phases of a vehicle realized by exclusive associations

---

Algorithm 1. OCL invariant for the exclusivity of vehicle phases in the PIM

---

context v : Vehicle **inv** exclusivePhaseAssociations :
v . available <> OclVoid **xor** v . in_maintenance <> OclVoid

---

4.2 Transformation of PIM into PSM

The second step is the transformation of the UML PIM into a PSM of a relational database. The UML Data Model profile – an extension to the UML class diagrams – is used in the examples to define the structure of relational databases in UML [15].

In general, when performing transformation from a UML PIM into a PSM of a relational database, classes are transformed into database tables, class's attributes into table columns and associations into FOREIGN KEY constraints. Also, PRIMARY KEY constraints are defined for unique identification of individual rows in the tables.

Roles. In UML PIM, the Role universals are represented as standard classes with an association to the class of their identity bearer. Therefore, the classes can be simply transformed into database tables.

The relation between the role's class and its identity bearer's class is transformed into standard reference between the tables. As the relation is one-to-one relationship, the direction is determined by the minimal multiplicity 1 of the identity bearer, as discussed in [16]. Therefore, the reference and the FOREIGN KEY constraint are defined in the table of the role referring to the table of the identity bearer. Furthermore, as the role is existentially-dependent on the identity bearer and the maximal multiplicity is 1, it is considered to be a weak entity and therefore, the reference should also be part of the PRIMARY KEY to make it unique. Example of this transformation for the running example is shown in Fig. 5, where the relation between the Vehicle and the Company_vehicle is realized by the FOREIGN KEY on the vehicle_id column.

Similar transformation is used for the relation between the role and the relationship truthmaker. However, the only strictly defined multiplicity derived from the Role universal is the minimal multiplity 1 of the truthmaker. Therefore, the

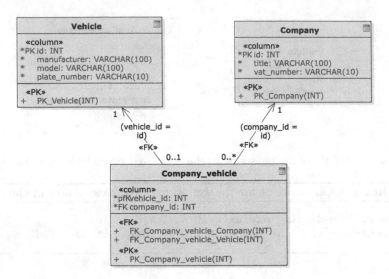

Fig. 5. PSM of the role of a company vehicle

direction of the reference must be determined according to the other multiplicities as discussed in [14]. For the running example shown in Fig. 5, the reference is defined in the Company_vehicle as it can be defined with the NOT NULL constraint to enforce the minimal multiplicity and no other constraints are needed.

Phases. In the UML PIM, the phases are represented by standard classes. Therefore, they are transformed into standard database tables in the PSM. However, the transformation of the phase partition depends on the variant used for its representation in the UML PIM.

When the phase partition is represented by the *exclusive associations* as shown in Fig. 4, all the classes can be transformed into standard database tables and all the associations into standard references. The suggested direction of the reference is from the phase tables to the identity bearer table, as shown in Fig. 6. Otherwise, there would be multiple references in the same table, while only one of them can be used because of the exclusivity constraint defined by the exclusivePhaseAssociations invariant shown in Algorithm 1. This constraint must be transformed into a constraint on the tables as shown in Algorithm 2.

When the phase partition is represented by the *abstract phase* and its generalization set of phases in the UML PIM, as shown in Fig. 3, they are transformed the same way as the generalization sets of Subkinds, as discussed in the parallel paper [5]:

Single Table. In this variant, a single table is used for the combination of all the phases and the abstract phase. It is possible to define the reference for the relation between the abstract phase and the identity bearer. However, this variant

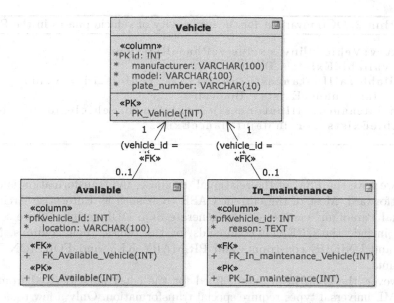

Fig. 6. PSM of the phases of a vehicle realized by exclusive references

would lead to complicated phase-specific constraints (e.g. the NOT NULL constraints for phase columns) and the exclusivity constraint as discussed in more details in [5]. Therefore, we would not recommend this variant and we will not discuss it any further.

Subclasses' Tables. In this variant, a separate table is used for each phase class. This supports independent definition of constraints for individual phases. The problem of duplicating superclass attributes discussed in [5] is overcome by the fact that the abstract phase's class contains no attributes. However, the relation between each phase and the identity bearer must be realized the same way as in the case of the *exclusive associations* discussed above.

Superclass and Subclasses' Tables. In this variant, separate tables are used for the abstract phase and for each of the phases. It is possible to define the reference between the abstract phase and the identity bearer. However, exclusive references between the abstract phase and the individual phases would also be needed to define as discussed above. Beside that, the table of the abstract phase would require to be joined in the queries even when not containing any useful data. Therefore, we would not recommend this variant and we will not discuss it any further.

4.3 Transformation of PSM into ISM

The last step is the transformation of the PSM of a relational database into an ISM consisting of SQL scripts for the creation of the database tables, constraints and other constructs.

Algorithm 2. OCL invariant for the exclusivity of vehicle phases in the PSM

```
context v:Vehicle inv exclusivePhaseReferences:
def: availableExists: Boolean =
   Available.allInstances()−>exist(a|a.vehicle_id = v.id)
def: inMaintenanceExists: Boolean =
   In_maintenance.allInstances()−>exist(m|m.vehicle_id = v.id)
availableExists xor inMaintenanceExists
```

As we have the PSM of the relational database, the transformation is quite straightforward. Most of the current CASE tools such as Enterprise Architect or Visual Paradigm[2] can be used to generate SQL DDL scripts. These scripts usually include the CREATE commands for the tables, their columns, NOT NULL and UNIQUE constraints and PRIMARY KEY and FOREIGN KEY constraints.

However, the OCL invariants defined for the constraints derived from the OntoUML universal types require special transformation. Only a few tools currently seem to offer transformation of such constraints – e.g. DresdenOCL[3], OCLE[4] and USE[5].

There are various options for the realization of OCL invariants from the PSM: using database views to access only valid data; using CHECK constraints to check all the values stored in a table; or using triggers to prevent violating the constraint before and after various DML operations. These options can be used for the realization of the special multiplicity constraints, as discussed in [14], as well as for the constraints derived from the OntoUML universal types. In the following, we discuss only the example of the realization using the database views.

The only constraint derived from the OntoUML Anti-rigid Sortal universal types requiring a special realization is the exclusivity constraint defined in Algorithm 2. Its realization using database views is shown in Algorithm 3. The view `Valid_Vehicles` is used to query only such rows from the `Vehicle` table that have a row either in the `Available` or in the `In_maintenance` table referring to it. Therefore, using this view, we can access data about such vehicles that are either available or in maintenance; the vehicles having invalid data are hidden from the view.

To query the data of valid *available* phases, the view `Valid_Available` can be used, which filters out invalid phases using the `Valid_Vehicles` view. By analogy, the view `Valid_In_maintenance` can be used to query only the valid phases of *in maintenance*.

---

[2] http://www.visual-paradigm.com/.

[3] https://github.com/dresden-ocl.

[4] http://lci.cs.ubbcluj.ro/ocle/.

[5] http://sourceforge.net/projects/useocl/.

Algorithm 3. Database views to query only valid data from the `Vehicle`, `Available` and `In_maintenance` tables

```
CREATE VIEW Valid_Vehicles AS
SELECT * FROM Vehicle v WHERE
    (EXISTS (SELECT 1 FROM Available a
        WHERE a.vehicle_id = v.id)
        AND NOT EXISTS (SELECT 1 FROM In_maintenance m
            WHERE m.vehicle_id = v.id))
    OR
    (NOT EXISTS (SELECT 1 FROM Available a
        WHERE a.vehicle_id = v.id)
        AND EXISTS (SELECT 1 FROM In_maintenance m
            WHERE m.vehicle_id = v.id))

CREATE VIEW Valid_Available AS
SELECT * FROM Valid_Vehicles v
    JOIN Available a ON (v.id = a.vehicle_id)

CREATE VIEW Valid_In_maintenance AS
SELECT * FROM Valid_Vehicles v
    JOIN In_maintenance m ON (v.id = m.vehicle_id)
```

All of these views are updatable – meeting the criteria for an *updatable view* – and therefore they can be defined WITH CHECK OPTION and used when manipulating the vehicles to prevent creating vehicles without a single phase record. However, it would not be possible to insert data into any of the views, as inserting into the `Valid_Vehicles` would violate the view condition, while inserting into the `Valid_Available` or `Valid_In_maintenance` would violate the FOREIGN KEY constraint. Therefore, the FOREIGN KEY constraint must be defined as *deferrable*, so it is checked at the end of the transaction and not at the time of execution of the command. Then it is possible to first insert data into the `Valid_Available` or `Valid_In_maintenance` views, while referring to a not-existing vehicle, and then to insert data into the `Valid_Vehicles` view.

However, as the vehicle data can still be manipulated directly in the tables and thus violating the constraints, it is necessary to strictly insist on using the views. Otherwise, CHECK constraints or triggers might be defined to enforce the constraint in a similar way as discussed in [14].

5   Discussion

As mentioned in Subsect. 4.3, our approach to the realization of the OCL constraints derived from the OntoUML Anti-rigid Sortal universal types is inspired by the approach discussed in [14]. In that paper, the authors use database views and triggers to maintain the database consistency in context of special multiplicities defined in a conceptual model. The authors also provide some experiments comparing the efficiency of DML operations and queries with and without such constraints, proving that their realization guarantees database consistency for the price of only slight decrease of efficiency.

The OCL constraints derived from the OntoUML Anti-rigid Sortal universal types are based on multiplicities – either on the exclusivity of relationships or on the mandatory source entity multiplicity. Therefore, the results of the experiments discussed in [14] apply even for such OntoUML constraints discussed in this paper. Still, some separate experiments should be executed to prove that.

In this paper, we discussed the constraints for the most common situation of mandatory attributes (attribute multiplicity [1..1]). In case of other multiplicities, the transformation vary and some of the constraints may be simplified. Moreover, in each transformation step, certain simplification of the model can be made based on the domain and other factors.

6   Conclusion

In this paper, we introduced our approach to the transformation of an OntoUML PIM of application data into an ISM of a relational database. This transformation is separated into three sequential steps: a transformation of OntoUML PIM into a UML PIM, a transformation of the UML PIM into a PSM for relational database and a transformation of the PSM into an ISM of a relational database.

During these transformations, specific relations and additional constraints are defined to maintain the semantics defined by the OntoUML universal types. In this paper, we discussed details of the transformation of Anti-rigid Sortal universal types – Roles and Phases. When transforming the roles, the transformation of the generalization relation to its identity bearer is discussed. When transforming the phases, the transformation of the phase partition is discussed with several options. All the situations are described using a running example of a simple OntoUML PIM of company vehicles.

As a following research, similar research should be elaborated for the Non-sortal universal types – e.g. Category, Mixin, RoleMixin – and relational constructs – part-whole relations, Relators, etc. Also, experiments should be carried out to study the finer points of individual variants of the constraints realization.

References

1. Ghezzi, C., Jazayeri, M., Mandrioli, D.: Fundamentals of Software Engineering, 2nd edn. Prentice Hall PTR, Upper Saddle River (2002)
2. Mellor, S.J., Clark, A.N., Futagami, T.: Model-driven development. IEEE Softw. **20**(5), 14 (2003)
3. Guizzardi, G.: Ontological Foundations for Structural Conceptual Models, vol. 015. University of Twente, Enschede (2005)
4. Rybola, Z., Pergl, R.: Towards OntoUML for software engineering: introduction to the transformation of OntoUML into relational databases. In: EOMAS 2016. LNBIP. Springer, Ljubljana, Slovenia (2016, in press)

5. Rybola, Z., Pergl, R.: Towards OntoUML for software engineering: transformation of rigid sortal types into relational databases. In: Proceedings of FedCSIS 2016. IEEE, Gdansk, Poland (2016, in press)
6. Arlow, J., Neustadt, I.: UML 2.0 and the Unified Process: Practical Object-Oriented Analysis and Design, 2nd edn. Addison-Wesley Professional, Boston (2005)
7. Stahl, T., Völter, M., Bettin, J., Haase, A., Helsen, S.: Model-Driven Software Development: Technology, Engineering, Management. Wiley, Chichester (2013)
8. da Silva, A.R.: Model-driven engineering: a survey supported by the unified conceptual model. Comput. Lang. Syst. Struct. **43**, 139–155 (2015)
9. OMG: UML 2.4.1. http://www.omg.org/spec/UML/2.4.1/. Accessed 08 Feb 2016
10. OMG: UML 2.5. http://www.omg.org/spec/UML/2.5/. Accessed 08 Feb 2016
11. OMG: Object constraint language (OCL), version 2.4, February 2014. http://www.omg.org/spec/OCL/2.4/. Accessed 23 Feb 2016
12. Guizzardi, G., Wagner, G., Guarino, N., van Sinderen, M.: An ontologically well-founded profile for UML conceptual models. In: Persson, A., Stirna, J. (eds.) CAiSE 2004. LNCS, vol. 3084, pp. 112–126. Springer, Heidelberg (2004). doi:10.1007/978-3-540-25975-6_10
13. Kuskorn, W., Lokcharoen, S.: An adaptive translation of class diagram to relational database. In: International Conference on Information and Multimedia Technology, ICIMT 2009, pp. 144–148, December 2009
14. Rybola, Z., Richta, K.: Possible realizations of multiplicity constraints. Comput. Sci. Inf. Syst. **10**(4), 1621–1646 (2013). WOS: 000327912000006
15. Sparks, G.: Database Modeling in UML. http://www.eetimes.com/document.asp?doc_id=1255046. Accessed 02 Feb 2016
16. Richta, K., Rybola, Z.: Transformation of relationships from UML/OCL to SQL. In: Zborník príspevkov prezentovaných na konferencii ITAT, ITAT 2011, vol. 11. Terchová, Slovakia, University of P. J. Šafárik, Košice, Slovakia, September 2011

Automatic Generation of Ecore Models for Testing ATL Transformations

Jesús M. Almendros-Jiménez[✉] and Antonio Becerra-Terón

Department of Informatics, University of Almería, 04120 Almería, Spain
{jalmen,abecerra}@ual.es

Abstract. Model transformation testing is crucial to detect incorrect transformations. Buggy transformations can lead to incorrect target models, either violating target meta-model requirements or more complex target model properties. In this paper we present a tool for testing ATL transformations. This tool is an extension of a previously developed tool for testing XML-based languages. With this aim an Ecore to XML Schema transformation is defined which makes to automatically generate random Ecore models possible. These randomly generated Ecore models are used to test ATL transformations. Properties to be tested are specified by OCL constraints, describing input and output conditions on source and target models, respectively.

1 Introduction

Model transformation is a key component of *Model Driven Engineering (MDE)* [19]. Several transformation languages (*ATL, QVT, AGG, VIATRA, Fujaba*, among others) have been proposed to define transformations making the definition of *(M2M) Model to Model* and *(M2T) Model to Text* transformations possible. Transformation languages work on source and target meta-models establishing a mapping from source to target models. Transformation programs are based on rules and range from imperative to declarative software.

Testing [17] is essential for ensuring software quality. The automation of testing enables the programmer to reduce time of testing and also makes to repeat testing after each modification to a program possible. A testing tool should determine whether a test is passed or failed. When failed, the testing tool should provide evidences of failures, that is, counterexamples of the properties to be checked. Additionally, a testing tool should generate test cases automatically [2]. Fully random generation of tests could not be suitable for an effective and efficient tool. Distribution of test data should be controlled, by providing user-defined test cases, that is, data distribution should be put under the human tester's control.

Testing of model transformations has been studied in several recent works [3–9,11,12,14,16,18]. The quoted works have basically the same goal: specification of properties on transformations and meta-models in order to ensure correct

---

This work was supported by the EU (FEDER) and the Spanish MINECO Ministry (*Ministerio de Economíay Competitividad*) under grant TIN2013-44742-C4-4-R.

L. Bellatreche et al. (Eds.): MEDI 2016, LNCS 9893, pp. 16–30, 2016.
DOI: 10.1007/978-3-319-45547-1_2

transformations. Properties on transformations range from termination, determinism, rule independence, rule applicability and reachability of states, while properties on meta-models establish input (respectively, output) properties on source (respectively, target) meta-models, as well as input-output properties on both source and target models. Here we will focus on meta-model properties, and our goal will be to build a testing tool able to detect buggy transformations from automatically generated test models.

In our research group we have developed a tool [1] to test XML-based applications. In particular, this tool has been previously used to test XQuery programs from automatically generated XML data. In this paper, we adapt the tool to model based transformation languages. In particular, we are able to automatically generate *Ecore* models, which are the selected format of ATL (ATLAS transformation language) [13] programs for source/target models. Additionally, we have extended the tool to test ATL applications, in such a way that given a source meta-model S, an ATL transformation TR, a set of input properties IP on the source meta-model and a set of output properties OP on the target meta-model, the tool is able to determine whether the output models of TR satisfy OP for each randomly generated test model of the meta-model S satisfying IP. In case of success, that is, each output model of TR satisfies the properties OP, then the tool answers "Ok", otherwise the tool shows counterexamples, that is, input test models which do not satisfy OP, together with the result of the transformation for the counterexamples.

Test models are randomly generated from source meta-models in an automatic way. The input of the testing is an Ecore source meta-model which is automatically transformed into an XML Schema. The resulting XML Schema is used by the tool to generate XML data tests. However, the human tester has to select the XML elements and attributes, and the number and value of them, for which test cases are randomly generated. In terms of Ecore models, the human tester has to prune the meta-model (similarly to [15]), selecting classes, attributes and associations to which generate instances. The idea is to select the smallest subset of the input meta-model that is relevant for the transformation (i.e., the classes, attributes and associations accessed by the transformation code). Thus, even when the generation of test models is fully random, the human tester can control the size and diversity of test models. The choice depends on the transformation to be tested as well as the input/output properties to be checked. Test models are randomly generated as combinations of values and a number of classes, attributes and associations, enabling a high level of diversity in test cases. Since the number of test cases can be potentially infinite, the human tester can select a limit of the size, and moreover, the test cases are generated in increasing size. In fact, most of ATL programming bugs can be detected from a small set of test models in a short time. The tool has been designed to interrupt testing when the output property is not satisfied by a test model, and thus even when the number of test models selected by the human tester can be bigger, the tool stops when a counterexample has been found.

The tool (i.e., Ecore to XML Schema transformation, test models generation, and property-based testing) has been implemented in the XQuery language. We use the *BaseX* XQuery interpreter to test ATL transformations. We have integrated the ATL EMFTVM virtual machine in XQuery, using the Java binding mechanism, in order to execute ATL transformations from XQuery and to test input/output properties.

The structure of the paper is as follows. Section 2 will define the transformation of Ecore meta-models to XML Schemas and will show examples of randomly generated test models. Section 3 will report several examples of ATL transformation testing. Section 4 will describe related work. Finally, Sect. 5 will present conclusions and future work.

2 Automatic Generation of Ecore Models

The process of automatic generation of Ecore test models is as follows. Firstly, the Ecore meta-model is transformed into an XML Schema. Next, the human tester selects items (elements and attributes) and number of items of the XML Schema (setting values for *minOccurs/maxOccurs* of elements, and values optional/required in *use* of attributes), and provides values for each type of the XML Schema (adding values to the *enumeration* section of each type). Finally, the test case generator reports random combinations of values and items.

With this aim, an Ecore to XML Schema transformation has been defined. Basically, *EClass* elements are mapped to *XML elements*, and *EAttribute* elements are mapped to *XML attributes*. Moreover, *EReference* elements are mapped to *XML elements* and *XML Attributes*. In the case of *EReference* elements with *containment* set to *true* the are mapped to *XML elements*, otherwise to *XML attributes*. In the second case, *XML Attributes* of XML Schemas have been modified enabling *minOccurs* and *maxOccurs* attributes. A similar solution was previously adopted in other works[1]. Thus XML Schemas have been extended to cover with Ecore references. Additionally, Ecore *lowerBound* and *upperBound* have been mapped to XML Schema *minOccurs* and *maxOccurs*, respectively. Finally, Ecore *datatypes* are mapped to XML *datatypes*.

For example, the *class* meta-model of the well-known *Class2Relational* transformation[2] of the *ATL Zoo*, is translated into the XML Schema of Fig. 1.

There are two types of XML attributes. The first one is the standard XML attribute: `<xs:attribute name="name" type="nameType" use= "required"/>` and the second one is a reference to an element: `<xs:attribute name="super" type="Class" class="yes" minOccurs="1" maxOccurs="unbounded"/>` in which *class* = *"yes"* means that *type* is a reference to an XML element (in the example, the XML element *Class*), and *minOccurs* and *maxOccurs* represent the number of allowed references. The test case generator will generate values *//@Class.1*, *//@Class.2*, etc., of references to elements. For instance, this is an example of test model generated by the tool:

---

[1] https://www.eclipse.org/modeling/emf/docs/overviews/XMLSchemaToEcoreMapping.pdf.

[2] http://www.eclipse.org/atl/atlTransformations/#Class2Relational.

```
<xs:complexType name="attr">
  <xs:attribute name="name" type="nameType" use="required"/>
  <xs:attribute name="type" type="Classifier" class="yes"
                minOccurs="1" maxOccurs="1"/>
  <xs:attribute name="multiValuod" type="multiValuedType" use="required"/>
</xs:complexType>
<xs:element name="xmi:XMI">
  <xs:complexType><xs:sequence>
      <xs:element name="Classifier" minOccurs="1" maxOccurs="unbounded">
      <xs:complexType>
      <xs:attribute name="name" type="nameType" use="required"/>
      </xs:complexType></xs:element>
      <xs:element name="DataType" minOccurs="0" maxOccurs="unbounded">
      <xs:complexType>
      <xs:attribute name="name" type="nameType" use="required"/>
      </xs:complexType></xs:element>
      <xs:element name="Class" minOccurs="1" maxOccurs="unbounded">
      <xs:complexType>
      <xs:attribute name="name" type="nameType" use="required"/>
      <xs:attribute name="super" type="Class" class="yes"
                    minOccurs="1" maxOccurs="unbounded"/>
      <xs:attribute name="isAbstract" type="isAbstractType" use="required"/>
      <xs:sequence>
      <xs:element ref="attr" minOccurs="1" maxOccurs="unbounded"/>
      </xs:sequence>
      </xs:complexType></xs:element>
  </xs:sequence></xs:complexType>
</xs:element>
```

Fig. 1. XML Schema of class meta-model

```
<xmi:XMI>
  <Classifier name="Default"/>
  <Class super="//@Class.1" isAbstract="true" name="Default"/>
  <Class isAbstract="true" name="Default">
    <attr type="//@Classifier.0" multiValued="true" name="Default"/>
  </Class>
</xmi:XMI>
```

The test case generator of [1] has been modified to include the second kind of attributes, and values of references to elements. The tool generates Ecore models of increasing size. Basically, starting from an initial step (step *0*) with minimal models according to *minOccurs* values for elements and *optional/required* for attributes, it generates new models in each step (step *n + 1*) adding new attributes and elements to models of step *n*, up to *maxOccurs* for elements and *required* for attributes is reached. In other words, the test case generator adds new classes, attributes and associations in each step, increasing the size of Ecore models. Additionally, it randomly takes values for attributes from the *enumeration* section. These values are manually added by the human tester, and the test case generator randomly combines values to produce different models. In the case a certain type is not defined in the *enumeration* section, the test case generator assigns as values *"Default"* for strings, *"0"* for numbers and *"true"* for Boolean. The number of steps *n* is a parameter of the tester, in order to limit the size of test models. The human tester can play with this parameter generating a large number of models. Also, the human tester can play with *minOccurs* (and *maxOccurs*) values for XML elements/XML Attributes, in order to generate a large number of classes and associations for each model. Playing with steps and

```
module Book2Publication;
create OUT : Publication from IN : Book;

rule Book2Publication1 {
  from
     b : Book!Book (b.getSumPages() > 100 and b.keyword='Biology')
  to
     out : Publication!Publication (
       title <- b.title,
       authors <- b.getAuthors(),
       nbPages <- b.getSumPages()
       keyword <- b.keyword)
}
rule Book2Publication2 {
  from
     b : Book!Book (b.getSumPages() < 100 and b.keyword='Romance')
  to
     out : Publication!Publication (
       title <- b.title,
       authors <- b.getAuthors(),
       nbPages <- b.getSumPages(),
       keyword <- b.keyword)
}
```

Fig. 2. *Book2Publication* transformation

minOccurs, the human tester can have a stronger confidence about the soundness of the program.

3   Testing of ATL Transformations

Let us consider the following (buggy) transformation *Book2Publication* defined by the code of Fig. 2. The transformation tries to map *book* into *publication* classes with two rules for *Biology* and *Romance* books, respectively. *Book* class is defined as a set of *chapters* each one with a *title*, an *author* and a number of pages *nbPages*. The transformation summarizes *book*s as a *publication* in which *title* is the same, *author*s of *chapters* are concatenated and the total number of pages is computed. ATL helpers *getAuthors* and *getSumPages* have been defined with this end (omitted in the Figure). However, the mapping is only required for a total number of pages greater than 100.

The human tester can now define OCL constraints for the transformation (see Fig. 3). The OCL constraints on the source meta-model describe the required properties on the source model. In this case, source model constraints require that all the *book*s and *chapters* have a title, and all the *book*s have a *keyword*. The target meta-model OCL constraints describe the required properties on the target model. They require that the *title* of *publication*s is not empty, all the *publication*s are Biology or Romance *publication*s, and finally, the number of pages *nbPages* is greater than 100. The Ecore source meta-model and the corresponding XML Schema are shown in Figs. 4 and 5, respectively.

The human tester can now edit the XML Schema in order to select relevant elements (XML elements and attributes) and values for the transformation and testing. In the *Book2Publication* transformation, the elements *book* and *chapters*

```
(1)  Book!Book->allInstances()->select(b | b.title->size()=0)->isEmpty()
(2)  Book!Chapter->allInstances()->select(ch | ch.title->size()=0)->isEmpty()
(3)  Book!Book->allInstances()->select(b | b.keyword->size()=0)->isEmpty()
(4)  Publication!Publication->allInstances()->
         select(p | p.title->size()=0) >isEmpty()
(5)  Publication!Publication->allInstances()->
     select(p | not(p.keyword='Biology' or p.keyword='Romance'))->isEmpty()
(6)  Publication!Publication->allInstances()->
         select(p | not(p.nbPages>100))->isEmpty()
```

Fig. 3. Input and output properties of *Book2Publication* transformation

```
<eClassifiers xsi:type="Ecore:EClass" name="Book">
<eStructuralFeatures
  xsi:type="Ecore:EAttribute" name="title" lowerBound="1" eType="EString"/>
<eStructuralFeatures
  xsi:type="Ecore:EAttribute" name="keyword" eType="EString"/>
<eStructuralFeatures
  xsi:type="Ecore:EReference" name="chapters" upperBound="-1"
  eType="#//Chapter" containment="true" eOpposite="#//Chapter/book"/>
</eClassifiers>
<eClassifiers xsi:type="Ecore:EClass" name="Chapter">
<eStructuralFeatures
  xsi:type="Ecore:EAttribute" name="title" lowerBound="1" eType="EString"/>
<eStructuralFeatures
  xsi:type="Ecore:EAttribute" name="nbPages" lowerBound="1" eType="EInt"/>
<eStructuralFeatures
  xsi:type="Ecore:EAttribute" name="author" lowerBound="1" eType="EString"/>
<eStructuralFeatures
  xsi:type="Ecore:EReference" name="book" lowerBound="1"
  eType="#//Book" eOpposite="#//Book/chapters"/>
</eClassifiers>
```

Fig. 4. Source meta-model of *Book2Publication* transformation

are relevant, and the same can be said for attributes *title*, *author*, *keyword* and *nbPages*. In order to force the generation of *book*s with at least one *chapter* the human tester can set *minOccurs* to 1:

```
<xs:element ref="chapters" minOccurs="1" maxOccurs="unbounded"/>
```

Next, the human tester selects relevant values for the transformation. In this case, the idea is to generate test models in which books have as *keyword* "Biology" and "Romance", and some other value (for instance "Computers") in order to validate (3) and (5) of the OCL constraints. Additionally, it would be useful to have chapters with different number of pages, greater than 100, and smaller than 100, in order to validate (6). A good choice would be to generate test models with chapters of size 50, 100, 150, etc. Thus the values for *nbPages* will be selected to be "50" and "150". With regard to *title*, and the validation of (1), (2) and (4), it is only required to have at least one value, for instance "a". *Author* element is not required by the OCL constraints, but required by the transformation, thus we can add just one value "b". Values for attributes and elements are added to the XML Schema in the *enumeration* section as shown in Fig. 6. The tester call is as follows:

```
<xs:complexType name="chapters">
    <xs:attribute name="title" type="titleType" use="required"/>
    <xs:attribute name="nbPages" type="nbPagesType" use="required"/>
    <xs:attribute name="author" type="authorType" use="required"/>
</xs:complexType>
<xs:element name="xmi:XMI">
    <xs:complexType><xs:sequence>
        <xs:element name="Book" minOccurs="1" maxOccurs="unbounded">
            <xs:complexType><xs:sequence>
                <xs:element ref="chapters" minOccurs="0" maxOccurs="unbounded"/>
                </xs:sequence>
                <xs:attribute name="title" type="titleType" use="required"/>
                <xs:attribute name="keyword" type="keywordType" use="required"/>
            </xs:complexType></xs:element>
    </xs:sequence></xs:complexType>
</xs:element>
```

Fig. 5. Source XML Schema of *Book2Publication* transformation

```
<xs:simpleType name="titleType">
    <xs:restriction base="xs:string">
        <xs:enumeration value="a"/>
    </xs:restriction></xs:simpleType>
<xs:simpleType name="keywordType">
    <xs:restriction base="xs:string">
        <xs:enumeration value="Biology"/>
        <xs:enumeration value="Romance"/>
        <xs:enumeration value="Computers"/>
    </xs:restriction></xs:simpleType>
<xs:simpleType name="nbPagesType">
    <xs:restriction base="xs:integer">
        <xs:enumeration value="50"/>
        <xs:enumeration value="150"/>
    </xs:restriction></xs:simpleType>
<xs:simpleType name="authorType">
    <xs:restriction base="xs:string">
        <xs:enumeration value="b"/>
    </xs:restriction>
</xs:simpleType>
```

Fig. 6. Values for source model of *Book2Publication* transformation

```
atl:tester("Schema.xsd","Book.Ecore","Book","Publication.Ecore",
        "Publication","MyPath","Book2Publication","Input_prop","Output_prop
        ",1)
```

where the number *"1"* is the number of steps, and *Input_prop* and *Output_prop* are selected to be (3) and (6), respectively, of Fig. 3. The ATL tester reports in 639 ms the following answer:

```
Output Property Falsifiable after 2 tests.
Counterexample:

<xmi:XMI>
    <Book keyword="Romance" title="a">
        <chapters author="b" nbPages="50" title="a"/>
    </Book>
</xmi:XMI>

Result:

<publication:Publication title="a" authors="b" nbPages="50"
                keyword="Romance"/>
```

which means that after two test models, the ATL tester found that the output property cannot be satisfied. The tester shows a counterexample, that is, a test model fulfilling the input properties, but violating the output property. In addition, the tester shows the result of the transformation for the test model. In the counterexample, we can see that given as source model an *Romance* book with one chapter of 50 pages, the target model does not satisfy the output property. This is due to the (intentionally added) *bug* in the transformation: *Romace* books are transformed when the number of pages is smaller than 100. Once the bug is removed, the ATL tester answers (in 8,722 ms) as follows: `Ok: passed 54 tests, 54 valid`. Which means that 54 models have been proven, and all of them satisfy the output property, and in addition, it reports the number of models that satisfy the input property (i.e., valid models). When the number of models satisfying the input property is zero, the ATL tester answers: `Unable to test the property`.

```
module ER2RL;
create OUT : REL from IN : ER;

rule S2S { from s : ER!ERSchema
           to t : REL!RELSchema (name<-s.name,relations <- s.entities,
                  relations <- s.relships)}
rule E2R { from s : ER!Entity
           to t : REL!Relation ( name  <- s.name) }

rule R2R { from s : ER!Relship
           to t : REL!Relation ( name  <- s.name ) }

rule EA2A { from att : ER!ERAttribute, ent : ER!Entity (att.entity = ent)
            to t : REL!RELAttribute (name <- att.name, isKey <- att.isKey,
                   relation <- ent) }

rule RA2A { from att : ER!ERAttribute, rs  : ER!Relship (att.relship = rs)
            to t : REL!RELAttribute (name <- att.name, isKey <- att.isKey,
                   relation <- rs ) }

rule RA2AK { from att : ER!ERAttribute, rse : ER!RelshipEnd
             (att.entity = rse.entity and att.isKey = true)
        to   t : REL!RELAttribute (name <- att.name, isKey <-  att.isKey,
                 relation <- rse.relship )}
```

Fig. 7. *Class2Relational* transformation

Let us now consider the *Class2Relational* transformation defined in Fig. 7. This ATL program transforms entity-relationship (*ERSchema*) schemas into relational (*RELSchema*) ones, in which each *Entity* and relationship (*Relship*) is transformed into a *Relation*. Additionally, attributes (*ERAttribute*) of entities and relationships are transformed into attributes (*RELAttribute*) of relations. Finally, key attributes of entities (*isKey* is set to *true*) become attributes of the relations in which entities participate (*RelshipEnd*). This is a simplified version of the Class2Relational transformation of the ATL Zoo[3], but enough for showing several examples of testing.

---

[3] http://www.eclipse.org/atl/atlTransformations/#Class2Relational.

```
(1)  ER!Entity->allInstances()->forAll(e | e.attrs->forAll(a1,a2 | a1.name=
     a2.name implies a1=a2));
(2)  ER!Relship->allInstances()->forAll(r | r.attrs->forAll(a1,a2 | a1.name =
     a2.name implies a1=a2));
(3)  ER!Relship.allInstances()->forAll(e | e.attrs->collect(a | a.isKey)->
     size()=1) and ER!Entity.allInstances()->forAll(e | e.attrs->collect(a |
     a.isKey)->size()=1);
(4)  REL!Relation->allInstances()->forAll(r | r.attrs->forAll(a1,a2 | a1.name
     =a2.name implies a1=a2));
(5)  REL!Relation->allInstances()->forAll(r | r.attrs->collect(a | a.isKey)->
     size()=3 or r.attrs->collect(a | a.isKey)->size()=1);
```

Fig. 8. Input and output properties of *Class2Relational* transformation

Let us also consider the following set of input and output properties defined as OCL constraints (see Fig. 8). The OCL constraints on the source model establish that (1) all entities have attributes with distinct names, (2) all relationships have attributes with distinct names and (3) all entities and relationships have exactly one key. The OCL constraints on the target model establish that (4) all attributes of a relation have distinct names and (5) all relations have one or three keys (one for relations coming from entities, and three for relations coming from relationships). Let us suppose the human tester uses our tool to test the previous OCL constraints. Firstly, the human tester can select (1) and (2) as input properties and try to test (4) as output property. For the selected properties, the XML Schema should be modified in order to ensure that each entity and relationship have at least one attribute (setting *minOccurs* in *attrs* of *entities* and *relships* to one). Otherwise, entities and relationships will be generated without attributes, and the tester could not be able to test the properties (see example bellow). Now, the human tester calls the tester adding a couple of values for attribute names ("a" and "b") to *enumeration* section of the XML Schema in the *nameType* simpleType. The tester answers (in 5,249 ms) as follows:

```
Output Property Falsifiable after 33 tests.
Counterexample:

<xmi:XMI>
  <ERSchema name="a">
    <entities name="a">
      <attrs isKey="true" name="a"/>
    </entities>
    <relships name="a">
      <attrs isKey="true" name="a"/>
      <ends entity="//@ERSchema.0/@entities.0" name="a"/>
      <ends entity="//@ERSchema.0/@entities.0" name="a"/>
    </relships>
  </ERSchema>
</xmi:XMI>

Result:

<xmi:XMI>
  <rel:RELSchema name="a">
    <relations name="a">
      <attrs isKey="true" name="a"/>
      <attrs isKey="true" name="a"/>
      <attrs isKey="true" name="a"/>
```

```
    </relations>
  </rel:RELSchema>
  <rel:Relation name="a">
    <attrs isKey="true" name="a"/>
  </rel:Relation>
</xmi:XMI>
```

The test model illustrates that when entities and relationships share an attribute with the same name, the output property is violated. Thus, a stronger condition than (1) and (2) is required. Let us focus now on properties (3) and (5). In this case, names are not relevant and thus the human tester can use a different version of the XML Schema, in which he or she introduces two values (*true* and *false*) for *isKey*, adding them to *enumeration* section of the XML Schema, in the *isKeyType* simpleType. Additionally, *minOccurs* of *attrs* in *entities* and *relships* is set to one. In this case, the ATL tester answers (in 15,233 ms and number of steps 2):

```
Output Property Falsifiable after 109 tests.
Counterexample:

<xmi:XMI>
  <ERSchema name="a">
    <entities name="a">
      <attrs isKey="true" name="a"/>
    </entities>
    <relships name="a">
      <attrs isKey="true" name="a"/>
      <ends entity="//@ERSchema.0/@entities.0" name="a"/>
      <ends entity="//@ERSchema.0/@entities.0" name="a"/>
      <ends entity="//@ERSchema.0/@entities.0" name="a"/>
    </relships>
  </ERSchema>
</xmi:XMI>
```

which means that the output property is violated after 109 tests when the number of relationship *ends* is three. Thus, the human tester should restrict the number of relationship ends to ensure the output property. Setting *maxOccurs* of *ends* in *relships* to two, the following answer (in 170,740 ms and number of steps 3) is reported: Ok: **passed 1296 tests, 464 valid.** which means that 464 models satisfy the input and output properties from 1,296 randomly generated examples.

Let us now suppose that *attrs* is set to zero in *entities* and *relships*, and the number of steps is set to zero. In this case the ATL tester answers as follows: **Unable to check the property,** which means that from the models generated none of them satisfies the input property. This kind of answer is in most of cases reported when the selected number of steps is not enough to get valid source models. In this case, the solution is to increase the number of steps, or more appropriately and efficiently, to increase the number of elements, by setting a greater value of *minOccurs*. Sometimes, it can be solved by adding more values to types. For instance, in case of checking distinct values of a certain attribute at least two values are required. On the other hand, in the case of a buggy rule (of Fig. 7) is defined as follows:

```
rule RA2A { from att : ER!ERAttribute, rs   : ER!Relship
             to t : REL!RELAttribute
                     ( name <- att.name, isKey <- att.isKey, relation <- rs ) }
```

in which the condition *att.relship = rs* is omitted, the ATL tester answers (in 528 ms and number of steps 1) as follows:

```
Output Property Falsifiable after 5 tests.
Counterexample:

<xmi:XMI>
    <ERSchema name="a">
    <entities name="a">
        <attrs isKey="true" name="a"/>
    </entities>
    <relships name="a">
        <attrs isKey="true" name="a"/>
        <ends entity="//@ERSchema.0/@entities.0" name="a"/>
        <ends entity="//@ERSchema.0/@entities.0" name="a"/>
    </relships>
    </ERSchema>
</xmi:XMI>
```

3.1   Benchmarks

Finally, we would like to show the benchmarks of ATL testing for several examples. Table 1 shows the execution time of the testing for four examples: Book2Publication (B2P), Families2Persons (F2P), Composed2Simple (CSP) and ER2RL transformation. Code of transformations is omitted. The execution times have been measured (in milliseconds, ms) for different number of steps (2, 3, 4 and 5). Additionally, the table shows the number of test models (m), and which of them are valid (v). We have not modified the XML Schema generated from the Ecore model, except in the XML Schema of Entity Relationship meta-model in which *maxOccurs* of *ends* is set to two (in order to satisfy source OCL constraints). We can see in this table that the ATL tester is able to generate up to 5,998 models in reasonable time (ER2RL transformation), and test input and output properties of 1,202 models in short time (F2P transformation). Let us remark that modifying XML Schema elements (i.e., *minOccurs*, *maxOccurs* and values of types of enumerations) execution time can be drastically altered. To take the original XML Schema is not usually recommended, but for validating the performance of our test model generator we have decided to leave XML Schema unchangeable. Usually, XML Schema should be modified to avoid large and useless models (non valid models). Obviously, when the output property is not satisfied the ATL tester is faster.

Table 1. Benchmarks

Transformation	Steps = 2	Steps = 3	Steps = 4	Steps = 5
B2P	7 m. 7 v. 1,068 ms.	16 m. 16 v. 1,331 ms.	38 m. 38 v. 3,363 ms.	97 m. 97 v. 14,631 ms.
F2P	7 m. 7 v. 553 ms.	32 m. 32 v. 2,585 ms.	177 m. 177 v. 18,382 ms.	1202 m. 1202 v. 207,670 ms.
C2S	14 m. 4 v. 1,945 ms.	61 m. 9 v. 4,360 ms.	274 m. 23 v. 19,024 ms.	1374 m. 69 v. 95,741 ms.
ER2RL	16 m. 0 v. 4,205 ms.	144 m. 4 v. 15,567 ms.	841 m. 22 v. 106,848 ms.	5998 m. 306 v. 1,089,177 ms.

4   Related Work

From related works about test modeling we can distinguish two main lines of research. Those ones generating source test models using black-box techniques, and others using white-box techniques. Black box techniques do not use the transformation code or the specification (i.e., properties) to generate source test models. White box techniques use the transformation code or the specification to generate source test models. Most of white box techniques are based on OCL analysis and use constraint solvers.

In case of black-box approach, the authors of [18] use tracts to certify that a transformation works for some source test models generated from a script defined with the ASSL language. Tracts are pieces of specification focused on a particular scenario and each transformation can be specified by a set of tracts, enabling the partition of the full input space into smaller units. Tracts are specified by OCL constraints. The authors of [6] introduce model transformation testing in which an expected target model is used to validate transformations in which testing results are difference models. MANTra tool has been proposed in [4] to define test models for QVTO (QVT Operational) in terms of a transformation. The testing report is therefore also a model. MANTra checks output properties on target models. Test models are manually defined for each transformation, and they are used to show testing results. The authors of [8] adapt the classical category partition method to qualify source models of transformations. They established partitions on meta-models in order to automatically generate test models. The specification language PAMOMO is used in [11] to express contracts: input, output properties as well as input-output properties (called invariants). These contracts are compiled into executable QVT transformations which are run to certify transformations. In case of properties are violated, detailed information (parts of the model in which a contract fails) is given to the user.

Our approach follows the same proposal as [18]: that is, it is able to partially validate a transformation concentrating on specific input and output properties. Due to the automation of our approach, the human tester can play with several combinations of input and output properties. The difference of our approach with this work is that we are able to automatically generate test models from the meta-model, while in [18] the human tester has to program a test model generator for each transformation using the ASSL language. Even more, the human tester in our approach can play with several sizes and values for model elements enabling the definition of a high diversity of test models. Properties on target models are specified in our approach by OCL constraints instead of using an expected output model like in [6]. Nevertheless, we plan to study the possibility of providing other techniques for checking output properties. Source test models are, in our approach, automatically generated from the source meta-model, but we plan to consider the testing procedure as a transformation, similarly to [4]. In our approach the human tester is responsible of the customization of test models, selecting from the source meta-model the elements and number of elements required to test the transformation. Thus, the partition is defined by the human tester, compared to the work [8]. This is an advantage given that the partition can be more precise and suitable in some examples. We use OCL to express properties, and we are able to certify ATL transformations for the test models automatically generated. So far, the information provided to the human tester is limited to "Ok" and in the case of fail, the tool shows counterexamples, which are source models, together with the result of the transformation for the counterexamples. The human tester uses the counterexamples in order to detect the bugs in the transformation, enough in most of cases. However, we plan to study the possibility of extending our work in the same line as [11], providing richer information to the human tester about rules and parts of the target model in which properties are not satisfied.

With regard to white box approaches, the authors of [7] use a constraint solver to generate test models from the source meta-model OCL constraints, and similarly the proposal of [9], using also the dependence graph of ATL trans-formation. The authors of [10] use a category-partition based method adapted to OCL and an EMFtoCSP tool to generate test models. Generation of test models using SAT-solving techniques to complete hand-crafted partial models from the source meta-model is proposed in [16]. The authors of [12] derive test models from the transformation. The source test models are computed using SAT-solving techniques on OCL expressions generated from the specification. Typing errors of ATL transformations are studied in [5], and the authors are able analyzing ATL code to generate test cases for most common typing errors. OCL constraints are used to generate test cases from constraint solving. Finally, fault analysis in ATL rules is carried out in [3] by using OCL constraints. Our approach is black box, but we would like to extend our work in the future to white box techniques. In our case, white box testing means to be able to automatically select the number and value of elements (classes, attributes and associations) to which test models are generated. In other words, automatize the selection made by the human tester. It involves to analyze ATL code and OCL constraints like in the quoted approaches.

5   Conclusions and Future Work

In this paper we have presented how to automatically generate random Ecore models for testing ATL transformations. We have described an Ecore to XML Schema transformation that makes to generate Ecore models according to human tester's choices possible. We have showed how the developed ATL tester is able to show counterexamples of OCL constraints on target models, when the testing fails, and to certify ATL transformations when OCL constraints on source and target models are satisfied. As future work, we would like to extend our approach as follows. Firstly, we would like to extend our tool with input-output properties (called invariants in the context of model transformation). Input-output property testing is of great interest since transformations can fulfill input and output properties but fail in source and target model mapping, which is only detected from input-output properties. Secondly, we plan to work in the improvement of the ATL tester, showing better results of tests: which property is not satisfied, and which part of the model is involved. Thirdly, we would like to work on white box testing, using ATL code to automatically generate a pruned XML Schema with values taken from the transformation code. Our approach is black-box, and the human tester designs the test models by selecting items, number of them and values. Thus, test coverage, for instance, is decided by the human tester. In white-box testing, we will study test coverage. Finally, we would like to implement a Web tool to test ATL programs.

References

1. Almendros-Jiménez, J.M., Becerra-Terón, A.: XQuery testing from XML schema based random test cases. In: Chen, Q., Hameurlain, A., Toumani, F., Wagner, R., Decker, H. (eds.) DEXA 2015. LNCS, vol. 9262, pp. 268–282. Springer, Heidelberg (2015)
2. Anand, S., Burke, E.K., Chen, T.Y., Clark, J., Cohen, M.B., Grieskamp, W., Harman, M., Harrold, M.J., McMinn, P., et al.: An orchestrated survey of methodologies for automated software test case generation. J. Syst. Softw. **86**(8), 1978–2001 (2013)
3. Burgueno, L., Troya, J., Wimmer, M., Vallecillo, A.: Static fault localization in model transformations. IEEE Trans. Softw. Eng. **41**(5), 490–506 (2015)
4. Ciancone, A., Filieri, A., Mirandola, R.: Testing operational transformations in model-driven engineering. Innovations Syst. Softw. Eng. **10**(1), 19–32 (2014)
5. Cuadrado, J.S., Guerra, E., de Lara, J.: Uncovering errors in ATL model transformations using static analysis and constraint solving. In: 2014 IEEE 25th International Symposium on Software Reliability Engineering, pp. 34–44. IEEE (2014)
6. Finot, O., Mottu, J.-M., Sunyé, G., Attiogbé, C.: Partial test oracle in model transformation testing. In: Duddy, K., Kappel, G. (eds.) ICMB 2013. LNCS, vol. 7909, pp. 189–204. Springer, Heidelberg (2013)
7. Fiorentini, C., Momigliano, A., Ornaghi, M., Poernomo, I.: A constructive approach to testing model transformations. In: Tratt, L., Gogolla, M. (eds.) ICMT 2010. LNCS, vol. 6142, pp. 77–92. Springer, Heidelberg (2010)
8. Fleurey, F., Baudry, B., Muller, P.-A., Le Traon, Y.: Qualifying input test data for model transformations. Softw. Syst. Model. **8**(2), 185–203 (2009)
9. González, C.A., Cabot, J.: ATLTest: a white-box test generation approach for ATL transformations. In: France, R.B., Kazmeier, J., Breu, R., Atkinson, C. (eds.) MODELS 2012. LNCS, vol. 7590, pp. 449–464. Springer, Heidelberg (2012)
10. González, C.A., Cabot, J.: Test data generation for model transformations combining partition and constraint analysis. In: Di Ruscio, D., Varró, D. (eds.) ICMT 2014. LNCS, vol. 8568, pp. 25–41. Springer, Heidelberg (2014)
11. Guerra, E., de Lara, J., Wimmer, M., Kappel, G., Kusel, A., Retschitzegger, W., Schönböck, J., Schwinger, W.: Automated verification of model transformations based on visual contracts. Autom. Softw. Eng. **20**(1), 5–46 (2013)
12. Guerra, E., Soeken, M.: Specification-driven model transformation testing. Softw. Syst. Model. **14**(2), 623–644 (2015)
13. Jouault, F., Allilaire, F., Bézivin, J., Kurtev, I.: ATL: a model transformation tool. Sci. Comput. Program. **72**(1), 31–39 (2008)
14. Selim, G.M.K., Cordy, J.R., Dingel, J.: Model transformation testing: the state of the art. In: Proceedings of the First Workshop on the Analysis of Model Transformations, pp. 21–26. ACM (2012)

15. Sen, S., Moha, N., Baudry, B., Jézéquel, J.-M.: Meta-model pruning. In: Schürr, A., Selic, B. (eds.) MODELS 2009. LNCS, vol. 5795, pp. 32–46. Springer, Heidelberg (2009)
16. Sen, S., Mottu, J.-M., Tisi, M., Cabot, J.: Using models of partial knowledge to test model transformations. In: Hu, Z., de Lara, J. (eds.) ICMT 2012. LNCS, vol. 7307, pp. 24–39. Springer, Heidelberg (2012)
17. Utting, M., Pretschner, A., Legeard, B.: A taxonomy of model-based testing approaches. Softw. Test. Verification Reliab. 22(5), 297–312 (2012)
18. Vallecillo, A., Gogolla, M., Burgueño, L., Wimmer, M., Hamann, L.: Formal specification and testing of model transformations. In: Bernardo, M., Cortellessa, V., Pierantonio, A. (eds.) SFM 2012. LNCS, vol. 7320, pp. 399–437. Springer, Heidelberg (2012)
19. Völter, M., Stahl, T., Bettin, J., Haase, A., Helsen, S.: Model-Driven Software Development: Technology, Engineering, Management. Wiley, Chichester (2013)

Towards a Methodological Tool Support for Modeling Security-Oriented Processes

Jacob Geisel[1(✉)], Brahim Hamid[1], David Gonzales[2], and Jean-Michel Bruel[1]

[1] IRIT, University of Toulouse, Toulouse, France
{geisel,hamid,bruel}@irit.fr
[2] Ikerlan, Mandragon, Spain
DGonzalez@ikerlan.es

Abstract. Development processes for software construction are common knowledge and widely used in most development organizations. Unfortunately, these processes often offer only little or no support in order to meet security requirements. In our work, we propose a methodology to build domain specific process models with security concepts on the foundations of industry-relevant security approaches, backed by a security-oriented process model specification language. Instead of building domain specific security-oriented process models from the ground, the methodology allows process designers to fall back on existing well established security approaches and add domain relevant concepts and repository-centric approaches, as well as supplementary information security risk management standards (e.g., Common Criteria), to fulfill the demand for secure software engineering. Supplementary and/or domain specific concepts can be added trough our process modeling language in an easy and direct way. The methodology and the process modeling language we propose have been successfully evaluated by the TERESA project for specifying development processes for trusted applications and integrating security concepts into existing process models used in the railway domain.

Keywords: Process modeling · Secure software engineering · Model-Driven Engineering · MDE toolchain · Repository · Reuse

1 Introduction

Development processes for software construction are common knowledge and mainstream practice in most development organizations. Unfortunately, these processes offer little support in order to meet security requirements and are rarely formalized. As a consequence, there are increased risks of security vulnerabilities that are introduced into software in various stages of development. Secure software (or software security) engineering aims to avoid security vulnerabilities in software by considering security aspects from the very beginning and throughout the life cycle. From another perspective, formalizing processes offers the ability to teach and communicate them and to reason about them.

© Springer International Publishing Switzerland 2016
L. Bellatreche et al. (Eds.): MEDI 2016, LNCS 9893, pp. 31–41, 2016.
DOI: 10.1007/978-3-319-45547-1_3

The SEMCO project [15] aims at closing this gap by offering a framework for modeling and formalizing, on the one hand, modeling a set of artifacts (e.g., security patterns) and on the other hand to provide methodologies for model-based development (e.g., pattern-based security-oriented development). The modeling is becoming a major paradigm in system engineering, engineering of embedded systems, and particularly in system software engineering [14], but also in process engineering with the appearance of process metamodels [5]. Model-Driven Engineering (MDE) offers tools to deal with the development of complex systems improving their quality and reducing their development cycles.

In this work, we propose a process modeling environment, which associates model-driven paradigms and established security engineering concepts, to support the design of repository-centric security-oriented process models. In this context, we propose a methodology to build domain specific process models with security concepts on the foundations of industry-relevant security approaches, backed by a security-oriented process model specification language. To enable reuse, common industry-relevant approaches for considering security aspects in process models are made available to process designers through process model skeletons. The methodology allows process designers to build domain specific security-oriented process models based on existing industry-relevant security-oriented approaches and potentially add supplementary information security risk management and/or repository concepts. As part of the assistance for the modeling of process models for secure applications, we implement a tool-chain based on the Eclipse platform to support the different activities of process modeling and a repository, providing a set of reusable process skeletons and process type libraries. The proposed solutions were evaluated in the TERESA project through a case study from the metrology domain.

The rest of this paper is organized as follows. Section 2 outlines existing work on (security-oriented) process metamodels and models. Section 3 outlines our approach on building security-oriented process models based on solid foundations. Section 4 introduces RCPM (Repository Centric Process Metamodel) and details the packages used for security. Section 5 describes the concrete syntax of the RCPM modeling language. Moreover, it presents possibilities of analyzing the process model under various points of view and describes our proposed toolset to support the methodology, including a textual process model editor and a repository of process artifacts. Section 6 concludes this paper, discussing the advantages and limits of our approach and giving an outlook on future work.

2   Related Work

We will give an overview on the existing approaches on formalizing process models, on industry-relevant process models as well as on approaches on taking into account security concepts.

Process metamodeling. Different process metamodels are proposed [8,12] for modeling software engineering processes. These process metamodels are divided into different categories according to [7]. The viewpoint of process metamodel concentrates different aspects of methodologies that are used by these metamodels. In our context, process models will be created with the viewpoint of activity-oriented, as the development of security-oriented systems is more directly modeled in this viewpoint. SPEM2 (Software & Systems Process Engineering Metamodel) [12] was created by the OMG as a *de facto*, high-level standard for processes used in object-oriented software development. The scope of SPEM is purposely limited to the minimal elements necessary to define any software and system development process, without adding specific features for particular development domains or disciplines (e.g., project management, security). Other commonly used process metamodels like UMA or OPEN have similar characteristics.

Process models. The V-Model [3] development process, also called verification & validation model, is suggested by the standard IEC61508. It is a trustworthy software development model, which aims at taming the complexity of project management, and which is used by big companies. The Rational Unified Process (RUP), an implementation of the Unified Process, is a comprehensive process framework that provides industry-tested practices for software engineering [8]. It is an iterative software development process framework, providing prototypes during each iteration.

Security engineering. The focus is put on three forefront representatives, namely Microsofts Security Development Life cycle (SDL), OWASPs Comprehensive, Lightweight Application Security Process (CLASP) and McGraw Touchpoints, as they are recognized as the major players in the field. Microsoft's Security Development Life (SDL) cycle [10] is probably the most rigorous, most tool-supported and more oriented towards large organizations (e.g., Microsoft uses it internally). Microsoft defined this process in 2002 to address security issues frequently faced in development. It contains an extensive set of (security oriented) activities, which can be used as supporting activities in development process models. These activities are often related to functionality-oriented activities and complement them by adding security aspects. Proposed activities are grouped into classical development phases (i.e., Education, Design, Implementation, Verification, Release) to ease the introduction into existing approaches. Vast guidance, such as detailed description of methods and tool support, is available, enabling even less qualified practitioners to achieve the required outcome. These guidance go as far down as to give coding and compiling guidelines, which do not map to process model activities any more.

The Comprehensive, Lightweight Application Security Process [13] by the OWASP Consortium is a lightweight process containing 24 main activities. It can be customized to fit different projects (activities can be integrated) and focuses on security as the central role of the system. CLASP also offers a rich set of security support resources.

McGraw's work [9] is based on industrial experience and has been validated over time. It provides a set of best practices regrouped into 7 so-called touchpoints. The activities focus on risk management and flexibility and offer white-hat and black-hat approaches to increase security.

Common Criteria for Information Technology Security Evaluation [1] is a ISO/IEC standard for computer security certification. It is defined as a generic framework offering process designers and project managers can specify security functional requirements through protection profiles.

3   Approach

The methodology we propose is based on a repository of modeling artifacts. Once the repository is set up and populated with process model skeletons and process type libraries, the (end-user) process engineer begins building domain specific process models. The central idea of our methodology consists of building on existing security-oriented process models, which then are extended by the process designer to meet the domain demands and additional security-oriented concepts. The methodology is illustrated in Fig. 1.

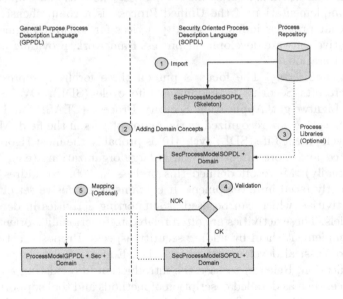

Fig. 1. From scratch methodology overview

In the following we detail the different steps of this methodology and describe the alternatives the process designer has.

1. In a first step (**Step 1**) the process designer chooses a security model skeleton as a template for the process model. The designer then imports the process model from the repository and creates a local copy of it in the process model design environment. The proposed framework makes available some process skeletons, based on the aforementioned secure development approaches, and offers process engineers to deposit process skeletons (as well as complete process models) to the repository.

2. In a second step (**Step 2**) the process designer uses this process skeleton and adds domain specific phases, activities, roles, etc. to the process model coming from project-related recommendations e.g., in-house guidelines, non-formalized domain standards. In this step the process designer customizes the process skeleton, which is a rather generic (security-oriented) approach to fit the approaches used in the application domain.

3. In the following optional step (**Step 3**) the designer has the possibility to select additional process type libraries to augment the process model (either domain specific process model libraries derived from standards or process type libraries for specific purposes, such as repository-centric or pattern-based libraries). The integration of the process libraries will be manual or semi-automatic, depending on the complexity of the process model and the library.

4. As next step (**Step 4**) the designer validates the process model and iterates over the second step until validation passes. The designer has the choice between different validations, on the hand conformance validation towards the process metamodel and on the other hand supplementary validations, such as validations concerning correct implementation of the process type libraries.

5. Finally, the process designer can choose in a optional step (**Step 5**) to map the created process model to a General Purpose Process Description Language (GPPDL) or to stay in a Security-Oriented Process Description Language (SOPDL). This allows the process designer to take advantages of both modeling environments, and to either use existing tools and frameworks to analyze and enact the process model, in the case of the initial *GPPDL* or any other *GPPDL*, or to take advantage of the proposed framework, in the case of the *SOPDL*, or to use both.

In the next section we will detail a metamodel to define a security-oriented process description language and concepts for reusing knowledge in process engineering, allowing process designers to follow the proposed methodology. In addition to the concepts of metamodel and the concrete syntax, we offer a repository with process model skeletons and process type libraries to give an infrastructure to build on to process designers. This repository includes process skeleton, like the SDL skeleton, and process type libraries for security (e.g., CLASP, Touchpoints) and repository-centric development approaches (e.g., PBSE).

4   RCPM Concepts for Security and Reuse

The RCPM is a metamodel defining a new formalism for security process modeling based on a repository of modeling artifacts. The concepts of the metamodel, which are only briefly outlined have been presented in previous work [4,6]. The complete description of the abstract syntax of the RCPM are available online via http://www.semcomdt.org/semco/resources/RCPM.pdf.

To illustrate the concepts presented in this paper, we will use the working example described in the following.

4.1   Working Example: Simplified V-Modell XT

The *V-Modell XT* [2] is a high level framework and model for planning and realizing projects developed by the German government. It is the successor of the established *V-Modell 97*. The *V-Modell XT* allows to be tailored to specific needs of projects (e.g., size, budget, time constraints).

For demonstration purposes and better understandability, we simplify the process and focus on the software development part. Decision making and management phases and activities up to specifications upstream to the system development, as well as product maintenance are not treated.

4.2   Metamodel Description

The Repository-Centric Process Metamodel (RCPM) is divided into the following six sub-packages: (1) CORE, regrouping basic concepts; (2) PROCESS, for concepts related to process engineering, based on CORE; (3) SAFETY, for safety related concepts, based on PROCESS; (4) SECURITY, for security phases, activities, based on PROCESS and SECURITY; (5) REPOSITORY, for interactions with a pattern repository, based on PROCESS and CORE and (6) TYPES, for typing process elements and enforcing reuse of process elements, based on CORE.

Core Concepts

Core package. The Core Package contains the elements which are used as top-level elements throughout the other packages and contain the basic attributes of all elements. These concepts include basic concepts (e.g., Element, Association) and their attributes (e.g., name, description).

Process package. The Process Package contains all the concepts used for process engineering, the basic concepts, like Process Model, concepts of a work breakdown structure (e.g., Phase, Activity, Task) and a breakdown structure (e.g., Role, Tool, WorkProduct) and concepts needed for detailing activities (e.g., Steps and Relationships as Responsible, Workdirection, Performer). This package is largely inspired by either existing process metamodels, such as SPEM2.0, UMA and/or OPF as well as by industry used process models such as the V-Modell XT.

Safety Engineering Package. Based on the Process Package, the Safety Engineering Package regroups recurring Safety Engineering Concepts and extends and enhances process concepts. The safety concepts of this package are derived from process models which are safety oriented, such as the V-Model XT.

Security Engineering Package. The Security Engineering Package regroups recurring Security Concepts, like Activities, Phases or Checkpoints. It is based on the Process and the Safety Package and reuses their concepts to express security-oriented concepts.

- **Recurring Elements**
  - *SecurityEngineer.* A Role describing a Security Engineer of the system-under-development.
  - *ThreatModeling.* Recurring Activity to define sets of possible attacks on system assets.
  - *SecurityReview.* Checkpoint targeting the entire system with a focus on highest-risk components. This is normally a checkpoint at the end of each phase.
  - *AttackSurfaceReduction.* Activity to minimize attack surface (reduction of privileges and/or access points).
  - *RiskAssessment.* Checkpoint to determine the quantitative or qualitative value of risk related to a concrete situation and a recognized threat.
- **Education and Project Inception**
  - *Education Phase.* Commonly used Phase for learning of security aspects. This phase also allows to create common security knowledge in the team.
  - *SecurityTeamBuilding Activity.* Addressing the set-up of security-oriented responsibilities, project or company-wide.
  - *SecurityLogistics Activity.* Addressing logistic aspects (e.g., tools, type of security bugs to be handled).
  - *SecurityMetrics Activity.* Assessing the security posture of the product as well as enforcing accountability of security issues.
- **Analysis and Requirements**
  - *AnalysisLevelThreatModeling.* A refinement of ThreatModeling, using different approaches on threat modeling, such as use case driven, resource driven and/or knowledge driven, assessing whether known attacks can be valid and useful
  - *SecurityRequirements.* An Activity specialized on defining the security requirements of the system-under-development. These requirements contain legal, financial, contractual and functional security requirements. This activity also resolves deficiencies and conflicts between requirement sets.
- **Architecture**
  - *ThirdPartyRiskAssessment.* Refinement of RiskAssessment to analyze weaknesses that arise by using third party software such as off-the-shelf components.
  - *RequirementsAudit.* Checkpoint to audit security (and non-security) requirements in order to assess their completeness.
  - *ArchitectureLevelThreatModeling.* A refinement of ThreatModeling focussing on threat identification and risk assessment where risks in the system are identified and mitigated.
  - *SecurityArchitecture.* Activity to take into account the security requirement in the architecture of the system-under-development.

Type Package. The Types Package is used to define libraries for reuse of process blocks and to create constraints on Breakdown, Work Breakdown and Association Elements. The type elements correspond to the existing process elements and associations in the other packages (i.e., process, safety, security, repository).

- *TypeLibrary.* Library enabling reuse of process blocks (e.g., Phases, Activities), containing types and links among types.
- *ProcessElementTypes.* Generic Process Element Type.
- *AssociationTypes.* An Element allowing to type different kinds of associations.
- *WorkBreakdownElementTypes.* An Element (and especially its derived Elements) allowing to build a Work Breakdown structures. for reuse.
- *BreakdownElementTypes.* An Element (and especially its derived Elements) allowing to build a Breakdown structures for reuse.

5 Security-Oriented Process Modeling

5.1 Concrete Syntax

Most metamodels and/or abstract syntaxes offer one or more concrete syntaxes to instantiate their concepts. The standards UML and SPEM2, for example, provide concrete syntaxes with diagrams for different viewpoints, in a graphical manner with icons and links. Other metamodels and especially domain-specific modeling languages often come with a textual syntax. We provide a tree-based concrete syntax, derived automatically from the metamodel, but which is not as convenient as using a well domain-adapted concrete syntax. A text-based syntax offers process modeling engineers a common and accustomed way to model their processes. We choose to use an EBNF grammar to define a concrete syntax for the RCPM language.

5.2 Process Model Analysis and Documentation

In this section we detail the possibilities of analyzing the process model under various points of view. We allow process designers to check the conformance of their model to the metamodel, helping to find concepts and relationships breaking the conformance. Another analysis approach is to extract metrics on the process model. Process Model Metrics is an important tool to analyze and understand process models. By these metrics it is possible to point out problems and find ways to improve the process model (e.g., reduce complexity, error probability).

The metrics offered by the framework are (1) *Size*, the number of nodes (and/or arcs) in the process model or the number of nodes referenced by or nested in an element (approximately equivalent to LoC metric, (2) *Diameter*, longest path from start to end, exploring the process model from the beginning to the end, checking the different alternatives and taking into account different parameters for computation, (3) *Depth*, depth of nesting of elements in a process model and listing these according to a root element shows a depth metric for taking the process model as root element) and (4) Control Flow Complexity, summing up all the choices in a process model. In addition to these quality-oriented metrics we offer also metrics used by project managers helping evaluate time and resources consumption for the aimed project. These metrics include estimations on resource consumption (e.g., a Security Engineer intervenes in a certain number of Activities and Tasks, Security Documentation is made up of a certain number of Work Products) and time consumption (e.g., the longest path, regarding estimated time, from possible alternatives from Activity A to Activity B).

In addition to giving analysis approaches on process models to process engineers and project managers, we allow through generation of documentation to extract process information and guidelines for enacting practitioners of the process model from different viewpoints and for different parts of the process model.

5.3 Tool Support

Using the proposed metamodels and the Eclipse Modeling Framework, ongoing experimental work is done with SEMCoMDT as a MDE tool-chain supporting the proposed approach metamodels. We build a set of software tools, for designing process models, for populating and for retrieval from the repository. Moreover, we provide tools to support the management of the repository (SEMCO Gaya Repository), the generation of documentation and the transformations for refinement and analysis. We choose to derive a text-based syntax to create instances of the metamodel using the Xtext Framework (SEMCO Naravas Process Model Editor). For the description of the model transformations, the QVT Operational language is used and for metrics generation the Acceleo transformation engine [11] is used to build static HTML pages based on the Bootstrap Framework. An Example of the output is given in Fig. 2.

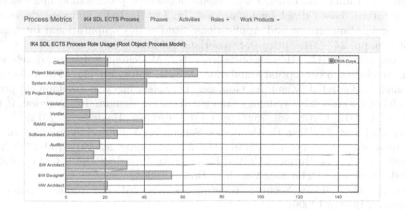

Fig. 2. NaravasX: metrics on security engineer effort days

6   Conclusion

In this paper we propose a methodology to design process models with security aspects based on industry-relevant best-practices. This is realized by reusing and building upon security concepts from established security-oriented approaches. The security aspects of the modeling language are detailed and demonstrated on a working example through a text-based concrete syntax. The methodology and the security-oriented process modeling language are validated by a use case from the railway domain through the modeling of a process model for a Train Control System. The advantages of the approach are a more direct and intuitive way of building process models on existing security-oriented approaches and adding security concepts for domains having strong security requirements. In addition, to easing the process modeling from the ground up, assistance is given to the process designer by model type libraries, guiding the designer to conform with domain specific guidelines and/or best practices. Despite the advantages of the approach and the modeling language, there are limits to the approach. Our security-oriented process modeling language is not able to represent all of the concepts given in SPEM2.0 or other GPPDLs (General Purpose Process Description Language), although this might not raise an issue, since the process concepts needed for security engineering are kept. Derived from this, the transformation from our process modeling language to a GPPDL might not be able to represent all the security concepts in the generic process description language in an explicit way.

References

1. Common Criteria: common criteria for information technology security evaluation v3.1r4. Technical report CCMB-2012-09-001/002/003, Common Criteria (2012)
2. Die Beauftragte der Bundesregierung für Informationstechnik. V-modell XT (2005)
3. Forsberg, K., Mooz, H., Cotterman, H.: Visualizing Project Management. A Model for Business and Technical Success, 2nd edn. Wiley, New york (2000)
4. Geisel, J., Hamid, B., Bruel, J.-M.: Repository-centric process modeling – example of a pattern based development process. In: Lee, L. (ed.) Software Engineering Research, Management and Applications. Studies in Computational Intelligence, vol. 496, pp. 247–261. Springer, Switzerland (2014)
5. Gonzalez-Perez, C., Henderson-Sellers, B.: Modelling software development methodologies: a conceptual foundation. J. Syst. Softw. 80(11), 1778–1796 (2007)
6. Hamid, B., Geisel, J., Ziani, A., Gonzalez, D.: Safety lifecycle development process modeling for embedded systems - example of railway domain. In: Avgeriou, P. (ed.) SERENE 2012. LNCS, vol. 7527, pp. 63–75. Springer, Heidelberg (2012)
7. Hug, C., Front, A., Rieu, D., Henderson-Sellers, B.: A method to build information systems engineering process metamodels. J. Syst. Softw. 82(10), 1730–1742 (2009)
8. Kruchten, P.: The Rational Unified Process: An Introduction, 3rd edn. Addison-Wesley Longman Publishing Co., Inc., Boston (2003)
9. McGraw, G.: Software Security: Building Security, 3rd edn. Addison-Wesley Professional, Boston (2006)
10. Microsoft: Microsoft Security Development Lifecycle (SDL) process guidance - version 5.2 (2012)

11. OBEO: Acceleo (2014). http://www.eclipse.org/acceleo/
12. OMG: Software and systems process engineering metamodel specification (SPEM) version 2.0. Technical report, Object Management Group Inc. (2008)
13. OWASP: OWASP CLASP V1.2. OWASP, November 2007
14. Selic, B.: The pragmatics of model-driven development. IEEE Softw. **20**(5), 19–25 (2003)
15. SEMCO: System and software engineering for embedded systems applications with multi-concerns support (2010)

ResilientStore: A Heuristic-Based Data Format Selector for Intermediate Results

Rana Faisal Munir[1]([⊠]), Oscar Romero[1], Alberto Abelló[1], Besim Bilalli[1], Maik Thiele[2], and Wolfgang Lehner[2]

[1] Universitat Politécnica de Catalunya (UPC), Barcelona, Spain
{fmunir,oromero,aabello,bbilalli}@essi.upc.edu
[2] Technische Universität Dresden (TUD), Dresden, Germany
{maik.thiele,wolfgang.lehner}@tu-dresden.de

Abstract. Large-scale data analysis is an important activity in many organizations that typically requires the deployment of data-intensive workflows. As data is processed these workflows generate large intermediate results, which are typically pipelined from one operator to the following. However, if materialized, these results become reusable, hence, subsequent workflows need not recompute them. There are already many solutions that materialize intermediate results but all of them assume a fixed data format. A fixed format, however, may not be the optimal one for every situation. For example, it is well-known that different data fragmentation strategies (e.g., horizontal and vertical) behave better or worse according to the access patterns of the subsequent operations. In this paper, we present ResilientStore, which assists on selecting the most appropriate data format for materializing intermediate results. Given a workflow and a set of materialization points, it uses rule-based heuristics to choose the best storage data format based on subsequent access patterns. We have implemented ResilientStore for HDFS and three different data formats: SequenceFile, Parquet and Avro. Experimental results show that our solution gives 18 % better performance than any solution based on a single fixed format.

Keywords: Big data · Data-intensive workflows · Intermediate results · Data format · HDFS

1 Introduction

Large-scale data analysis is an important activity for many organizations. It is typically performed by deploying pipelined workflows (known as Data Intensive Workflows (DIW)) on Hadoop[1] clusters. Many high-level languages (namely as Hive[2] and Pig[3]) have been introduced to facilitate the execution of analysis

---

[1] https://hadoop.apache.org.
[2] http://hive.apache.org.
[3] http://pig.apache.org.

© Springer International Publishing Switzerland 2016
L. Bellatreche et al. (Eds.): MEDI 2016, LNCS 9893, pp. 42–56, 2016.
DOI: 10.1007/978-3-319-45547-1_4

tasks on Hadoop. These languages aim at decomposing the tasks into multiple pipelined MapReduce [4] jobs. Each task produces results that are commonly referred to as intermediate results. Intermediate results are used by multiple subsequent tasks. An in-depth study of MapReduce workloads for seven enterprises [3] shows that 80% of intermediate results are re-accessed in different parts of DIWs. This study demonstrates the importance of materializing the right intermediate results for speeding up the flows that re-access them. However, the study gives rise to two questions as well: "What to materialize?" and "How to materialize?".

Answers to the first question have already been given. In [6,16], they provide tools which help in choosing what to materialize. However, these solutions do not provide help in terms of how to materialize the intermediate results. They typically store them directly on HDFS [10], where I/O operations are expensive. Hence, unnecessary reads and writes performed, increase the execution costs of DIWs.

Researchers have come up with different data formats that help in reducing the amount of read and write operations. The proposed data formats are built on top of HDFS and are designed for fast loading, fast query processing and efficient storage utilization. Among the most popular formats, we find: Record Columnar File (RCFile) [11], Optimized Row Columnar (ORC)[4], Avro[5], Parquet[6] and SequenceFile[7]. They differ from each other in terms of their layout. Avro, for instance, uses a horizontal layout, whereas Parquet uses a hybrid layout. None of them is the universal best choice; different workloads require different layouts to achieve optimal performance [2].

Note also that, none of the solutions that answer the first question consider different formats and they store intermediate results using a single fixed format. A single fixed format though, is not appropriate for all types of workloads[8] and this is already identified in previous works [2,9,13]. These works clearly demonstrate the importance of the second question. Ideally, the materialized results should be stored in the most appropriate format for their later reuse.

We contend that a properly chosen data format reduces the load time of the intermediate results in their subsequent use, and overall, reduces the execution cost of DIW. That is why, in this paper we present ResilientStore, which decides the most appropriate data format for intermediate results using heuristic rules and considering the subsequent access characteristics. The contributions of this paper are as follows:

- We show the performance bottleneck of data formats in different workloads.
- We define a set of heuristic rules to select the appropriate data format based on the access characteristics of the workloads.
- We show that by using ResilientStore in selecting the data format we can reduce the load time of the intermediate results.

---

[4] https://orc.apache.org.
[5] http://avro.apache.org.
[6] http://parquet.apache.org.
[7] http://wiki.apache.org/hadoop/SequenceFile.
[8] http://www.svds.com/how-to-choose-a-data-format.

The remainder of this paper is organized as follows. In Sect. 2, we discuss the Hadoop data formats and provide the motivating example of our work. In Sects. 3 and 4, we discuss the heuristic rules, the architecture of ResilientStore and its implementation. In Sect. 5, we show our experiment results. In Sect. 6, we have a discussion of the related work. Finally in Sect. 7, we conclude the paper and discuss our future work.

2   Background and Motivating Example

In this section, we discuss different storage layouts and their Hadoop representative formats. Moreover, we present an example to show the performance of different formats for different workloads. This example motivates our work and shows the importance of considering different formats for the materialization of intermediate results. Note that, in the context of this paper, layout refers to the fragmentation strategy (e.g., horizontal, vertical) and format refers to the file format (e.g., Avro, Parquet, SequenceFile).

2.1   Hadoop Data Formats

One of the most commonly used formats in Hadoop is the raw format. Despite its extensive use, it suffers from many problems. For instance, it is not splittable after compression or it does not store schema information. Different binary formats have been proposed in order to overcome these problems [9] and they can be classified according to the layout they follow: horizontal, vertical or hybrid.

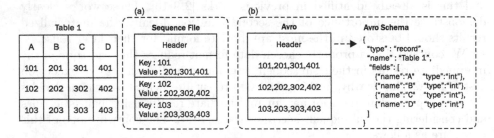

Fig. 1. High level representation of SequenceFile and Avro

Horizontal Layout. A format implementing a horizontal layout organizes data in rows. These formats excel when workloads require full scans. If all the columns are not required, they perform unnecessary reads from disk, since non-required columns will be read anyway. However, these formats are good for data insertion. In Hadoop, the SequenceFile and Avro formats implement a horizontal layout. Figure 1 shows an example table and its corresponding format in SequenceFile (i.e., Fig. 1a) and Avro (i.e., Fig. 1b).

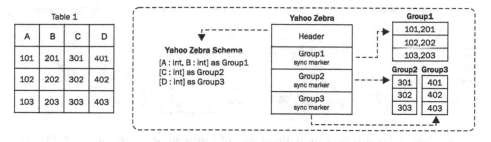

Fig. 2. High level representation of Yahoo Zebra

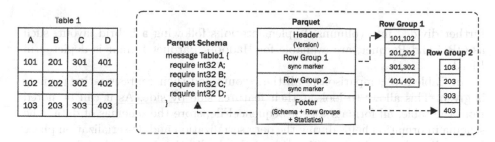

Fig. 3. High level representation of Parquet

Vertical Layout. Formats following a vertical layout organize data in columns and each row is split into different groups of columns. Each group consists of multiple columns stored together. This kind of structure helps on reading less data when a query requires only a subset of columns (i.e., improves the effective read ratio). In Hadoop, Yahoo Zebra[9] implements a vertical layout. Figure 2 exemplifies the Yahoo Zebra format.

Hybrid Layout. A hybrid layout combines the horizontal and vertical layouts. Data stored is divided into row groups and each row inside the row group is

Table 1. Comparison of data formats

Features	Horizontal		Vertical	Hybrid	
	SequenceFiles	Avro	Yahoo Zebra	ORC	Parquet
Schema	No	Yes	Yes	Yes	Yes
Column pruning	No	No	Yes	Yes	Yes
Predicate pushdown	No	No	No	Yes	Yes
Indexing information	No	No	No	Yes	Yes
Statistics information	No	No	No	Yes	Yes
Nested records	No	No	Yes	Yes	Yes

---

9 http://pig.apache.org/docs/r0.9.1/zebra_pig.html.

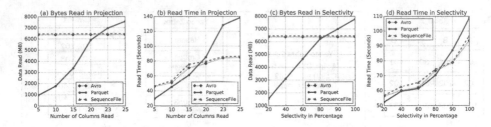

Fig. 4. Table is created by materializing join of Lineitem and Part tables of TPC-H (Scale Factor: 4)

further divided into columns. Implementations following a hybrid layout, such as ORC and Parquet, are available for Hadoop. Parquet format is depicted in Fig. 3.

In Table 1, a comparison of all the layouts and their representative formats is given. This allows to look at their features side by side. As it can be noted from the table, all formats except SequenceFile, store the schemas of data. The schema information helps during the data serialization and de-serialization phase by avoiding the need to cast the data at the application level - which is a costly operation. Moreover, the table shows that both vertical and hybrid layouts provide support for column pruning. It means, they only read the required columns and do not perform unnecessary reads. Hybrid layouts can also push down the selection predicates into the storage layer because they store indexing information that helps in filtering the records while reading. Furthermore, since hybrid layouts store statistical information for each column, they enable easier computation of aggregates. Additionally, vertical and hybrid layouts have support for nested records which helps in storing bag, map and custom user data types. It can also be noted that hybrid layouts have more features but they also have a significant overhead when writing and therefore when reading the same amount of data (due to the amount of metadata stored with data).

In summary, these formats have different features that make them perform better or worse for different workloads. Generally, hybrid layouts perform well if a subset of data is read. On the other hand, horizontal layouts perform well if all, or most of the data is read.

2.2 Motivating Example

In this section we present the results drawn by storing the intermediate results of a DIW in different formats. Note that we do not consider the raw format because of the drawbacks mentioned in the previous section. Consequently, nowadays, mostly binary formats are used in real-world scenarios [2]. The results show that the different features of each binary format prevents them from being a universal solution for all types of workloads. Even more now, when mixed workloads are present, consisting of reporting, interactive, or data mining queries. For instance, Parquet is good for reporting and interactive queries whereas Avro is good for data mining queries where most data is read. Different types of queries can be found in different parts of DIWs. As a matter of fact, queries must be analyzed in order to find the proper format for the materialization.

In this example we create a DIW from the TPC-H benchmark[10] queries and materialize in different Hadoop formats a join between the Lineitem and Part tables. In Fig. 4, results of our example are shown for SequenceFile, Parquet and Avro. We present now the results of reading such materialization by considering two subsequent operators in the DIW: Projection and Selection. Figures 4a and b depict the case when a Projection follows with different numbers of columns to be read from HDFS. In Fig. 4a we measure the size of the data read and in Fig. 4b we measure the needed time to read the data. Note that Parquet is performing better in the first 20 columns but after that SequenceFile and Avro take the lead. Similarly, Fig. 4c and d show the same type of experiment but for Selection.

From the results of this example, we can observe that performance depends on the data format and the subsequent operation in the DIW (i.e., the kind of workload). As a matter of fact, this supports our proposed hypothesis that different formats must be chosen depending on the workload characteristics.

3   System Model and Heuristic Rules

This section presents a formal notation of our problem, which we use to define the rules used to decide the data format for materialized intermediate results. As first approach, we opt for heuristics rules. Lightweight approximations have consistently been used in databases before as they yield a good balance between the performance gain obtained and the extra overhead introduced. For example, [6] uses heuristic rules to decide what nodes to materialize given a DIW. The reason is that, unlike cost-based solutions, heuristic rules do not require to gather run-time statistics (e.g., selectivity factor per operation) and thus do not yield any extra performance overhead. Yet, such lightweight approaches can yield significant improvements.

System Model. We formally define a DIW as follows:

$$DIW \leftarrow DAG(V, E), \text{ where}$$
$$V = \{v_1, v_2, ..., v_n\} \text{ and } E = \{e_1, e_2, ..., e_n\}$$
$$M \subseteq V \text{ and } \forall x \in M, O(x) \subseteq E$$
$$getOP : E \rightarrow \{op_1, op_2, ..., op_n\}$$
$$getType : E \rightarrow \{Type_1, Type_2, ..., Type_n\}$$
$$getCol_{op} : op \rightarrow \mathcal{P}\{col_1, col_2, ..., col_n\}$$
$$getCol_v : V \rightarrow \mathcal{P}\{col_1, col_2, ..., col_n\}$$
$$getBest : M \rightarrow \{format_1, format_2, ..., format_n\}$$

A *DIW* is a *DAG* that consists of vertices (V) and edges (E). A vertex represents a set of data and an edge represents an operator. More precisely, an

---

[10] http://www.tpc.org/tpch.

edge represents an operator applied to the data in its starting vertex. The ending vertex represents the data delivered by the operator after processing the input data. Note that an edge is adorned with schema information; i.e., the columns to which the operator applies. Function **getOP** and **getType** are used to get the instance and type of an operator for a given edge, respectively. Additionally, function **getCol**$_{op}$ is used to get the set of columns on which an operator is executed. Similarly, the function **getCol**$_v$ is used to extract the set of columns of a vertex. In the above notation, M denotes the materialized nodes, which are a subset of V. $O(x)$ represent the outgoing edges from a materialized node, which is a subset of E. Finally, given that our set of rules may decide that more than one format is suitable for a materialized node. We introduce the function **getBest** in order to choose one among them. This function compares the different formats and chooses the one which has more features.

Heuristic Rules for Format Selection. We now introduce the heuristic rules used to decide what format to choose for a given materialized node. These rules derive from the well-known properties of horizontal, vertical and hybrid layouts and the specific format features presented in Sect. 2:

$\forall x \in M$

$rule1 : x \rightarrow$ SequenceFile, IF $size(getCol_v(x)) = 2$

$rule2 : x \rightarrow$ Parquet, IF $\exists e \in O(x)$, WHERE $getType(e) \in \{AggregationOps\}$

$rule3 : x \rightarrow$ Parquet, IF $\exists e \in O(x)$, WHERE $getCol_{op}(getOP(e)) \subseteq getCol_v(x)$

$rule4 : x \rightarrow$ Avro, IF $\forall e \in O(x)$, WHERE $getCol_{op}(getOP(e)) = getCol_v(x)$

$rule5 : x \rightarrow$ Avro, IF $\exists e \in O(x)$, WHERE $getType(e) \in \{Join, CartesianProduct,$
$GroupALL, Distinct\}$

`Rule1` chooses SequenceFile for the materialization of nodes that have exactly two columns. This is an immediate application of the SequenceFile format (which stores data as key-value pairs). Otherwise, several columns need to be combined (e.g., with a separator marker such as "-" or ";") either in the key or the value and parsed at the application level. `Rule2` chooses Parquet when performing aggregations on data. Since Parquet stores statistical information for each column, it is the most efficient when computing aggregates. Since Parquet implements a hybrid layout, it is also the best choice when it comes to read subsets of data or when operators apply on subsets of columns (see Table 1). This rationale is behind `rule3`. Oppositely, Avro is chosen when all the data is read or when the operator does not apply on a certain subset of columns. This is a consequence of Avro implementing a horizontal layout. Hence, `rule4` (the operator affects all columns) and `rule5` (the operator requires to read the whole data without filtering) recommend using Avro in these respective cases. The heuristic rules defined are mutually exclusive. They can be applied independently of each other and without any fixed order. Note that, these rules do not consider vertical layouts because they are subsumed by hybrid layouts. However, using our formal notation other formats can be added easily.

After applying the heuristic rules, there exist some cases where multiple choices are suitable. In order to circumvent this problem, we have defined the function `getBest`. This function gives highest priority to Parquet owing to the fact that Parquet has more features and a more flexible behavior. The second highest priority is assigned to Avro because it stores schema information about the data which speeds up the reading. Finally, the lowest rank belongs to SequenceFile which is only chosen for key-value data.

4   ResilientStore

In this section, we first discuss about the materialization of intermediate results. Then, we discuss the architecture of our system and its implementation. Finally, we discuss its format selection algorithm.

4.1   Materialization of Intermediate Results

In previous sections, we mentioned that re-accessing of data occurs very often (i.e., 80 % of the time [3]), and there are already available solutions [6,16] for deciding on the materialization of intermediate results. Hence, we use one of these solutions for the materialization phase, namely, ReStore [6]. However, any other solution can be used as long as it provides the nodes to be materialized. The heuristics used in ReStore are categorized into conservative and aggressive. Conservative heuristics refer to the materialization of the outputs from PROJECT and FILTER operators, because they reduce the size of data. Whereas, aggressive heuristics are used to materialize the outputs of JOIN, GROUP and CoGROUP[11] operators, because they are computation intensive. These heuristics are used to decide about the materialization of the results to be reused by subsequent operators in DIWs. However, note that ReStore does not consider the data format to be used for the materialization. Our approach fills this gap by using the aforementioned heuristic rules for selecting the most appropriate data format when materializing intermediate results.

4.2   System Architecture

In Fig. 5, we depict the architecture of ResilientStore. It takes a workflow (DIW) as input and returns a DIW where the nodes to be materialized are tagged and the most appropriate data format is selected. First, ResilientStore applies the ReStore heuristic rules to choose the best nodes for materialization and then applies format selection heuristic rules (Sect. 3) to decide the most suitable data format.

Our prototype is implemented using Pig as this is the most popular language for executing DIWs on a Hadoop cluster [3] and also because of compatibility reasons with ReStore. Thus, we first instantiated the conceptual operations mentioned in our format selection heuristic rules with Pig Operators. The *Aggregation Ops* (see `rule2`) provided by Pig include SUM, MIN, MAX and COUNT.

---

[11] A Pig operation combining GROUP BY and JOIN.

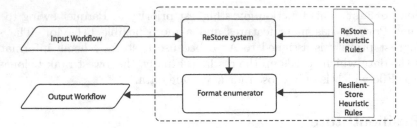

Fig. 5. System architecture

The set of Pig operations to be considered in `rule5` are JOIN, CROSS (Cartesian Product), COGROUP, GROUPALL and DISTINCT. However, our rules are independent of Pig. We can use any other language (e.g., Apache Drill or Apache Hive) just by instantiating the conceptual operators with the operators of that language.

Algorithm 1. ResilientStore data format selection algorithm

1: **procedure** RS–FORMAT(x)
2:     ruleSet = $getResilientStoreRules()$
3:     formatSet = $\emptyset$
4:     **for each** $rule \in$ ruleSet **do**
5:         format = $rule$(x)
6:         formatSet.$append$(format)
7:     **end for**
8:     bestFormat = $getBest$(formatSet)
9:     **return** bestFormat
10: **end procedure**

In order to choose the nodes to be materialized, our solution first applies the heuristic rules of ReStore on each Pig script. Then, once the nodes to be materialized are chosen, the scripts containing them are further analyzed using our heuristic rules to decide the most appropriate data format. Note that, our heuristic rules only consider the first operator of subsequent scripts which are reading these materialized nodes. The reason is that, only the first operator has effect on reading the data from the disk and subsequent operators read the data from the memory. After the data format is decided, the serialization in the selected format needs to be carried out. The serialization process is straightforward for Avro and Parquet because they automatically infer the tuples' schema during the serialization and de-serialization phases. SequenceFile, however, requires explicit key-value pairs for the serialization and de-serialization. Hence, our system automatically converts each tuple into a key-value pair (one attribute is set as key, and the other as value).

4.3   Format Enumerator Algorithm

Our algorithm is shown in Algorithm 1. The algorithm, takes a materialized node as input and finds the best storage format for it. In lines 4 to 7, it iteratively applies all the ResilientStore rules which we have defined in Sect. 3 and gets their suggested formats. Then, in line 8 it gets the best format among the ones that were suggested. Finally, in line 9 it returns the chosen format. Note that, this algorithm is then iteratively run on every materialized node in order to choose the best format for each one of them.

5   Experiments

This section reports on our experimental findings. Note, first, that we are not considering compression for a fairer comparison between different formats. Second, we are assuming data is uniformly distributed.

5.1   Setup and Dataset

Our experiments are performed on a 8-machine cluster[12]. Each machine has a Xeon E5–2630L v2 @2.40 GHz CPU, 128 GB of main memory and 1 TB SATA-3 of hard disk. Each machine runs Hadoop 2.6.0 and Pig 0.15.0 on Ubuntu 14.04 (64 bit). We have dedicated one machine for the name node and the remaining seven machines for data nodes.

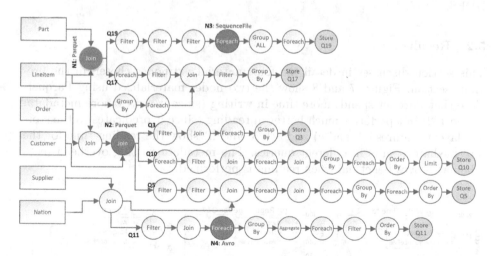

Fig. 6. DIW of six TPC-H queries

We use the TPC-H[13] benchmarking tool to generate datasets and queries. In order to create a complex DIW, we use Quarry [15]. Quarry is used to combine all

---

[12] http://www.ac.upc.edu/serveis-tic/altas-prestaciones.
[13] http://www.tpc.org/tpch.

TPC-H queries into one integrated DIW as shown in Fig. 6. We are using TPC-H because it is a standard benchmarking tool and it contains queries which cover all possible cases.

In order to perform more realistic experiments, we generate data with scale factor ranging from 1 GB to 128 GB. In our experiments, ReStore chooses 8 nodes to be materialized after applying both its aggressive and conservative heuristics. The aggressive heuristics decide the materialization of the output of 6 JOINs and the conservative heuristics decide to materialize that of 2 FOREACH operations. We then apply our heuristic rules (see Sect. 3) to choose the format of the materialized nodes. For the 6 JOINs, we choose Parquet, while Avro and SequenceFile are chosen, respectively, for the first and second FOREACH. ResilientStore choose the best format in all cases. For discussion, we choose 4 nodes which cover the three formats, as shown in Fig. 6. The DIW used in our experiments is available online[14]. Additionally, we choose two metrics to analyze our approach, namely write time and read time, and measure them for each materialized node using the following formulas.

- `write_time = # of HDFS blocks * cost of writing one HDFS block`
- `read_time = (# of HDFS blocks * cost of reading one HDFS block)`
  `+ execution cost of the first operator of the query`

We only consider the first operator in `read_time` because the subsequent operators are executed in memory and hence they read from memory instead of HDFS.

5.2   Results

This section discusses in detail the four materialized nodes chosen in the previous section. Figures 7 and 8 show the two nodes materialized using Parquet. Note that Parquet spends more time in writing (since it writes more metadata; see Sect. 2) but performs much better in reading (since it predicates to the storage layer). Figures 7(b and c) and 8(b, c and d) show the reading time for the intermediate results in different queries. The metadata writing overhead (e.g., schema) proves beneficial when reading is performed.

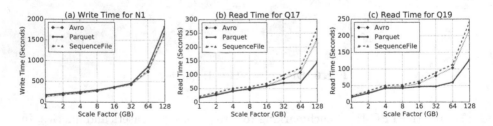

Fig. 7. Experiment results for N1 (Q17 & Q19)

[14] http://ranafaisal.info/?attachment_id=153.

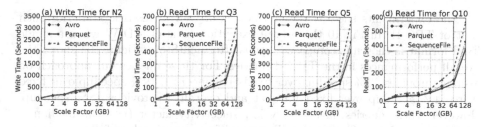

Fig. 8. Experiment results for N2 (Q3, Q5 & Q10)

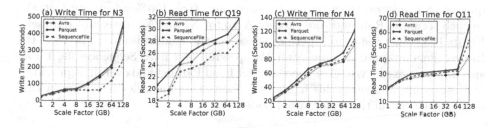

Fig. 9. Experiment results for N3 (Q19) and N4 (Q11)

Furthermore, as it can be noted from Fig. 9a and b, SequenceFile is a better choice for N3. For all the other nodes SequenceFile takes more time in writing than Avro, because it stores data as key-value pairs and for columns stored in the value it needs markers to separate them. However, in N3 SequenceFile writes less data since two columns are written (one as key, the other as value) and no marker is necessary. In N3, SequenceFile performs also good when reading because it does not need to convert key-value pairs back to tuples.

In Fig. 9c and d, we show the performance for N4, which chooses Avro. Note that Avro writes less data for all nodes except for N3. This is the reason why Avro performs well in N4, since all the data needs to be read. However, in the other nodes, Avro does not perform that well because of the column pruning applied by Parquet.

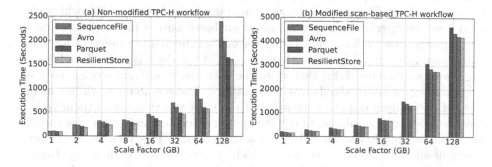

Fig. 10. Single fixed format vs. ResilientStore

The experiments show that our rules work well in realistic scenarios such that of TPC-H. In Fig. 10 the overall execution time of a DIW when a single fixed format is chosen is compared against ResilientStore. Figure 10a shows the overall performances in the TPC-H queries. For these queries our approach on average provides 32 % speedup over fixed SequenceFile, 19 % speedup over fixed Avro, 4 % speedup over fixed Parquet and overall, it provides 18 % speedup. However, these queries have a very low selectivity factor (i.e., the median is 0.8 %) [1], which benefits Parquet. To exemplify a scenario where full-scans would dominate (e.g., for computing data mining algorithms), we modified the TPC-H queries to transform them into scan-based ones (i.e., 100 % selectivity factor). In such scenario, ResilientStore chooses Avro for N1 and N2 instead of Parquet. Figure 10b shows the overall performances for the modified queries of TPC-H. In average, our approach provides a 9 % speedup over fixed SequenceFile, 1.5 % speedup over fixed Avro, 21 % speedup over fixed Parquet and overall, it provides 10 % speedup. Moreover, this figure also shows that our rules have chosen the right format for all the materialized nodes.

6   Related Work

The fixed format problem has been identified by the research community and many solutions have been proposed. The existing solutions allow using multiple layouts together. For instance, the in-memory DBMS SAP HANA [8] uses horizontal and vertical layouts for On-line Transaction Processing (OLTP) and On-line Analytical Processing (OLAP) workloads, respectively. In a similar way, in DB2 [17] horizontal and vertical layouts can be used for the same table-space. However, these layouts are fixed and non-modifiable at runtime. There are also solutions that consider workloads in order to decide for the most suitable layout. These systems, however, work in multi-database environments. Polybase [5] for instance, is a system that uses both a Hadoop cluster and a DBMS for data storage. Based on the workloads, it dynamically decides which solution is the best. According to this decision, it also moves the data from one system to another for executing queries. This solution focuses on utilizing the processing power of the Hadoop cluster and it always uses an horizontal layout to store data on Hadoop. Similar to Polybase, there is a hybrid system [12], which can read raw files directly and choose the layout based on the input queries. However, they propose to keep multiple copies of the same data in different formats. But this might not be feasible when the size of the data is huge. In addition, there are two systems [7,18] that store the data inside different storage engines by taking into account the data access patterns. These systems work like mediators, they analyze the characteristics of the data and then route them to the most suitable storage engine. In [7], the system requires training in order to take the right decision in choosing the best storage engine. This training runs every query in all available systems to see which system fits best each query. Hence, this requires extra processing and adds extra cost. In [18], the solution relies on annotations which are defined by the user during the requirements definition process of an application. These annotations help the mediator to decide where to store the application data. The annotations, however cannot be defined at run-time. Moreover, this solution mainly focuses on choosing a storage engine according to the application requirements without considering the data format.

H2O [2] can dynamically decide the layout of the data based on the current workload. However, it only considers vertical layouts by creating different column groups. As discussed in [2], creating column groups is a NP-hard problem and it is not feasible for tables with many columns. Similarly, Trojan [13] is an adaptable column storage for Hadoop, which takes advantage of the data replication feature of HDFS. It analyzes the workload access patterns and stores different column groups on each replica according to the different access patterns. Then, it routes a query to the most suitable replica format. However, it only considers vertical layouts. Finally, WWHow [14] proposes a data layer which is independent of the physical storage. This layer enables an adaptable physical storage engine by analyzing the application needs. However, they are considering general storage systems such as file-systems, databases and cloud storage without considering the physical formats. Moreover, once decided, the storage system remains fixed.

7   Conclusion and Future Work

Analytical querying introduces variable types of workloads that co-exist in the same system, and a fixed data format does not yield the best performance for all types of workloads. Thus, we discussed the need to introduce flexibility in the data format and decide it based on the characteristics of the subsequent operators accessing data. Specifically, we have shown for the Hadoop ecosystem that selecting the data format according to the access patterns helps in reducing the load time of the intermediate results. In this paper we introduced ResilientStore a tool to assist on selecting the most appropriate data format. ResilientStore analyzes the access patterns of intermediate results and chooses a format by applying heuristic rules. Our experiments on the Hadoop ecosystem show the benefits on performance. In the future work we plan to combine our approach with a cost-based one in a two-phase approach. In the first phase, we use our rule-based approach to choose a format, so we can immediately react to new flows with no overhead. In the second phase, we plan to refine our first decision by gathering the needed statistics (e.g., the operators selectivity factor) and follow an off-line cost-based approach. This way, for future executions of these intermediate results we can refine the rule-based decision made once the needed statistics have been gathered.

Acknowledgments. This research has been funded by the European Commission through the Erasmus Mundus Joint Doctorate "Information Technologies for Business Intelligence - Doctoral College" (IT4BI-DC).

References

1. Abelló, A., Ferrarons, J., Romero, O.: Building cubes with MapReduce. In: Proceedings of the DOLAP (2011)
2. Alagiannis, I., Idreos, S., Ailamaki, A.: H2O: a hands-free adaptive store. In: Proceedings of the SIGMOD (2014)
3. Chen, Y., Alspaugh, S., Katz, R.: Interactive analytical processing in big data systems: a cross-industry study of MapReduce workloads. In: Proceedings of the VLDB (2012)
4. Dean, J., Ghemawat, S.: MapReduce: Simplified data processing on large clusters. In: Proceedings of the OSDI (2004)
5. DeWitt, D.J., Halverson, A., Nehme, R., Shankar, S., Aguilar-Saborit, J., Avanes, A., Flasza, M., Gramling, J.: Split query processing in polybase. In: Proceedings of the SIGMOD (2013)
6. Elghandour, I., Aboulnaga, A.: ReStore: reusing results of MapReduce jobs. In: Proceedings of the VLDB (2012)
7. Elmore, A., Duggan, J., Stonebraker, M., Balazinska, M., Gadepally, V., Heer, J., Howe, B., Kepner, J., Kraska, T., Madden, S., Maier, D., Mattson, T., Papadopoulos, S., Parkhurst, J., Tatbul, N., Vartak, M., Zdonik, S.: A demonstration of the BigDAWG polystore system. In: Proceedings of the VLDB (2015)
8. Färber, F., Cha, S.K., Primsch, J., Bornhovd, C., Sigg, S., Lehner, W.: SAP HANA database - data management for modern business applications. In: Proceedings of the SIGMOD Record (2011)
9. Floratou, A., Patel, J.M., Shekita, E.J., Tata, S.: Column-oriented storage techniques for MapReduce. In: Proceedings of the VLDB (2011)
10. Ghemawat, S., Gobioff, H., Leung, S.-T.: The Google file system. In: Proceedings of the SOSP (2003)
11. He, Y., Lee, R., Huai, Y., Shao, Z., Jain, N., Zhang, X., Xu, Z.: RCFile: a fast and space-efficient data placement structure in MapReduce-based warehouse systems. In: Proceedings of the ICDE (2011)
12. Idreos, S., Alagiannis, I., Johnson, R., Ailamaki, A.: Here are my Data Files. Here are my Queries. Where are my Results? In: Proceedings of the CIDR (2011)
13. Jindal, A., Quian-Ruiz, J.-A., Dittrich, J.: Trojan data layouts: right shoes for a running elephant. In: Proceedings of the SOCC (2011)
14. Jindal, A., Quian-Ruiz, J.-A., Dittrich, J.: WWHow! freeing data storage from cages. In: Proceedings of the CIDR (2013)
15. Jovanovic, P., Romero, O., Simitsis, A., Abelló, A.: Incremental consolidation of data-intensive multi-flows. In: Proceedings of the TKDE (2016)
16. Kalavri, V., Shang, H., Vlassov, V.: m2r2: a framework for results materialization and reuse. In: Proceedings of the BDSE (2013)
17. Raman, V., Attaluri, G., Barber, R., Chainani, N., Kalmuk, D., KulandaiSamy, V., Leenstra, J., Lightstone, S., Liu, S., Lohman, G.M., Malkemus, T., Mueller, R., Pandis, I., Schiefer, B., Sharpe, D., Sidle, R., Storm, A., Zhang, L.: DB2 with BLU acceleration: so much more than just a column store. In: Proceedings of the VLDB (2013)
18. Schaarschmidt, M., Gessert, F., Ritter, N.: Towards automated polyglot persistence. In: Proceedings of the BTW (2015)

Bulk-Loading xBR$^+$-trees

George Roumelis[1], Michael Vassilakopoulos[2]($\boxtimes$), Antonio Corral[3],
and Yannis Manolopoulos[1]

[1] Department of Informatics, Aristotle University of Thessaloniki,
Thessaloniki, Greece
{groumeli,manolopo}@csd.auth.gr
[2] Department of Electrical and Computer Engineering,
University of Thessaly, Volos, Greece
mvasilako@uth.gr
[3] Department of Informatics, University of Almeria, Almeria, Spain
acorral@ual.es

Abstract. Spatial indexes are important in spatial databases for efficient execution of queries involving spatial constraints. The xBR$^+$-tree is
a balanced disk-resident quadtree-based index structure for point data,
which is very efficient for processing such queries. Bulk-loading refers
to the process of creating an index from scratch as a whole, when the
dataset to be indexed is available beforehand, instead of creating (loading) the index gradually, when the dataset items are available one-by-one.
In this paper, we present an algorithm for bulk-loading xBR$^+$-trees for
big datasets residing on disk, using a limited amount of RAM. Moreover, using real and artificial datasets of various cardinalities, we present
an experimental comparison of this algorithm vs. the algorithm loading
items one-by-one, regarding performance (I/O and execution time) and
the characteristics of the xBR$^+$-trees created. We also present experimental results regarding the efficiency of bulk-loaded xBR$^+$-trees vs.
xBR$^+$-trees where items are loaded one-by-one for query processing.

Keywords: Spatial indexes · Bulk-loading · xBR$^+$-trees · Query
processing

1 Introduction

Spatial indexes are designed to facilitate spatial database operations that involve
retrieval of spatial objects according to specific spatial constraints [1]. An important issue in the implementation of such spatial indexes is the time needed to
build them from a specific dataset. If the dataset is static (i.e. when insertions
and deletions are rarely executed or even they are not performed at all), we can
focus on building the spatial index in a way that permits the efficient execution
of queries. However, it is also desirable that the index creation time is as short
as possible. For this reason, the fast construction of an optimized spatial index
structure regarding certain index characteristics (e.g. storage overhead minimiza-
tion, storage utilization maximization, etc.) is an interesting challenge, since it

© Springer International Publishing Switzerland 2016
L. Bellatreche et al. (Eds.): MEDI 2016, LNCS 9893, pp. 57–71, 2016.
DOI: 10.1007/978-3-319-45547-1_5

is anticipated that, due to these characteristics, query processing performance will be improved. This is known in the literature as *packing* or *bulk-loading*.

Bulk-loading refers to the process of creating an index from scratch for a given dataset [2], and here we use this term to characterize building of a disk-based spatial index for an entire dataset without any intervening queries [17]. Index bulk-loading of large datasets has been an important direction of database research. Bulk-loading is necessary when an index is built up for the first time. It is well known that loading indexes by inserting items (tuples) one-by-one (i.e. *tuple-loading* [2]) is less efficient than specially designed bulk-loading algorithms that can be executed with the same complexity as external sorting [2]. Bulk-loading is therefore an interesting option for building spatial indexes when the data are known in advance and not many updating operations are executed.

The bulk-loading process, in general, consists of two sub-processes: data partitioning and index construction. In the *data partitioning process*, a dataset is partitioned into subsets whose cardinality is at maximum a certain number of data objects, called *fanout*. Data objects are sorted according to particular methods and are assigned linearized orders. In the *index construction process*, geometric shapes (as Minimum Bounding Rectangles, MBR) are formed from partitioned subsets and inserted as entries to intermediate or terminal nodes of the spatial index structure. *Top-down* approach builds intermediate nodes first, whereas *bottoms-up* builds terminal nodes first.

In this paper, we study the efficiency of building a quadtree-based index structure. In particular, wel focus on the xBR$^+$-tree [3], a balanced disk-based index structure for point data that belongs to the Quadtree family, and hierarchically decomposes space in a regular manner. The xBR$^+$-tree improves the xBR-tree [4,19] in the node structure and the splitting process. Moreover, it outperforms xBR-trees and R*-trees with respect to several well-known spatial queries, such as Point Location, Window Query, K-Nearest Neighbor, etc.

In this paper, we present the first algorithm for bulk-loading xBR$^+$-trees for big datasets residing on disk, using a limited amount of RAM. Moreover, using real and artificial datasets of various cardinalities, we present an experimental comparison of this algorithm vs. the algorithm of loading items one-by-one, regarding creation time and the characteristics of the tree created. We also present experimental results regarding the (I/O and execution time) efficiency of bulk-loaded xBR$^+$-trees vs. xBR$^+$-trees, where items are loaded one-by-one for query processing of single dataset queries (Point Location − *PLQ*, Window Query − *WQ*, Distance Range Query − *DRQ*, K-Nearest Neighbors Query − *KNNQ*, Constrained K-Nearest Neighbors Query − *CKNNQ*) and of dual dataset spatial queries (*K*-Closest Pairs Query − *KCPQ* and Distance Join Query − *DJQ*).

This paper is organized as follows. In Sect. 2 we review related work on bulk-loading and provide the motivation of this paper. In Sect. 3, we describe the most important characteristics of xBR$^+$-tree, from the implementation point of view. Section 4 presents our bulk-loading method for the xBR$^+$-tree. In Sect. 5, we discuss the results of our experiments. And finally, Sect. 6

provides the conclusions arising from our work and discusses related future work directions.

2   Related Work and Motivation

This section reviews previous bulk-loading methods in general, whose main target is to reduce the loading time, the query cost of the resulting index structure, or both. In [2] the bulk-loading methods are roughly classified into three categories: sort-based, buffer-based and sampled-based methods.

- The *sort-based bulk-loading* methods are characterized by the following two steps: first, the dataset is sorted and second, the tree is built in a bottom-up fashion. The advantages of these methods are their simplicity of implementation and their good query performance.
- The *buffer-based bulk-loading* methods use the *buffer-tree* techniques [6], and they can be considered as a hybrid of top-down and bottom-up strategies. They employ external queues (*buffers*) attached to the internal nodes of the tree except for the root node. An insertion of a record can be viewed as a process temporarily blocked after having arrived at a node. Instead of continuing the traversal down to the leaf, the record is inserted into the *buffer*. Whenever the number of records in a *buffer* exceeds a threshold, a large portion of the records of the buffer is transferred to the next level.
- The *sample-based bulk-loading* methods use a sample of the input that fits into memory to build up the target index. In general, this method randomly samples objects, so-called *representatives*, from the input and builds up a structure. Then, the remaining records of the input are assigned to one of the *representatives*. For each representative, the associated data objects are treated again in the same way.

There are several methods that belong to the *sort-based bulk-loading* category, but the most characteristic ones are proposed in [8–11]. In [8], a method (so-called *packed R-tree*) that uses a heuristic for aggregating rectangles into nodes is introduced. It suggests to sort the data with respect to minimum value of the objects in a certain dimension. In [9] a variant of the packed R-tree is proposed, so-called *Hilbert-packed R-tree*, wherein the order is based purely on the Hilbert code of the objects' centroids. Another sort-based method for bulk-loading R-trees is presented in [10]. The method starts sorting the data source with respect to the first dimension (e.g. using the center of the spatial objects). Then, $(N/B)^{1/d}$ contiguous partitions are generated, each of them containing (almost) the same number of objects, where N is the number of objects, B is the node capacity and d are the dimensions of the input dataset. In the next step, each partition is sorted individually with respect to the next dimension. Again, partitions are generated of almost equal size and the process is repeated until each dimension has been treated. The final partitions will eventually contain at most B objects. In [10], it was also shown that this method of sort-based bulk-loading creates R-trees whose search quality is superior to R-trees created with respect to the Hilbert-ordering. However, the method also requires the input being sorted d times. Recently, in [11] a sort-based query-adaptive loading for building R-trees optimally designed for a given query profile is presented. Finally, in [12] a scalable alternative MapReduce approach to parallel loading of R-trees using a level-by-level design, based on [11], is introduced.

The most representative of *buffer-based bulk-loading* methods are proposed in [6,7,13]. In [13], the R-tree is built recursively bottom-up. In each stage, an intermediate tree structure is built, where the lowest level corresponds to the next level of the final R-tree. The non-leaf nodes in the intermediate tree structures have a high fan-out (determined by available internal memory) as well as a buffer that receives insertions. [6] achieves a similar effect by using a regular R-tree structure (i.e. where the non-leaf nodes have the same fan-out as the leaf nodes) and attaching buffers to nodes only at certain levels of the tree. In [7], a generic algorithm for bulk-loading based on *buffer-trees* for a broad class of index structures (e.g. R-trees) is proposed. Instead of sorting, the split and merge routines of the target index structure are exploited for building an efficient temporary structure (based on *buffer-tree*). From this structure, the desired index structure is built up incrementally bottom-up, one level at a time.

The most remarkable *sample-based bulk-loading* algorithms have been proposed in [2,14,15]. In [14] a method to build an M-tree was proposed. This algorithm selects a number of *seed* objects (by sampling) around which other objects are recursively clustered to build an unbalanced tree, which must later be re-balanced. In [15], a kd-tree structure is built up using a fast external algorithm for computing the median (or a point within an interval centered at the median). The sample is used for computing the skeleton of a kd-tree that is kept as an index in an internal node of the index structure. In [2], the two generic sample-based bulk-loading algorithms proposed, recursively partition the input by using a main-memory index of the same type as the target index to be built.

The most representative contributions related to bulk-loading techniques for Quadtree index structures are [16–18]. In [16], the bulk-loading is characterized by the process of building a disk-based spatial index for an entire set of objects without any intervening queries. The proposed approaches, trying to speed up the bulk-loading process on PMR-quadtrees, are based on the idea of trying to fill up memory with as much of the Quadtree as possible (using *buffers*) before writing some of its nodes on disk. The first approach focuses on the problem on B-tree level, increasing the amount of buffering done by the B-tree (*B-tree buffing*). The second approach focuses on the problem of PMR-quadtree level, reducing the number of accesses to the B-tree as much as possible by storing parts of the PMR-quadtree in main memory (*Quadtree buffering*). In [17], improved versions of the bulk-loading algorithms studied in [16] for PMR-quadtrees are presented, assuming that the algorithms are implemented using a linear quadtree, a disk-resident representation that stores objects contained in the leaf nodes of the quadtree in a linear index (B-tree) ordered on the basis of a space-filling curve (*Morton curve*). Finally, the extended version of [16,17] is presented in [18], where the detailed algorithms for the proposed *sort-based bulk-loading* method, analytic observations, an extensive experimental study and interesting discussions are presented.

The main motivation of this work is the proposal of a new bottom-up, sort-based like approach for bulk-loading of a space-driven quadtree variant, the xBR$^+$-tree. Note that the xBR$^+$-tree [4,19] (for more details, see Sect. 3) is unlike any other quadtree variant, since it is a totally disk-based, height-balanced, pointer-based, multiway tree for multidimensional points and no other quatree variant has all these characteristics.

3 The xBR$^+$-tree

The xBR$^+$-tree [3] (an extension of the xBR-tree [4,19]) is a hierarchical, disk-resident Quadtree-based (space-driven access method) index structure for multi-dimensional points. For 2d space, the space indexed is a *square* and is recursively subdivided in 4 equal subquadrants. The nodes of the tree are disk pages of two kinds: *leaves*, which store the actual multidimensional data themselves and *internal nodes*, which provide a multiway indexing mechanism.

Internal node entries in xBR$^+$-trees contain entries of the form (*Shape, qside, DBR, Pointer*). Each entry corresponds to a child-node pointed by *Pointer*. The region of this child-node is related to a subquadrant of the original space. *Shape* is a flag that determines if the region of the child-node is a complete or non complete square (the area remaining, after one or more splits; explained later in this subsection). This field is heavily used in queries. *DBR* (Data Bounding Rectangle) stores the coordinates of the rectangular subregion of the child-node region that contains point data (at least two points must reside on the sides of the *DBR*), while *qside* is the side length of the subquadrant of the original space that corresponds to the child-node.

The subquadrant of the original space related to the child-node is expressed by an *Address*. This *Address* (which has a variable size) is not explicitly stored in the xBR$^+$-tree, although it is uniquely determined and can be easily calculated using *qside* and *DBR*. Each *Address* represents a subquadrant that has been produced by Quadtree-like hierarchical subdivision of the current space (of the subquadrant of the original space related to the current node). It consists of a number of directional digits that make up this subdivision. The NW, NE, SW and SE subquadrants of a quadrant are distinguished by the directional digits 0, 1, 2 and 3, respectively. For 2d space, we use two directional bits each of every dimension. The lower bit represents the subdivision on horizontal (X-axis) dimension, while the higher bit represents the subdivision on vertical (Y-axis) dimension [4,19]. For example, the *Address* 1 represents the NE quadrant of the current space, while the *Address* 10 the NW subquadrant of the NE quadrant of the current space. The address of the left child is * (has zero digits), since the region of the left child is the whole space minus the region of the right child.

However, the actual region of the child-node is, in general, the subquadrant of its *Address* minus a number of smaller subquadrants, the subquadrants corresponding to the next entries of the internal node (the entries in an internal node are saved sequentially, in preorder traversal of the Quadtree that corresponds to the internal node). For example, in Fig. 1 an internal node (a root) that points to 2 internal nodes that point to 7 leaves is depicted. The region of the root is the original space, which is assumed to have a quadrangular shape. The region of the right child is the NW quadrant of the original space. The region of the left child is the whole space minus the region of the NW quadrant - a non-complete square. The * symbol is used to denote the end of a variable size address. The *Address* of the right child is 0*, since the region of this child is the NW quadrant of the original space. The *Address* of the left child is * (has zero directional digits), since the region of this child refers to the remaining space. Each of these *Addresses* is expressed relatively to the minimal quadrant that covers the internal node (each *Address* determines a subquadrant of this minimal quadrant). For example, in Fig. 1, the *Address* 3* is the SE subquadrant of the NW subquadrant of whole space (absolute *Address* 03*). During a search, or an insertion of a data element with specified coordinates, the appropriate leaf and its region is determined by descending the tree from the root.

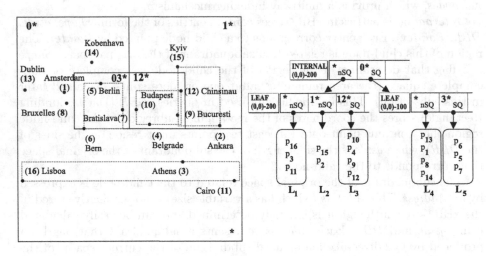

Fig. 1. A collection of points, its grouping to xBR$^+$-tree nodes and its xBR$^+$-tree.

External nodes (leaves) of the xBR$^+$-tree simply contain the data elements and have a predetermined capacity C. When C is exceeded, due to an insertion in a leaf, the region of this leaf is partitioned in two subregions. The one (new) of these subregions is a subquadrant of the region of the leaf, which is created by partitioning the region of the leaf according to hierarchical (Quadtree like) decomposition, as many times as needed so that the most populated subquadrant (that corresponds to this new subregion) has a cardinality that is smaller than or equal to C. The other one (old) of these subregions is the region of the leaf minus the new subregion.

4   Bulk-Loading xBR$^+$-tree

In this section, we present the method that we developed for bulk-loading xBR$^+$-trees. This method consists of four phases.

The first phase is a technical one. Since the initial dataset file is usually in text format, we transform this file to binary format (for efficiency during reading from and writing to secondary memory) and at the same time we split it in two files, based on the middle of the axis of the last dimension. These transformation and splitting are a preprocessing step for the next phase (the resulting files are used as input item files for the next phase).

During the second phase we partition each of the two input item files into item blocks of size $\leq$ *MemoryLimit* in a regular fashion (we alternate between splitting axes and always split in the middle of the current subregion). We use a temporary helper file, which is paired with each of the input item files. When the partition of one of these input item files starts, the item file is used for input and the helper is used for output. While there exist blocks of size $>$ *MemoryLimit*, we continue splitting and each time we alternate between splitting axes the roles of input and output files are interchanged. The resulting blocks are transferred in main memory, as input for the next phase.

During the third phase, for each block of items, a Quadtree is built in main memory by splitting nodes as long as they correspond to regions (quadblocks) containing more items than the capacity of xBR$^+$-tree leaves. This Quadtree is gradually transformed to an xBR$^+$-tree in main memory, referred to as m-xBR$^+$-tree for the rest of the paper. Initially, in a bottom-up fashion, the subtrees of this Quadtree that will form the leaves of the m-xBR$^+$-tree having the largest possible occupancy of items are determined. When all the leaves of the m-xBR$^+$-tree have been created in main memory, they are transferred to secondary memory, since they will not be altered for the rest of the bulk-loading process and the pointers pointing them (entries of internal nodes) are updated. This transfer to secondary memory is uninterruptible for the whole set of leaves, since this is more efficient (I/O with the data file hosting the whole set of leaves for large chunks of time) than several transfers of single leaves that are intermixed with other I/O operations. Afterwards, the rest of the Quadtree is transformed to the index part of the m-xBR$^+$-tree (internal nodes), level-by-level. Again, for each level, in a bottom-up fashion, the subtrees of the Quadtree that will form the internal nodes of the m-xBR$^+$-tree of this level having the largest possible occupancy of children are determined. The process followed to form the nodes of the leaf level and the levels of internal nodes has similarities to the way we split overflowed xBR$^+$-tree nodes when we insert items one-by-one into them [3,4,19]. The difference lies in the number of subtrees that form the m-xBR$^+$-tree nodes of a level, as now they may be more than two. This process is repeated a number of times equal to the final height of the m-xBR$^+$-tree (up to the root level) for the current item block.

During the last phase, the m-xBR$^+$-tree created in main memory is merged with the xBR$^+$-tree already built in secondary memory (existing xBR$^+$-tree). This xBR$^+$-tree was created during the previous iteration of the bulk-loading process. For the merging process to be feasible, two properties (that are satisfied by the previous phases of the bulk-loading process) should hold. Either the regions R_0 of the existing xBR$^+$-tree holding P_0 points and R_1 of the m-xBR$^+$-tree holding P_1 points are completely disjoint ($R_0 \cap R_1 = \emptyset$), or the existing xBR$^+$-tree has no data items into the R_1 region ($\forall p \in R_0, p \notin R_1$). The merge process proceeds as follows:

- If there is an empty xBR$^+$-tree in disk (since this is the first block processed), the internal nodes of the m-xBR$^+$-tree are transferred to disk in a post-order fashion and become the existing xBR$^+$-tree. As mentioned before, the leaves of the m-xBR$^+$-tree have already been saved into disk.
- If the the existing xBR$^+$-tree and the m-xBR$^+$-tree have the same height, all internal nodes of the m-xBR$^+$-tree are transferred to disk in a post-order fashion, except for the root. The root of the xBR$^+$-tree ($|R_0| = n_0$) must be merged with the root of the m-xBR$^+$-tree ($|R_1| = n_1$). There are two cases in this phase. If $n_0 + n_1 \leq C$ then all entries of R_1 are added to R_0. Else, if $n_0 + n_1 > C$, a new root of the xBR$^+$-tree must be created having the roots of the two trees as children. In this case, the merge process leads to an increase of the height of the existing xBR$^+$-tree.
- If the m-xBR$^+$-tree has a smaller height (h_1) than the existing xBR$^+$-tree (h_0), all internal nodes of the m-xBR$^+$-tree are transferred to disk in a post-order fashion, except for the root. The xBR$^+$-tree is searched from its root in order to find the internal node (with region N_0, where $|N_0| = n_0$) of height h_1, that can host the region of the root of the m-xBR$^+$-tree ($|R_1| = n_1$). If $n_0 + n_1 \leq C$ then all entries of R_1 are added in N_0. Else, if $n_0 + n_1 > C$, a new entry for R_1 is created and added to the parent node of N_0. As long as overflows continue to appear, this process continues upwards and may even cause an increase of the tree height.
- If the m-xBR$^+$-tree has a larger height than the existing xBR$^+$-tree ($h_1 > h_0$), the m-xBR$^+$-tree is traversed from its root down to the h_0 level (without transferring any nodes above h_0 level to disk) and the process of merging trees of one of the last two previous cases (trees of equal heights, or m-xBR$^+$-tree with a smaller height) is executed for each of the nodes (roots of subtrees) of the m-xBR$^+$-tree at the h_0 level and the existing xBR$^+$-tree.

The bulk-loading process continues as long as m-xBR$^+$-trees that host an item sub-dataset (block) are created and terminates when the whole dataset has been processed.

Note that the four phases are pipelined (phase one produces an output file as input to phase two that produces a block as input to phase three that produces an m-xBR$^+$-tree as input to phase four). Note also that partitioning data items in a regular (Quadtree-like) fashion is a way of two dimensional sorting. Moreover, m-xBR$^+$-trees are built bottom-up. Therefore, we characterize our technique as a bottom-up, sort-based like approach for bulk-loading the xBR$^+$-tree.

5   Experimental Results

We designed and run a large set of experiments to compare the Process of Bulk-Loading xBR$^+$-trees *(PBL)* to the Process of Loading items in xBR$^+$-trees One-by-One *(PLObO)*. We used 4 real spatial datasets of North America, representing cultural landmarks (NAclN with 9203 points) and populated places (NAppN with 24491 points), roads (NArdN with 569082 line-segments) and railroads (NArrN with 191558 line-segments). To create sets of 2d points, we have transformed the MBRs of line-segments from NArdN and NArrN into points by taking the center of each MBR (i.e. |NArdN| = 569082 points, |NArrN| = 191558 points). Moreover, in order to get the double amount of points from NArrN and NArdN, we chose the two points with *min* and *max* coordinates of the MBR of each line-segment (i.e. |NArdND| = 1138164 points, |NArrND| = 1138188 points). The data of these 6 files were normalized in the range $[0, 1]^2$. We have also created synthetic clustered datasets of 125000, 250000, 500000 and 1000000 points, with 125 clusters in each dataset (uniformly distributed in the range $[0, 1]^2$), where for a set having N points, $N/125$ points were gathered around the center of each cluster, according to Gaussian distribution. We also used two big real datasets[1] to justify the use of spatial query algorithms on disk-resident data instead of using them in-memory. They represent water resources of North America (Water) consisting of 5836360 line-segments and world parks or green areas (Park) consisting of 11503925 polygons. To create sets of points, we used the centers of the line-segment MBRs from Water and the centroids of polygons from Park. The experiments were run on a Linux machine, with Intel core duo 2×2.8 GHz processor and 4 GB of RAM.

We run experiments for tree building, counting tree characteristics and creation time. We also run experiments for several single dataset spatial queries *(PLQ, WQ, DRQ, KNNQ, CKNNQ)* and for two dual dataset spatial queries *(KCPQ* and *DJQ)*, counting disk read accesses (I/O) and total execution time.

5.1   Experiments for Tree Building

In Table 1, for the *PBL*, we present for four indicative datasets (two big and one smaller real datasets and one synthetic dataset) the effect of the *MemoryLimit (ML)* as a percentage of the cardinality of each dataset to the tree characteristics: tree height (H), internal nodes occupancy percentage (Iocc), leaf nodes occupancy percentage (Locc), size of the tree in disk (Size) and the total creation time of the tree (Time). For each each dataset, we added a line that presents the same tree characteristics and the total creation time of tree created by *PLObO*.

Regarding the efficiency of the *PBL*, we observe the following.

– The tree takes the best (smallest) height value using as *MemoryLimit* a percentage of at least 1 % for all datasets, except for the big real dataset, Park. For Park a *MemoryLimit* greater than or equal to 2 % is needed.

---

[1] Retrieved from http://spatialhadoop.cs.umn.edu/datasets.html.

Table 1. Tree creation characteristics, using the *PBL* and the *PLObO* .

ML (%)	H	Iocc (%)	Locc (%)	Size (MB)	Time (s)	ML %)	H	Iocc (%)	Locc (%)	Size (MB)	Time (s)
		Dataset : Water						Dataset : 1000KCN			
1/4	6	55.62	65.08	351	16.93	1/4	7	19.72	64.20	63	1.31
1/2	5	59.82	65.08	350	16.41	1/2	5	48.29	64.20	61	1.28
1	4	65.52	65.08	350	17.37	1	4	57.30	64.19	61	1.43
2	4	67.52	65.08	350	16.41	2	4	60.03	64.19	61	1.26
4	4	68.50	65.08	350	16.34	4	4	64.76	64.19	61	1.25
8	4	68.80	65.08	350	16.63	8	4	65.66	64.19	61	1.45
—	4	57.38	64.69	353	116.0	—	4	63.73	64.57	60	13.0
		Dataset : Park						Dataset : NArdND			
1/4	7	55.55	63.35	711	33.87	1/4	7	20.30	65.15	71	1.67
1/2	6	64.03	63.35	709	34.77	1/2	4	52.42	65.15	68	1.61
1	5	68.07	63.35	708	35.05	1	4	56.15	65.15	68	1.58
2	4	69.03	63.35	708	34.68	2	4	59.45	65.15	68	1.50
4	4	69.25	63.35	708	33.43	4	4	63.74	65.15	68	1.76
8	4	69.34	63.35	708	32.74	8	4	64.51	65.15	68	1.63
—	4	57.20	64.95	693	208.0	—	4	56.83	64.87	69	16.0

- The internal nodes occupancy is increasing as the *MemoryLimit* increases. This is expected if we think that the most compact tree would be created if all the data were present in main memory. However, we observe that the rate of increase of internal nodes occupancy decreases significantly for exponential rate of increase of the *MemoryLimit*.
- The leaves occupancy (and the highly correlated tree size), as it is expected, is independent to the *MemoryLimit*, since the number of items that correspond to *MemoryLimit* is always larger than C, the capacity of the leaves.
- For all *MemoryLimit* values in each dataset, the creation time takes similar values.

The observations are analogous for the rest of the datasets used. Considering the above observations, we propose a *MemoryLimit* value of 2 %. This value achieves either the best, or a good enough value for any tree characteristic.

Comparing the *PBL* to the *PLObO*, we observe the following:

- The smallest height of the *PBL* (for an appropriate value of *MemoryLimit*) is equal to the height of the *PLObO*, for all datasets.
- The *PBL* builds more compact indexes (larger internal nodes occupancy) than the *PLObO*, for most datasets, using *MemoryLimit* larger than 0.5 %.
- The leaves occupancy (and the highly correlated tree size) is comparable in all cases for the two processes.
- The time that the *PBL* takes to create the tree (this is mainly time for I/O) is more than 6 times smaller than the *PLObO*.

The conclusions are analogous for the rest of the datasets used.

5.2   Experiments for Single Dataset Spatial Queries

For *PLQs*, we executed two sets of 60 experiments (12 datasets × 5 node sizes). In the first set, we used as query input the original datasets (existing points). When searching for existing points the number of disk accesses in xBR$^+$-trees is equal to their height. This set of experiments is summarized in the 1st data line of Table 2. In this table, for each query, regarding disk read accesses and execution time, we present percentages of experimental cases where trees created by the two processes perform equivalently (Columns 2 and 5, respectively) and where trees created by *PBL/PLObO* have a performance that is more than 5 % better than their rivals (Columns 3 and 6/4 and 7, respectively). The *MemoryLimit* used was equal to 4 %, although a value of 2 % gives analogous results. It is evident that, for this set of experiments, both types of trees perform almost equivalently. In the second set, we used as query input the centroids of the query windows (non-existing points). While searching for non existing points in the dataset, the disk accesses may be less than the tree-height of xBR$^+$-trees (due to *DBRs*). This set of experiments is summarized in the 2nd data line of Table 2. It is clear that trees created by *PBL*, on the average, perform better in both metrics.

Table 2. Percentages of cases of Disk Accesses and Execution Time winners.

Query	Number of disk read accesses			Execution time		
		PBL	PLObO		PBL	PLObO
	tie	wins	wins	tie	wins	wins
	diff ≤ 5 %	diff > 5 %	diff > 5 %	diff ≤ 5 %	diff > 5 %	diff > 5 %
PLQ-existing points	95.0	00.0	05.0	61.7	23.3	15.0
PLQ-non-existing points	58.3	35.0	06.7	40.0	36.7	23.3
WQ	85.0	13.9	01.1	68.1	21.9	10.0
DRQ	84.7	14.2	01.1	69.7	19.2	11.1
KNNQ	58.3	24.6	17.1	45.8	35.8	18.3
CKNNQ	50.4	43.8	05.8	55.4	31.7	12.9
KCPQ	20.4	79.6	00.0	24.8	75.2	00.0
DJQ	22.8	77.2	00.0	25.6	74.0	00.4

For *WQs*, we executed 360 experiments (12 datasets × 5 node sizes × 6 query window sizes). In Table 3, we depict the average number of disk read accesses and average execution time (in μs), per query window, of 3 real and 2 synthetic datasets having node size of 8KB, as particular examples[2]. The experiments were executed for 4096 query windows (having size 1/4096 of the total space) for each data set. Regarding disk accesses, the two trees perform almost equivalently in 3/5 cases, while, in the other 2/5 cases, the trees created by *PBL* perform

---

[2] Due to space limitations, results for particular datasets are presented for some queries, only.

better. Regarding execution time, the two trees perform almost equivalently in 2/5 cases, while, in the other 3/5 cases, the trees created by *PBL* perform better. All the 360 experiments are summarized in the 3rd data line of Table 2. It is clear that the trees created by *PBL*, on the average, perform better in both metrics.

For *DRQs*, five algorithms, four versions of depth-first (DF) and one version of best-first (BF) were tested in 360 experiments (12 datasets × 5 node sizes × 6 sets of query circles), each. Both trees responded best with DF algorithm in most cases (so, the performance comparison was based on this algorithm). All the 360 experiments are summarized in the 4rd data line of Table 2. It is clear that the trees created by *PBL*, on the average, perform better in both metrics.

For *K-NNQs*, five algorithms, four versions of DF and one version of BF were tested in 240 experiments (12 datasets × 5 node sizes × 4 *K*-values, using 4096 query points, in all cases), each. Both trees responded best with the HDF algorithm (DF search that utilizes a local *MinHeap*, keyed by *mindist* between query point and *DBR*) in most cases (so, the performance comparison was based on this algorithm). In Table 4, we depict the results of 3 real and 2 synthetic datasets having node size of 8 KB, as particular examples. The experiments were executed for 4096 query points (asking for K=1000 nearest neighbors to each query point) for each data set. In these experiments, the trees created by *PBL* always perform better regarding disk read accesses. Regarding execution time, the two trees perform almost equivalently in 1/5 cases, while, in the rest 4/5 cases, the trees created by *PBL* perform better. All the 240 experiments are summarized in the 5rd data line of Table 2. It is clear that the trees created by *PBL*, on the average, perform better in both metrics.

Finally, for *CK-NNQs*, five algorithms, four versions of DF and one version of BF were tested in 240 experiments (12 datasets × 5 node sizes × 4 *K*-values, using 4096 query circles, in all cases), each. Both trees responded best with BF algorithm in most cases, especially in execution time (so, the performance comparison was based on this algorithm). All the 240 experiments are summarized in the 6th data line of Table 2. It is clear for this query, too, that trees created by *PBL*, on the average, perform better in both metrics.

Overall, trees created by *PBL*, perform better regarding both metrics, for all the single dataset queries, except for the *PLQ* for existing points, where the two trees appear almost equivalent. The explanation for the improved performance

Table 3. WQs: average number of Disk Accesses and Execution Time, per query.

Dataset name	Disk read accesses		Relative diff (%)	Time (μs)		Relative diff (%)
	PBL	PLObO		PBL	PLObO	
NArrN	1.925	2.154	10.6	6.59	7.056	6.62
NArdN	2.830	3.102	8.76	9.90	10.48	5.55
500KCN	3.340	3.406	1.93	12.2	12.44	1.85
1000KCN	4.056	4.081	0.60	15.0	15.28	1.83
Water	12.34	12.72	2.98	34.0	35.97	5.54

Table 4. KNNQs: average number of Disk Accesses and Execution Time, per query.

Dataset name	Disk read accesses		Relative diff (%)	Time (μs)		Relative diff (%)
	PBL	PLObO		PBL	PLObO	
NArdN	17.008	22.714	25.1	131.69	202.85	35.1
500KCN	17.478	18.877	7.41	137.78	146.53	5.97
1000KCN	16.932	18.385	7.90	145.76	148.56	1.88
Water	18.875	32.313	41.6	154.92	328.53	52.9
Park	21.237	27.424	22.6	172.36	281.28	38.7

of trees created by *PBL* is related to the structural difference between the two trees. The *PBL* can achieve better grouping of subregions, since all data/entries are known before each node is created.

5.3   Experiments for Dual Dataset Spatial Queries

For *K-CPQs/DJQs*, four algorithms, three versions of DF and one version of BF were tested in 250 experiments (10 combinations of datasets × 5 node sizes × 5 *K*-values, in all cases), each. Both trees responded best with HDF algorithm (that utilizes *minmindist* between *DBRs*, instead of *mindist* between query point and *DBR*) in most cases (so, the performance comparison was based on this algorithm).

Table 5. KCPQs: average number of Disk Accesses and Execution Time, per query.

Dataset name	Disk read accesses		Relative diff (%)	Time (ms)		Relative diff (%)
	PBL	PLObO		PBL	PLObO	
NArrND×NArdND	14351	24559	41.6	100.7	143.8	30.0
500KC2N×1000KC1N	16969	18123	6.37	109.7	116.2	5.58
1000KC1N×1000KC2N	21913	22788	3.84	136.7	141.0	3.04
NArdND×Water	2095	10987	80.9	23.05	104.2	77.9
Water×Park	56783	111960	49.3	360.4	570.7	36.8

In Table 5, we depict the results of 3 combinations of real and 2 combinations of synthetic datasets having node size of 8KB, as particular examples. The experiments were executed for K=1000 closest pairs for each combination. In these experiments, the two trees perform almost equivalently in 1/5 cases, while, in the rest 4/5 cases, the trees created by *PBL* perform better, in both metrics. All the 250 experiments are summarized in the 7th/8th data line of Table 2. It is clear that trees created by *PBL* perform, on the average, significantly better in both metrics. The explanation for the significantly improved performance of trees created by *PBL* is related to the better grouping of subregions and the fact that the execution of *K-CPQs/DJQs* corresponds to multiple *K-NNQs/DRQs*, maximizing the benefits resulting from the *PBL*.

6   Conclusions and Future Work

In this paper, for the first time in the literature, we present an algorithm for bulk-loading xBR$^+$-trees for big datasets residing on disk, using a limited amount of RAM. This bottom-up, sort-based like algorithm was implemented and extensive experimentation was performed for comparing the characteristics and the query performance of trees created by the new algorithm and trees created by the traditional way of inserting items one-by-one. These experiments show that, using a RAM buffer $\geq 2\%$ of the dataset size, bulk-loaded trees that have comparable structural characteristics to non bulk-loaded trees and perform better/significantly better in processing single/dual dataset queries are created.

In the future, we plan to examine alternative ways of bulk-loading xBR$^+$-trees (for example, to avoid using a RAM based Quadtree for gradually building the respective xBR$^+$-tree in main memory, working directly with items and entries). Moreover, we plan to compare bulk-loaded xBR$^+$-trees to other types of spatial indexes (like R*-trees produced by the bulk-loading algorithm of [10]). Last but not least, we plan to embed bulk-loaded xBR$^+$-trees in SpatialHadoop[3].

References

1. Shekhar, S., Chawla, S.: Spatial Databases - A Tour. Prentice Hall, Upper Saddle River (2003)
2. Van den Bercken, J., Seeger, B.: An evaluation of generic bulk loading techniques. In: VLDB Conference, pp. 461–470 (2001)
3. Roumelis, G., Vassilakopoulos, M., Loukopoulos, T., Corral, A., Manolopoulos, Y.: The xBR$^+$-tree: an efficient access method for points. In: Chen, Q., Hameurlain, A., Toumani, F., Wagner, R., Decker, H. (eds.) DEXA 2015. LNCS, vol. 9261, pp. 43–58. Springer, Heidelberg (2015)
4. Roumelis, G., Vassilakopoulos, M., Corral, A.: Performance comparison of xBR-trees and R*-trees for single dataset spatial queries. In: Eder, J., Bielikova, M., Tjoa, A.M. (eds.) ADBIS 2011. LNCS, vol. 6909, pp. 228–242. Springer, Heidelberg (2011)
5. Beckmann, N., Kriegel, H.P., Schneider, R., Seeger, B.: The R*-tree: an efficient and robust access method for points and rectangles. In: SIGMOD Conference, pp. 322–331 (1990)
6. Arge, L., Hinrichs, K.H., Vahrenhold, J., Vitter, J.S.: Efficient bulk operations on dynamic R-trees. Algorithmica **33**(1), 104–128 (2002)
7. Van den Bercken, J., Seeger, B., Widmayer, P.: A generic approach to bulk loading multidimensional index structures. In: VLDB Conference, pp. 406–415 (1997)
8. Roussopoulos, N., Leifker, D.: Direct spatial search on pictorial databases using packed R-trees. In: SIGMOD Conference, pp. 17–31 (1985)
9. Kamel, I., Faloutsos, C.: On packing R-trees. In: CIKM Conference, pp. 490–499 (1993)
10. Leutenegger, S.T., Edgington, J.M., Lopez, M.A.: STR: a simple and efficient algorithm for R-Tree packing. In: ICDE Conference, pp. 497–506 (1997)

---

[3] http://spatialhadoop.cs.umn.edu/.

11. Achakeev, D., Seeger, B., Widmayer, P.: Sort-based query-adaptive loading of R-trees. In: CIKM Conference, pp. 2080–2084 (2012)
12. Achakeev, D., Schmidt, M., Seeger, B.: Sort-based parallel loading of R-trees. In: BigSpatial Workshop, pp. 62–70 (2012)
13. Van den Bercken, J., Seeger, B., Widmayer, P.: A generic approach to bulk loading multidimensional index structures. In: VLDB Conference, pp. 406–415 (1997)
14. Ciaccia, P., Patella, M.: Bulk loading the M-tree. In: Australian Database Conference, pp. 15–26 (1998)
15. Berchtold, S., Böhm, C., Kriegel, H.-P.: Improving the query performance of high-dimensional index structures by bulk load operations. In: Schek, H.-J., Saltor, F., Ramos, I., Alonso, G. (eds.) EDBT 1998. LNCS, vol. 1377, pp. 216–230. Springer, Heidelberg (1998)
16. Hjaltason, G.R., Samet, H., Sussmann, Y.J.: Speeding up bulk-loading of quadtrees. In: ACM GIS Conference, pp. 50–53 (1997)
17. Hjaltason, G.R., Samet, H.: Improved bulk-loading algorithms for quadtrees. In: ACM GIS Conference, pp. 110–115 (1999)
18. Hjaltason, G.R., Samet, H.: Speeding up construction of PMR quadtree-based spatial indexes. VLDB J. 11(2), 109–137 (2002)
19. Vassilakopoulos, M., Manolopoulos, Y.: External balanced regular (x-BR) trees: new structures for very large spatial databases. In: Advances in Informatics: Selected Papers of the 7th Panhellenic Conference on Informatics. World Scientific Publishing Co., pp. 324–333 (2000)

A Meta-advisor Repository for Database Physical Design

Abdelkader Ouared[1(✉)], Yassine Ouhammou[2], and Amine Roukh[3]

[1] National High School for Computer Science (ESI), Algiers, Algeria
a_ouared@esi.dz
[2] LIAS/ISAE-ENSMA, Futuroscope, Poitiers, France
yassine.ouhammou@ensma.fr
[3] University of Mostaganem, Mostaganem, Algeria
roukh.amine@univ-mosta.dz

Abstract. The physical design is one of the crucial phases of advanced database design life cycle. This is due to its important role in selecting optimization structures such as materialized views, indexes, and partitioning to speed up the performance of queries. This phase has been amplified by the continually needs of storing and managing in efficient way the deluge of data in storage systems. This situation motivates the editors of commercial and non-commercial Database Management Systems (e.g. SQL Tuning Advisor - Oracle and Parinda - PostgreSQL) to propose tools (called advisors) to assist database administrators in their tasks when selecting their relevant optimization structures for a given database/data warehouse schema and a workload. The maturity of research performed in the physical design motivates us to go further and capitalize the knowledge and expertise in terms of processes, the algorithms, the cost models used to quantify the benefit of the selected optimization structures, etc. used by the research community. In this paper, we first propose a physical design language called *PhyDL* that allows describing all inputs and outputs of the physical design phase. Secondly, to increase the reuse of the existing advisors, we elaborate a repository called *Meta-Advisor* that persists all components of the physical design. Finally, a case study of our contribution is presented to stress the meta-advisor repository and highlights its importance.

1 Introduction

Nowadays, the database trends evolve regularly due to the advances in database technology and the hardware progress. This evolution makes the database systems more and more challenging. In other words, database systems requires to satisfy several non-functional requirements (NFRs) (such as such as query performance, reliability, usability, etc.). The physical design is one of the main phases in database life-cycle, which is devoted to take important design choices in order to satisfy these NFR. By design choices we mean selecting physical structures like indexes and materialized views [12]. In order to help database administrators (DBAs) to do their physical design choices, many *optimization*

© Springer International Publishing Switzerland 2016
L. Bellatreche et al. (Eds.): MEDI 2016, LNCS 9893, pp. 72–87, 2016.
DOI: 10.1007/978-3-319-45547-1_6

algorithms [18] and *cost models* [4] have been proposed by the research database community. Since there are a lot of possible design choices (a.k.a solutions) for a given system design (a.k.a problem), optimization algorithms explore the solution space and propose optimal ones. For this purpose, optimization algorithms are driven by cost models enabling to quantify the cost (e.g. Input/output CPU, network transfer cost, etc.) of each possible solution.

By exploring the literature, we notice that several academic and industrial tools, known as advisors, have automated the physical design process by invoking programs based on optimization algorithms and cost models. Indeed, the databases and the workloads may be evaluated by being submitted to advisor tools which propose design solutions to the DBA, who may decide to deploy them in the real system.

However, since algorithms and cost models are scattered in the literature, to study, compare and reuse them for extension purposes is complex and requires a good background. Despite the variety of existing advisor tools, the usage of appropriate ones depends on the nature of system under design and the DBA needs. Besides, several commercial advisor tools are black-box and do not give enough details about the algorithms and cost models on which proposed solutions are based. Moreover, to the best of our knowledge, there is neither a work that orients DBA to easily use optimization algorithms, nor a referential that helps researchers for comparing their own optimization algorithms with the existing ones. Comparing algorithms and/or cost models and determining the appropriate advisor for a given design is difficult since there is no formalism of physical design phase that enables to describe system configurations. This research aims to capitalize the knowledge relaying on the database physical design in order to decrease the difficulty related to the constant evolution of this domain.

In this paper we firstly propose *PhyDL* a design language dedicated to describe the system which need to be optimized. Secondly, we elaborate a repository called *Meta-Advisor* to store optimization algorithms and cost models by taking specificities of their dedicated problems into consideration. This repository also enables to enhance the re-usability of existing advisors.

The remainder of the paper is organized as follows. In Sect. 2, we introduce the physical design domain. Section 3 describes the architecture of our proposal, highlights its different capabilities and presents how such framework can be used. A proof of concept is presented in Sect. 4. Section 5 to discuss some related works. Finally, the paper concludes and describes directions for the future work in Sect. 6.

2   Background

In order to make this paper self-contained and straightforward, this section introduces at large the challenges of the physical design.

2.1   Physical Design in Database

The physical design phase consists of choosing a specific database physical configuration on the storage media in order to improve the performance of queries [14]. In general, a physical configuration represents the result of deploying one or several physical structures. Then, the main difficulty of the physical design phase is to decide which appropriate physical structures have to be chosen for a given system. This leads to a set of design decision problems related to the choice of physical structures, such as: materialized views [1], indexes, horizontal partitioning, [6,8], buffer management [5], query scheduling and buffer management [15], system sizing [27], tuning and admission control [8,10]. These kinds of problems fall under the category of constraint optimization problems. In other words, each problem needs *solutions*, which have to satisfy one or several *NFR* (such as query performance, reliability, usability) without violating system *constraints* (such as storage cost, maintenance cost). The challenge of DBAs in this design phase is to find solutions/answers to *problems* such as: What are possible indexed attributes? Which view can be materialized? What are objects to store in the buffer? What is the optimal partitioning schema?

In addition, each physical structure can be deployed on different ways in the system, where each one represents a possible solution of the questions presented above. Thus, the selection of the best solutions is known to be a NP-complete *problem* [12] due to the fact that solution space grows exponentially as the problem size increases. Usually, problems of selections are solved using *optimization algorithms*, which span deterministic algorithms, randomized algorithms, etc. (For more details, please refer to the survey [18]). Furthermore, the objective functions of algorithms are driven by *cost models* which use parameters related to databases schema, architecture, hardware, query workload, constraints etc. Then, the cost models enable to measure the solutions quality based on metrics like CPU time, number of input/output, etc.

Figure 1 sketches the general overview of the physical design process. It shows three principal areas. The first area is dedicated to DBAs, where the system characteristics and the DBA needs are defined. Note that the system characteristics can also be related to previous design phases of the life-cycle (i.e. conceptual and/or logical database design phases). Once the DBA specifies his/her needs, this latter can be evaluated by one or several advisor tools. Obviously, the used tools have to support as inputs the specificities of the system under design. Although some white-box advisor tools provide the algorithms and cost models that are behind their recommendations, the step which consists of choosing adapted advisors is not automatic, and can be laborious and error-prone, due to the variety of the parameters which have to be considered and their impact on the recommendation, its quality and its correctness. In this paper, we focus on the transition from the expressed needs to the algorithms chosen by DBA. The underlying idea behind this focus is to propose an approach capitalizing the physical design research and carrying ideas from knowledge-based design to model-based process.

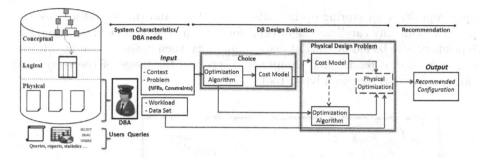

Fig. 1. Conceptual processes of the database physical design

2.2 Example

We present an example of a physical design problem that has been presented in [22]. This example will be reclaimed in case study section. The authors of [22] consider *problem* of "views", where the objective is to minimizing energy consumption and response time with respect of the storage space and the maintenance cost constraints. Non-dominated Sorting in Genetic Algorithms (NSGA-II) has been chosen as an optimization algorithm in order to solve the problem for a given workload. The authors also propose a cost model to estimate the total energy consumption and execution time of queries by considering their I/O and CPU costs. The system under design is described by several parameters related to the database, queries, and the platform. The database parameters are: *relational* schema, *row-oriented storage*, no data compression, and a *pipeline*[1] query processing strategy. The queries parameters considered are: OLAP queries type with no concurrency execution. The platform parameters are: *centralized* deployments architecture, *main memory* as a primary storage device, and *hard disk drive* as a secondary storage device.

3 Our Contribution: A Meta-advisor Approach

As we have presented previously in Sect. 2, concepts related to the database physical design are numerous, inter-dependant and evolve increasingly. Thus, the choice of suitable optimization algorithms and/or cost models can be tedious and requires a good expertise and up to date knowledge.

3.1 Contribution Overview

Our contribution consists of proposing a model-based approach in order to cope with the gap related to the transition from the characteristics of the system under-design and the choice of advisors/algorithms. Our objective is to help DBAs by allowing them (i) to express their needs formally, (ii) to suggest an

---

[1] A pipeline is a set of query operators running concurrently.

open repository for storing optimization algorithms, and (iii) to automatize the process to identify candidate algorithms for a given system. The idea behind the repository is to be fed by the database community, then optimization algorithms can be reused, extended and compared. Therefore, the usage of the repository can be viewed as a meta-advisor tool.

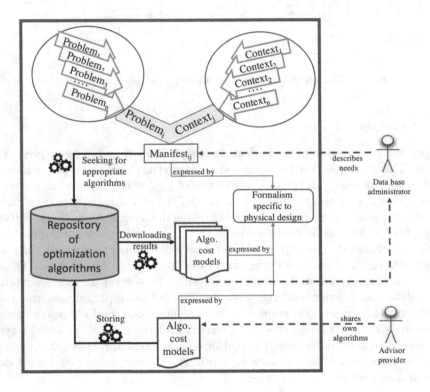

Fig. 2. Overview of our approach

Our contribution is based on the facilities of the model-driven engineering paradigm [23]. Figure 2 gives an overview of our meta-advisor approach. We classify concepts of the physical design into two categories: *problem* category and *context* category. While the problem means the considered physical structures and the questions asked by DBA, the context represents the set of parameters related to the databases schema, architecture, hardware, etc. Each combination of a context and problem leads to get a *manifest*. Thus, by varying the problem, we can get different manifests for the same context. This separation between the problem and the context intends to bring flexibility on the database physical design in terms of reuse and comparison.

Figure 2 also highlights the need of a formalism dedicated to the domain of the physical design. On the one hand, this formalism has to be used to express manifests in order to seek optimization algorithms that match the manifest.

On the other hand shared and found algorithms (and their cost models) have also to be described in the formalism in question. We believe that having an unified formalism will ease the reuse of existing optimization algorithms for different purposes, like: (i) their use as advisors, (ii) comparing the efficient algorithms when several ones can be used for the same manifest, and also (iii) simplify the extension and the up to date of existing algorithms. Therefore, we propose *PhyDL* a Physical Design specific Language.

3.2   PhyDL: Physical Design Specific Language

The *PhyDL* language is a domain specific language (DSL) dedicated to physical design process. As every DSL, *PhyDL* language is defined by three elements:

- Abstract syntax: it is the structure of the language based on elements and their relationships. This structure corresponds on the meta-model. We have used a diagram class UML-like [21] formalism called Ecore [24] to express our meta-model. It is one of various MOF implementations.
- Concrete syntaxes: they correspond to specific representations of the design language in order to instantiate its meta-model. A syntax may be graphical or textual.
- Semantic: which means the meaning of meta-model concepts and how can be represented on the instantiation.

The objectives of the *PhyDL* language are as follows. An instance of the *PhyDL* language can represent a *manifest* (i.e. needs of DBA which look for suitable advisors). In this case, the DBA has to specify the context of his/her system and the problem on which the DBA needs helps. By instantiating *PhyDL* language, we can also get a description of an optimization algorithm and cost models on which its objective function is based. In this case, the users of *PhyDL* language are academic or industrial researchers who would like to share their advisors (based on optimization algorithms). Obviously, researchers have to specify the problem(s) addressed by their advisors and also the context of system on which their proposed algorithms can be used. Hereafter, we focus on core elements of *PhyDL* meta-model and their semantics.

Figure 3 depicts the elements dedicated to express optimization algorithms and their characteristics. Then, the root element of the meta-model is the `Algorithm` class. Every `Algorithm` instance is composed of a problem (instance `Problem` class), a context (instance `Context` class) and cost model (instance `CostModel` class). An instance of the `Problem` class can be characterized by several types (e.g. index selection, view selection, horizontal partitioning selection). Moreover, `Problem` instances are also defined by the type of selection. It means that when the problem addresses many physical structures, one can specify if those structures will be treated one by one (`isolated` item), or together at the same time conjointly or sequentially (`multiple` item). Every problem has to satisfy one or many non functional requirement (`NFRequirement`) under some constraints (instances of `Constraint` class). Every context (instance of

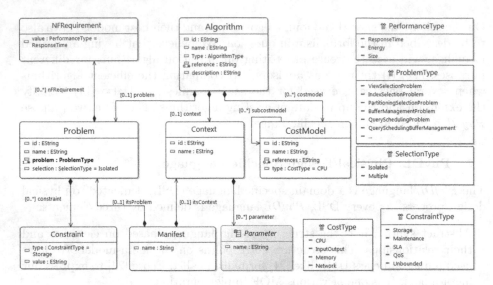

Fig. 3. Excerpt of PhyDL meta-model: core entities

`Context` class) of a given Manifest/Algorithm/cost-model is described by a set of database system parameters. Those parameters are related to different categories. Meta-modeling these parameter categories and their attributes lead to numerous classes and enumerations. Then, Fig. 4 gives only an brief view of our meta-model classes that correspond to context parameters. There are various types of parameters scattered in the literature. To organize them, we propose four categories of parameters:

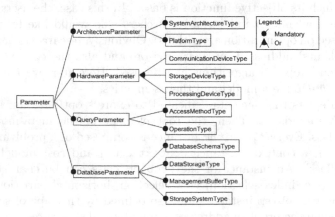

Fig. 4. Excerpt of PhyDL meta-model: focus on context parameters and their categories

- *Database parameters:* elements of this category are related to the database and different functionalities that have to be provided by the database management system (DBMS). Through this category we precise context parameters of storage systems (for instance relational or non-relational), buffer management (e.g. the buffer pool size) and database schema (e.g. tables/columns, partitioning table).
- *Hardware parameters:* generally, the hardware context parameters define device characteristics, such as processing device (e.g. CPU, *Graphical Processing Units* GPU, etc.), different storage device (e.g. *Main-Memory, Solid State Drives* SSD or *Hard Disk Drive* HDD) and communication device.
- *Query parameters:* the query parameters mean concepts used to perform a set of algebra operations (*join, select, etc.*). The operation can be unary or binary function. The result of the query can be restricted by a set of predicates. These operators should perform as fast as possible by exploiting underlying an access method (e.g., index methods or in-memory access methods [19]).
- *Architecture parameters:* elements of this category contain the deployment architecture such as: distributed or parallel database systems, database clusters, or cloud environments. These category parameters feed the cost model context on the type of the system architecture (e.g. shared memory, shared disc, etc.) and their parameters like the number of nodes in parallel environment.

Figure 5 focuses on Algorithm class and its related elements. We recall, that the meta-modeled classes are only related to the domain of the physical database design. Each algorithm is characterized by a name and references which indicate the scientific papers presenting the optimization algorithm. Every instance of the Algorithm class also has at least one algorithm type: constraint programming, deterministic, random and hybrid. Furthermore, each algorithm has several parameters AlgorithmParameter. All parameters considered in the algorithm fall into one of the following categories: *VariationOperator, StoppingCriteria, SolutionCodding, FitnessFunction, Initialization* and *UserDefinedParamter*) (see Fig. 5). The optimization algorithms are coupled with the characteristics of the system under design (i.e. context). Since, the context is also defined by a set of parameters (as shown in Fig. 4), some of the algorithm parameters may be matched to those of the context thanks to the ContextMappingRelation class (see Fig. 5).

Figure 6 depicts the CostModel class. Every CostModel instance is composed of a metric (instance Metric class) and a cost function (instance CostFunction class). A cost model can have its own context. The parameters of this latter are a sub set of the global context of the algorithm. The cost model is also characterized by references to indicate the scientific papers where it is presented. Every instance of the CostModel class also has at least one cost type. Thanks to the CostFunction class, the mathematical formula of a cost model is supported in a structured way. The CostFunction class consists of two parts of operands: logical costs and physical costs. In fact, an operand may be a given real value (i.e. instance of ConstantValue class) or derived from other context parameters.

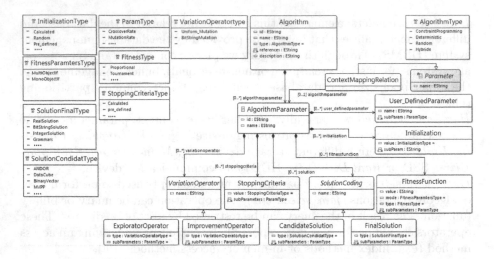

Fig. 5. Excerpt of PhyDL meta-model: focus on algorithm class and its relationships

In this case, the operand is represented by an instance of `CalculatedValue` class. Indeed, that corresponds to what we have previously highlighted, when we have said that the main math formula assigned to a cost function may be composed of other basic ones. We integrate the MathML [2] package into *Meta-Advisor* meta-model. Thanks to this, the math formulas of `CostFunction` and `CalculatedValue` classes can be expressed (instance of `MathType` class). Note that to keep the traceability and the origin of all math formulas operands, the `Parameter`, `LogicalCost` and `PhysicalCost` classes inherit from the `MiType` class of the MathML package. We recall that `MiType` class allows to define variables of equations.

3.3   Meta-advisor Repository

Figure 7 depicts the high-level workflow of how our repository can be used. Two kinds of users (providers and seekers) interact with the repository via the two interface skeletons. Thus, our system produces different views based on users roles. The skeletons of the user API (Application Programming Interface) have been developed based on *PhyDL* design language. In the following, we detail the possible scenario usage of the repository.

Enrichment Flow: A provider (e.g. academic researcher) should use the providing interface to insert own optimization algorithms and cost models. Through this interface (which plays the role of a design tool), the modeling of the optimization algorithm, its cost models, its context and the addressed problem is possible. Once the provider obtains a model conforms to the *PhyDL* meta-model,

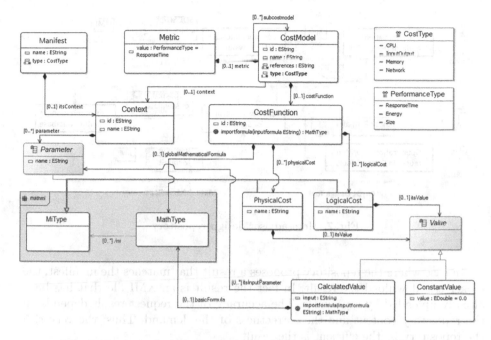

Fig. 6. Excerpt of of PhyDL meta-model: focus on Cost-Model class

the providers can upload it. A model conforms to a meta-model is like a program conforms to the programming languages grammar in which it is written. In fact, the uploaded model is serialized an XML file (based on XML Metadata Interchange schema) [11]). We developed an enrichment process which deals transforming the uploaded model to SQL statements. The SQL statements is mainly based on "INSERT" queries. This transformation is implemented in a model-to-text language called Acceleo [20]. Therefore, we store in the database the information related to the algorithms contained in the XML file and also the link of file location. This process should be repeated for each algorithm eligible to be shared. Actually, the trust of the repository is managed manually by a moderator. Thus, the insertion process passes by a staging area.

Selection Flow: This flow should help seekers to reuse optimization algorithms and cost models provided by other researchers. A seeker (e.g. DBA) should use the selection interface to search for appropriate optimization algorithms and cost models. The seeker has first the design tool in order to express the manifest. Each expressed manifest is a model conforms to the *PhyDL* meta-model, and it is serialized as an XMI file. The developed selection process deals with transforming the manifest model to a SQL statements. The SQL statements is based on "SELECT" queries.

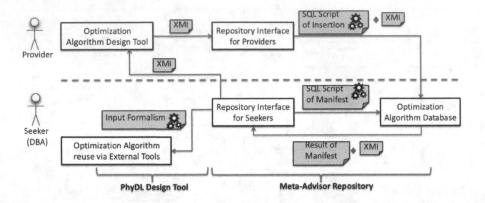

Fig. 7. Meta-advisor design repository

In case where the repository proposes a result that matches the manifest, the seeker can download the result. In fact the result is an XMI file that has been already uploaded by a provider. The accuracy of the request result depends on the repository content and the correctness of the demand. Thus, the very rich the repository is, the efficient is the result.

4   Case Study

This section is devoted to stress the proof of concept of our contribution. The goal is to show the implementation of our tools.

We have developed a design tool allowing to create and visualize a physical design problem conform to the *PhyDL* design language. The design tool is based on Java EMF (Eclipse Modeling Framework) API and has been integrated as a plugin in Eclipse[2] which is an Integrated development Environment. Hereafter, we present two usage scenarios showing the selection and enrichment of the Meta-Advisor repository. This latter refers to the example presented in Sect. 2.2.

4.1   Storing in the Repository

The model of Fig. 8 is an instance of the optimization algorithm. This model is expressed by *PhyDL* language. As it is shown in Fig. 8, the model contains also the context elements, the problem, the cost models.

Figure 9 shows how the XMI file of the model can be downloaded in order to be stored in the repository. As we have presented in the contribution section (see Sect. 3.3), the insertion process is based on a code generator component enabling to generate the SQL script. The script serves to insert the different kinds (context, algorithms, problems, cost models, etc.) of instances contained in the model. Listing 1.1 shows an example of the generated script.

---

[2] Eclipse Modeling Project. www.eclipse.org/modeling/.

```
INSERT INTO Algorithm (AlgorithmID, name, type, selectionType, reference,
    description) VALUES ( 'ALG_0010', 'NSGA II', 'Random', 'Multiple' , 'A.
    Roukh, L. Bellatreche, ..','we provide a multi-objective...');
INSERT INTO Context (id, name, Algorithm_id) VALUES ('CXT_10', 'Context 1','
    ALG_0010');
INSERT INTO ArchitectureParameter (id , architecture, type, value ,
    Context_id) VALUES ('10','Centralized', 'SharedNothing', 'ALG_0010','
    CXT_10');
.....
```

Listing 1.1. Excerpt of SQL queries to insert a new algorithm

```
SELECT Algorithm.*
FROM Algorithm, Context, Problem, DatabaseParameter, HardwareParameter,
    ArchitectureParameter, QueryParameter
WHERE Problem.Algorithm_id = Algorithm.id
AND CostModel.PhysicalDesign_id = Algorithm.id
...
AND Problem.type= 'VSP' AND Problem.constraint in ('storageCost', '
    maintenanceCost') AND Problem.NFR= IN ('energy', 'responseTime')
AND DatabaseParameter.optmizationStruture='materializedView' AND
    DatabaseParameter.dataStorageType='rowOriented' AND DatabaseParameter.
    storageSystem='conventionalDatabaseSql' AND ArchitectureParameter.type='
    centralized' AND ArchitectureParameter.kind='sharedNothing' AND
    QueryParameter.type='OLAP';
```

Listing 1.2. Excerpt of SQL query to select algorithms

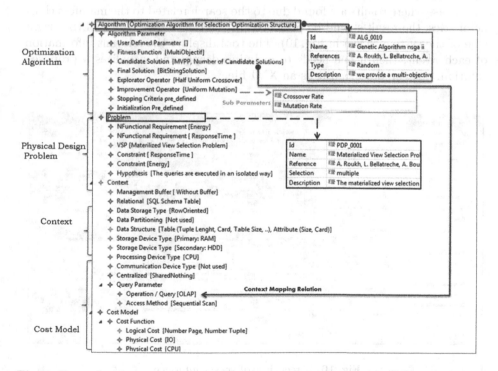

Fig. 8. Example of an optimization algorithm, as it is presented in [22] expressed in PhyDL

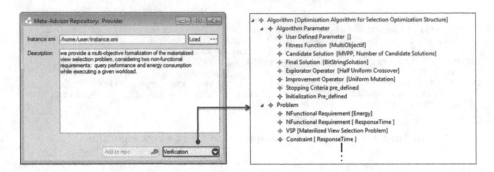

Fig. 9. Screenshot of the provider interface

4.2   Searching from the Repository

In this part of the case study, we illustrate how one can use the seeker interface to search in our repository. The left part of the system depicted in Fig. 10 is an example showing how a manifest can be specified. Each manifest represents a specific search, and each search is based on the execution of a generated SQL script. Listing 1.2 shows the SQL query corresponding to the characteristics of the manifest.

In case where results are found due to the search related to the manifest characteristics, the result should be presented in the right side of the tool (See right side of the system shown in Fig. 10). The tool displays the relevant information of each result, then if one needs to examine deeply and visualizes a proposed solution, one can download it as an XMI file.

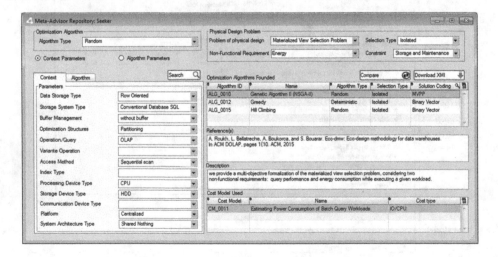

Fig. 10. Screenshot of seeker interface

5 Related Work

By exploring the literature, numerous research works and design tools have tackled the physical database design problems. At the core of designer tools are optimization algorithms and cost models which is used to estimate and compare the performance of query. The industrial design tools have been proposed such as (e.g., *Index Tuning Wizard* [1], *Tuning Advisor* in Microsoft SQL Server [8], *Teradatas Index Wizard* [7], IBM *DB2s Design Advisor* [28], Oracles *SQL Tuning Adviser* [9]. Other types of design problems include project selection in columnar database such as *Verticas DBD* [26]. Design tools have the advantage of automate and facilitate the database optimization and maintenance. However, each design tool suffer from several limitations. First, it depends on the nature of the system which needs modeling. Second, the optimization algorithms is specific to a particular problem and can't be generalized. Third, the proposed tools cannot offer all optimization algorithms and cost models. Last, they are provided as a black-box (i.e., without modifying their internal implementations). Also, open source paradigms and academic tools have been proposed, such as *SimulPh.D* [3] and *Parinda* for Postgres [17] which assists DBA selecting horizontal partitioning and indexes optimization structures, they use some advanced algorithms such as genetic, simulated annealing, etc. Similarly to industrial solutions, the academic researches and tools have their limitations. For instance, to reuse an existing optimization algorithm for both producing and reproducing analysis result of research papers, generally one extracts them manually. Thus, this penalizes the reuse and the comparison of existing algorithms. Based on this discussion, in this paper we propose the construction of physical design repository, inspired by the database physical design and making it evolving to consider the evolution of the database and the technology. Recently, the computational science community spends a lot of efforts in building repositories of data issued from their experiments and simulations for analysis, reuse and reproduction purposes. The *cTuning*[3] repository is an example of these initiatives. It is open-source, customizable Collective Knowledge Repository for physics domain. Similar efforts have been conducted by the process community. *APROMORE* (Advanced Process Model Repository) is an example of these initiative [16]. [25] propose a repository for APIs (Application programming interface) to facilitate the development of new advanced applications. [13] propose A Model Repository Description Language *MRDL* for the development and use of model repositories.

6 Conclusion

In this paper, we focused on the database physical design by studying optimization algorithms and analyzing their usage. This study was motivated by the existence of a panoply of optimization algorithms and their important impact on the databases physical design. To enhance the reuse of existing optimization algorithms and help the database community to cope with the various concept of

---

[3] http://ctuning.org/index.html.

this domain, we suggested a model-based approach called *Meta-Advisor*. First, we suggested *PhyDL* a Physical Design specific Language dedicated to database Physical Design. The goal of the language is to offer to the database community an unified formalism to express the optimization algorithms and cost models. The language can also be used to express the manifest of users, especially DBAs. Secondly, we proposed an open repository in order to capitalize the knowledge relaying on the database physical design in order to decrease the difficulty related different usages such as the *visualization*, the *evolution*, the *sharing* and the *reuse* of existing *advisors*. A proof of feasibility and practicability of our proposition was also presented.

Currently, we are testing our propositions by students following our Advanced Databases course in order to get their feed-backs for possible improvements. We are also proposing a mechanism making our system trustworthy from the provider side (to replace the moderator).

References

1. Agrawal, S., Chaudhuri, S., Narasayya, V.: Materialized view and index selection tool for microsoft SQL server 2000. ACM SIGMOD Rec. **30**(2), 608 (2001)
2. Asperti, A., Padovani, L., Coen, C.S., Guidi, F., Schena, I.: Mathematical knowledge management in HELM. Ann. Math. Artif. Intell. **38**(1–3), 27–46 (2003)
3. Bellatreche, L., Boukhalfa, K., Alimazighi, Z.: SimulPh.D.: a physical design simulator tool. In: Bhowmick, S.S., Küng, J., Wagner, R. (eds.) DEXA 2009. LNCS, vol. 5690, pp. 263–270. Springer, Heidelberg (2009)
4. Bellatreche, L., Bress, S., Kerkad, A., Boukorca, A., Salmi, C.: The generalized physical design problem in data warehousing environment: towards a generic cost model. In: MIPRO, pp. 1131–1137. IEEE (2013)
5. Bellatreche, L., Cheikh, S., et al.: How to exploit the device diversity and database interaction to propose a generic cost model? In: IDEAS. ACM (2013)
6. Boukorca, A., Bellatreche, L., Cuzzocrea, A.: SLEMAS: an approach for selecting materialized views under query scheduling constraints. In: COMAD, pp. 66–73. Computer Society of India (2014)
7. Brown, D.P., Chaware, J., Koppuravuri, M.: Index selection in a database system, 3 March 2009. US Patent 7,499,907
8. Chaudhuri, S., Narasayya, V.: Self-tuning database systems: a decade of progress. In: VLDB, pp. 3–14. VLDB Endowment (2007)
9. Dageville, B., Das, D., Dias, K., Yagoub, K., Zait, M., Ziauddin, M.: Automatic SQL tuning in Oracle 10g. In: VLDB, pp. 1098–1109. VLDB Endowment (2004)
10. Giurgiu, I., Botezatu, M., Wiesmann, D.: Comprehensible models for reconfiguring enterprise relational databases to avoid incidents. In: CIKM. ACM (2015)
11. O.M. Group: OMG MOF 2 XMI mapping specification. Version 2.4.1 (2011). http://www.omg.org/spec/XMI/2.4.1/. Accessed 4 June 2016
12. Gupta, H., Mumick, I.S.: Selection of views to materialize under a maintenance cost constraint. In: Beeri, C., Bruneman, P. (eds.) ICDT 1999. LNCS, vol. 1540, pp. 453–470. Springer, Heidelberg (1998)
13. Hamid, B.: A Model Repository Description Language - MRDL. In: Kapitsaki, G., Santana de Almeida, E. (eds.) ICSR 2016. LNCS, vol. 9679, pp. 350–367. Springer, Heidelberg (2016). doi:10.1007/978-3-319-35122-3_23

14. Iman, E., Ashraf, A., Daniel, C.Z., Calisto, Z.: Recommending XML physical designs for XML databases. VLDB J. **22**(4), 447–470 (2013)
15. Kerkad, A., Bellatreche, L., Richard, P., Ordonez, C., Geniet, D.: A query beehive algorithm for data warehouse buffer management and query scheduling. IJDWM **10**(3), 34–58 (2014)
16. La Rosa, M., Reijers, H.A., et al.: Apromore: an advanced process model repository. Expert Syst. Appl. **38**(6), 7029–7040 (2011)
17. Maier, C., Dash, D., Alagiannis, I., Ailamaki, A., Heinis, T.: PARINDA: an interactive physical designer for PostgreSQL. In: EDBT, pp. 701–704. ACM (2010)
18. Mami, I., Bellahsene, Z.: A survey of view selection methods. ACM SIGMOD Rec. **41**(1), 20–29 (2012)
19. Manegold, S., Boncz, P.A.: Optimizing database architecture for the new bottleneck: memory access. VLDB J. Int. J. Very Large Data Bases **9**, 231–246 (2000)
20. Musset, J., Juliot, E., Lacrampe, S.: Acceleo référence. Technical report, Obeo et Acceleo (2006)
21. Object Management Group. OMG Unified Modeling Language. Superstructure, Version 2.4.1. http://www.omg.org/spec/UML/2.4.1/
22. Roukh, A., Bellatreche, L., Boukorca, A., Bouarar, S.: Eco-DMW: Eco-design methodology for data warehouses. In: ACM DOLAP, pp. 1–10. ACM (2015)
23. Schmidt, D.C.: Model-driven engineering. Comput. IEEE Comput. Soc. **39**(2), 25 (2006)
24. Steinberg, D., Budinsky, F., et al.: EMF: Eclipse Modeling Framework. The Eclipse Series (2008). Gamma, E., Nackman, L., Wiegand, J. (eds.)
25. Sun, Y.-J.J., Barukh, M.C., Benatallah, B., Beheshti, S.-M.-R.: Scalable SaaS-based process customization with casewalls. In: Barros, A., Grigori, D., Narendra, N.C., Dam, H.K. (eds.) ICSOC 2015. LNCS, vol. 9435, pp. 218–233. Springer, Heidelberg (2015). doi:10.1007/978-3-662-48616-0_14
26. Varadarajan, R., Bharathan, V., et al.: DBdesigner: a customizable physical design tool for vertica analytic database. In: ICDE, pp. 1084–1095. IEEE (2014)
27. Zhang, N., Tatemura, J., Patel, J.M., Hacigümüş, H.: Towards cost-effective storage provisioning for DBMSS. VLDB **5**(4), 274–285 (2011)
28. Zilio, D.C., Zuzarte, C., et al.: Recommending materialized views and indexes with the IBM DB2 design advisor. In: ICAC, pp. 180–187. IEEE (2004)

Linked Service Selection Using the Skyline Algorithm

Mahdi Bennara[1(✉)], Michael Mrissa[2], and Youssef Amghar[1]

[1] Université de Lyon, LIRIS, INSA-Lyon - CNRS UMR5205, 69621 Lyon, France
{mahdi.bennara,youssef.amghar}@liris.cnrs.fr
[2] Université de Lyon, LIRIS, Université Lyon 1 - CNRS UMR5205,
69622 Lyon, France
michael.mrissa@liris.cnrs.fr

Abstract. Recently, resource oriented computing has changed the way Web applications are designed. Because of the increasing number of APIs, centralized repositories are no longer a viable option for discovery. As a consequence, a decentralized approach is needed in order to enable value-added applications. In this paper, we propose a client-side QoS-based selection algorithm that can be executed along the discovery stage. Our solution provides different alternatives based on the skyline approach to select resources and maintain acceptable time performance.

Keywords: RESTful linked web services · Discovery · Selection · Quality of service

1 Introduction

In the past twenty years, SOAP-based Web services have helped reaching syntactic level interoperability for distributed applications on the Web. More recently, resource-oriented computing, and in particular the REST architectural style [5], has revised the way we interact with services, bringing in new advantages such as uniform interface (and consequently generic client), HATEOAS[1] (hypertext-driven applications), cacheability, etc. In parallel, the Web of services has started an evolution towards semantic-level interoperability, with a lot of work around semantically described Web services [6,7] to allow services to exchange semantically annotated data. This evolution has moved towards linked data. Combining the RESTful architectural style with semantic annotations has unlocked the benefits of using linked data for Web applications. We talk about Linked Web Services which are RESTful services described with linked data and that exchange linked data. Despite the evolution of service technologies, the need for service composition to build complex applications is still present. However, the challenges have changed. As centralized solutions for service discovery have proven not to scale well [2], the need for distributed service discovery has emerged [9].

---

[1] Hypermedia As The Engine Of the Application State.

© Springer International Publishing Switzerland 2016
L. Bellatreche et al. (Eds.): MEDI 2016, LNCS 9893, pp. 88–97, 2016.
DOI: 10.1007/978-3-319-45547-1_7

The discovery of services that fulfill a certain task in the process of answering the user's request also brings in the need for selecting the most suitable of these candidates to actually execute the task needed.

In this paper, we introduce a set of algorithms for discovering and selecting semantically described resources. As we work in the context of resource oriented Web, the discovery of new resources that can potentially participate in answering the user's request is done progressively following the principle of HATEOAS. We rely on semantic annotations developed in previous work [3] to describe resources. Such descriptions include resource attributes, available HTTP operations and relations with other resources. We also rely on breadth-first search algorithm combined with a skyline-based approach [4] to select the appropriate resources while maintaining acceptable performance.

The remainder of this paper is organized as follows. Section 2 presents related work and highlights the originality of our solution. Section 3 introduces a scenario that motivates our approach. Section 5 details our contribution and shows the different setups for discovery-selection as well as the algorithms. Section 6 discusses the choices we made in the contribution section and highlights the advantages of our approach. Section 7 resumes our approach and lists some elements of future work.

2 State of the Art

2.1 Quality of Service in Service Oriented Web

During the last years, QoS has been a key challenge for research community.

Ran [8] proposed a model for QoS in Service oriented Web that divides QoS attributes into several different categories. This is one of the efforts to provide a complete set of attributes that describe the QoS aspects of a service. It is designed for the service-oriented architectures and particularly the Web.

AgFlow [13] is a solution that enables quality-driven composition of Web services. It proposes two different approaches to select Web services for a given task within a composite service. The local optimization approach suggests to leave the selection to the last possible moment. In the global planning approach, the selection is done for each task individually but by taking into account the other tasks.

2.2 QoS-Based Web Service Selection

The problem of selection of Web services is a part the composition process that involves the QoS aspect to choose the most suitable services for the user. Finding the optimal solution for this problem with multiple QoS constraints is a NP-hard combinatorial optimization problem [12]. This problem can be modeled as follows: the user emits a request that requires several Web services to be answered. The solution for this request is divided into several tasks, every task can be performed by a single Web service. Every task has several candidate Web services. Finding a solution amounts to select the best candidate for each task in order to obtain the highest overall QoS. In the current paper we follow a different setup where the search space of candidates progressively discovered by following links between resources.

Wang et al. [10] propose an approach for selecting services based on Generic and Domain-related QoS attributes (DGQOS). Generic QoS attributes (GQoS) can apply on any type of Web service. Domain QoS attributes (DQoS) apply only on a certain class of Web services. The authors define evaluation models for DQoS and GQoS attributes, which help calculate the overall QoS of composite Web services based on its components. They use the C-MMAS (Cultural Min-Max Ant System) algorithm in order to solve the selection problem.

Alrifai et al. [1] propose a solution for selection Web services based on the skyline approach. The goal is to identify for each task the services that will never be part of the final solution simply because they are outclassed by another candidate service in every QoS-related aspect. The authors try to keep the set of candidates as small as possible in order to apply constraint optimization algorithms to obtain the best solution. They also propose a solution to further reduce the size of the set of candidates by identifying representative candidates that replace a subset of candidates that have similar QoS parameters.

2.3   Analysis

We have to highlight that in our context, the set of candidate resources to be selected is progressively discovered. Indeed, the setup of a centralized registry for all resources is not adapted to the distributed and large scale nature of the Web. Therefore, the discovery process gradually discovers resources that can fulfill a given task and does not have all the candidates until the end of the algorithm. Plus, the space of solutions expands as the discovery algorithm finds new candidates which increases the computational time of the selection process. Here, we face two possibilities. The first one is to run the selection algorithm while the discovery algorithm is exploring the resources on the Web. When a new candidate is discovered, it may be a part of the final solution. The second possibility is to run the selection algorithm at the end after having all candidates for every resource, the selection algorithm is run a single time after the end of the discovery algorithm.

3   Scenario and Motivation

In order to motivate our work, we consider a scenario where a user wants to buy a book online. We assume there are three book selling Web resources, three shipment Web resources and two online payment Web resources in competition. Every Web resource has its own quality of service properties, and the user has its own preferences. The disposal of the scenario setup includes the human user, the machine client software and the set of Web resources listed above.

The process of buying a book requires shipment and online payment, and is described as follows: the user emits a request explaining his needs e.g. "buy book". This request is combined with a set of QoS-related information which guide the machine in the processing of his request, we agree to call this set of information "user profile". For example, the user may want the services with the best performance and then the best rated among these and does not care about their availability. The client-side reasoner infers that it needs to discover a book selling, a shipping service and a payment service. The process of deduction is achieved through a reasoner with a simple subsumption technique. If we take the example of the user's request: "buy book", the reasoner infers that there is a need for a service that sells books in order to allow the user to buy books. The ontology we use for this scenario can be found here: http://soc.univ-lyon1. fr/bookselling.owl. The client begins to crawl the Web looking for the resources needed to answer the user's request. The client needs to discover three services according to the reasoning on the request: the book selling service, the shipping service and the online payment service. The client may find multiple services that fulfill each functionality and has to select one based on the user's QoS profile.

4   Problem Statement

We consider a user request that involves a set of tasks, each task is represented by an ontology concept. The set of tasks is organized as a workflow that represents the series of actions that the client needs to perform in order to deliver the result to the user. The Web resource that can fulfill a specific task is not unique due to the nature of the Web and the client can discover many candidate resources to fulfill the given task. However, not all these candidates match the user requirements in terms of QoS, and therefore a selection phase is needed in order to determine the most suitable candidate for each task.

$T = \{OntologyConcept\}^N$ is the set of tasks in the workflow, where N is the total number of tasks.

$C_i = \{(URI, operation)\}^{m_i}$ is the set of candidates for a task t_i, where m_i is the total number of candidates for the task t_i. The candidate number j for the task t_i is therefore c_{ij}.

Finding a solution for the user's request amounts to finding the set of candidates c_k for each task t_k, where every candidate meets the hard constraints for the user at least (and preferably the soft constraints) and the overall QoS of the set is the best among all combinations. We define hard constraints as conditions that must be fulfilled by a discovered resource otherwise it is not eligible for the task. On the other hand soft constraints are optional conditions that are not necessary to select a candidate for a task.

As we have opted for a hypermedia-driven approach for exploring the Web, we need an on-the-fly selection strategy in order to be able to select relevant resources along the discovery process. In the remainder of this section, we detail a "select while you discover" strategy to enable on-the-fly selection.

4.1   A Minimal QoS Model for Web Resources

In this paper, we rely on a minimal model based on [8] in order to describe some important non-functional properties of a Web resource. QoS : {Performance: [0–10], Availability: [0–100], Reputation: [0–5]}

4.2   QoS-Based Resource Selection Problem Specification

The problem of selection of resources is part of the composition problem. This problem has been proven to be NP-Complete (c.f. Sect. 2). The process of reasoning on the user's request, as described in the scenario (c.f. Sect. 3), can be assimilated to a Web service selection problem. Every task of the composite solution can be fulfilled by a resource, that has to be discovered. Multiple resources can be candidates for a single task. Tasks are semantically identified by the concepts the reasoner infers after analyzing the user's request. We start with N tasks and for each task i we have M_i candidates. The problem is to identify the set of candidates S where each candidate s_j fulfills the task t_j and the overall QoS of the set is the best according to the user's preferences.

5   Contribution

In this paper, we propose a quality-driven approach that relies on a minimal QoS model to improve selection of RESTful resources. We want the QoS attributes to be a guide together with the resource descriptions (including links between resources) for the selection process. We rely on a minimal QoS model based on a set of quality attributes in order to incorporate it on the resource descriptions according to the Descriptor concept [3]. The selection phase is the step where we have multiple candidates for each task of the process aiming to answer the user's request. The selection phase aims at selecting the best candidate for each task to obtain an overall QoS that matches with the user's QoS profile. In this paper, we present two configurations of the discovery and selection processes.

5.1   On-The-Fly Selection

In this configuration, the selection process is executed at the same time as the discovery goes on. Each time a resource is discovered, the selection algorithm is run in order to verify if this new resource can be the best candidate for its task among the other previously discovered resources for that same task while, at the same time, making sure the set of selected candidates for all the tasks verify certain conditions (best overall QoS matching with user's profile, compatibility between resources, etc.).

In Table 1, we present four different setups to enable the on-the-fly selection (select as you discover)

Table 1. Different on-the-fly selection setups

Setup	Advantage	Drawback
Selection of the first solution that matches the user's QoS profile	Fast solution	Low overall QoS, may not match with the user's soft constraints
Selection of the best candidate for each task	Selection of the best candidate for each task	May not be the best solution to obtain the best overall QoS
Selection of the best solution, by exploring all combinations	Ensures the best solution amongst all combinations	Slow solution, exponential processing time
Selection of the best solution while eliminating irrelevant candidates using skyline approach	Ensures the best solution amongst all combinations, while having less candidates to work with	Still a relatively solution but a lot better than naive exploring of all combinations

The general selection algorithm takes as input the set of all candidates T for each resource, the current set of best candidates s and the new candidate c resource as well as the user's QoS preferences qos and returns a new set of best candidates and updates If it is selected the set of best candidates is updated with the better new solution. For this purpose, we consider a discovered candidate as an object composed of two attributes resource URI and HTTP operation (uri and operation) plus the concept that matches is with the operation (concept). In the context of the algorithms presented below, we define the concept of domination as follows: a candidate c_1 dominates another candidate c_2 if all of c_1's QoS attributes are equal of better compared to c_2's QoS attributes.

Algorithm 1 shows the optimized global planning method. This algorithm eliminates the candidates that will not be part of the final solution before reevaluating the solution. If the new candidate cannot be added to the set of candidates (is irrelevant), the algorithm does nothing and skips this iteration.

Algorithm 2 shows how to insert the new candidate and how the irrelevant ones are removed right after.

5.2 N-Periodic Selection

Launching the selection every time we have N new candidates for a given task can reduce processing time for the selection phase, with the skyline based setup. Note that the number of new candidates for a given task t is n_t where $\sum_{i=1}^{M} n_t = N$ (M being is the total number of tasks).

Algorithm 3 shows how to apply the skyline approach to reduce the size of candidates for a given task t when n_t new candidates are discovered in each iteration of the selection process, instead of only one.

We know that the set of old candidates for the task t is a skyline i.e. no old candidate in $T[t]$ is dominated by another one in the same set. The first step is to eliminate the new candidates in $(N[t])$ that are dominated at least one

---

Algorithm 1. On-The-Fly optimized selection algorithm

    Input: s: **array of Candidate**
    Input: c: **Candidate**
    Input: qos : **QoSprofile**
    Input: T : **array of array of Candidate**
    Output: s: **array of Candidate**
1 **var** s2: **array of Candidate** = s
2 // If the new candidate matches user requirements :
3 **if** $QoSmatch(c, qos)$ **then**
4   // add c while removing irrelevant candidates
5   // if c is irrelevant quit if (skyline(T, c) = **true**) **return**
6   // and verify if there is a new best solution :
7   **for** $i = 0$ **to** $T.size$ **do**
8   **for** $j = 0$ **to** $T[i].size$ **do**
9   s2[i] = T[i,j]
10   **if** $QoScalculate(s2, qos) > QoScalculate(s, qos)$ **then**
11   s = s2

Algorithm 2. Inserting the new candidates and removing the irrelevant ones using the skyline approach

---

    Input: c: **Candidate**
    Input: T : **array of array of Candidate**
    Output: T : **array of array of Candidate**
1 **var** x : **type** = init
2 // if c is not dominated by any other candidate for the same task
3 **for** $i = 0$ **to** $T[c.concept].size$ **do**
4   **if** $dominate(T[c.concept][i], c)$ **then**
5   **return true**
6 // insert it T[c.concept].insert(c);
7 // remove candidates dominated by c **foreach** $c2$ **in** $T[c.concept]$ **do**
8   **if** $dominate(c, c2)$ **then**
9   T[c.concept].remove(c2);
10 **return false**

---

candidate of the same set. After that, we eliminate the new candidates (which is now a skyline) that are dominated by at least one old candidate ($T[t]$). Next, we eliminate old candidates dominated by at least one new candidate. Now we know that no candidate in $T[t]$ or $N[t]$ is dominated by any other candidate in the two sets. Finally, we merge the two sets in order to obtain the skyline of candidates for the task t.

Algorithm 3. Selection of n resources at a time instead of one

---

Input: N : **array of array of Candidate**
Input: T : **array of array of Candidate**
Output: T : **array of array of Candidate**
1 // apply the skyline on the set of new candidates first
2 **for** $i = 0$ **to** $N[t].size$ **do**
3 | **for** $j = i+1$ **to** $N[t].size$ **do**
4 | | **if** $dominate(N[t][i], N[t][j])$ **then**
5 | | | $N[t].remove(j)$;
6 | | **if** $dominate(N[t][j], N[t][i])$ **then**
7 | | | $N[t].remove(i)$; **break**;

8 // remove new candidates dominated by old ones
9 **for** $i = 0$ **to** $N[t].size$ **do**
10 | **for** $j = 0$ **to** $T[t].size$ **do**
11 | | **if** $dominate(T[t][j], N[t][i])$ **then**
12 | | | $N[t].remove(i)$; **break**;

13 // remove old candidates dominated by new ones
14 **for** $i = 0$ **to** $T[t].size$ **do**
15 | **for** $j = 0$ **to** $N[t].size$ **do**
16 | | **if** $dominate(N[t][j], t[t][i])$ **then**
17 | | | $T[t].remove(i)$; **break**;

18 // merge the two new sets
19 $T[t].merge(N[t])$;

---

6 Discussion and Theoretical Evaluation

6.1 One-Periodic Selection Versus N-Periodic Selection

Executing the selection algorithm every time a new candidate is discovered can hinder the processing performance to answer the user's request. With the skyline-based solution the overall execution time can be optimized through waiting for N new candidates to start the selection.

Lets suppose the number of new candidates for each task t is m_t, where $\sum_{i=1}^{N} m_i = n$ where N is the number of tasks. Let us suppose the number of the old candidates for each task is l_t.

In the worst case (i.e. no new nor old candidate is dominated by another), the number of iterations is exactly the same with One-periodic or N-periodic selection : $2l_t m_t + \frac{m(m-1)}{2}$. But in the general case, the number of iterations in N-periodic selection is lower. Indeed, we eliminate the irrelevant candidates in the set $s1$ of the newly discovered n candidates to obtain a set $s2$ of $m \leq n$ candidates. After that, we consider $s2$ and eliminate the candidates that are dominated by at least one element of $T1$ to obtain $s3$ with $|s3| \leq |s2|$. Next, we consider the complete set of candidates $T1$ and eliminate the candidates that are dominated by at least one element of $s2$ to obtain a new set $T2$ where $|T2| \leq |T1|$. Finally we merge $T2$ and $s3$ to obtain the final set $T3$ that represents the whole set of candidates without irrelevant candidates.

6.2 Selection Algorithms of the Skyline Set of Services

After reducing the number of candidates with the skyline algorithm, we need to choose the best solution for selection. In our contribution we show the naive combinatorial algorithm in order to explore the reduced space of solutions. We use a double loop in order to explore the two dimension array of candidates. There are some optimized algorithms [11] specifically aimed at obtaining better performances for this class of optimization problems.

In some cases, the size of the set of candidates is very large that, even with the algorithms we proposed, the solution can not be obtained in a reasonable amount of time. Some solutions have been proposed to resolve this problem, such as the representative skyline services proposed in [1].

7   Conclusion

In this paper, we propose a skyline-based approach to enable Web resource selection. We show that a solution based on the HATEOAS principle, where we select the Web resource candidates along the discovery stage, is more efficient for selection than a classical solution that consists in waiting for discovery results before the selection stage. We rely on a minimal QoS model to demonstrate our approach. We provide four different setups in order to satisfy the user requirements according to the QoS profile and preferences. We enhance the performance of our solution with a skyline-based algorithm in order to reduce the set of candidates for a given task and demonstrate that it gives the same output as with a fully combinatorial algorithm but with less candidates and therefore less overall computational time.

As future work, we envision to consider constraints between candidates for different tasks while running the selection process. In other words, the set of candidates for a given task can be different depending on the chosen candidate for other tasks and also on the user's preferences.

Acknowledgment. We would like to thank Karim Benouaret for his fruitful discussions about the application of the skyline approach over the selection-on-the-fly setup.

References

1. Alrifai, M., Skoutas, D., Risse, T.: Selecting skyline services for qos-based web service composition. In: Proceedings of the 19th International Conference on World Wide Web, pp. 11–20. ACM (2010)

2. Anadiotis, G., Kotoulas, S., Lausen, H., Siebes, R.: Massively scalable web service discovery. In: Awan, I., Younas, M., Hara, T., Durresi, A. (eds.) The IEEE 23rd International Conference on Advanced Information Networking and Applications, AINA 2009, Bradford, UK, pp. 394–402. IEEE Computer Society, 26–29 May 2009. http://dx.doi.org/10.1109/AINA.2009.106
3. Bennara, M., Amghar, Y., Mrissa, M.: Managing web resource compositions. In: Reddy, S. (ed.) 24th IEEE International Conference on Enabling Technologies: Infrastructure for Collaborative Enterprises, WETICE Workshops 2015, Larnaca, Cyprus, pp. 176–181. IEEE, 15–17 June 2015
4. Borzsony, S., Kossmann, D., Stocker, K.: The skyline operator. In: Proceedings of 17th International Conference on Data Engineering, pp. 421–430. IEEE (2001)
5. Fielding, R.T.: Architectural styles and the design of network-based software architectures. Ph.D. thesis, University of California, Irvine (2000). aAI9980887
6. Kopecký, J., Vitvar, T., Bournez, C., Farrell, J.: SAWSDL: semantic annotations for WSDL and XML schema. IEEE Internet Comput. 11(6), 60–67 (2007)
7. Martin, D., Paolucci, M., McIlraith, S.A., Burstein, M., McDermott, D., McGuinness, D.L., Parsia, B., Payne, T.R., Sabou, M., Solanki, M., Srinivasan, N., Sycara, K.: Bringing semantics to web services: the OWL-S approach. In: Cardoso, J., Sheth, A.P. (eds.) SWSWPC 2004. LNCS, vol. 3387, pp. 26–42. Springer, Heidelberg (2005)
8. Ran, S.: A model for web services discovery with QOS. SIGecom Exchanges 4(1), 1–10 (2003). http://doi.acm.org/10.1145/844357.844360
9. Verborgh, R., Hausenblas, M., Steiner, T., Mannens, E., de Walle, R.V.: Distributed affordance: an open-world assumption for hypermedia. In: Carr, L., Laender, A.H.F., Lóscio, B.F., King, I., Fontoura, M., Vrandecic, D., Aroyo, L., de Oliveira, J.P.M., Lima, F., Wilde, E. (eds.) WWW (Companion Volume), pp. 1399–1406. International World Wide Web Conferences Steering Committee/ACM (2013)
10. Wang, Z.J., Liu, Z.Z., Zhou, X.F., Lou, Y.S.: An approach for composite web service selection based on DGQOS. Int. J. Adv. Manufact. Technol. 56(9–12), 1167–1179 (2011)
11. Wolsey, L.A., Nemhauser, G.L.: Integer and Combinatorial Optimization. Wiley, New York (2014)
12. Yu, T., Zhang, Y., Lin, K.: Efficient algorithms for web services selection with end-to-end QOS constraints. TWEB 1(1) (2007)
13. Zeng, L., Benatallah, B., Ngu, A.H.H., Dumas, M., Kalagnanam, J., Chang, H.: Qos-aware middleware for web services composition. IEEE Trans. Software Eng. 30(5), 311–327 (2004)

Toward Multi Criteria Optimization of Business Processes Design

Nadir Mahammed[(✉)] and Sidi Mohamed Benslimane

LabRi Laboratory, Higher School of Computer Science,
BP 73, ELWIAM, 22000 Sidi Bel Abbes, Algeria
{n.mahammed, s.benslimane}@esi-sba.dz

Abstract. In enterprise, optimization is seen as making business decisions by varying some parameters to maximize profit and reduce loss. We focus on business processes design optimization. It is known as the problem of creating feasible business processes while optimizing their criteria such as resource cost and execution time. In this paper, we propose an approach that focuses on tasks composing a business process, their resources and attributes rather than a full representation of a business process for its evaluation according to certain criteria. The main contribution of this work is a framework capable of (i) generating business processes using an enhanced version of evolutionary algorithm NSGAII. (ii) Verifying the feasibility of each business process created using an effective algorithm. At last, (iii) selecting Pareto optimal solutions in a multi criteria optimization environment up to three criteria, using an effectual fitness function. The experimental results showed that our proposal generates efficient business processes in terms of qualitative parameters compared with existing solutions.

Keywords: Business process · Multi criteria optimization · Evolutionary computing

1 Introduction

A business process (BP) has multiple definitions [1, 2]. [3] testified that "BP is a set of activities that takes one or more kinds of input and creates an output that has value to the customer". The business processes multi criteria optimization (BPMCO) can be defined according to [4] as follows [14]:

$P = (BPS, F, C)$ with (*i*) BPS is the search space of BPs ($sol \in BPS$), (*ii*) F is the Fitness function that assigns a numerical score $F(sol)$ for each business process instance (BP) in the search space, (*iii*) C is a set of constraints. The aim of the optimization problem is to find either the instance of global optimal BP sol_{opt}, such as $\forall sol \in BPS$, $F(sol_{opt}) < F(sol)$ or a near-optimal BP sol_{nopt}, such that $F(sol_{opt}) - F(sol_{nopt}) < \delta$.

This work presents a new and original approach for multi criteria optimization of the design of BPs, using an evolutionary algorithm. This approach uses business process tasks and their attributes *e.g.* cost of resources, duration and customer satisfaction, while neglecting other characteristic components of BPs. [4] noted that business processes optimization is a difficult issue because of the nonlinear nature,

© Springer International Publishing Switzerland 2016
L. Bellatreche et al. (Eds.): MEDI 2016, LNCS 9893, pp. 98–107, 2016.
DOI: 10.1007/978-3-319-45547-1_8

and often discontinuous mathematical models involved. For its part, [5] asserted there is relatively little work for BPMCO with a fixed design and optimizing the participating tasks. The contributions of this work are threefold. First, the verification of the feasibility of BPs is provided by the Reverse Process Verification Algorithm (ReProVA). Second, this work uses an enhanced evolutionary algorithm (xNSGAII) for the generation of BPs. Third, the optimization criteria are: cost resources, execution time and customer satisfaction.

The remainder of this paper will present a state of the art on the BPMCO with evolutionary computing in Sect. 2. This is followed by an exhaustive description of the proposed approach in Sect. 3. Finally, Sect. 4 presents experimental results. We close this paper with the conclusion and perspectives.

2 Related Work

[6] are considered to be the first to really have worked on BPMCO with an evolutionary algorithm, a genetic algorithm (AG) in this case. However, their work has not achieved satisfactory results, due to limitations in mathematical formulas. [7, 8] proposed to optimize the allocation of resources and time in BPs. The first study used a simple AG, while the second was called to hybridization between NSGA[1] and the idea of random weighting from HLGA[2]. Subsequently, [9–14] explored and advanced the state of BPMCO with evolutionary computing. The idea of their approach was simple, bold and smart. They just used two matrices to represent a BP: a task/resource matrix and a task/attribute matrix. In their early works, they refined an algorithm by keeping the same design as the proposed business process model [11]. Afterward, this algorithm allowed reviewing and optimizing the design of a BP [12]. This work was applied with different evolutionary algorithms: NSGAII[3], SPEA2[4], PESA2[5], PAES[6] and MOPSO[7]. [4, 15] are other works worthy to be cited. [4] proposed to optimize the design of BPs using a causal matrix, a domain ontology containing principles, properties and BP rules (cited but not detailed), and finally the use of an optimization algorithm based on fireflies. [15] proposed to represent a BP by an ordered sequence of tasks, starting with the result (product and/or service) and go backward. Using two evolutionary algorithms ACO[8] and BCO[9], at the optimization phase and compare the results. Two other interesting work, [16] which proposed to use NSGAII and Petri nets for modeling BP, and [17] which took the work of [11] and modified NSGAII operators. [18] proposed a

---

[1] Non-dominated Sorting Genetic Algorithm.
[2] Hajela's and Link Genetic Algorithm.
[3] Non-dominated Sorting Genetic Algorithm II.
[4] Strength Pareto Evolutionary Algorithm 2.
[5] Pareto Envelope-based Selection Algorithm 2.
[6] Pareto Archived Evolution Strategy.
[7] Multi-objective Particle Swarm Optimization Algorithm.
[8] Ant Colony Optimization.
[9] Bee Colony Optimization.

decision model support based on BP aligned with the business goals using a simple AG. Last but not least, [19] suggested using BP semantics and AG to generate solutions, to obtain and optimize business process execution plans. [20] proposed an approach to bring out BP models from another BP models and their event logs. They used an AG without crossover operator to obtain results. In this paper, we present an approach for BPMCO based on [14].

3 Proposed Approach

This section details the quantitative representation of BPs and the formulation of the proposed BPMCO matter. In the following lines, ReProVA is presented. It deals with checking the BPs feasibility. Subsequently, the details of the enhanced evolutionary algorithm used (xNSGAII) for generating solutions candidates are exposed.

3.1 Business Process Quantitative Representation

The proposed work draws on the work of [14]. A BP is viewed as a collection of tasks that ensures a business transaction *i.e.*, any operation that results is a service or product, if tasks are connected properly. Quoted by [11], before turning on the BPMCO, BPs must be represented in such a way that they are manageable and flexible enough for evolutionary optimization techniques. This involves formally represent a BP to be quantitatively evaluable, and ensure the ability to generate alternative solutions. The elements taken into consideration are the tasks, their resources and the attributes involved in a BP. A task is atomic, similar and homogeneous, but differs in its functionality within a BP. The attributes of a task involving its measurable properties are cost in resource, duration in time and customer satisfaction, in our case. Finally, resources are the task inputs and outputs. The resource nature and type are irrelevant. A BP is made of linked tasks together with its inputs and outputs. The design of a BP is formulated with TRM matrix (Matrix Task/Resource). The membership of a task to a process is irrelevant. With a set of rules, TRM allows transcribing the different forms that a BP design may take.

For a task t_i, a resource r_i, I_i set of t_i input resources and O_i set of a t_i output resources:

- If $r_i \in I_i$ then $TRM_{ij} = 1$ (A resource belongs to task's input resources).
- If $r_i \in O_i$ then $TRM_{ij} = 2$ (A resource belongs to task's output resources).
- If $r_i \notin I_i$ and $r_i \notin O_i$ then $TRM_{ij} = 0$ (A resource does not belong to task's input and output resources).

3.2 Reverse Process Verification Algorithm (ReProVA)

One of the main contributions of this paper is the Reverse Process Verification Algorithm (ReProVA). (i) It represents a BP as a directed graph, which the nodes symbolize BP tasks, the edges represent the used resources. (ii) ReProVA allows updating the tasks composing the solution design. It is achieved by updating TRM, for two reasons:

- Delete any task not involved in a BP composition.
- Swap any task of TRM by another task (from library) which ensures BP feasibility.

```
Algorithm 1 Reverse Process Verification Algorithm (ReProVA)
Input TRM /* initial business process design */
      Library (N) /* Library of tasks to design BPs */
      Min length, max length /* BP measures */
Output TRM updated /* Feasible BP design */
       Nd updated /* Set of tasks composing BP */
Insert "START" and "END" nodes /* Start and End nodes of BP */
Fix "END" as the parent level /* 1st parent level */
For all son levels do
    Generate input resources of son level
    If all BP input resources are produced
        Update TRM.
        If all BP output resources are used
        If BP length is between min and max
            Keep the BP design
        Stop Feasible business process design
    else If unused tasks in Library exist
            Fix the son as the new parent
        else
            Stop Infeasible BP design
End For
```

To produce outputs by a BP, it is necessary that all inputs are used. In ReProVA, outputs not mentioned indicate a failure of the corresponding tasks. ReProVA adds the step backward aspect. Hence, its originality is due to start from BP outputs to produce and go backward to BP inputs. The proposed work applies the logic behind working backwards is a forward step in the solution [21].

Algorithm 1 presents the outline of ReProVA. It constructs a directed graph, and verifies the satisfaction of the BP requirements (inputs, outputs and measures). Two additional nodes are added, "START" and "END" for input resources and output resources of a BP, respectively. These nodes facilitate the interconnection of BP resources with the other participating tasks to produce a feasible solution. The concept of "father-son" is used so that father level indicates the nodes set already included in the graph. Consequently, the son level is the nodes set newly added to the design based on parent nodes input resources. Once all son level tasks developed, the result is the new father level. And so on for the edification of proposed solution. In the best case, the ReProVA result is a feasible BP design, in which (i) all the design tasks are interconnected, (ii) all process output resources are used, (iii) all process input resources are produced and (iv) the proposed length limits are respected.

3.3   xNSGAII

Therefore, the last contribution of the authors work is using a modified version of NSGAII [22], which is called "xNSGAII". The difference with the original algorithm is by adopting a random keys representation for solutions, combined with selective crossover. Random key representation of an individual was proposed by [23] and frequently used for combinatorial optimization problems [24]. One of the particularities of this coding is the use of random numbers as tags to represent solutions. These random numbers are taken from a space $[0, 1]^n$. The search algorithm sees this space as a sample of the solution space. For evaluation, the points in the random keys space are mapped to points in space solutions. Another feature is the feasibility of the children resulting from the crossing using it [23].

The authors' readings were conducted to confirm that works on random keys representation involved using a traditional AG, and exceptionally a NSGAII [25]. No serious study has been done with multi criteria optimization problem related to BPs.

By adopting genetics terminology: a chromosome is the encoding of a solution, in the form of a vector in R^n. A gene is an element of this chromosome. An allele is the value given to this gene. The representation in random keys used tags which crossover uses to reorganize the solution. [23] presents the general structure of random keys representation, as well:

1. For each solution forms a chromosome by generating random real numbers, *e.g.*, a solution with 5 tasks (t3, t5, t1, t2, t4) gives the sequence $2 \rightarrow 4 \rightarrow 5 \rightarrow 1 \rightarrow 3$.
2. From a given chromosome is derived a solution by sorting the random numbers affected. Referring to the above example, $1 \rightarrow 2 \rightarrow 3 \rightarrow 4 \rightarrow 5$ (*i.e.*, t2, t3, t4, t5, t1).
3. [26] advised to apply the crossover operator on random keys representation, not the solution itself. The authors choose to apply the selective crossover.

Thereafter, the authors propose to combine random keys representation with selective crossover lauded by [27]. The selective crossover may be summary as the use of an additional vector that accompanies an individual. The vector main objective is to accumulate the knowledge of what happened (gene flow) in previous generations. This knowledge is used to promote the use of best genes during crossover on futures generations. It avoids stagnation at the search space (see [28] for details).

3.4   Business Process Optimization Framework

The proposed framework aims to generate and optimize a series of BPs, using xNSGAII and respecting defined constraints. Each solution obtained has (Fig. 1a): (1) BP tasks stored in N_d, (2) Graph of optimized BP and (3) BP attributes values.

It would be good to point out that the proposed framework involves a distinctive feature in the optimization process (Fig. 1a): results (1) and (2) are ReProVA products. Only BP attributes values are fitness function results. Figure 2b shows the main steps of the proposed framework.

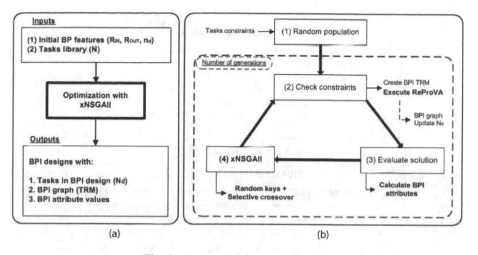

Fig. 1. Proposed framework features.

1. Generate a random population. This step occurs only once in the optimization process. Afterward, the population evolves for a number of generations. The random generation of populations creates a fixed number of tasks sets. However, for each of them, there is a constraint on the tasks random distribution "a task must appear only once in the same set". After the random population is generated, the steps 2–4 are repeated for a predefined number of generations.

2. Check the constraints. For each solution of the population, the problem constraints are verified. To do so, two actions are triggered on the basis of the proposed BP representation (i) TRM is created and (ii) ReProVA is executed. It uses information stored in TRM to design a solution based on process requirements.

3. Evaluate the solution. It is done in three stages. First, BP attributes are calculated on the basis of BP updated version involving design and its attributes values. Second, the various attributes of a solution are calculated on the basis of its Fitness function. Third, the solution is evaluated in terms of BP attributes values.

4. xNSGAII. It is applied to generate new BP designs. The crossover is carried out on N_d of each solution; in two steps. First, the random keys representation is applied to each selected solution. Second, the selective crossover is applied on the random keys results. Mutation operator is applied normally.

4 Experimentation and Results

The proposed framework's aim is to generate satisfactory solutions. To get there, it has to (i) guarantee to obtain an optimal BP design *i.e.,* convergence to optimal Pareto front, (ii) respect BP size diversity *i.e.,* keep population's diversity during various iterations. (iii) Use diversity criteria includes in tasks *i.e.,* utilize task's attributes, to assess each BP. This work focuses on three criteria. It seeks to maximize as much as possible the BP size, while being limited to a small library (n = 20 tasks).

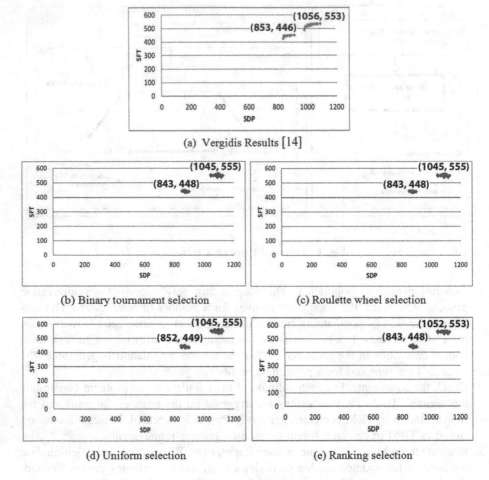

(a) Vergidis Results [14]

(b) Binary tournament selection

(c) Roulette wheel selection

(d) Uniform selection

(e) Ranking selection

Fig. 2. Experimentation results.

Table 1 shows the test scenario with selected parameters used by the framework's evolutionary algorithm. The values proposed for BP features (n_{min} and n_{max}), population size, number of iterations, mutation's probability and resources numbers (r_d) are taken from [14]. R_{IN}, R_{OUT}, r_d and P are referring to the initial BP set of inputs, set of outputs, number of resources and number of optimization criteria, respectively. The authors used these values for the sake of objectivity in results comparison.

The challenge for the proposed framework is to identify non-dominated solutions in the search space, from all generated solutions by xNSGAII. Figure 2a shows the results of Vergidis according to two criteria. [22] explained that NSGAII used binary tournament selection, because of its more efficient time complexity. The authors opted for changing xNSGAII selection operator, in order to explore more search space. To our knowledge, it has never been used in such type of problem. Figure 2(b–e) show the proposed framework results according to three criteria, using binary tournament

Table 1. Parameters used by the proposed framework.

Parameter	Value		
n	20	Mutation	0,2
n_{min}	4	SDP	[200 230]
n_{max}	6	SFT	[100 115]
r_d	8	SDD	[300 390]
R_{IN}	{3, 6}	Population	500
R_{OUT}	{8}	Iteration	25000
P	3	Algorithm	xNSGAII
		Crossover	Random keys + Selective crossover

selection (Fig. 2b), Roulette wheel selection (Fig. 2c), uniform selection (Fig. 2d) and ranking selection (Fig. 2e). The optimized solutions were produced by executing the framework with Table 1 values. The generated solutions represent feasible BPs with minimized cost (SDP), minimized duration (SDD) and maximized customer's satisfaction (SFT). Considering limited drafting space, the authors opted for representing the SDP/SFT graphs.

Table 2 shows the best results obtained by Vergidis [14], while Table 3 presents the different results obtained by the proposed framework. However, it turns out that these same results can be obtained with an initial population of 200 individuals and 50 iterations. This leads to significantly reduce the execution time. The authors note that the solutions are similar with the tournament or roulette wheel selection operators.

Table 2. Results of Vergidis's framework [14].

Selection type	BP	SDP	SFT
Binary	1	853	446
tournament	2	1056	553

Table 3. Results of the proposed framework.

Selection type	BP	SDP	SFT	SDD
Binary	1	843	448	1395
tournament	2	1045	555	1752
Roulette	1	843	448	1395
wheel	2	1045	555	1752
Uniform	1	852	449	1357
	2	1045	555	1752
Ranking	1	843	448	1395
	2	1052	553	1729

Another finding is the assistance provided by the use of a different crossover to quickly find new solutions. Therefore, the proposed work results have achieved better results compared to [14], with each type of selection used.

It appears from this study that, for such problems, the crossover as much as the selection operators have a moderate effect on the quality of generated solutions. What made the difference is the ReProVa algorithm, according to the authors' interpretation.

5 Conclusion

The presented study developed a structured and efficient framework based on (i) xNSGAII; a modified evolutionary algorithm for generating optimized BPs. (ii) ReProVA; an operational algorithm for verifying the feasibility of resulting BPs of xNSGAII. (iii) Cost, duration and customer's satisfaction are the three optimization criteria for selecting optimal solutions, from the proposed solutions.

By developing the proposed framework, a test scenario was provided to demonstrate the proper functioning of the latter. Then, the test scenario was implemented on the algorithm and its results were compared to reported results in [14]. Success of used framework was demonstrated compared to previous studies in terms of efficiency of the proposed improvements by evaluating optimal BPs designs (i) using qualitative criteria including size, fitness value and (ii) using quantitative criteria including cost, duration and customer's satisfaction. Previous studies put too little effort on customizing evolutionary algorithms for optimizing BPs, and even less effort when using more than two optimization criteria. To fill this gap, the authors combined modified evolutionary operators of NSGAII and a real multi criteria optimization to generate solutions.

The proposed framework allows using more evolutionary algorithms; to do so, PAES2 and SPEA2 can be considered. Also, the authors plan to improve the proposed framework by using quantitative and qualitative parameters to evaluate alternative designs as operational power, productivity. Another interesting direction is to add the concept of purpose to different tasks, when designing a BP.

References

1. Porter, M.E.: Competitive Strategy: Techniques for Analyzing Industries and Competitors. The Free Press, New York (1980)
2. Dahman, K.: Gouvernance et Etude de L'impact du Changement des Processus Métiers sur les Architectures Orientées Services. Ph.D. thesis. University of Lorraine (2012)
3. Hammer, M., Champy, J.: Reengineering the Corporation: A Manifesto for Business Revolution. HarperCollins, New York (1993). 35 p.
4. Salomie, I., Chifu, V.R., Pop, C.B., Suciu, R.: Firefly-based business process optimization. In: IEEE Conference on Intelligent Computer Communication and Processing, pp. 49–56 (2012)
5. Tiwari, A., Vergidis, K., Turner, C.: Evolutionary multi-objective optimisation of business processes. In: Gao, X.-Z., Gaspar-Cunha, A., Köppen, M., Schaefer, G., Wang, J. (eds.) Soft Computing in Industrial Applications. AISC, vol. 75, pp. 293–301. Springer, Heidelberg (2010)
6. Hofacker, I., Vetschera, R.: Algorithmical approaches to business process design. Comput. Oper. Res. **28**, 1253–1275 (2001)
7. Zhou, Y., Chen, Y.: Business process assignment optimization. In: IEEE International Conference on Systems, Man and Cybernetics, vol. 3 (2002)
8. Zhou, Y., Chen, Y.: Project-oriented business process performance optimization. In: Proceedings of Industrial Electronics Conference (2003)

9. Tiwari, A., Vergidis, K., Turner, C.: Evolutionary multi-objective optimization of business processes. In: IEEE Congress on Evolutionary Computation, pp. 3091–3097 (2006)
10. Vergidis, K., Tiwari, A., Majeed, B.: Business process improvement using multi-objective optimisation. BT Technol. J. **24**(2), 229 (2006)
11. Vergidis, K., Tiwari, A.: Business process design and attribute optimization within an evolutionary framework. In: Congress on Evolutionary Computing, pp. 668–675 (2008)
12. Tiwari, A., Turner, C., Ball, P., Vergidis, K.: Multi-objective optimisation of web business processes. In: Bhattacharya, A., Chakraborti, N., et al. (eds.) SEAL 2010. LNCS, vol. 6457, pp. 573–577. Springer, Heidelberg (2010)
13. Vergidis, K., Tiwari, A., Saxena, D.: An evolutionary multi-objective framework for business process optimisation. Appl. Soft Comput. **12**, 2638–2653 (2012)
14. Vergidis, K., Turner, C., Alechnovic, A., Tiwari, A.: An automated optimization framework for the development of re-configurable business processes: a web services approach. Int. J. Comput. Integr. Manuf. **28**, 41–58 (2015)
15. Pop, C.B., Chifu, V.R., Salomie, I., Kovacs, T., Niculici, A.N., Suia, D.S.: Business process optimization using bio-inspired methods - ants or bees intelligence. In: IEEE International Conference on Intelligent Computer Communication and Processing, pp. 65–71 (2012)
16. Wibig, M.: Dynamic programming and genetic algorithm for business processes optimization. Int. J. Intell. Syst. Appl. **5**, 44–51 (2013)
17. Farsani, S.T., Aboutalebi, M., Motameni, H.: Customizing NSGAII to optimize business processes designs. Res. J. Recent Sci. **2**, 74–79 (2013)
18. Malihi, E., Aghdasi, M.: A decision framework for optimisation of business processes aligned with business goals. Int. J. Bus. Inf. Syst. **15**, 22–42 (2014)
19. Bae, H., Lee, S., Moon, I.: Planning of business process execution in business process management environments. Inf. Sci. **268**, 357–369 (2014)
20. Molka, T., Redlich, D., Gilani, W., Zeng, X.-J., Drobek, M.: Evolutionary computation based discovery of hierarchical business process models. In: Abramowicz, W. (ed.) BIS 2015. LNBIP, vol. 208, pp. 191–204. Springer, Heidelberg (2015)
21. Drake, R.F.: Working backwards is a forward step in the solution of problems by dimensional analysis. J. Chem. Educ. **62**, 414 (1985)
22. Deb, K., Pratap, A., Agarwal, S., Meyarivan, T.: A fast and Elitist multi-objective genetic algorithm: NSGAII. Evol. Comput. IEEE **6**, 182–197 (2002)
23. Bean, J.C.: Genetic algorithms and random keys for sequencing and optimization. ORSA J. Comput. **6**, 157–160 (1994)
24. Mason, S.J., Kurz, M.E., Pfund, M.E., Fowler, J.W., Pohl, L.M.: Multi-objective semiconductor manufacturing scheduling: a random keys implementation of NSGA II. In: Symposium on Computational Intelligence in Scheduling, pp. 159–164. IEEE (2007)
25. Zheng, F., Simpson, A.R., Zecchin, A.C.: An efficient hybrid approach for multiobjective optimization of water distribution systems. Water Resour. Res. **50**(5), 3650–3671 (2014)
26. Gonçalves, J.F., Resende, M.G.C.: Biased random-key genetic algorithms for combinatorial optimization. J. Heuristics **17**, 487–525 (2011)
27. Vekaria, K., Clack, C.: Selective crossover in genetic algorithms: an empirical study. In: Eiben, A.E., Bäck, T., Schoenauer, M., Schwefel, H.-P. (eds.) PPSN 1998. LNCS, vol. 1498, pp. 438–447. Springer, Heidelberg (1998)
28. Verkaria, K.: Selective crossover as an adaptive strategy for genetic algorithms. Ph.D. thesis, Department of Computer Science, University College London (2000)

Semantic-Enabled and Hypermedia-Driven Linked Service Discovery

Mahdi Bennara[1](✉), Michael Mrissa[2], and Youssef Amghar[1]

[1] Université de Lyon, LIRIS, INSA-Lyon - CNRS UMR5205, 69621 Lyon, France
{mahdi.bennara,youssef.amghar}@liris.cnrs.fr
[2] Université de Lyon, LIRIS, Université Lyon 1 - CNRS UMR5205,
69622 Lyon, France
michael.mrissa@liris.cnrs.fr

Abstract. Automating discovery and composition of RESTful services with the help of semantic Web technologies is a key challenge to exploit today's Web potential. In this paper, we show how semantic annotations on resource descriptions can drive discovery algorithms on the Web. We propose a semantically-enabled variant of the BFS discovery algorithm that aims at minimizing the number of links explored while maximizing result diversity. Our algorithm calculates semantic distances between resource descriptions and user request concepts to rank explored resources accordingly. We demonstrate the applicability of our solution with a typical scenario and provide an evaluation with a prototype.

Keywords: Linked Web services · Semantic Web · Discovery · Composition

1 Introduction

During the last few years, both the overall number of Web APIs exposed on the Web[1] and the increasing ratio of RESTful APIs has shown the interest of a Web of resources. Resources can be combined to answer complex user requests, in other words: to build Web applications. The emergence of RESTful services[2] has been a major success to enable interoperation on the Web. Moreover, service composition, or mashups, enables valued-added processes that combine several services to answer complex user needs. The success of Web services is highlighted via Web sites such as http://www.programmableweb.com that referenced 105 APIs available on the Web in 2005 and more than 15000 APIs in 2016, not counting mashups. The uniform interface, that comes with the correct use of HTTP verbs and their semantics, replaces the typical API build around functions and sets of input/output parameters. The operations handled by server-side modules are now shifting towards the client modules. On top of that, recent

---

[1] http://www.programmableweb.com/api-research.
[2] In the remainder of this paper, we use "resource" to describe a RESTful service accessed through a URI endpoint.

© Springer International Publishing Switzerland 2016
L. Bellatreche et al. (Eds.): MEDI 2016, LNCS 9893, pp. 108–117, 2016.
DOI: 10.1007/978-3-319-45547-1_9

advances in the semantic Web research area have been promoting linked data [2] and a set of languages and tools, such as RDF [10], that allow to annotate Web data, resources and services with explicit, machine-readable semantics that can be utilized in conjunction with advanced reasoning mechanisms to connect resources to each other. Linked services [13] benefit from these machine-readable semantic annotations.

Our paper is organized as follows. Section 2 introduces the motivating scenario of our contribution and details the research problem. Section 3 explains some background knowledge in order to understand our contributions. Section 4 presents related work and highlights the advantages our solution offers. Section 5 details how we semantically annotate resource descriptions and hypermedia links. Section 6 gives an evaluation and discusses the choices made and results obtained. Section 7 resumes our approach and lists some elements of future work.

2 Motivating Scenario and Research Problem

2.1 Scenario and Motivation

We motivate our contribution with an online book selling scenario where a user wants to buy a book, make a payment online then get the book shipped to the given address. The process of buying involves selecting a set of books, choosing a shipping method, and paying with the appropriate solution. We assume that the URI of one of the book selling resources is known to the user. Our work is motivated by the need to enable distributed affordance principle [14], which means that the resource discovery process should be automated and hypermedia-driven (consisting in following links between resources). The advantages of distributed affordance include the possibility of generating opportunities of use for resources while exploring the Web as well as respecting the user preferences. Automating the discovery process can typically be achieved with the help of semantic annotations that can aid software agents decide what are the relevant links to follow. Building a solution to enable distributed affordance includes two elements. Discovery requires **semantic description of resources**. Semantic annotations provide the means to reason about the descriptions. Such descriptions should follow the HATEOAS principle[3]. Exploring the Web requires a **resource discovery algorithm**. It must make appropriate use of the semantic annotations on resources to optimize the search response time. The end user should only provide high level objectives to the software program, as well as an entry point (URI to start the discovery process). The software program should be in charge of interpreting the user request, finding out that buying a book online includes selecting a set of books, choosing a delivery option and paying online. It should explore the Web of resources to discover the ones that help answering the query, orchestrate the interactions and execute the created process. These are the challenges we address in the current paper.

---

[3] Hypermedia as the Engine of Application State.

2.2   Problem Statement and Research Contribution

Typical approaches to discover, compose, orchestrate and utilize linked services on the Web require complete overhauling of existing technique in order to harness the benefits provided by the REST principles and the semantic Web. In the present paper, we propose a generic solution to automate resource discovery based on semantic reasoning and following the HATEOAS principle. We follow the distributed affordance principle [14] and rely on an extension [1] to the Hydra [8] specification for semantically describing resources. Our contribution is two-fold:

- Resource description: The extension of our previous work on descriptions (presented in Sect. 5) describes the business-level semantics of HTTP operations on resources as well as links to other resources. Annotations on operations allow to automate the identification the tasks required by the user, and annotations on links guide the discovery process to other resources.
- Resource discovery: we extend the BFS[4] algorithm with semantic-awareness to improve its response time. Our annotation extends the social model presented in [9] to semantically qualify the relationships between resources.

3   Background Knowledge

3.1   Graph Search Algorithms

Breadth-First-Search: Exploring very large graphs like the Web [11] needs high performance algorithms in order to obtain low response times. Efficiency of the exploration algorithm is key for our work, as we are discovering resources on the Web. Breadth-First-Search [7] algorithm yields high performances in large graphs, according to [12]. In addition, BFS is a natural search strategy in the context of Web. Also, compared to other efficient search algorithms, it has a relatively low computational cost for a large scale graph such as the Web. In our approach, BFS finds the most relevant resources to answer a user's request early enough to be considered efficient.

Depth-First-Search: DFS is also one of the well-known graph exploring algorithms [7]. It explores branches one by one and it stops only when it reaches the deepest node of that branch, the deepest node being the one with no successor. The application of DFS in Web crawling has proved to be difficult. This is due to the fact that the Web is a very large graph, and exploring one branch only can be extremely difficult, performance-wise. Most relevant nodes to the current research are generally not very deep but rather in different branches, which is the main weakness of the algorithm.

---

[4] Breadth First Search [7].

3.2   Web Resource Description

In this paper, we rely on the RESTful resource descriptor mechanism as well as and the discovery solution introduced in [1] in order to propose a solution for resource discovery problem in the context of semantic Web. The descriptor notion separates resource representation from its description and states that every resource must have a descriptor and a representation. The reason for detaching the representation from the description is to separate different concerns, in order to ease the resolution of each one apart. Resource representations relate to user Web browsing, while resource descriptions relate to M2M interactions and operations such as discovery and composition processes. The descriptor is typically accessed by calling a GET/HEAD operation on the resource URI, and retrieving the LINK header element in the HTTP response. A GET on the retrieved link returns a HTTP response whose body contains the descriptor itself.

4   Related Work

4.1   Semantic Description of Resources

Hydra Core Vocabulary: The Hydra core vocabulary [8] is a small vocabulary aimed to describe RESTful Web APIs. The purpose of developing the Hydra vocabulary is to simplify the development of RESTful APIs by leveraging the advantages offered by Linked Data. The basic idea of Hydra vocabulary is to allow RESTful APIs to publish valid state transitions to clients. As a result, the clients can utilize this information in order to construct valid HTTP requests in order to modify the resource, request/delete another one or create a new one. All this information is exchanged between server and client at run-time and is not hard-coded into client at design time. Hence, the clients can be decoupled from the servers and adapt their execution according to changes.

RESTdoc: RESTdoc [5] is a description solution that combines multiple microformats in order to semantically describe RESTful resources. RESTdoc offers also a discovery mechanism that distinguishes two different aspects of REST services discovery problem: (1) the discovery as a client concerns the client-side browsers. This discovery uses on HTML Link element on a Web site in order to point to other resource descriptions, and (2) the discovery as a service which is the ability for a service to access and link to other related resources in the same application domain. This solution describes a fully peer to peer discovery mechanism. In our work we combine both discovery modes.

4.2   Resource Discovery and Composition

LinkedWS: LinkedWS [9] is a Web service discovery model based on human interactions in social networks in the context of SOA. The idea behind LinkedWS is to establish a social network of Web services where nodes are actual Web services and edges are relations between these Web services. What is really important about this work in the current paper is the categorization established on exposed functionality. These functionalities are either Similar so the Web services compete for participation in compositions or Complementary, so the Web services work towards the same compositions.

RESTdesc: RESTdesc [15] is a work about semantic description of Web APIs based on the Notation3 RDF syntax. The purpose of the description is to allow for an efficient way to discover the features that Web APIs offer. It uses operational semantics of Notation3 in order to allow a flexible discovery. e think that the N3 descriptions require a lot of effort to work with, even though N3 reasoning has seen a good advance. Our descriptor mechanism is aimed specifically to render descriptions use simple for both machines and Web API developers.

4.3   Analysis

Using semantic Web advances to automate resource composition is a recent topic and has only been explored by few works in the literature [6]. The contribution we propose in this paper relies on exploring the semantic annotations over the links between resources, which are found in descriptors, in order to guide the discovery process into the links with the most potential to match with the request concepts. We reuse the Hydra core vocabulary in order to establish descriptions. However Hydra does not provide a good support for semantic annotations over links and operations. We extend hydra in order to allow resources description to have semantically annotated elements that can be exploited by discovery, selection and composition algorithms in order to enable a completely automated process to answer user's requests. The simplicity of our solution lies in the separation between resource representation and description as well as the separation between links and operations in the descriptions. In order to discover resources that can answer the user's request, the generic client has to start exploring the description of the resource given as an entry point by the user. Based on the semantic annotations given by the description, the decision making of (1) whether to account the current resource in the final composition and (2) what are the next resources to explore is easy to establish.

5   Contribution

5.1   Semantically Annotating Descriptor Links

Our descriptor-based solution allows generic clients to crawl from one resource to another in order to select interesting resources to answer the user's query. However, due to the huge number of resources on the Web, there is a need to improve the discovery algorithm that we use (i.e. BFS [7]) to only select the most interesting resources. The vocabulary we use to implement the descriptor concept is Hydra core vocabulary [8]. We introduce semantic annotations on descriptor links, and extend the BFS algorithm to take advantage of these annotations. The semantic annotations will guide the algorithm by excluding irrelevant links to the current application. Figure 1 illustrates the semantic annotation of descriptor links. Our semantic annotation is inspired from existing work [9] to define the properties that link resources to each other. We define that:

- Two resources are `similar` if they provide functionally substitutable services, sometimes varying in terms of non-functional properties.
- Two resources are `complementary` if they can be combined in the same process to answer user's needs, for example: a flight booking service and a hotel booking service in the context of a trip.
- Two resources are `incompatible` if they cannot be involved together in the same process because of a given reason, for example: the eBay online seller could decide not to work with the UPS delivery company.

bs: http://soc.univ-lyon1.fr/bookselling.owl rr : http://soc.univ-lyon1.fr/resourcerelation.owl		
Operations		**Links**
GET bs:consultBooks PUT bs:updateBookList	http://amazon.com rr:IsSimilar http://dhl.com rr:IsComplementary http://paypal.com rr:IsIncompatible	

Fig. 1. Descriptor example with annotated links

5.2 Semantic-Enabled Discovery

Our solution builds a generic client that interacts with the resources through their respective APIs. The client software program needs to be able to automate the process of composing the functionality of the three resources of the scenario to answer the user's query. This includes the discovery of the resources. The maximum number of `similar` links to be operated can be limited in order to increase the performance of the BFS algorithm. However, this will limit the choices given to the user. A compromise between performance and result diversity is to be established using this parameter.

We also propose a solution inspired by the weight-based approach presented in [3] in order to:

- Sort the links on a resource description in order to guide the discovery algorithm while exploring similar links.
- Sort the results obtained after positive matching with a query concept

In other words, the set of similar resources inside a resource descriptor are sorted from the most similar link into the least similar one. Based on the query nature, the discovery algorithm starts exploring the most similar resources if the priority is to find more alternatives to the current resource or the least similar resources if the priority is to find more complementary and diverse resources. Many formulas to calculate semantic distance have been proposed in the state of the art [3,4]. The one we adopt in our work is weight-based formula proposed in [3] because it can be directly used with our approach without any further calculation of additional parameters. Note that the work of annotating links and sorting them is not done during the discovery.

The discovery algorithm details are given in Algorithm 1.

Algorithm 1. BFS-based discovery algorithm

Input: conceptList: **array of string**
Input: currentLink: **string**
Input: similarLimit: **integer**
Output: result: **array of string**
1 bfsQueue: **array of string**
2 visited: **array of string**
3 **while** *not conceptList.empty() and not bfsQueue.empty()* **do**
4 | **if** *not currentLink in visited* **then**
5 | | visited.insert(currentLink)
6 | | **Descriptor** descriptor = getDescriptor(currentLink)
7 | | **foreach** *operation in descriptor.operations* **do**
8 | | | **foreach** *concept in conceptList* **do**
9 | | | | **if** *conceptMatch(operation.annotation, concept)* **then**
10 | | | | | result.insert([concept, currentLink])
11 | | | | | conceptList.remove(concept)
12 | | similarCount: **integer** = 0
13 | | **foreach** *link in descriptor.links* **do**
14 | | | **if** *link.annotation = IsComplementary* **then**
15 | | | | bfsQueue.insert(link)
16 | | | **else**
17 | | | | **if** *link.annotation = IsSimilar and similarCount < similarLimit* **then**
18 | | | | | bfsQueue.insert(link)
19 | | | | | similarCount = similarCount + 1
20 | | //and if it is incompatible we do not take it into account in the first place
21 | currentLink = bfsQueue.next()

The algorithm takes as input three parameters:

- `conceptList` (array): contains the list of concepts that describe the operations needed in order to answer the user's query.
- `currentLink` (string): contains the URI of the resource being processed.
- `similarLimit` (int): is the maximum number of similar links per resource to be taken into account by the algorithm.

The algorithm returns as output the `result` array which contains all the pairs [`concept`, `URI`] where the resource identified by `URI` can perform an operation that semantically matches the paired `concept` classified by semantic distance from the query concept.

The set of variables used in this algorithm are the following:

- The `bfsQueue` is the queue that contains the ordered set of URIs for the next nodes to be explored by the BFS algorithm.
- The `visited` array contains URIs of resources already traveled. This variable's main objective is to prevent loops if the graph is cyclic. Further improvements on this part of the algorithm are possible in order to obtain better performance.
- The `similarCount` variable introduced in line 12 counts the number of `similar` links that are inserted in the BFS queue to be traveled. This counter cannot exceed `similarLimit`.

The algorithm consists of a main `While` loop. The exit condition is verified when there are no concepts to look for or no further resources in the graph to travel or when a certain amount of time passed since the beginning of the loop (timeout). Each iteration of this loop discovers a single resource whose link is `currentLink`. The algorithm verifies if it has not been visited yet, if not it is marked as visited. If the resource has not been processed yet, the algorithm gets its descriptor then checks if any of the operations provided by the resource is annotated by one of the remaining concepts. If so, the concept along with the resource URI are inserted into `result` then the concept is removed from `conceptList`. After that, the algorithm inserts the URIs of the related resources into `bfsQueue`, while respecting the fact that similar resources links inserted cannot exceed `similarLimit`.

6 Evaluation and Discussion

The resources composing the services previously presented in the scenario are implemented using Java TM Servlets using Jersey framework 7. We use Apache Tomcat 8 as a server-side software in order to accommodate our resources. The demonstration Web page can be found here: https://liris.cnrs.fr/~mbennara/doku.php?id=medi2016.

We show the number of traveled nodes as well as response time (in milliseconds) gain compared to the raw BFS algorithm respectively in Figs. 2 and 3. Each column represents a separate query that involves an increasing number of resources in the Web. We get better response times for the same request with the enhanced algorithm because it explores less nodes than the regular. This is due to the fact that when we travel the Web graph, we find more similar resources. The similar resources are ignored by the enhanced algorithm but taken into account by the regular one. However, this decrease in response time can also be accompanied by a decrease in result diversity.

Enabling semantic annotations on links between resources allows the automation of the discovery process. Without the semantic annotations, the discovery algorithm has to explore every link in order to search for resources to answer the user's query. Having similar and complementary annotations on links allows

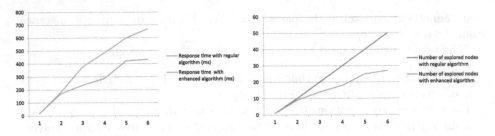

Fig. 2. Response time in ms   **Fig. 3.** Number of explored nodes

the algorithm to explore the requested links based on selectivity measures. The maximum number of similar links to be explored is limited. This limit determines the performances of the discovery algorithm as well as the diversity of the results obtained. The lack of diversity is due to the possibility for similar resources to contain links into useful complementary resources. Sorting the similar resource links in the description is important in order to optimize the discovery algorithm. Depending on the user's query, the discovery process will prioritize the most or the least similar links while taking into account the similar limit as well.

7   Conclusion

In this paper we propose an annotation of Web resource descriptions based on a social model that relies on similar and complementary relations. These annotations provide information for the discovery process in order to respond to the user's request faster and more accurately. Then, we provide a semantically-enhanced BFS-based algorithm to discover resources. It relies on the semantic annotations in order to determine whether a resource is worth exploring.

Future work includes exploring advanced heuristics to reach a better compromise between performance and result diversity. We envision to extend our model to support quality of service aspects in order to further enhance the discovery and selection processes. We aim also to enable an automatic service composition process in order to fully automate answering users' requests.

Acknowledgment. We would like to thank Mehdi Terdjimi for his support and help with the implementation of the algorithm, the ontology and the concept matching component.

References

1. Bennara, M., Amghar, Y., Mrissa, M.: Managing web resource compositions. In: Reddy, S. (ed.) 24th IEEE International Conference on Enabling Technologies: Infrastructure for Collaborative Enterprises, WETICE Workshops 2015, Larnaca, Cyprus, 15–17 June 2015, pp. 176–181. IEEE (2015)

2. Bizer, C., Heath, T., Berners-Lee, T.: Linked data - the story so far. Int. J. Semant. Web Inf. Syst. **5**(3), 1–22 (2009)
3. Ge, J., Qiu, Y.: Concept similarity matching based on semantic distance. In: Fourth International Conference on Semantics, Knowledge and Grid, SKG 2008, pp. 380–383. IEEE (2008)
4. Hau, J., Lee, W., Darlington, J.: A semantic similarity measure for semantic web services. In: Web Service Semantics Workshop at WWW, pp. 10–14 (2005)
5. John, D., Rajasree, M.S.: RESTDoc: describe, discover and compose RESTful semantic web services using annotated documentations. Int. J. Web Semant. Technol. (IJWesT) **4**(1), 37 (2013)
6. Kovatsch, M., Hassan, Y.N., Mayer, S.: Practical semantics for the internet of things: physical states, device mashups, and open questions. In: 2015 5th International Conference on the Internet of Things (IOT), pp. 54–61. IEEE (2015)
7. Kozen, D.: Depth-first and breadth-first search. In: The Design and Analysis of Algorithms. Texts and Monographs in Computer Science, pp. 19–24 (1992). http://dx.doi.org/10.1007/978-1-4612-4400-4_4
8. Lanthaler, M., Guetl, C.: Hydra: a vocabulary for hypermedia-driven web APIs. In: Bizer, C., Heath, T., Berners-Lee, T., Hausenblas, M., Auer, S. (eds.) CEUR Workshop Proceedings on LDOW, vol. 90. CEUR-WS.org (2013)
9. Maamar, Z., Wives, L.K., Badr, Y., Elnaffar, S., Boukadi, K., Faci, N.: LinkedWS: a novel web services discovery model based on the metaphor of "social networks". Simul. Model. Pract. Theor. **19**(1), 121–132 (2011)
10. Manola, F., Miller, E.: RDF Primer. W3C Recommendation. http://www.w3.org/TR/rdf-primer/
11. Meusel, R., Vigna, S., Lehmberg, O., Bizer, C.: The graph structure in the web-analyzed on different aggregation levels. J. Web Sci. **1**(1) (2015)
12. Najork, M., Wiener, J.L.: Breadth-first crawling yields high-quality pages. In: Proceedings of the 10th International Conference on World Wide Web, pp. 114–118. ACM (2001)
13. Pedrinaci, C., Domingue, J.: Toward the next wave of services: linked services for the web of data. J. UCS **16**(13), 1694–1719 (2010)
14. Verborgh, R., Hausenblas, M., Steiner, T., Mannens, E., de Walle, R.V.: Distributed affordance: an open-world assumption for hypermedia. In: Carr, L., Laender, A.H.F., Lóscio, B.F., King, I., Fontoura, M., Vrandecic, D., Aroyo, L., de Oliveira, J.P.M., Lima, F., Wilde, E. (eds.) International World Wide Web Conferences Steering Committee, WWW (Companion Volume), pp. 1399–1406. ACM (2013)
15. Verborgh, R., Steiner, T., Deursen, D.V., Roo, J.D., de Walle, R.V., Vallés, J.G.: Description and interaction of RESTful services for automatic discovery and execution. In: Proceedings of the FTRA 2011 International Workshop on Advanced Future Multimedia Services, December 2011

Multi-level Networked Knowledge Base: DDL-Reasoning

Sihem Klai[1]([✉]), Antoine Zimmermann[2], and Med Tarek Khadir[1]

[1] Labged, Department of Computer Science, University of Badji Mokhtar of Annaba, Po-Box 12, 2300 Annaba, Algeria
{klai,khadir}@labged.net
[2] Univ Lyon, MINES Saint-Étienne, CNRS, Laboratoire Hubert Curien UMR 5516, 42023 Saint-Étienne, France
antoine.zimmermann@emse.fr

Abstract. This paper describes a new formalism based on multi-level networked knowledge (MLNK), a combination of different ontologies describing heterogeneous and complementary domains aligned with semantic correspondences. Ontology alignments make explicit the correspondences between terms from different ontologies and must be taken into account in reasoning, where two explicit form of correspondences are given: mappings represent predefined relations such as subsumption, equivalence, or disjointness, that have a fixed semantics in all interpretations; as well as links that can relate complementary ontologies by introducing terms defined by experts, and their semantics varies according to interpretations. The proposed MLNK formalism can be transformed into a Distributed System capable of supporting DDL semantics. It permits to apply a contextual reasoning where ontologies and alignments by pairs of ontologies are developed in different and incompatible contexts. The semantic of the proposed formalism is extensively described along with an illustrative example.

Keywords: Multi-level networked knowledge base · Ontologies · Ontology-alignment · DDL-reasoning

1 Introduction

In information systems, and more recently in the Semantic Web, a number of heterogeneous, independently developed ontologies may be exploited in a single application that needs to share some knowledge. These ontologies are developed in different contexts and may well cover complementary domains.

In order to overcome the heterogeneity problem, complementary knowledge may be introduced in order to describe correspondences between ontologies to be exploited. These correspondences, represent relations between entities (terms or formulas) belonging to different ontologies. This set of correspondences is named ontology alignment.

© Springer International Publishing Switzerland 2016
L. Bellatreche et al. (Eds.): MEDI 2016, LNCS 9893, pp. 118–131, 2016.
DOI: 10.1007/978-3-319-45547-1_10

In order to exploit, during reasoning, a number of heterogeneous ontologies as well as correspondences, a simple solution consists in viewing the ontology system as a unique global ontology. Therefore, each local ontology as well as each alignment, is then considered as a knowledge complement over a larger domain. Taking into account all this knowledge, namely ontologies and alignments, may be performed using a fusion process obtaining a centralized system, or using distributed reasoning algorithms based on classical logic, (as shown in: SomeRDFS [2] and SomeOWL [1]). Such approaches consider ontologies and alignments describing a unique global theory, however, presenting inconvenient if the ontologies to be combined are highly heterogeneous. They will, therefore, describe different contexts and points of view, potentially incompatible.

The other possible solution consists in managing the set of ontologies as well as the corresponding alignments as a complex semantic network, where each node is represented by an ontology formalizing a given domain, with a different context than the ones given by the rest of the ontologies within the network. Such an approach, needs strong formalism modeling the already aligned ontology network, offering specific algorithms and techniques for contextual reasoning. In that sense, a number of formalisms have been proposed to model an aligned ontology network for contextual reasoning. These formalisms may be divided into two categories based on definition and application purposes. Alignment is a major concern, as it constitutes an important element of the complete system, distinguishing two major types of correspondences in order to define them.

The first type is for instance given by Distributed Description Logic [5] and Iqntegrated Distributed Description Logics [11] that define relations, named *mappings*, in order to reduce semantic heterogeneity problems between terms and entities belonging to different ontologies. These correspondences are associated with a predefined set of relations such as subsumption, equivalence, disjunction where the given semantic is fixed for all interpretations (*e.g.*, $\mathtt{mt{:}belong} \xleftrightarrow{\equiv} \mathtt{eq{:}belong}$).

The second type of alignments is used to link ontologies covering complementary domains. It is the case of $\mathcal{E}$-connection [8]. It is represented by inter-ontological links between entities, termed simply *links* (*e.g.*, $\mathtt{pr{:}T_1} \xleftrightarrow{\mathrm{compose}} \mathtt{eq{:}FD_1}$). This type of relations is defined by experts in the context of domain ontology combination, as well as semantic representation of context links.

However, a number of other works on contextual reasoning do not use corrspondences as defined here. Indeed, knowledge from multiple contexts are jointly exploited via a meta description of the contexts themselves. Established relations between contexts play a similar role, ensured by alignments between ontologies, (We can quote the recent work: [6]).

In this paper, we focus on proposing a formalism which supports both types of correspondences in order to permit heterogeneous ontology combination associated with different contexts covering complementary domains as is the case of [10]. Regarding the second point of difference, which is the application or treatment of alignments, the majority of proposed formalisms, such as Distributed Description Logic [5], $\mathcal{E}$-connection [8] and Package-based Description Logic [3]), consist in integrating alignment as external knowledge for the corresponding target ontology. The alignment is then defined and exploited following the target ontology point of view. In order to ensure reasoning over the ontology network, each ontology must be enriched with a reasoning mechanism which supports external knowledge.

The other way of looking at the problem is to consider alignments to be exploited at a higher level independent from local ontologies and termed global level [11]. In this approach, the alignment language may be more expressive than the languages defining local ontologies, allowing better alignment reuse. However, only mappings are considered in this work, and no proposition concerning the integration of links at the global level is made.

Links are, supposedly, introduced by experts. However, this may be unfeasible if experts covering all ontologies domain cannot be found. Therefore, if distinct pairs of ontologies are aligned by different experts with different terms and points of view, then it is likely that the heterogeneity problem will need to be considered this time between links.

The proposed contribution consists in defining and giving a semantics to a formalism named *Multi Level Networked Knowledge* (or MLNK for short). Here, we extend the work of [7] and provide an alternative, more distributed semantics for such networks.

The organization of the rest of the article is as follows: Sect. 2 describes a scenario representing an ontology network aligned using heterogeneous pairs ontology alignments. Section 3, describes the syntax formalism of the MLNK components. In Sect. 4, we recall the basic concepts of DDL. In Sect. 5, a possible interpretation using DDL semantics for automating reasoning tasks is proposed. Section 6 finishes the article with a general conclusion.

2   Motivating Example

In this section, a real life application example of gas turbine ontological representation is presented. Due to their wide usage in electricity production, gas turbine are often found in the center of large power systems that need to be managed in terms of knowledge and maintenance. Four ontologies describing gas turbine have been developed for the purpose of this example, namely:

- an ontology for equipment (eq) that describes turbine components, such as the concept flame-detector given by instance FD_1. A set of equipments forms the group instrumentation;
- an ontology termed (Pr), modeling spare parts, such as the concept trim given by the instance T_1. They compose the equipment and they can be replaced;
- an ontology for modeling the position of the equipment in the turbine hierarchy (zn);
- an ontology created from an existing database mt, using a semi automatic approach, covering maintenance operations (both preventive and after breakdown), defining the symptoms, the defects, the causes and the remedies for each case. The mt ontology exploits the first ontologies (eq, Pr and zn) in order

to provide details on equipments and spare parts concerned by maintenance operations.

Exploiting these ontologies requires their alignment and the integration of the latter in all reasoning or search strategies. For this purpose a number of alignment tools have been applied in order to provide *mappings* such as: mt:belong $\xleftrightarrow{\perp}$ eq:belong between (mt, eq) ontologies pair and pr:trim $\xleftrightarrow{\sqsubseteq}$ eq:instrumentation between (pr, eq). These sets of correspondences (or *mappings*) are enriched in a semi-automatic manner using *links* as well as consulting domain experts, an expert for a pair of ontologies. This operation revealed the existence of semantic heterogeneity problems between ontology alignments, and more precisely between links. As an example of heterogeneity, the links $A_{\text{pr-eq}}$:**compose** and $A_{\text{eq-zn}}$:**part-of** have similar semantics but appear in different alignments, namely $A_{\text{pr-eq}}$ and $A_{\text{eq-zn}}$. It is clear that reasoning on the set of ontologies and their existing alignments, semantic heterogeneity problem between *links* need to be solved. For the previous case, inserting an equivalence relation between *links* $A_{\text{pr-eq}}$:**compose** and $A_{\text{eq-zn}}$:**part-of** becomes necessary.

Example 1. An excerpt of ontologies and associated alignments are presented in Table 1.

Table 1. An excerpt of ontologies and associated alignments

Ontologies	Axioms
eq:	flame-detector(FD_1)
	flame-detector $\sqsubseteq$ $\exists$belong.instrumentation
pr:	trim(T_1)
zn:	zone(ANNA1TG01)
mt:	intervention(I_1)
	team(TE_1)
	intervene(TE_1, I_1)
	member $\sqsubseteq$ $\exists$belong.team
Alignments	
$A_{\text{eq-zn}}$:	eq:FD_1 $\xleftrightarrow{\text{part-of}}$ zn:ANNA1TG01
$A_{\text{pr-eq}}$:	pr:trim $\xleftrightarrow{\sqsubseteq}$ eq:instrumentation
	pr:T_1 $\xleftrightarrow{\text{compose}}$ eq:FD_1
$A_{\text{mt-eq}}$:	mt:I_1 $\xleftrightarrow{\text{concern}}$ eq:FD_1
	eq:belong $\xleftrightarrow{\perp}$ mt:belong
$A_{A_{\text{pr-eq}}-A_{\text{eq-zn}}}$:	pr-eq:**compose** $\xleftrightarrow{\equiv}$ eq-zn:**part-of**

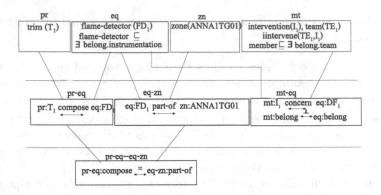

Fig. 1. Knowledge representation levels.

In order to solve semantic heterogeneity problem between links, it is essential to represent and understand the semantics of the MLNK. Further than semantic connections of a MLNK representing local knowledge, we may find semantic connections between alignments themselves, Fig. 1 represents the turbine example showing alignment levels.

3   Multi-level Networked Knowledge Base Syntax

Representation and formalization of MLNK implies on the one hand, represent each component of this network and formalize the semantics and on the other hand, that the relationships between these components can be represented. This section, is dedicated to the syntactic representation of a multi-level networked knowledge components, such as ontologies, alignments and knowledge nodes.

3.1   Knowledge Representation Languages and Ontologies

A knowledge representation language L, is defined by a syntax (how formulas are expressed) and a semantic (the meaning and sense of formulas). We then speak of signatures or vocabulary in order to design structured terms which are subsets of a given language symbols. Each signature permits the definition of a set of formulas defined by the used language, and a set of formulas constructed from a common signature form an ontology. Local ontologies or knowledge sources in a multi-level networked knowledge are linked using alignments.

3.2   Alignment Language

An alignment L_A language permits the description of correspondences between two vocabularies. It is also caracterised by a syntax (how correspondences are expressed) and a semantic (how correspondences are interpreted). The syntax of L_A is defined by:

– a set of terms, called links, specific to the alignment language noted $V(L_A)$;
– a function $E(L_A)$, which associate to each signature of a representation language L, a set of entities that can be aligned;
– a set of relation's symbols $R(L_A)$.

Thus, the syntax of an alignment language L_A is defined by the triple $\langle V(L_A), E(L_A), R(L_A)\rangle$, noted $\langle V, E, R\rangle$ when no ambiguity exists. Two types of correspondences might be defined as *mapping* and *link* correspondences.

Definition 1 (*mapping* correspondence). *Let V_1 and V_2 two aligned vocabularies and $L_A \langle V, E, R\rangle$ an alignment language. A* mapping *correspondence is a triple $\langle e_1, e_2, r\rangle$ noted $e_1 \xleftrightarrow{r} e_2$ where:*

– *$e_1 \in E(V_1)$ and $e_2 \in E(V_2)$ are matchable entities;*
– *$r \in R$ denotes an existing relation between e_1 and e_2.*

Referring to Example 1, $\texttt{eq:belong} \xleftrightarrow{\perp} \texttt{mt:belong}$ is a *mapping* correspondence. The term **belong** can be found in both ontologies vocabulary, for instance $\texttt{eq}$ and $\texttt{mt}$, formalized in description logic, with different meanings. *Mappings* are constructed using the set of relations $R = \{\sqsubseteq, \equiv \perp, \in =\}$.

Definition 2 (*link* correspondence). *Let V_1 and V_2 be two aligned vocabularies and $L_A \langle V, E, R\rangle$ an alignment language. A* link *correspondence is a formula in the form $e_1 \xleftrightarrow{l} c_2$ where:*

– *$e_1 \in E(V_1)$ and $c_2 \in E(V_2)$ are matchable entities;*
– *$l \in V$ denotes an existing relation between e_1 and e_2.*

Again referring to Example 1, $\texttt{eq:FD}_1 \xleftrightarrow{\text{part-of}} \texttt{zn:ANNA1TG01}$ and $\texttt{mt:I}_1 \xleftrightarrow{\text{concern}} \texttt{eq:FD}_1$ are *link* correspondences. Terms **part-of** and **concern** do not appear in the ontologies vocabularies, they were introduced at the alignment level in order to link different vocabularies entities. The alignment, now, possesses its own vocabulary and therefore may be aligned with other vocabularies in order to avoid heterogeneity problems.

Definition 3 (Alignment). *Let V_1 and V_2 be two vocabularies. An alignment of V_1 and V_2 is a tuple $\Lambda = \langle V, \kappa, \lambda\rangle$ where:*

– *V is an alignment vocabulary;*
– *κ is a set of* mapping *correspondences, $e_1 \xleftrightarrow{r} e_2$ where $e_1 \in E(V_1)$, $e_2 \in E(V_2)$ et $r \in R$;*
– *λ is a set of* link *correspondences, $e_1 \xleftrightarrow{l} e_2$ where $e_1 \in E(V_1)$, $e_2 \in E(V_2)$ and $l \in V$;*

Example 2. In DDL or in IDDL, alignments are between the ontologies signatures and the sets V, λ are all empty. In $\mathcal{E}$-connections, cross-ontology knowledge can involve terms from more than two ontologies. However, if one restricts to $\mathcal{E}$-connection axioms of the form $\langle E_i\rangle^j (a_i, b_j)$, where E_i is a link relation, a_i is an individual in ontology O_i and b_j is an individual in ontology O_j, then this can be represented as a correspondence in λ, with l being a term in the alignment vocabulary (the set κ is empty).

3.3   Knowledge Node

It is now possible to introduce the notion of knowledge node, which generalize the notion of ontology. Informally, an ontology is a level 0 knowledge node, while all knowledge node of level $m > 0$ is constructed from a number of nodes with inferior levels, linked using alignment (Fig. 2). Formally the node is defined as:

Definition 4 (Knowledge node). *A knowledge node is a pair* $K = \langle V_K, A_K \rangle$ *where* V_K *is a vocabulary, also written* $\text{Voc}(K)$ *and both* V_K *and* A_K *are defined recursively:*

- *an ontology O is a knowledge node with vocabulary* $\text{Voc}(O) = \text{Sig}(O)$ *and* A_K *is the set of axioms;*
- *for $n \geq 1$, if $K_1, \ldots, K_n$ are knowledge nodes with vocabularies* $\text{Voc}(K_1), \ldots,$ *$\text{Voc}(K_n)$, and for all $i, j \in [1, n]$, Λ_{ij} is an alignment of $\text{Voc}(K_i)$ and $\text{Voc}(K_j)$, then $K = \langle V_K, A_K \rangle$ is a knowledge node with the vocabulary:*

$$V_K = \bigcup_{i,j \in [1,n]} \{ij : l \mid l \in \text{Voc}(\Lambda_{ij})\} \cup \bigcup_{i \in [1,n]} \{i : e \mid e \in \text{Voc}(K_i)\}$$

and $A_K = \langle (K_i)_{i \in [1,n]}, (\Lambda_{ij})_{i,j \in [1,n]} \rangle.$

If a knowledge node includes only ontologies and ontology alignments, we call it a *network of aligned ontologies*. If a knowledge node is neither a single ontology, nor a network of aligned ontologies, we call it a *multi-level networked knowledge base* (see Fig. 2).

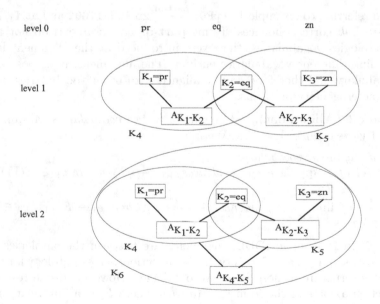

Fig. 2. Recursive representation of nodes.

4 Distributed Description Logics: Preliminaries

[4] introduces *Distributed Description Logics* (DDL) to connect and reason with multiple existing ontologies formalized in DL with different contexts. Ontologies are interconnected through (*Bridge rules*) which are the relationships between concepts, roles and individuals belonging to different ontologies. The bridge rules are oriented because they are established between a source ontology and a target one with the viewpoint of the target ontology. To represent distributed description logics system, a concrete syntax based on OWL has been defined.

4.1 Syntax

Ontologies in DDL are formalized in DL and the syntax of bridge rule is defined as follows.

Definition 5 (Bridge rules). *Let O_i et O_j two ontologies. Bridge rule from O_i to O_j ($i \neq j$) is an expression of one of the following forms: $i{:}X \xrightarrow{\sqsubseteq} j{:}Y$ is an into bridge rule; $i{:}X \xrightarrow{\sqsupseteq} j{:}Y$ is an onto bridge rule; $i{:}a \xrightarrow{\equiv} j{:}b$ is an individual correspondence where X (respectively Y) is either a concept or a role of O_i (respectively O_j) and a (respectively b) is an individual of O_i (respectively O_j). The notation $i{:}X \xrightarrow{\equiv} j{:}Y$ is expressing the combination of $i{:}X \xrightarrow{\sqsubseteq} j{:}Y$ and $i{:}X \xrightarrow{\sqsupseteq} j{:}Y$ and denotes the equivalence bridge rule.*

DDL knowledge system is composed of a family of local and prefixed ontologies and a set of bridge rules expressing mappings between entities belonging to these ontologies.

Definition 6 (DDL distributed system). *A DDL distributed system is a pair $\langle (O_i)_{i \in [1,n]}, (\mathcal{B}_{ij})_{i,j \in [1,n], i \neq j} \rangle$ where (O_i) is a family of local ontologies and $\mathcal{B}_{ij}$ is a set of bridge rules between O_i and O_j for all $i, j \in [1, n]$ et $i \neq j$.[1]*

4.2 Semantics

Interpreting DDL distributed system by assigning to each ontology a local interpretation, then defining relationships between different local interpretations. A domain relation r_{ij} represents a relationship between O_i domain interpretation and O_j domain interpretation.

Definition 7 (Distributed interpretation). *Let S be a distributed system $S = \langle \{O_i\}, \{\mathcal{B}_{ij}\} \rangle$. A distributed interpretation of S is a pair $\mathcal{I} = \langle \{I_i\}, \{r_{ij}\} \rangle$, for all $i \in [1, n]$, $I_i = \langle \Delta^{I_i}, \cdot^{I_i} \rangle$ is an ontology interpretation O_i for $i, j \in [1, n]$ and $i \neq j$, $r_{ij} \subseteq \Delta^{I_i} \times \Delta^{I_j}$ is a relation domain.*

---

[1] In the rest of the paper, for readability, we omit the set of indices by writing, e.g., (O_i) instead of $(O_i)_{i \in [1,n]}$.

Distributed interpretation is a model of the DDL distributed system if every local interpretation is a model of its associated ontology, and if the domain relation satisfies all the bridge rules.

Definition 8 (satisfaction relation). *Let $\mathcal{I}$ a distributed interpretation $\mathcal{I} = \langle\{I_i\}, \{r_{ij}\}\rangle$. We define the satisfaction relation in DDL $\models_d$ as follows: if α is an axiom then $\mathcal{I} \models_d i : \alpha$ if and only if $I_i \models \alpha$; if X, Y are concepts or roles then $I \models_d i{:}X \overset{\sqsubseteq}{\rightarrow} j{:}Y$ if and only if $r_{ij}(X^{I_i}) \subseteq Y^{I_j}$; if X, Y are concepts or roles then $I \models_d i{:}X \overset{\sqsupseteq}{\rightarrow} j{:}Y$ if and only if $r_{ij}(X^{I_i}) \supseteq Y^{I_j}$; if a and b are individuals then $I \models_d i{:}a \overset{\equiv}{\rightarrow} j{:}b$ if and only if $r_{ij}(a^{I_i}) = \{b^{I_j}\}$; $\mathcal{I} \models_d B_{ij}$ if and only if for all $\beta \in B_{ij}$, $\mathcal{I} \models_d \beta$.*

$\mathcal{I}$ is a model of S if and only if: for all $i \in [1, n]$ and all axioms α in O_i, $\mathcal{I} \models_d i : \alpha$ and for all $i, j \in [1, n]$, $i \neq j$, $\mathcal{I} \models B_{ij}$. After recalling the fundamentals of description logics, we will, in the next section use DDL to interpret multi-level networked knowledge semantics.

5   Multi-level Networked Knowledge Semantics

The representation of MLNK was defined independently of any language and can support multiple semantics. In this paper, we adopt distributed description logics (DDL) which is one of the most popular and contextual semantics to interpret the multi-level knowledge network.

The presented approach, consists in transforming the multi-level networked knowledge into a DDL distributed system. An ontology in description logic (called alignment-ontology) is created from the alignment then bridge rules between local ontologies and alignment-ontologies are generated. All local ontologies, alignment-ontologies and the set of bridge rules constitute the DDL distributed system. We will start by detailing the alignment-ontology building process.

Generating Alignment-Ontology. The alignment-ontology is a DL-ontology generated from the transformation of the alignment between a pair of nodes which is composed of a signature and a set of axioms. The signature of this ontology is made from terms (concepts, roles or individuals) contained in the left and right of mappings belonging to local aligned vocabularies. It also contains the links terms that belong to the alignment vocabularies. Before defining the new notions of alignement-ontology signature and formulas, a complementary function permitting the indexing of the ontology elements is firstly defined.

Definition 9 (Index the element of ontology). *Let i be an indice. We define the function* prefix *on the terms, axioms and ontologies, such that* prefix$(X, i) = \{i{:}X\}$ *when X is an atomic concept, atomic role or an individual, and if X is a formula,* prefix(X, i) *is a formula where all terms are prefixed by i.*

Definition 10 (Alignment-ontology signature). *Let K a multi-level knowledge node, alignment-ontology signature Σ_A is defined as follows according to the case:*

- *if K is an ontology then $\Sigma_A = \emptyset$;*
- *if K a multi-level knowledge node composed of sub nodes $K_1, \ldots, K_n$ and A_{ij} which is alignment between K_i and K_j for $i, j \in [1, n]$, then:*

$$\Sigma_A(K) = \bigcup_{i,j \in [1,n]} \{\mathsf{prefix}(X, i), \mathsf{prefix}(Y, j) \mid i{:}X \xrightarrow{r} j{:}Y \in A_{ij}\} \cup \bigcup_{i,j \in [1,n]} \mathrm{Voc}(A_{ij})$$

where X and Y are the concepts, roles or individuals and $r \in \{\sqsubseteq, \equiv, \bot, \in, =\}$, and $\mathrm{Voc}(A_{ij})$ means the alignment vocabulary, the links of A_{ij}.

Alignment-ontology formulas is the set of generated formulas from correspondences. Firstly, the function associating each correspondence in to an axiom is defined.

Definition 11 (Correspondence transformation in to axiom). *Let A_{ij} for $i, j \in [1, n]$ an alignment between a node i and a node j. We define* trans *a function which assigns to each correspondence of A_{ij} a DL axiom:* $\mathsf{trans}(\{i{:}A \xleftrightarrow{\sqsubseteq} j{:}B\}) = \{\mathsf{prefix}(A, i) \sqsubseteq \mathsf{prefix}(B, j)\}$; $\mathsf{trans}(\{i{:}A \xleftrightarrow{\equiv} j{:}B\}) - \{\mathsf{prefix}(A, i) \equiv \mathsf{prefix}(B, j)\}$; $\mathsf{trans}(\{i{:}A \xleftrightarrow{\ } j{:}B\}) = \{\mathsf{prefix}(A, i) \sqsubseteq \neg\mathsf{prefix}(B, j)\}$; $\mathsf{trans}(\{i{:}u \xleftrightarrow{\in} j{:}A\}) = \{\mathsf{prefix}(A, j)(i{:}u)\}$; $\mathsf{trans}(\{i{:}u \xleftrightarrow{=} j{:}u'\}) = \{i{:}u = j{:}u'\}$; $\mathsf{trans}(\{i{:}u \xleftrightarrow{l} j{:}u'\}) = \{\mathsf{role}(l)(i{:}u, j{:}u')\}$; $\mathsf{trans}(\{i{:}A \xleftrightarrow{l} j{:}B\}) = \{\mathsf{prefix}(A, i) \sqsubseteq \exists\mathsf{role}(l).\mathsf{prefix}(B, j)\}$, *where A, B, u et u' are the matchable entities and l is a* link.

Definition 12 (Alignment-ontology formulas). *Let K a multi-level knowledge node, the set of alignment-ontology formulas F_A is defined as follows according to the cases:*

- *if K is an ontology then $F_A = \emptyset$;*
- *if K a multi-level knowledge node composed of sub nodes $K_1, \ldots, K_n$ and alignments A_{ij} between K_i and K_j for $i, j \in [1, n]$ and* trans *is the function that associates to any correspondence of A_{ij} a DL-axiom (see Definition 11) and alignment-ontology-formula set $F_A(K) = \{f \mid f \in \mathsf{trans}(A_{ij})\}$.*

Definition 13 (Alignment-ontology). *Let a node $K = \langle\{K_i\}, \{A_{ij}\}\rangle$ for $i, j \in [1, n]$, K_i are local nodes and A_{ij} is an alignment between K_i and K_j. We define* OntoAlign *the alignment-ontology generated from A_{ij} of K,* $\mathsf{OntoAlign}(K) = \langle\Sigma_A(K), F_A(K)\rangle$.

The bridge rules of multi-level knowledge node represent the equivalence correspondences established between the terms of alignment-ontology and terms belonging to the corresponding local ontologies.

Definition 14 (Bridge rules toward alignment-ontology). *Let K be a knowledge node. We define the bridge rules oriented towards the alignment-ontology (noted $B(K)$) as follows depending on the cases:*

- *if K is an ontology then $B(K) = \emptyset$;*
- *if K a multi-level knowledge node composed of sub nodes $K_1, \ldots, K_n$ and of A_{ij} which is alignment between K_i and K_j for $i, j \in [1, n]$ then $B(K)$ contains a bridge rules defined as follows, for $i \in [1, n]$:*
  - *if K_i is an ontology and X is a concept or a role of K_i then $i{:}X \xrightarrow{\equiv} \mathsf{OntoAlign}(K){:}i{:}X \in B(K)$;*
  - *if K_i is an ontology a is an individual of K_i then $i{:}a \xrightarrow{=} \mathsf{OntoAlign}(K){:}i{:}a \in B(K)$;*
  - *if K_i is a composed node and X a concept or role of $\mathsf{OntoAlign}(K_i)$ then $\mathsf{OntoAlign}(K_i){:}X \xrightarrow{\equiv} \mathsf{OntoAlign}(K){:}k_i{:}X \in B(K)$;*
  - *if K_i is a composed node and a an individual of $\mathsf{OntoAlign}(K_i)$ then $\mathsf{OntoAlign}(K_i){:}a \xrightarrow{=} \mathsf{OntoAlign}(K){:}k_i{:}a \in B(K)$.*

The MLNK interpreted as a DDL system is composed of several local nodes connected to their alignment-ontology through a family on bridge rules.

Definition 15 (MLNK in DDL form). *Let K a knowledge node. $\mathsf{SystDis}$ is a DDL system of K, $\mathsf{SystDis}(K) = \langle \mathsf{Onto}(K), \mathsf{Bridge}(K) \rangle$ with $\mathsf{Onto}(K)$ a family of local ontologies which is recursively defined as follows*

- $\mathsf{Onto}(K) = \{K\}$, *if K is a DL-ontology;*
- $\mathsf{Onto}(K) = \mathsf{Onto}(K_1) \cup \mathsf{Onto}(K_2) \cup \cdots \cup \mathsf{Onto}(K_n) \cup \mathsf{OntoAlign}(K)$ *if K is a node with K_i local nodes.*

$\mathsf{Bridge}(K)$ *is a family of bridge rules of K recursively defined as follows:*

- $\mathsf{Bridge}(K) = \emptyset$ *if K is an ontology;*
- $\mathsf{Bridge}(K) = \mathsf{Bridge}(K_1) \cup \cdots \cup \mathsf{Bridge}(K_n) \cup B(K)$.

Example 3. Ontologies and alignments of Example 1 are used to build a DDL system. Figure 3 shows the structured knowledge nodes. Table 2 details the contents of those nodes.

Semantics. In this section, a multi-level knowledge base X is interpret in the same way as the DDL distributed system $\mathsf{SystDis}(X)$ built out of it using the previous definitions.

Definition 16 (Knowledge   node   DDL-interpretation). *A DDL-interpretation of knowledge node X is an interpretation in DDL formalism of the distributed system ($\mathsf{SystDis}(X)$).*

Distributed interpretation is a model of multi-level knowledge base if, each local interpretation is a model of associated local ontology and if domain relation satisfies the bridge rules.

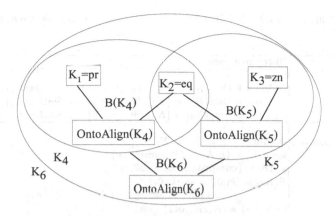

Fig. 3. Example of an MLNK in DDL form.

Definition 17 (DDL-based satisfaction relation of an MLNK). *Let X be a multi-level knowledge node, I is DDL-interpretation of X, then I DDL-satisfies X (noted $I \models_{N-DDL} X$) if and only if I satisfies SystDis(X) in DDL meaning (noted $I \models_{DDL}$ SystDis(X)). In this case, we say that I is a DDL-model of X.*

Additionally, X DDL-entails Y if and only if all DDL-models of X are also DDL-models of Y.

Property 1. *Let X be a multi-level knowledge node, composed of local nodes $N_1, \ldots, N_k$, then X DDL-entails all local nodes $(X \models_{N-DDL} N_i)$ for $i \in [1, k]$.*

Proof. Let a node $X = \langle \{N_i\}, \{A_{ij}\} \rangle$. $X \models_{N-DDL} N_i$ if it exists an interpretation I where I is a DDL-model of X then I is also DDL-model of N_i. We suppose that $I \models_{N-DDL} X$. This implies that $I \models_{DDL}$ SystDis(X) (Definition 17) and $I \models_{DDL} \langle$Onto(X), Bridge$(X)\rangle$ (Definition 15). Then $I \models_{DDL}$ Onto$(N_1) \cup$ Onto$(N_2) \cup \cdots \cup$ Onto$(N_n) \cup$ OntoAlign(X), Bridge(N_1), Bridge$(N_2) \cup \cdots \cup$ Bridge(N_n) and $I \models_{DDL}$ SystDis(N_i) for $i = [1..n]$ consequently I is a DDL-model of N_i

Example 4. With reference to Example 3, SystDis$(K_6) = \langle \{K_1, K_2, K_3, \mathsf{oa}_4, \mathsf{oa}_5, \mathsf{oa}_6\},$ Bridge$(K_6)\}\rangle$. We note that $I \models_{DDL} K_1, K_2, K_4$, $I \models_{DDL} k_1{:}\mathsf{G}_1 \xrightarrow{\equiv} \mathsf{oa}_4{:}k_1{:}\mathsf{G}_1$ and $I \models_{DDL} k_2{:}\mathsf{DF}_1 \xrightarrow{\equiv} \mathsf{oa}_4{:}k_2{:}\mathsf{DF}_1$ then I satisfies SystDis(K_4) and it implies that I a model of K_4. I satisfies also SystDis(K_5) then I is a model of K_5. So, we can conclude that K_6 implies a local nodes K_4 and K_5.

The transformation of a multi-level knowledge node allows us to relate it to distributed description logics which has an operational reasoning tool able to reason on the node, named DRAGO [9]. Therefore, the transformation provides us with an effective way of reasoning over multi-level networked knowledge.

Table 2. Example of an MLNK in DDL form. We rename $\mathsf{OntoAlign}(K_i)$ in oa_i for $i \in [4, 6]$.

Node	Distributed system
level 0	
$K_1 = \mathsf{pr}$	$B(K_1) = \emptyset, \mathsf{Onto}(K_1) = \{K_1\}, \mathsf{Bridge}(K_1) = \emptyset, \mathsf{SystDis}(K_1) = \{\{K_1\}, \emptyset\}$
$K_2 = \mathsf{eq}$	$B(K_2) = \emptyset, \mathsf{Onto}(K_2) = \{K_2\}, \mathsf{Bridge}(K_2) = \emptyset, \mathsf{SystDis}(K_2) = \{\{K_2\}, \emptyset\}$
$K_3 = \mathsf{zn}$	$B(K_3) = \emptyset, \mathsf{Onto}(K_3) = \{K_3\}, \mathsf{Bridge}(K_3) = \emptyset, \mathsf{SystDis}(K_3) = \{\{K_3\}, \emptyset\}$
niveau 1	
$K_4 = \{K_1, K_2, A_{K_1\text{-}K_2}\}$	$\mathsf{OntoAlign}(K_4) = \mathsf{oa}_4 = \langle \Sigma_4, F_4 \rangle,$ where $\Sigma_4 = \{k_1{:}\mathsf{G}_1, k_2{:}\mathsf{DF}_1, \mathbf{compose}\}$ and $F_4 = \{\mathbf{compose}(k_1{:}\mathsf{G}_1, k_2{:}\mathsf{DF}_1)\}$ $B(K_4) = \{k_1{:}\mathsf{G}_1 \xrightarrow{\equiv} \mathsf{oa}_4{:}k_1{:}\mathsf{G}_1,$ $\qquad\qquad k_2{:}\mathsf{DF}_1 \xrightarrow{\equiv} \mathsf{oa}_4{:}k_2{:}\mathsf{DF}_1\};$ $\mathsf{Onto}(K_4) = \{K_1, K_2, \mathsf{oa}_4\}$ $\mathsf{Bridge}(K_4) = B(K_4);$ $\mathsf{SystDis}(K_4) = \langle \mathsf{Onto}(K_4), \mathsf{Bridge}(K_4) \rangle$
$K_5 = \{K_2, K_3, A_{K_2\text{-}K_3}\}$	$\mathsf{OntoAlign}(K_5) = \mathsf{oa}_5 = \langle \Sigma_5, F_5 \rangle,$ where $\Sigma_5 = \{k_2{:}\mathsf{DF}_1, k_3{:}\mathsf{ANNA1TG01}, \mathbf{part\text{-}of}\}$ and $F_5 = \{\mathbf{part\text{-}of}(k_2{:}\mathsf{DF}_1, k_3{:}\mathsf{ANNA1TG01})\}$ $B(K_5) = \{k_2{:}\mathsf{DF}_1 \xrightarrow{\equiv} \mathsf{oa}_5{:}k_2{:}\mathsf{DF}_1,$ $\qquad\qquad k_3{:}\mathsf{ANNA1TG01} \xrightarrow{\equiv} \mathsf{oa}_5{:}k_3{:}\mathsf{ANNA1TG01}\};$ $\mathsf{Onto}(K_5) = \{K_2, K_3, \mathsf{oa}_5\}$ $\mathsf{Bridge}(K_5) = B(K_5)$ $\mathsf{SystDis}(K_5) = \langle \mathsf{Onto}(K_5), \mathsf{Bridge}(K_5) \rangle$
niveau 2	
$K_6 = \{K_4, K_5, A_{K_4\text{-}K_5}\}$	$\mathsf{OntoAlign}(K_6) = \mathsf{oa}_6 = \langle \Sigma_6, F_6 \rangle$ where $\Sigma_6 = \{\mathsf{oa}_4{:}\mathbf{compose}, \mathsf{oa}_5{:}\mathbf{part\text{-}of}\}$ and $F_6 = \{\mathsf{oa}_4{:}\mathbf{compose} \equiv \mathsf{oa}_5{:}\mathbf{part\text{-}of}\}$ $B(K_6) = \{\mathsf{oa}_4{:}\mathbf{compose} \xrightarrow{\equiv} \mathsf{oa}_6{:}\mathbf{compose},$ $\qquad\qquad \mathsf{oa}_5{:}\mathbf{part\text{-}of} \xrightarrow{\equiv} \mathsf{oa}_6{:}\mathbf{part\text{-}of}$ $\mathsf{Onto}(K_6) = \mathsf{Onto}(K_4) \cup \mathsf{Onto}(K_5) \cup \{\mathsf{oa}_6\}$ $\qquad\quad = \{K_1, K_2, K_3, \mathsf{oa}_4, \mathsf{oa}_5, \mathsf{oa}_6\}$ $\mathsf{Bridge}(K_6) = \mathsf{Bridge}(K_4) \cup \mathsf{Bridge}(K_5) \cup B(K_6)$ $\qquad\qquad = B(K_4) \cup B(K_5) \cup B(K_6)$ $\mathsf{SystDis}(K_6) = \langle \mathsf{Onto}(K_6), \mathsf{Bridge}(K_6) \rangle$

6   Conclusions

In this paper a formalism capable of reasoning on a network of heterogeneous, complementary aligned ontologies, is presented. The alignments have proper vocabularies and necessitate, sometimes, to be aligned at different levels which represent the novelty of the presented formalism called MLNK. The semantic interpretation of the formalism is based on an existing paradigm, having complete reasoning procedures, along with operational tools such as a distribute description logics DDL, used in this case. An implementation of the approach as well as experimentation and tests on significant examples will be presented in our future work, but preliminary experiments on a variant semantics of MLNK was provided in [7]. We have chosen in this work to use an existing paradigm but it would be interesting to think about other ways of interpreting multi-level networked knowledge semantics by defining a formal semantic built directly into the network structure and then propose a correct and complete reasoning algorithm better adapted in this structure. Finally, we consider of paramount importance the implementation of a system able to integrate knowledge of such networks and respond to queries in a formalism question that remains to be defined.

References

1. Adjiman, P., Chatalic, P., Goasdoué, F., Rousset, M.-C., Simon, L.: Distributed reasoning in a peer-to-peer setting: application to the semantic web. J. Artif. Intell. Res. **25**, 269–314 (2006)
2. Adjiman, P., Goasdoué, F., Rousset, M.-C.: SomeRDFS in the semantic web. J. Data Semant. **8**, 158–181 (2007)
3. Bao, J., Voutsadakis, G., Slutzki, G., Honavar, V.: Package-based description logics. In: Stuckenschmidt, H., Parent, C., Spaccapietra, S. (eds.) Modular Ontologies. LNCS, vol. 5445, pp. 349–371. Springer, Heidelberg (2009)
4. Borgida, A., Serafini, L.: Distributed description logics: directed domain correspondences in federated information sources. In: Meersman, R., Tari, Z. (eds.) CoopIS 2002, DOA 2002, and ODBASE 2002. LNCS, vol. 2519, pp. 36–53. Springer, Heidelberg (2002)
5. Borgida, A., Serafini, T.: Distributed description logics: assimilating information from peer sources. J. Data Semant. **1**, 153–184 (2003)
6. Joseph, M.: Query answering over contextualized RDF/OWL rules: decidable classes. Ph.D. thesis, University of Trento (2015)
7. Klai, S., Zimmermann, A., Khadir, M.T.: Multi-level networked knowledge: representation and DL-reasoning. Int. J. Metadata Semant. Ontol. (2016, to appear)
8. Kutz, O., Lutz, C., Wolter, F., Zakharyaschev, M.: E-connections of abstract description systems. Artif. Intell. **156**(1), 1–73 (2004)
9. Serafini, L., Tamilin, A.: DRAGO: distributed reasoning architecture for the semantic web. In: Gómez-Pérez, A., Euzenat, J. (eds.) ESWC 2005. LNCS, vol. 3532, pp. 361–376. Springer, Heidelberg (2005)
10. Vouros, G., Santipantakis, G.M.: Distributed Reasoning with E^{DDL}_{HQ+} SHIQ. In: Schneider, J., Walther, D. (eds.) Proceedings of the 6th International Workshop on Modular Ontologies, Graz, Austria, 24 July 2012, vol. 875. CEUR Workshop Proceedings. Sun SITE Central Europe (CEUR), July 2012
11. Zimmermann, A.: Integrated distributed description logics. In: Calvanese, D., Franconi, E., Haarslev, V., Lembo, D., Motik, B., Tessaris, S., Turhan, A.-Y. (eds.) Proceedings of the 20th International Workshop on Description Logics DL 2007, 8–10 June 2007, Brixen/Bressanone, Italy, pp. 507–514. Bolzano University Press, June 2007

Maintenance of Profile Matchings
in Knowledge Bases

Jorge Martinez-Gil[1], Lorena Paoletti[1], Gábor Rácz[2], Attila Sali[2],
and Klaus-Dieter Schewe[1(✉)]

[1] Software Competence Center Hagenberg, Softwarepark 21, 4232 Hagenberg, Austria
{jorge.martinez-gil,lorena.paoletti,kd.schewe}@scch.at
[2] Alfréd Rényi Institute of Mathematics, P.O.B.127, Budapest 1364, Hungary
gabee33@gmail.com, sali@renyi.hu

Abstract. A profile describes a set of properties, e.g. a set of skills a person may have or a set of skills required for a particular job. Profile matching aims to determine how well a given profile fits to a requested profile. Profiles can be defined by filters in a lattice of concepts derived from a knowledge base that is grounded in description logic, and matching can be realised by assigning values in [0,1] to pairs of such filters: the higher the matching value the better is the fit. In this paper the problem is investigated, whether given a set of filters together with matching values determined by some human expert a matching measure can be determined such that the computed matching values preserve the rankings given by the expert. In the paper plausibility constraints for the values given by an expert are formulated. If these plausibility constraints are satisfied, the problem of determining a ranking-preserving matching measure can be solved.

1 Introduction

A profile describes a set of properties, and profile matching is concerned with the problem to determine how well a given profile fits to a requested one. Profile matching appears in many application areas such as matching applicants for jobs to job requirements, matching system configurations to requirements specifications, etc.

Taking the profile just as a set of unrelated items is usually not appropriate for the problem, even though many distance measures between sets such as Jaccard or Sørensen-Dice [8] have proven to be useful in ecological applications. The reason is that many dependencies between the properties have to be

The research reported in this paper was supported by the Austrian Forschungsförderungsgesellschaft (FFG) for the Bridge project "Accurate and Efficient Profile Matching in Knowledge Bases" (ACEPROM) under contract [**FFG: 841284**]. The research reported in this paper has further been supported by the Austrian Ministry for Transport, Innovation and Technology, the Federal Ministry of Science, Research and Economy, and the Province of Upper Austria in the frame of the COMET center SCCH [**FFG: 844597**].

L. Bellatreche et al. (Eds.): MEDI 2016, LNCS 9893, pp. 132–141, 2016.
DOI: 10.1007/978-3-319-45547-1_11

taken into account. Therefore, in the human resources application area many taxonomies for skills, competences and education such as DISCO [2], ISCED [6] and ISCO [7] have been set up. On the grounds of these application-oriented dictionaries for profile matching a lattice structure for the individual properties can be assumed. This has been exploited by Popov and Jebelean in [13] defining a different asymmetric matching measure on the basis of filters in such lattices.

However, it can well be argued that the hierarchical dependencies in lattices are still insufficient for capturing the exact meaning of the properties in a profile. For instance, it is not common to request just "programming in Java" as a required skill, but it is more likely that further attributes are given such as years of experience associated with the skill, level of complexity of problems addressed with the skill, etc. Therefore, it appears favourable to not only assume a lattice structure, but to exploit sophisticated knowledge representation features for semantic matching problems as advocated by Falk, Mochol and others [3,10]. In our research we adopt this basic assumption how to represent knowledge about properties. That is, we exploit description logics [1] as the basis for knowledge representation using a rather expressive language similar to $SROIQ(\mathcal{D})$ [11]. On these grounds matching top-k queries have been addressed in [12]. In order to generalise matching to knowledge bases we exploit "blowing-up" roles, which means to enrich the concept lattice by inverse images defined by the roles [11]. In Sect. 2 we briefly review our general approach to profile matching in knowledge bases, formally defining a knowledge representation language and matching measures based on filters. Probabilistic extensions to the theory of matching measures have been investigated in [14].

The second question, which is the core problem handled in this paper concerns the relationship of rankings obtained through the matching measures and the judgements of human experts. An initial idea based on formal concept analysis [4] was already presented in [9] aiming to enrich the knowledge base by additional concepts that would justify the judgement of the human expert. In this paper we investigate the learning of the matching measure. Starting from the set of filters together with matching values or simply rankings determined by some human expert we derive plausibility constraints that should be satisfied to exclude unjustified bias, which could be grounded in the valuation of facts not represented in a knowledge base. Our key result is a proof that the satisfaction of the plausibility constraints implies the existence of a matching measure that preserves the human rankings. This key contribution will be presented in Sect. 3. We conclude with a brief summary.

2   Profile Matching in Knowledge Bases

In this section we present the formal definitions underlying our approach to profile matching in knowledge bases. We will start with the general approach to knowledge representation, proceed with the representation of profiles, and discuss filter-based matching.

2.1 Knowledge Representation

For the representation of knowledge we adopt the fundamental distinction between *terminological* and *assertional* knowledge that has been used in description logics since decades. For the former one we define a language, which defines the TBox of a knowledge base, while the instances define a corresponding ABox.

A TBox consists of concepts and roles. In addition, we will permit the denotation of individuals as supported by SROIQ($\mathcal{D}$) [1] and OWL2 [5]. For this assume that C_0, I_0 and R_0 represent not further specified sets of basic concepts, individuals and roles, respectively. Then *atomic concepts* A, *concepts* C and *roles* R are defined by the following grammar:

$$
\begin{aligned}
R &= R_0 \mid R_0^- \mid R_1 \circ R_2 \\
A &= C_0 \mid \top \mid \geq m.R \text{ (with } m > 0) \mid \{I_0\} \\
C &= A \mid \neg C \mid C_1 \sqcap C_2 \mid C_1 \sqcup C_2 \mid \exists R.C \mid \forall R.C
\end{aligned}
$$

Definition 1. A *TBox* is a finite set $\mathcal{T}$ of assertions of the form $C_1 \sqsubseteq C_2$ with concepts C_1 and C_2 as defined by the grammar above.

Each assertion $C_1 \sqsubseteq C_2$ in a TBox $\mathcal{T}$ is called a *subsumption axiom*. Note that Definition 1 only permits subsumption between concepts, not between roles, though it is possible to define more complex terminologies that also permit role subsumption. As usual, we use several shortcuts: (1) $C_1 \equiv C_2$ can be used instead of $C_1 \sqsubseteq C_2 \sqsubseteq C_1$, (2) $\bot$ is a shortcut for $\neg\top$, (3) $\{a_1,\ldots,a_n\}$ is a shortcut for $\{a_1\} \sqcup \cdots \sqcup \{a_n\}$, (4) $\leq m.R$ is a shortcut for $\neg \geq m+1.R$, and (5) $= m.R$ is a shortcut for $\geq m.R \sqcap \leq m.R$.

Definition 2. A *structure* $\mathcal{S}$ for a TBox $\mathcal{T}$ consists of a non-empty set $\mathcal{O}$ together with subsets $\mathcal{S}(C_0) \subseteq \mathcal{O}$ and $\mathcal{S}(R_0) \subseteq \mathcal{O} \times \mathcal{O}$ for all basic concepts R_0 and basic roles R_0, respectively, and individuals $\bar{a} \in \mathcal{O}$ for all $a \in I_0$. $\mathcal{O}$ is called the base set of the structure.

We first extend the interpretation of basic concepts and roles and to all concepts and roles as defined by the grammar above, i.e. for each concept C we define a subset $\mathcal{S}(C) \subseteq \mathcal{O}$, and for each role R we define a subset $\mathcal{S}(R) \subseteq \mathcal{O} \times \mathcal{O}$ as follows:

$$
\mathcal{S}(R_0^-) = \{(y,x) \mid (x,y) \in \mathcal{S}(R_0)\}
$$
$$
\mathcal{S}(R_1 \circ R_2) = \{(x,z) \mid \exists y.(x,y) \in \mathcal{S}(R_1) \wedge (y,z) \in \mathcal{S}(R_2)\}
$$
$$
\mathcal{S}(\top) = \mathcal{O} \qquad \mathcal{S}(\{a\}) = \{\bar{a}\} \qquad \mathcal{S}(\neg C) = \mathcal{O} - \mathcal{S}(C)
$$
$$
\mathcal{S}(\geq m.R) = \{x \in \mathcal{O} \mid \#\{y \mid (x,y) \in \mathcal{S}(R)\} \geq m\}
$$
$$
\mathcal{S}(C_1 \sqcap C_2) = \mathcal{S}(C_1) \cap \mathcal{S}(C_2) \qquad \mathcal{S}(C_1 \sqcup C_2) = \mathcal{S}(C_1) \cup \mathcal{S}(C_2)
$$
$$
\mathcal{S}(\exists R.C) = \{x \in \mathcal{O} \mid (x,y) \in \mathcal{S}(R) \text{ for some } y \in \mathcal{S}(C)\}
$$
$$
\mathcal{S}(\forall R.C) = \{x \in \mathcal{O} \mid (x,y) \in \mathcal{S}(R) \Rightarrow y \in \mathcal{S}(C) \text{ for all } y\}
$$

Definition 3. An *ABox* for a TBox $\mathcal{T}$ is a finite structure $\mathcal{S}$, such that $\mathcal{S}(C_1) \subseteq \mathcal{S}(C_2)$ holds for all assertions $C_1 \sqsubseteq C_2$ in $\mathcal{T}$.

For the following we always consider a concept C in a TBox as representation of abstract properties, e.g. "knowledge of Java", and individuals in the ABox as concrete properties such as the "Java knowledge of Lara". Therefore, given an ABox a *profile* is simply a subset of the base set $\mathcal{O}$.

2.2   Filter-Based Matching

Obviously, the concepts in a TBox define a lattice with $\sqcap$ and $\sqcup$ as operators for meet and join, and $\sqsubseteq$ for the partial order. So let us abstract for a moment from the specific definition of the knowledge base by TBox and ABox and assume to be given a lattice $(\mathcal{L}, \leq)$.

Definition 4. A *filter* in a lattice $(\mathcal{L}, \leq)$ is a non-empty subset $\mathcal{F} \subseteq \mathcal{L}$, such that for all C, C' with $C \leq C'$ whenever $C \in \mathcal{F}$ holds, then also $C' \in \mathcal{F}$ holds.

If $P \subseteq \mathcal{O}$ is a profile, then P defines in a natural way a filter $\mathcal{F}$ of the lattice $\mathcal{L}$ of concepts: $\mathcal{F} = \{C \in \mathcal{L} \mid \exists p \in P.\ p \in \mathcal{S}(C)\}$. Therefore, for determining matching relations we can concentrate on filters $\mathcal{F}$ in a lattice.

Definition 5. Let $(\mathcal{L}, \leq)$ be a lattice, and let $\mathbb{F} \subseteq \mathcal{P}(\mathcal{L})$ denote the set of filters in this lattice.

A *relative weight measure* on $\mathcal{L}$ is a function $m : \mathcal{P}(\mathcal{L}) \rightarrow [0, 1]$ satisfying (1) $m(\mathcal{L}) = 1$, and (2) $m(\bigcup_{i \in I} A_i) = \sum_{i \in I} m(A_i)$ for pairwise disjoint A_i $(i \in I)$.

A *matching measure* is a function $\mu : \mathbb{F} \times \mathbb{F} \rightarrow [0, 1]$ such that $\mu(\mathcal{F}_1, \mathcal{F}_2) = m(\mathcal{F}_1 \cap \mathcal{F}_2)/m(\mathcal{F}_2)$ holds for some relative weight measure m on $\mathcal{L}$.

Example 1. The matching measure μ_{pj} defined in [13] uses simply cardinalities: $\mu_{pj}(\mathcal{F}_1, \mathcal{F}_2) = \#(\mathcal{F}_1 \cap \mathcal{F}_2)/\#\mathcal{F}_2$. Thus, it is defined by the relative weight measure m on $\mathcal{L}$ with $m(A) = \#A/\#\mathcal{L}$.

It is easy to see that every matching measure μ is defined by weights $w(C) = m(\{C\}) \in [0, 1]$ for the elements $C \in \mathcal{L}$. With this we immediaely obtain $m(\mathcal{F}) = \sum_{C \in \mathcal{F}} w(C)$ and thus $\mu(\mathcal{F}_1, \mathcal{F}_2) = \sum_{C \in \mathcal{F}_1 \cap \mathcal{F}_2} w(C) \cdot \left(\sum_{C \in \mathcal{F}_2} w(C)\right)^{-1}$.

Example 2. Take a simple lattice $\mathcal{L}$ with only five elements: $\mathcal{L} = \{C_1, C_2, C_3, C_4, C_5\}$ with $C_5 < C_2 < C_1$ and $C_5 < C_4 < C_3 < C_1$. Then we obtain seven filters for this lattice, each generated by one or two elements of the lattice.

If we now define weights $w(C_1) = \frac{1}{10}$, $w(C_2) = \frac{3}{10}$, $w(C_3) = \frac{1}{5}$, $w(C_4) = \frac{3}{10}$, $w(C_5) = \frac{1}{10}$, then we obtain the matching measure values $\mu(\mathcal{F}, \mathcal{G})$ shown in Table 1. In the table the row label is $\mathcal{F}$ and the column label is $\mathcal{G}$.

The matching measures introduced so far are based solely on filters in a lattice, but a TBox is more than its concept lattice. In order to fully exploit the knowledge represented in a TBox we use blow-up operators. Formally, if C is a concept, for which $C \sqsubseteq \exists R.C'$ holds, then for any subconcept $C'' \sqsubseteq C'$ we can define the subconcept $\mathrm{bl}_{R,C''}(C) = C \sqcap \exists R.C''$ of C, which is called the result of the *blow-up* of R with respect to C'' on the concept C.

Table 1. A matching measure μ on the lattice $\mathcal{L}$

	$\langle C_1 \rangle$	$\langle C_2 \rangle$	$\langle C_3 \rangle$	$\langle C_2, C_3 \rangle$	$\langle C_4 \rangle$	$\langle C_2, C_4 \rangle$	$\langle C_5 \rangle$
$\langle C_1 \rangle$	1	$\frac{1}{4}$	$\frac{1}{3}$	$\frac{1}{6}$	$\frac{1}{6}$	$\frac{1}{9}$	$\frac{1}{10}$
$\langle C_2 \rangle$	1	1	$\frac{1}{3}$	$\frac{2}{3}$	$\frac{1}{6}$	$\frac{4}{9}$	$\frac{2}{5}$
$\langle C_3 \rangle$	1	$\frac{1}{4}$	1	$\frac{1}{2}$	$\frac{1}{2}$	$\frac{1}{3}$	$\frac{3}{10}$
$\langle C_2, C_3 \rangle$	1	1	1	1	$\frac{1}{2}$	$\frac{2}{3}$	$\frac{3}{5}$
$\langle C_4 \rangle$	1	$\frac{1}{4}$	1	$\frac{1}{2}$	1	$\frac{2}{3}$	$\frac{2}{5}$
$\langle C_2, C_4 \rangle$	1	1	1	1	1	1	$\frac{9}{10}$
$\langle C_5 \rangle$	1	1	1	1	1	1	1

In particular, this becomes relevant, if C'' is defined by individuals, say $C'' = \{a_1, \ldots, a_n\}$. Any subsumption between subconcepts of C' naturally induces subsumption on these blown-up subconcepts of C, i.e. we have $C_1 \sqsubseteq C_2 \Rightarrow \mathrm{bl}_{R,C_1}(C) \sqsubseteq \mathrm{bl}_{R,C_2}(C)$. By means of the blow-up operators we bring the information carried by the roles into additional concepts, to which the matching measures as discussed before can be applied.

3   Matching Analysis

Let $\mathcal{L}$ be a lattice with profiles defined by filters. Let $\mathbb{F}$ denote the set of all filters. Note that each filter $\mathcal{F} \in \mathbb{F}$ is uniquely determined by its minimal elements, so we can write $\mathcal{F} = \langle C_1, \ldots, C_k \rangle$. The matching knowledge of a human expert can be represented be a partial mapping $h : \mathbb{F} \times \mathbb{F} \to [0,1]$. Though human experts will hardly ever provide complete information, we will assume in the sequel that h is total.

The general question is whether there exists a matching measure μ on $\mathbb{F}$ as defined before such that $\mu(\mathcal{F}, \mathcal{G}) = h(\mathcal{F}, \mathcal{G})$ holds for all pairs of filters. As the matching values as such are merely used to determine rankings whereas their concrete value is of minor importance, this problem can be weakened to find a *ranking-preserving* matching measure μ on $\mathbb{F}$, i.e. the matching measure should imply the same rankings.

Definition 6. A matching measure μ on $\mathbb{F}$ is called *ranking-preserving* with respect to $h : \mathbb{F} \times \mathbb{F} \to [0,1]$ iff

(1) for all filters $\mu(\mathcal{F}_1, \mathcal{G}) \geq \mu(\mathcal{F}_2, \mathcal{G})$ holds, whenever $h(\mathcal{F}_1, \mathcal{G}) \geq h(\mathcal{F}_2, \mathcal{G})$ holds, and
(2) for all filters $\mu(\mathcal{F}, \mathcal{G}_1) \geq \mu(\mathcal{F}, \mathcal{G}_2)$ holds, whenever $h(\mathcal{F}, \mathcal{G}_1) \geq h(\mathcal{F}, \mathcal{G}_2)$ holds.

3.1   Plausibility Constraints

We are looking for plausibility constaints for the mapping h that should be satisfied in the absence of bias, i.e. the assessment of the human expert is not grounded in hidden concepts. If such plausibility conditions are satisfied we explore the existence of a ranking-preserving matching measure μ. First we show the following simple lemma.

Lemma 1. *Let μ be a matching measure on $\mathbb{F}$. Then for all filters $\mathcal{F}, \mathcal{F}_1, \mathcal{F}_2, \mathcal{G} \in \mathbb{F}$ the following conditions hold:*

(1) $\mu(\mathcal{F}, \mathcal{G}) = 1$ for $\mathcal{G} \subseteq \mathcal{F}$.
(2) $\mu(\mathcal{F}, \mathcal{G}) \leq \mu(\mathcal{F}, \mathcal{G} - \{C\})$ holds for $C \notin \mathcal{F}$.
(3) $\mu(\mathcal{F}, \mathcal{G}) \leq \mu(\mathcal{F} \cup \{C\}, \mathcal{G} \cup \{C\})$.
(4) If $\mathcal{F} \cap \mathcal{F}_1 \cap \mathcal{G} = \mathcal{F} \cap \mathcal{F}_2 \cap \mathcal{G}$ holds, then $\mu(\mathcal{F}_1, \mathcal{G}) > \mu(\mathcal{F}_2, \mathcal{G}) \Leftrightarrow \mu(\mathcal{F}, \mathcal{F}_1 \cap \mathcal{G}) < \mu(\mathcal{F}, \mathcal{F}_2 \cap \mathcal{G})$.

Proof. Property (1) is obvious from the definition of matching measures (Definition 5), as in this case $\mathcal{F} \cap \mathcal{G} = \mathcal{G}$ holds.

For property (2) let $C \in \mathcal{G}$ without loss of generality. Then we have

$$\mu(\mathcal{F}, \mathcal{G}) = \frac{m(\mathcal{F} \cap (\mathcal{G} - \{C\}))}{m(\mathcal{G} - \{C\}) + w(C)} \leq \frac{m(\mathcal{F} \cap (\mathcal{G} - \{C\}))}{m(\mathcal{G} - \{C\})} = \mu(\mathcal{F}, \mathcal{G} - \{C\}).$$

For property (3) the case $C \notin \mathcal{F}$ is trivial. In case $C \in \mathcal{G} - \mathcal{F}$ holds, we get

$$\mu(\mathcal{F}, \mathcal{G}) = \frac{m(\mathcal{F} \cap \mathcal{G})}{m(\mathcal{G})} \leq \frac{m(\mathcal{F} \cap \mathcal{G}) + w(C)}{m(\mathcal{G})} = \mu(\mathcal{F} \cup \{C\}, \mathcal{G} \cup \{C\}).$$

In case $C \notin \mathcal{G}$ first note that for any values a, b, c with $a \leq b$ we get $ab + ac \leq ab + bc$ and thus $\frac{a}{b} \leq \frac{a+c}{b+c}$. Thus, we get

$$\mu(\mathcal{F}, \mathcal{G}) = \frac{m(\mathcal{F} \cap \mathcal{G})}{m(\mathcal{G})} \leq \frac{m(\mathcal{F} \cap \mathcal{G}) + w(C)}{m(\mathcal{G}) + w(C)} = \mu(\mathcal{F} \cup \{C\}, \mathcal{G} \cup \{C\}).$$

For property (4) both sides of the equivalence are equivalent to $m(\mathcal{F}_1 \cap \mathcal{G}) > m(\mathcal{F}_2 \cap \mathcal{G})$, which completes the proof. $\square$

Informally phrased property (1) states that whenever all requirements in a requested profile $\mathcal{G}$ (maybe even more) are satisfied by a given profile $\mathcal{F}$, then $\mathcal{F}$ is a perfect match for $\mathcal{G}$. Property (2) states that if a requirement not satisfied by a given profile $\mathcal{F}$ is removed from the requested profile $\mathcal{G}$, the given profile will become a better match for the restricted profile. Property (3) covers two cases. If $C \in \mathcal{G}$ holds, then simply the profile $\mathcal{F} \cup \{C\}$ satisfies more requirements than $\mathcal{F}$, so the matching value should increase. The case $C \notin \mathcal{G}$ is a bit more tricky, as the profile $\mathcal{G} \cup \{C\}$ contains an additional requirement, which is satisfied by the enlarged profile $\mathcal{F} \cup \{C\}$. In this case the matching value should increase, because the percentage of requirements that are satisfied increases. Property (4) states that if the given profile $\mathcal{F}_1$ is better suited for the required profile $\mathcal{G}$ than the given profile $\mathcal{F}_2$, then relative to $\mathcal{G}$ the profile $\mathcal{F}_2$ is less over-qualified than

$\mathcal{F}_1$ for any other required profile $\mathcal{F}$, provided the intersections of $\mathcal{F} \cap \mathcal{G}$ with the two given profiles coincide.

Thus, disregarding for the moment our theory of matching measures, all four properties in Lemma 1 appear to be reasonable. Therefore, we require them as *plausibility constraints* that a human-defined mapping $h : \mathbb{F} \times \mathbb{F} \rightarrow [0, 1]$ should satisfy:

(1) $h(\mathcal{F}, \mathcal{G}) = 1$ for $\mathcal{G} \subseteq \mathcal{F}$,
(2) $h(\mathcal{F}, \mathcal{G}) \leq h(\mathcal{F}, \mathcal{G} - \{C\})$ for any concept $C \notin \mathcal{F}$, and
(3) $h(\mathcal{F}, \mathcal{G}) \leq h(\mathcal{F} \cup \{C\}, \mathcal{G} \cup \{C\})$ for any concept C.
(4) If $\mathcal{F} \cap \mathcal{F}_1 \cap \mathcal{G} = \mathcal{F} \cap \mathcal{F}_2 \cap \mathcal{G}$ holds, then $h(\mathcal{F}_1, \mathcal{G}) > h(\mathcal{F}_2, \mathcal{G}) \Leftrightarrow h(\mathcal{F}, \mathcal{F}_1 \cap \mathcal{G}) < h(\mathcal{F}, \mathcal{F}_2 \cap \mathcal{G})$.

3.2   Linear Inequations

Let h be a human-defined matching measure that satisfies the plausibility constraints. Assume the lattice $\mathcal{L}$ contains $n + 2$ elements $C_0, \ldots, C_{n+1}$ with top- and bottom elements C_0 and C_{n+1}, respectively.

Fixing a requested profile $\mathcal{G}$, then $h(\mathcal{F}_1, \mathcal{G}) < h(\mathcal{F}_2, \mathcal{G})$ defines a linear inequation of the form $\sum_{x \in U} x < \sum_{x \in V} x$ with $U = \{w(C) \mid C \in \mathcal{F}_1 \cap \mathcal{G}\}$ and $V = \{w(C) \mid C \in \mathcal{F}_2 \cap \mathcal{G}\}$. In these inequalities we may remove summands $w(C)$ on both sides for $C \in \mathcal{F}_1 \cap \mathcal{F}_2 \cap \mathcal{G}$. In particular, $w(C_0)$ never appears in the inequalities. Without loss of generality we can also ignore C_{n+1}, as it only appears for the trivial case.

If we fix a given profile $\mathcal{F}$, we also obtain linear inequalities of the form $\sum_{x \in U} x < \sum_{x \in V} x$ with disjoint sets U and V corresponding to sets of weights of concepts. If all these inequalities can be satisfied, then clearly the solution defines a matching measure μ that is order-preserving with respect to h.

The "worst case" arises, if we have a linear order on the set of all terms $\sum_{i \in I} x_i$, where x_i represents $w(C_i)$ and $I \subseteq \{1, \ldots, n\}$. This arises for the lattice $\mathcal{L}$, in which all C_i $(i = 1, \ldots, n)$ are pairwise incomparable. For all other lattices we can extend the set of inequalities derived from h to the "worst case".

So we reduce the problem of finding a ranking-preserving matching measure to a problem of solving a set of linear inequalities. Thus, let $\mathcal{P}$ be a linear order on the set of terms $\{\sum_{i \in I} x_i \mid I \subseteq \{1, \ldots, n\}\}$. We say that $\mathcal{P}$ is *realisable* iff there is a substitution $v : \{x_1, \ldots, x_n\} \rightarrow \mathbb{R}^+$ of the variables by positive real numbers such that $\sum_{i \in I} x_i$ precedes $\sum_{j \in J} x_j$ in $\mathcal{P}$ iff $\sum_{i \in I} v(x_i) < \sum_{j \in J} v(x_j)$ holds. As all sums are finite, it is no loss of generality to seek substitutions by rational numbers, and further using the common denominator it suffices to consider positive integers only.

As $\mathcal{P}$ is defined by h we can assume that $\sum_{i \in I} x_i$ precedes $\sum_{j \in J} x_j$ for $I \subset J$. We can then also extend $\mathcal{P}$ to a partial order $\hat{\mathcal{P}}$ on multisets of variables by adding the same variable(s) to both sides. Clearly, $\mathcal{P}$ is realisable iff $\hat{\mathcal{P}}$ is realisable. For convenience we introduce the notation $U \prec V$ for multisets U, V over

$\{x_1, \ldots, x_n\}$ to denote the inequality $\sum_{x_i \in U} m_U(x_i)x_i < \sum_{x_j \in V} m_V(x_j)x_j$, where m_U and m_V are the multiplicities for the two multisets.

Theorem 1. $\mathcal{P}$ *is realisable iff there is no positive integer combination of inequalities in* $\mathcal{P}$ *that results in* $A \prec B$ *with* $B \subseteq A$ *as multisets, i.e.* $m_B(x_i) \leq m_A(x_i)$ *for all* $i = 1, \ldots, n$.

Proof (sketch). The necessity of the condition is obvious. For the sufficiency we use *Fourier-Motzkin elimination.* □

3.3 Derivation of Matching Measures

We now use Theorem 1 to prove our main result:

Theorem 2. *Let* h *be a human-defined matching measure that satisfies the plausibility constraints. Then there exists a matching measure* μ *that is ranking-preserving with respect to* h.

Proof. Assume that $\mathcal{P}$ is not realisable. Then according to Theorem 1 there exist inequalities $U_1 < V_1, \ldots, U_k < V_k$ in $\mathcal{P}$ such that $V = \biguplus_{i=1}^{k} V_i \subseteq \biguplus_{i=1}^{k} U_i = U$ as multisets and

$$\sum_{x \in U} \sum_{j=i}^{k} m_{U_j}(x)x < \sum_{x \in V} \sum_{j=i}^{k} m_{V_j}(x)x.$$

Let this system of inequalities be minimal, so each subset violates the condition in Theorem 1. Taking the inequalities in the same order let

$$A_i = \sum_{x} \sum_{j=1}^{i} m_{U_j}(x)x \quad \text{and} \quad B_i = \sum_{x} \sum_{j=1}^{i} m_{V_j}(x)x.$$

Then for $i < k$ there always exists some x with $\sum_{j=1}^{i} m_{U_j}(x) < \sum_{j=1}^{i} m_{V_j}(x)$, while $A_i \prec B_i$. On the other hand $\sum_{j=1}^{k} m_{U_j}(x) \geq \sum_{j=1}^{k} m_{V_j}(x)$, while $A_k \prec B_k$.

Let V_i' be the multiset $B_i - A_i$, i.e. the multiset of all x with $m_{B_i}(x) > m_{A_i}(x)$ such that $m_{V_i'}(x) = m_{B_i}(x) - m_{A_i}(x)$ holds. Each $x \in V_i'$ is a witness for the violation of the condition in Theorem 1. In particular, we have $V_i' \neq \emptyset$ for all $i < k$, but $V_k' = \emptyset$.

Let $V_{i+1}'' = V_i \cap V_{i+1}$ as multisets, so $m_{V_{i+1}''}(x) = \min(m_{V_i'}(x), m_{V_{i+1}'}(x))$, i.e. x will at most be added to B_i to give B_{i+1}, but not to A_i. In particular, $V_{i+1}'' \subseteq V_i'$. Take the complement U_{i+1}' such that $V_i' = U_{i+1}' \uplus V_{i+1}''$.

As $U_i < V_i$ is in $\mathcal{P}$, we also have $U_i' < V_i$ in $\mathcal{P}$ for all $i > 1$ (U_1' is not yet defined).

Let $B_1' = V_1 = V_1'$. Then proceed inductively defining $W_i = B_i' - U_{i+1}'$ as well as $A_{i+1}' = U_{i+1}' \uplus W_i$ and $B_{i+1}' = V_{i+1} \uplus W_i$, which gives $A_{i+1}' < B_{i+1}'$ in $\hat{\mathcal{P}}$ and $B_i' = A_{i+1}'$. That is, we obtain a chain

$$B_1' = A_2' < B_2' = \cdots < B_{k-1}' = A_k' < B_k'.$$

Complement these definitions by $U_1' = B_k' \cap U_1 = A_1'$, and $X_0 = B_k' - U_1 = X_1$. Proceed inductively defining

$$C_1 = U_1' \uplus X_0 \prec V_1 \uplus X_1 = B_1' \uplus X_1 = D_1 \text{ and } X_{i+1} = X_i - (U_{i+1} - A_{i+1}')$$

This gives $C_{i+1} = A_{i+1}' \uplus X_i \prec B_{i+1}' \uplus X_{i+1} = D_{i+1}$ and $C_{i+1} = D_i$. Finally, due to this construction we also have $X_i \supseteq X_{i+1}$ for all i and $X_k = \emptyset$. This implies $D_k = C_1$, which means we have a cycle in $\hat{\mathcal{P}}$ contradicting the fact that it is a partial order. Therefore, $\mathcal{P}$ must be realisable.   □

Example 3. (1) To illustrate the construction in the proof take the inequalities $x_1 + x_2 < x_3 + x_4$, $x_2 + x_3 < x_5$, $x_4 + x_5 < x_1 + x_3$ and $x_3 < x_2$ in $\mathcal{P}$ which satisfy the condition in Theorem 1. From these we construct first the following inequalities in $\hat{\mathcal{P}}$: $x_3 + x_4 < x_4 + x_5$, $x_4 + x_5 < x_1 + x_3$ and $x_1 + x_3 < x_1 + x_2$. As the last right hand side is U_1, we get $X_0 = \emptyset$, which defines the additional inequality $x_1 + x_2 < x_3 + x_4$. These four inequalities define the contradictory cycle in $\hat{\mathcal{P}}$.

(2) If the third inequality had been $x_4 + x_5 < x_1 + x_2 + x_3$ instead, the constructed inequalities in $\hat{\mathcal{P}}$ would have been $x_3 + x_4 < x_4 + x_5$, $x_4 + x_5 < x_1 + x_2 + x_3$ and $x_1 + x_2 + x_3 < x_1 + 2x_2$. This defines $X_0 = \{x_2\}$, which gives the addition inequality $x_1 + 2x_2 < x_2 + x_3 + x_4$ and the modified inequality $x_2 + x_3 + x_4 < x_4 + x_5$, which again defines a cycle.

Note that our main result only states the existence of a ranking preserving matching measure μ. However, we obtain solutions for the linear inequations defined by h by minimising $x_1 + \cdots + x_n - 1$ under the conditions $\sum_{x_j \in V} x_j - \sum_{x_i \in U} x_i > 0$. For this linear optimisation problem the well-known *simplex algorithm* can be exploited.

4 Conclusion

In this paper we addressed the problem to determine matching measures for profiles that produce rankings, which are in accordance with the measures given by a human expert or at least imply the same rankings. For this we analysed linear inequalities that result from the human-defined rankings. We could show that if certain plausibility rules are obeyed by the human expert–i.e. the matching and the rankings are not biased by criteria not represented in the knowledge base–then we can indeed create such matching measures, with the help of which the human expertise can be approximated. This shows that the very general approach to matching based on filters provides the necessary flexibility required for diverse matching tasks.

This is only a starting point for even more sophisticated matching analysis aiming at consensus building among different experts and determination of the most suitable matching measure that is in accordance with the expert knowledge. We also have to take into account that valuations given by human experts will never be complete. This will be addressed in our future research.

References

1. Baader, F., et al. (eds.): The Description Logic Handbook: Theory, Implementation and Applications. Cambridge University Press, New York (2003)
2. European distionary of skills and competences. http://www.disco-tools.eu
3. Falk, T., et al.: Semantic-web-technologien in der Arbeitsplatzvermittlung. Informatik Spektrum **29**(3), 201–209 (2006)
4. Ganter, B., Wille, R.: Formal Concept Analysis - Mathematical Foundations. Springer, Heidelberg (1999)
5. Grau, B.C., Horrocks, I., Motik, B., Parsia, B., Patel-Schneider, P.F., Sattler, U.: OWL 2: the next step for OWL. J. Web Semant. **6**(4), 309–322 (2008)
6. International Standard Classification of Education. http://www.uis.unesco.org/Education/Pages/international-standard-classification-of-education.aspx
7. International Standard Classification of Occupations (2008). http://www.ilo.org/public/english/bureau/stat/isco/isco08/
8. Levandowsky, M., Winter, D.: Distance between sets. Nature **234**(5), 34–35 (1971)
9. Looser, D., Ma, H., Schewe, K.-D.: Using formal concept analysis for ontology maintenance in human resource recruitment. In: Ferrarotti, F., Grossmann, G. (eds.) Ninth Asia-Pacific Conference on Conceptual Modelling (APCCM 2013), vol. 143. CRPIT, pp. 61–68. Australian Computer Society (2013)
10. Mochol, M., Wache, H., Nixon, L.J.B.: Improving the accuracy of job search with semantic techniques. In: Abramowicz, W. (ed.) BIS 2007. LNCS, vol. 4439, pp. 301–313. Springer, Heidelberg (2007)
11. Paoletti, A.L., Martinez-Gil, J., Schewe, K.-D.: Extending knowledge-based profile matching in the human resources domain. In: Chen, Q., Hameurlain, A., Toumani, F., Wagner, R., Decker, H. (eds.) DEXA 2015. LNCS, vol. 9262, pp. 21–35. Springer, Heidelberg (2015)
12. Paoletti, A.L., Martinez-Gil, J., Schewe, K.-D.: Top-k matching queries for filter-based profile matching in knowledge bases. In: Ma, H., Hartmann, S. (eds.) Database and Expert Systems Applications (DEXA 2016), LNCS. Springer, Heidelberg (2016, to appear)
13. Popov, N., Jebelean, T.: Semantic matching for job search engines - a logical approach. Technical report 13–02, Research Institute for Symbolic Computation, JKU Linz (2013)
14. Rácz, G., Sali, A., Schewe, K.-D.: Semantic matching strategies for job recruitment: a comparison of new and known approaches. In: Gyssens, M., Simari, G. (eds.) FoIKS 2016. LNCS, vol. 9616, pp. 149–168. Springer, Heidelberg (2016). doi:10.1007/978-3-319-30024-5_9

Distributed Reasoning for Mapped Ontologies Using Rewriting Logic

Mustapha Bourahla[(✉)]

Laboratory of Pure and Applied Mathematics (LMPA),
Computer Science Department, University of M'sila,
BP 166 Ichebilia, 28000 M'sila, Algeria
mbourahla@hotmail.com

Abstract. The Ontology Web Language (OWL) implicitly maps the interconnected ontologies by its mechanism of ontology importation and it uses a global view (global reasoning procedure) for their interpretation. In this paper, we generate explicit context mappings from these same heterogeneous and interconnected OWL ontologies to adopt local view interpretation. Each separate OWL ontology is transformed to be described by a Maude module based on the Rewriting Logic (RL) and internally it executes a local reasoning procedure developed with Maude itself as extension to standard Description Logic Tableau. The combination of these local reasoning Maude modules, creates a distributed reasoning system for the heterogeneous and contextualized OWL ontologies.

Keywords: Semantic web · Maude and rewriting logic · Distributed reasoning · Heterogeneous ontologies · Ontology mapping · Description logics · Ontology web language

1 Introduction

The mapping between local ontologies called also context mapping, transforms the source ontology entities into the target ontology entities based on semantic relations defined at a conceptual level. This mapping provides interoperability between local ontologies and it is more appropriate and flexible for scaling up to the Semantic Web because the changes of local ontology could be done locally without regard to other mappings. This mapping is very suitable for ontologies having mutual inconsistency of their information. The primary application of this mapping is the Semantic Web because of its decentralized nature.

The language OWL [5] doesn't contain mappings but it can import (include) other ontologies using the "owl:imports" construct which allows to include by reference in a knowledge base the axioms contained in another ontology retrievable from the Web and identified by a URI. By this mechanism of importation, a set of local ontologies can be globalized in a unique shared ontology and then mappings implicitly exist in terms of mutual use of statements across ontologies. This means that all the linked ontologies are only merged into a single

© Springer International Publishing Switzerland 2016
L. Bellatreche et al. (Eds.): MEDI 2016, LNCS 9893, pp. 142–155, 2016.
DOI: 10.1007/978-3-319-45547-1_12

logical space. This mechanism does not support information hiding or filtering, everything in the imported ontologies gets into the original ontology which leads to unmanageable blow up of ontology size. The imported axioms or assertions (facts) don't retain their context and the OWL reasoning does not take such context into account.

In this paper, we generate contextual ontologies from a family of mapped OWL ontologies. These generated contextual ontologies described as Maude modules based on Rewriting Logic (RL) [3] keep the ontology contents local by using explicit mappings which gives a limited and completely controlled form of globalization. These Maude ontologies are inputs to a new developed distributed reasoner with Maude. The non-distributed reasoning procedure [7,10] performed across different ontologies, assumes that these ontologies should share the interpretation domain. Most of the existing efficient OWL reasoners are inmemory reasoners and work only on a single machine. Although their efficiency, they cannot scale up with the volume and velocity of the information.

The reasoning over contextualized ontologies is distributed; reasoning over each contextualized ontology uses a local domain of interpretation. Relations between these local interpretation domains are established by domain relations, which explicitly codify how elements in one domain map into elements of the other domain. The reasoning semantics rules of context mapping modify only the target context, leaving the source unaffected. The objective of this reasoner is to be able to reason on a set of independently developed ontologies that may overlap in concepts, roles and/or individuals but are following different modelling perspectives and granularity. To be able to do that, we assume that there exists explicit correspondences between different ontologies, which have been built by automatic ontology matchers, by humans, or partly by both.

Related Works: Distributed Description Logics (DDLs) [1] are extensions of OWL-DL to combine different ontologies where their identity and independence are preserved. The DDLs inherited a lot of ideas from the other logics for distributed systems (like, Multi Context Systems and Distributed First Order Logics). This combination is realised by a new set of inter-ontology axioms called bridge rules. These bridge rules are used for establishing view dependent subsumption relationships between classes and correspondences between individuals in different ontologies. The DDLs are very suitable for the vision of the Semantic Web in which the notion of a universal upper ontology is abandoned by the notion of a web of distributed, linked and independently developed ontologies.

The authors of [2] have proposed a language called Context OWL (C-OWL) whose syntax and semantics have been obtained by extending the OWL by DDL formalism for the representation of contextual ontologies. A distributed reasoner called DRAGO was developed by the authors of [11] as extension of Pellet and it uses the language C-OWL to generate a mapping box to be added to the Pellet Knowledge base. As extension, DRAGO implementation has added a bridge expansion rule and it supports only the bridge rules of inclusion axioms between atomic concepts.

The $\mathcal{E}$-connections formalism [9] is a method for integrating knowledge bases written with logical languages using n-ary link relations (it is strictly more expressive than DDLs where bridge rules can be seen as a special case of binary link relations). The authors of [4] have defined a syntax and semantic extension of OWL to integrate the $\mathcal{E}$-connections formalism. The extension is based on the definition of a new set of properties, called links (a link is interpreted as a cross-domain relation), that stand for the inter-ontology relations in the $\mathcal{E}$-connections framework.

The OWL-DL language is then enriched with a new set of constructors that basically allow defining new classes by placing restrictions on the link properties. This extension uses a sublanguage of $\mathcal{E}$-connections (it doesn't use inverses on link properties) and it is restricted to combinations of OWL-Lite (SHIF(D)) ontologies without ABoxes. This restricted case of $\mathcal{E}$-connections is implemented as extension of the OWL reasoner Pellet as a combined tableau which is selective global approach organized in a single reasoner which is not a distributed tableau that combines different reasoning procedures for mapped ontologies. The authors of the paper [8] have studied the problem of query answering over quads augmented with forall-existential bridge rules that enable interoperability of reasoning between the triples in various contexts.

The work in this paper has the capability of reasoning with ontologies coupled with semantic mappings using a distributed algorithm which uses ontologies and mappings published on the Web and it doesn't extend the language OWL by mapping constructors and associated semantics, instead we generate these mappings from OWL ontologies inter-connected by its mechanism of importation and we keep the different knowledge separate during the reasoning. The rest of this paper is organised as follows. Section 2 explains the generated description of contextualized OWL ontologies with Maude. In Sect. 3, we present in detail, the distributed reasoning system developed with Maude where its effectiveness and efficiency will be demonstrated with experimental results. At the end, conclusions and perspectives are given.

2   Ontology Description with Rewriting Logic

The formal description language OWL2 DL is a variant of the Description Logic (DL) SROIQ(D) [6] which consists of an alphabet composed of three sets of names. The set $\mathcal{C}$ of atomic concepts, the set $\mathcal{R}$ of atomic roles (abstract or concrete) and the set $\mathcal{I}$ of individuals (objects). It consists also of a set of constructors used to build complex concepts and complex roles from the atomic ones. OWL ontology can contain import references to other ontologies. So, OWL ontologies can be referenced by means of a URI. Let $\mathcal{X}$ be a set of indexes, standing for a set of pairs of ontology names and their URIs. For instance, we can reference an ontology O_i by the pair $\langle ontologyName = O_i, URI = $ "http://www.ontologies.com/O_i"$\rangle$. Each entity x from the ontology O_i can be referenced by the URI "http://www.ontologies.com/O_i#x". The formal semantics of DLs is given in terms of interpretations.

An ontology $O = \langle T, A \rangle$ is DL knowledge base which is composed of two sets, the intensional knowledge (Terminological) box T; it is a general knowledge about the problem domain, composed of a set of terminological axioms (statements) about concept inclusions, concept equivalences, characteristics of roles like statements asserting that a role is functional or transitive or is in inclusion (equivalence) relationships. The second set of an ontology (DL knowledge base) is the extensional knowledge (Assertional) box A which is a knowledge about specific situation (world description), where a specific state of affairs is described with respect to some individuals of an application domain in terms of concepts and roles.

An OWL space is a family of N ontologies $\mathcal{O} = \{O_i\}_{i=1,\cdots,N}$ such that every O_i is an ontology. An ontology $O_i = \langle T_i, A_i \rangle$ is developed independently with a description logic DL_i, where $\{DL_i\}_{i=1,\cdots,N}$ is a collection of description logics. We assume that each DL_i is description logic weaker or at most equivalent to SROIQ(D). We denote a refered name "$name$" of concept, role or individual in ontology O_i from (defined in) ontology O_j by $O_j(name)$. The mapping of ontologies $\{O_i\}$, $i = 1, \cdots, N$ will extend their sets of concepts C_i, their sets of roles $\mathcal{R}_i$ and their sets of individuals $\mathcal{I}_i$ by a set of foreign (non-local) concepts, roles and individuals, respectively from other ontologies in the OWL space.

Example 1. Let $\mathcal{O}$ be a OWL space of two ontologies O_1 and O_2 where their DL descriptions are below. We assume their indexes are $\mathcal{X}_1 = \langle O1,$ "http:// www.ontologies.com/O1"$\rangle$, $\mathcal{X}_2 = \langle O2,$ "http://www.ontologies.com/O2"$\rangle$. The terminology T_2 contains an axiom to state that the local individual b is the same individual as a in the ontology O_1.

Ontology O_1 (DL description)	Ontology O_2 (DL description)
$T_1 = \left\{ \begin{array}{l} NonFlying \equiv \neg FLying \\ Bird \sqsubseteq Flying \\ Individual(a) \end{array} \right\}$	$T_2 = \left\{ \begin{array}{l} Penguin \sqsubseteq O_1(Bird) \\ Penguin \sqsubseteq O_1(NonFlying) \\ individual(b) \equiv O_1(a) \end{array} \right\}$
$A_1 = \{ Bird(a) \}$	$A_2 = \{ Penguin(b) \}$

Description of the ontology O_2 with the language OWL imports the other ontology O_1 by the construct "imports http://www.ontologies.com/O1" to allow direct references to different foreign entities (for example, the axiom $Penguin \sqsubseteq O_1(Bird)$ can be $Penguin \sqsubseteq$ "http://www.ontologies.com/O1#Bird"). By this mechanism of importation, a set of local ontologies can be globalized in a unique shared ontology and then mappings implicitly exist in terms of mutual use of statements across ontologies.

The first contribution in this paper is to contextualize these OWL ontologies by transformation to contextual Maude ontologies and keeping their contents local, not shared with other ontologies. These Maude ontologies are mapped via explicit (context) mappings, which describe the contextual ontologies by the same way as OWL, except the importation mechanism is omitted and the context mappings are now very explicit.

2.1   Generation of Contextual Maude Ontologies

Maude is a language and tool which implements the Rewriting Logic (RL) theory [3]. The Maude specification formalism is based on first-order equational and rewriting logic specification techniques. In Maude the basic units of specification and programming are called modules. In Core Maude there are two kinds of modules, functional modules and system modules. The difference between functional and system modules resides in the statements they can have, functional modules admit equations, identifying data, and memberships, stating typing information for some data, while system modules also admit rules, describing transitions between states, in addition to equations and memberships. Full Maude provides additional support for object-oriented programming with classes, subclassing, and convenient abbreviations for rule syntax in object-oriented modules.

Each ontology $O_i = \langle T_i, A_i \rangle$ in a OWL space $\mathcal{O}$ of N mapped ontologies will be described by a RL system module "$mod\ O_i\ is\ \cdots\ endm$" using a RL signature defined in other Maude module called $OWL2 - SIGNATURE$ with respect to the syntax of OWL2. The entities in the terminological box T_i will be described by RL operators. There are RL abstract sorts for the different terminology elements. The assertional box is a list of instances, where each instance is of a defined sort. Due to space limit, this Maude module of OWL2 signature will not be presented. However, the given examples below will help understanding its syntax.

The inputs to distributed reasoning procedures are contextual Maude ontologies generated from OWL ontologies. The generation process takes in consideration the semantics based on local interpretation and context mappings. The OWL semantics assumes the existence of a unique shared domain for a global view, which means the OWL interpratation for the OWL space of N ontologies, $\{O_i\}_{i=1,\cdots,N}$, is a pair $I = (\Delta^I, (.)^I)$, where Δ^I contains a non-empty set of objects (the resources) and $(.)^I$ is an interpretation function. An OWL interpretation I satisfies an OWL space $\{O_i\}_{i=1,\cdots,N}$, if I satisfies each axiom and each assertion of O_i, for any $i \in \{1, \cdots, N\}$.

This global view semantics based on importing ontologies, has some drawbacks. The inconsistency of an ontology O_i will be automatically propagated to the whole space which implies that there is no interpretation for the whole OWL space. The directionality of logical consequences is not fulfilled when importing ontologies. This means, if an ontology imports other ontology and a statement is satisfied in the first ontology, there will no guarantee that is satisfied in the second ontology. Other issue of semantics globalisation is that sometimes it is not possible to merge different local domains in a single one because they are at different level of abstraction. On the other hand, two concepts can describe the same real-world class of objects from two different points of view, and there can be many reasons for integrating this information. This integration cannot be stated via OWL axioms.

This definition of interpretation is modified, where the main idea is that a global interpretation is split into a family of (local) interpretations, one for each ontology. The idea here is to associate to each ontology a local domain. Local domains may overlap as we have to cope with the case where two ontologies refer to the same object. An OWL interpretation with local domains for the OWL space $\{O_i\}_{i=1,\cdots,N}$, is a family $I = \{I_i\}, i = 1, \cdots, N$, where each $I_i = (\Delta^{I_i}, (.)^{I_i})$ is the local interpretation of the ontology O_i. We have to take care, however, that j-foreign concepts, roles, and individuals used in O_i could be interpreted (by the local interpretation I_j) in a (set of) object(s) which are not in the local domain Δ^{I_i}.

Indeed, to deal with this problem, we have to impose that any expression occurring in O_i should be interpretable in the local domain Δ^{I_i}. As a consequence, we restrict the interpretation of any foreign concept $C \in \mathcal{C}_j$, any foreign role $R \in \mathcal{R}_j$ and any foreign individual $a \in \mathcal{I}_j$ as follows. $(O_j(C))^{I_i} = (C)^{I_j} \cap \Delta^{I_i}$, $(O_j(R))^{I_i} = (R)^{I_j} \cap (\Delta^{I_i} \times \Delta^{I_i})$ and $(O_j(a))^{I_i} = (a)^{I_j}$. Notice that the last point implicitly imposes that if a j-foreign individual $O_j(a)$ is used in the ontology O_i, then its interpretation in O_j, i.e., $(a)^{I_j}$, must be contained in the domain Δ^{I_i}. Based on these notions, a XSL stylesheet is written to transform OWL2 ontologies to Maude ontologies using the defined RL signature with respect to the OWL2 syntax.

Example 2 (Example 1 continued). The OWL2 versions of the ontologies O_1 and O_2 are transformed to Maude modules called 01 and 02, respectively with respect to the RL signature in $OWL2 - SIGNATURE$. The ontology 02 contains references to entities from the ontology 01. This corresponding extends its set of concepts by the concepts $O1('Bird)$ and $O1('NonFlying)$, and its set of individuals by the individual $O1('a)$.

┌─ Ontology O_1 (RL description) ─┬─ Ontology O_2 (RL description) ─┐

```
mod 01 is
inc OWL2-SIGNATURE .
inc OWL2-REASONER .
eq ontologyName = '01 .
eq URI =
   "http://www.ontologies.com/01" .
---- As there is no reference to 02
---- The URI of 02 is not included
ops Bird Flying NonFlying : ->
   Concept .
eq subClassOf(Bird) = Flying .
eq disjointWith(Flying) =
   NonFlying .
op a : -> Individual .
eq ABox = { Bird(a) } .
endm
```

```
mod 02 is
inc OWL2-SIGNATURE .
inc OWL2-REASONER .
eq ontologyName = '02 .
eq URI = "http://www.ontologies.com/02" .
op 01 : -> Ontology .
eq URI(01) =
   "http://www.ontologies.com/01" .
op Penguin : -> Concept .
eq subClassOf(Penguin)=01('Bird).Concept.
eq subClassOf(Penguin) =
   01('NonFlying).Concept .
op b : -> Individual .
eq sameAs(b) = 01('a).Individual .
eq ABox = { Penguin(b) } .
endm
```

For mapping, the ontology O_2 has reference to the concept $Bird$ from the ontology O_1, then its module should contain the declaration 01 : -> Ontology to be able to use the correspondance 01('Bird).Concept. The RL operator for referencing a foreign concept is $op\ \_(\_).Concept : Ontology\ Qid \rightarrow Concept$, by the same way, an object property is $op\ \_(\_).ObjectProperty : Ontology\ Qid \rightarrow ObjectProperty$, a datatype property is $op\ \_(\_).DatatypeProperty : Ontology\ Qid \rightarrow DatatypeProperty$ and an individual is $op\ \_(\_).Individual : Ontology\ Qid \rightarrow Individual$. The predefined Maude sort Qid (Qualified identifier) is the class of all identifiers preceded by a quote.

Each Maude ontology in this mapped set $\{O_1, O_2\}$ includes a copy of a module called $OWL2 - REASONER$ implementing an extended DL reasoning procedure which is developed with Maude itself as a second contribution of this paper. Consequently, this set of contextual Maude ontologies will create a distributed DL reasoning system, supported by mapping semantics to propagate information between the Maude ontologies using the Maude sockets. The next section shows some aspects of its implementation and the end of this section will explain its effectiveness on the example of $\{O_1, O_2\}$ and demonstrates its efficiency by experimental results on very large ontologies.

3   Distributed Reasoning for Mapped Maude Ontologies

A DL system offers services that reason on axioms and assertions. Reasoning with a DL knowledge base is a process of discovering implicit knowledge entailed by the knowledge base. Reasoning services can be basic services, which involve the checking for the truth of a statement like knowledge base satisfiability, concept satisfiability, subsumption checking, and instance checking. The complex services are built upon these basic services, as concept classification using subsumption checking between concepts and query answering using instance checking.

Each Maude module of ontology O_i, $i = 1, \cdots, N$ from the set of N contextualized OWL ontologies includes a copy of the Maude module $OWL2 - REASONER$ to execute its own reasoning server. This module includes a predefined Maude module called *Socket* to create sockets for communication using the model client/server. In addition to the set of rewriting rules implementing the extended tableau expansion rules, this module declares server configuration $< OntServer : ServerClass \mid Attributes : AttributeSet >$, where $OntServer$ is the server object identifier which is of the class $ServerClass$.

Each ontology object server has a set of attributes of the sort $AttributeSet$. This set includes attributes for concepts $\mathcal{C}_i$, roles $\mathcal{R}_i$, individuals $\mathcal{I}_i$, axioms $\mathcal{A}_i$ and assertions $\mathcal{S}_i$ representing knowledge, which is extracted from the ontology O_i Maude module for offering reasoning services. The ontology O_i reasoning server creates sockets for communicating with the external objects representing other ontologies $(O_j, j \neq i)$ reasoning servers. It sends the external object $socketManager$ (defined in the socket Maude module) a message containing the port number associated with the ontology ($port(OntologyName)$) and a number of queue requests for connection that this ontology server will allow.

The external object $socketManager$ will create a socket (an object called $Listener_i$) for the ontology O_i server to listen on for clients attempting to make connections. If the ontology server accepts connection request from the server of another ontology say O_j, a new socket $Client_i$ is created where the ontology O_i server uses to communicate with that client. This new socket behaves just like a client socket for sending and receiving. The ontology server can always reuse the server socket $Listener_i$ to accept new clients until it explicitly closes it.

The distributed reasoning is based on the distributed expansion of a kowledge base structure called completion tree with respect to the axioms in $\mathcal{A}_i$. Each ontology O_i server has its own completion tree as an additional server attribute generated from the assertions in S_i. A completion tree T_i is composed of nodes with the signature $op < \quad _{-,\,-,\,-,\,-,\,-}\quad > : \quad Individual\ ConceptExpression$ $RoleConnections\ DataConstraints\ BlockingStatus \rightarrow Node$.

Each node of the completion tree will be represented by a Maude term $<$ $x, CL, RL, DL, BS >$, where x of sort $Individual$ is the name (abstract object from the set $\mathcal{I}_i$) of the node, CL is the concept label which is a concept expression ($ConceptExpression$) over atomic and restricted concepts which can be also imported (foreign) concepts. The label RL is the edge labels of x, which is a set of connections $R(y)$ (or $S(d)$) of sort $RoleConnections$ ($R(y)$ means that y is a successor of x by the abstract role R and $S(d)$ means the data d is data property of x by the concrete role S). These roles can also be imported roles.

The label DL of sort $DataConstraints$ is used to label the node by data constraints that can be generated during the expansion. For example, if the label CL contains an existential or universal restriction sub-expression over a datatype role (of the form $\exists S.P$ or $\forall S.P$) and the label RL contains a data successor $S(d)$ then the data restriction $P(d)$ will be inserted into the set of data constraints DL. The label BS of sort $BlockingStatus$ (which is a subsort of Boolean sort), it is used to mark if the node is blocked to not be expanded further or not. A node is blocked if a clash is observed either within the assertions represented by the label CL or within the data constraints DL. The cases of clash are:

1. If $CL - noThing$ then $BS = true$, a contradiction is observed like CL contains a subterm $C \wedge \neg C$ which is reduced by a rewriting equation to the term $noThing$.
2. If a contradiction is observed in the set of data constraints, like $P(25)$, where $P = maxInclusive(20)$, which means $25 \leq 20$.
3. If the node of the individual x is blocked then all its successors will be blocked. This means, for all $< x', CL', RL', DL', BS' >$, where $R(x') \in RL \wedge BS = true \implies BS' = true$.

In context mappings, we have concepts, roles and individuals local to different ontologies and domains of interpretation. A context mapping allows us to state that a certain property holds between elements of two different ontologies. Thus, for instance, one possible mapping could allow us to say that the concept $Penguin$ in the ontology O_2 is subclass of (or, as we say, is contextually subclass of) the concept $Bird$ defined in the ontology O_1. This cannot be done via local axioms within an ontology. The pseudo code of implemented Maude reasoning server is presented in Algorithm 1. Due to space limit, this algorithm offers two services (the other reasoning services can be added easily), the satisfiability check of concepts in C_i and the implicit Knowledge entailment from T_i.

For knowledge propagation, the algorithm can generate from the ontology Maude module the sets of ontology indexes $\mathcal{X}_i$ and individual mappings $\mathcal{V}_i$ as additional server attributes. The ontology indexes information are $\mathcal{X}_i = \{\langle O_j, URI_j \rangle \mid O_j : \rightarrow Ontology \wedge URI(O_j) = URI_j \in O_i\}$. The individual mappings $\mathcal{V}_i = \{\langle O_i(x), O_j(y) \rangle \mid sameAs(x), O_j(y) \in O_i \vee sameAs(O_j(y)) = x \in O_i\}$, is a subset of the mappings $\mathcal{M}_i = \{M_{ij}\}$. Given a OWL space

---

Algorithm 1. Pseudo code for ontology O_i server

1: Generate from the ontology description Maude module: the set of concepts C_i, the
   set of individuals $\mathcal{I}_i$, the set of axioms $\mathcal{A}_i$, the set of assertions $\mathcal{S}_i$, the completion
   tree $\mathcal{T}_i$, the set of indexes $\mathcal{X}_i$, and the set of individual mappings $\mathcal{V}_i$
2: $Listener_i \leftarrow createSocketServer(port(O_i), queueRequestsNumber)$
3: Accept client connections on $Listener_i$
4: **while** $true$ **do**
5:     **Switch** Service **do**
6:         **case** ConceptSatisfiabiliyCheck
7:             **for** each $C \in C_i$ **do**
8:                 **if** expand($\langle x, C, \emptyset, \emptyset, false \rangle$) = $\langle x, CL, RL, DL, true \rangle$ **then**
9:                     The concept C is not satisfied
10:                **end if**
11:            **end for**
12:        **case** knowledgeEntailment
13:            $\mathcal{T}_i = expand(\mathcal{T}_i)$; $sendKnowledge()$; receiveKnowledge()
14:            **if** communications are terminated **then**
15:                **for** each $\langle x, CL, RL, DL, true \rangle \in \mathcal{T}_i$ **do**
16:                    Assertions on x are not satisfied
17:                **end for**
18:            **end if**
19:    **end Switch**
20: **end while**

$\{O_i\}, i = 1, \cdots, N$ a mapping $\mathcal{M}_{ij}$, from O_i to O_j is a set of statements. If C
and D stand for concepts, a and b for individuals, each statement can be one of
$O_i(C) \sqsubseteq O_j(D)$ (subsumption), $O_i(C) \sqsupseteq O_j(D)$ (supsumption), $O_i(C) \equiv O_j(D)$
(equivalence), $O_i(C)\#O_j(D)$ (disjointness). The same thing can be applied for
abstract and concrete roles. For individual mappings, $O_i(a) = O_j(b)$ (same as),
and $O_i(a) \neq O_j(b)$ (different from).

Mappings are directional, i.e., $\mathcal{M}_{ij}$ is not the inverse of $\mathcal{M}_{ji}$. A mapping
$\mathcal{M}_{ij}$ might be empty. This represents the impossibility for O_j to interpret any
i-foreign concept into some local concept. Dually $\mathcal{M}_{ij}$ might be a set of statements of the form $O_i(x) \equiv O_j(y)$ for any element x (concept, role, and individual) of O_i. This represents the operation of mapping all of O_i into an equivalent
subset of O_j. If this subset is O_j itself then this becomes the contextual mapping
version of the OWL import operation. However, notice that importing O_i into
O_j is not the same as mapping O_i to O_j with $\mathcal{M}_{ij}$. In both cases information
goes from i to j. The difference is that, in the former case, O_j duplicates the
information of i-foreign elements without any change, while, in the latter, O_j
translates (via the mapping $\mathcal{M}_{ij}$) the semantics of O_i into its internal (local)
semantics.

The expansion process (the call to the function $expand()$ in Algorithm 1) is
repeatedly applying the completion SROIQ(D) DL rules [7,10] that either update
the node labels and/or add new leaf nodes; such completion rules correspond
to the logical constructors as well as role axioms provided by the description

language. A set of rewriting equations for expanding tree nodes are written to reduce the concept expressions in the concept labels with respect to the axioms in $\mathcal{A}_i$. This rewriting will update the other node labels and/or add other nodes if necessary.

If the concept label or the role label set of a node contains an imported (foreign) entity and the node name (individual) has a semantic relation with a foreign individual that is from the same ontology, then the distributed reasoning algorithm communicates this information to its owner local ontology server by calling the function $sendKnowledge()$ (its pseudo code is defined below), which uses the defined context mappings. More clearly, if the concept label CL or role label RL of a node named x in the expanded completion tree contains a reference to a foreign concept $O_j(C)$ or to a foreign role $O_j(R)(y)$ $(O_j(S)(d))$, where y is the object successor (d is the data property) of the object x and the node name x is related to a foreign individual say $O_j(z)$ by the mapping statement $sameAs(x) = O_j(z)$, then the ontology O_i server will communicate the information $C(z)$, $R(z, O_i(y))$ or $S(z, d)$ to the ontology O_j server.

```
1: function SENDKNOWLEDGE( )
2:     for each ⟨O_i(x), O_j(y)⟩ ∈ V_i where ⟨O_j, URI_j⟩ ∈ X_i do
3:         for each < x, CL, RL, DL, false >∈ T_i do
4:             msg ← "#"
5:             if O_j(C) ∈ CL then
6:                 msg ← msg + "C(y)#"
7:             end if
8:             if O_j(R)(z) ∈ RL then  // R is abstract (or concrete) role
9:                 msg ← msg + "R(y, z)#"  // z is an object (or data)
10:            end if
11:            if msg ≠ "#" then
12:                Client_i ← createClientSocket(address(URI_j), port(O_j))
13:                if Connection accepted then
14:                    send(Client_i, msg); closeClientSocket(Client_i)
15:                end if
16:            end if
17:        end for
18:    end for
19: end function
```

In this case the ontology O_i server plays the role of a client of the ontology O_j server and it uses the information in its index attribute $\langle O_j, URI_j \rangle \in \mathcal{X}_i$ to create a client socket by sending the external object $socketManager$ a message "$createClientTcpSocket(socketManager, OntServer_i, address(URI_j),$ $port(O_j))$", where $OntServer_i$ is the name of the object the reply should be sent to, and $address(URI_j)$ is the address of the server of the ontology O_j the ontology O_i server wants to connect to (this is an IP dotted address or "localhost" for the same machine where the Maude system is running on), and $port(O_j)$ is the port the ontology O_i server wants to connect to. The reply to the object $OntServer_i$ will be $createdSocket(OntServer_i, socketManager, Client_i)$, where $Client_i$ is the name of the newly created socket. The server of the ontology O_i can then send messages to the server of O_j with $send(Client_i, OntServer_i, message)$, which can be confirmed by $sent(OntServer_i, Client_i)$.

Similarly, the server $OntServer_i$ of the ontology O_i can receive requests (see the function $receiveKnowledge()$ below) for services from other ontologies servers that are indexed in its index attribute $\mathcal{X}_i$. To receive these requests it should accept connection ($acceptedClient(OntServer_i, Listener_i, IP, Client_j)$) from the socket manager. The address IP can help to identify the ontology server asking for the service using the index attribute. At this point the ontology server $OntServer_i$ can ask to receive message from this connected client by sending the message $receive(Client_j, OntServer_i)$ (it is a not blocking procedure) to the socket manager. A received message msg is confirmed by receiving the message "$received(OntServer_i, Client_j, msg)$" from the socket manager. When the server of the ontology O_i is done with the socket, it should close it with a message $closeSocket(Client_j, OntServer_i)$.

```
 1: function RECEIVEKNOWLEDGE( )
 2:     if Client_j connection request is accepted then
 3:         if received(Client_j, msg) then
 4:             for each C(x) ∈ msg do
 5:                 if ∃⟨x, CL, RL, DL, false⟩ ∈ T_i then
 6:                     T_i[⟨x, CL[C ∧ CL], RL, DL, false⟩] // update CL by C ∧ CL
 7:                 else
 8:                     T_i ← T_i ∪ ⟨x, C, ∅, ∅, false⟩
 9:                 end if
10:             end for
11:             for each R(x, z) ∈ msg do
12:                 if ∃⟨x, CL, RL, DL, false⟩ ∈ T_i then
13:                     T_i[⟨x, CL, RL[R(z)RL], DL, false⟩] // update RL by R(z)RL
14:                 else
15:                     T_i ← T_i ∪ ⟨x, Thing, R(z), ∅, false⟩
16:                 end if
17:             end for
18:             Accept client connections on Listener_i
19:             T_i = expand(T_i); sendKnowledge(T_i); receiveKnowledge()
20:         end if
21:     end if
22: end function
```

This distributed reasoning algorithm terminates either when the completion tree is complete (no further completion rules can be applied and all the communication canals are empty) or when an obvious contradiction, or clash has been revealed. The concept is unsatisfiable if every expansion leads to a contradiction and it is satisfiable if any possible expansion leads to the discovery of a complete clash-free tree. This principle of concept satisfiability check can be used for offering other reasoning services like concept subsumption, instance checking, knowledge base satisfiability, concept classification and query answering.

A context space is a pair composed of a Maude space $\{O_i\}_{i \in \{1,\cdots,N\}}$ and a family $\{\mathcal{M}_{ij}\}_{i,j \in \{1,\cdots,N\}}$ of mappings from i to j, for each pair $i,j \in \{1,\cdots,N\}$. To give the semantics of Maude context mappings we extend the definition of OWL interpretation with local domains with the notion of domain relation. A domain relation $dr_{ij} \subseteq \Delta^{I_i} \times \Delta^{I_j}$ states, for each element in Δ^{I_i} to which element in Δ^{I_j} it corresponds to. It can be determined by $dr_{ij}(O_i(a))^{I_i}) = \{(O_i(b))^{I_j} | \langle O_i(a), O_j(b) \rangle \in \mathcal{V}_i\}$. When dr_{ij} is determined with respect to the individual mappings between ontologies and the local interpretation domain of each ontology, the semantics for context mapping statements from i to j can then be given with respect to dr_{ij}.

- $subClassOf(O_i(C)) = O_j(D) \Leftrightarrow dr_{ij}((C)^{I_i}) \subseteq (D)^{I_j}$
- $subClassOf(O_j(D)) = O_i(C) \Leftrightarrow dr_{ij}((C)^{I_i}) \supseteq (D)^{I_j}$
- $equivalentClass(O_i(C)) = O_j(D) \Leftrightarrow dr_{ij}((C)^{I_i}) = (D)^{I_j}$
- $disjointWith(O_i(C)) = O_j(D) \Leftrightarrow dr_{ij}((C)^{I_i}) \cap (D)^{I_j} = \emptyset$
- $a \in O_j(D) \Leftrightarrow dr_{ij}((a)^{I_i}) \in (D)^{I_j}$
- $sameAs(O_i(a)) = O_j(b) \Leftrightarrow dr_{ij}((a)^{I_i}) = (b)^{I_j}$
- $differentFrom(O_i(a)) = O_j(b) \Leftrightarrow dr_{ij}((a)^{I_i}) \neq (b)^{I_j}$

An interpretation for a context space of N ontologies $(\{O_i, \mathcal{M}_i = \{\mathcal{M}_{ij}, j \in \{1,\cdots,N\}, i \neq j\}), i \in \{1,\cdots,N\}$ is composed of a pair $(I = \{\Delta^{I_i}, (.)^{I_i}\}, \{dr_{ij}, i \neq j\})$, where $i,j \in \{1,\cdots,N\}$. The first component I is the set of local interpretations, where each $(.)^{I_i}$ is an OWL interpretation over local domain Δ^{I_i} of the ontology O_i and the second component dr_{ij} is the domain relations from i to j which is a subset of $\Delta^{I_i} \times \Delta^{I_j}$. An interpretation for a context space is a model if all the local interpretations and the domain relations are satisfied.

Example 3. The completion trees of the ontologies in the context space $\{O_1, O_2\}$ of Example 2 are $\mathcal{T}_1 = \{\langle a, Bird, \emptyset, \emptyset, false \rangle\}$, $\mathcal{T}_2 = \{\langle b, Penguin, \emptyset, \emptyset, false \rangle\}$. The mappings sets are, $\mathcal{V}_1 = \emptyset$, $\mathcal{V}_2 = \{\langle b, O_1(a) \rangle\}$, $\mathcal{X}_1 = \emptyset$ and $\mathcal{X}_2 = \{\langle O_1 = O1, URI_1 = \text{"http://www.ontologies.com/O1"}\}$. After expansion of local completion trees, we have $\mathcal{T}_1$ stays unchanged and $\mathcal{T}_2$ is updated to be $\{\langle b, Penguin \wedge O1('Bird') \wedge O1'(NonFlying), \emptyset, \emptyset, false \rangle\}$. Then, the ontology servers begin exchanging knowledge using the information in their sets of mappings. The ontology O_2 server will propagate the knowledge "$\#Bird(a)\#NonFlying(a)\#$" to the ontology server of O_1 as it has mappings to its ontology.

After receiving this information, the ontology O_1 server updates its completion tree to be $\mathcal{T}_1 = \{\langle a, Bird \wedge NonFlying, \emptyset, \emptyset, false \rangle\}$. Consequently, this updated completion tree will be reexpanded to become $\mathcal{T}_1 = \{\langle a, noThing, \emptyset, \emptyset, true \rangle\}$. This means, a clash is observed on the node of a as consequence of the disjointness of $Bird$ and $NoFlying$ stated in $\mathcal{A}_1$ of O_1. Although the local domains of this context space are satisfied, it cannot have a model for its interpretation. For instance, if $(a)^{I_1} = a$ and $(b)^{I_2} = b$ then $dr_{21} = \{a\}$, because we have $sameAs(b) = O_1(a)$. Now, as $(O_1(Bird)(b))^{I_2} = \{b\}$ using the statement from 2 to 1, $O_1(Bird)(b) \Leftrightarrow (O_1(Bird)(b))^{I_2} = (Bird(dr_{21}(b)))^{I_1} = Bird(a)$, which yields a contradiction.

3.1   Experimental Results

This distributed reasoning system is extensively tested on interconnected ontologies with small sizes. To show its scalability, many experiments were run on a network of eight PCs with CPU of 1.70 Ghz and RAM of 8 Go. A set of eight context spaces is developed over large ontologies for experimenting this distributed reasoning system. The context space number i, where $i = 1, \cdots, 8$ is composed of i mapped OWL ontologies. The experiment results are compared to experiment results of running Pellet on original mapped OWL ontologies using implicit mapping with global view strategy. Figure 1 (left) shows the percentages of the sizes of entailed knowledge bases using the context mappings with local view strategy (distributed reasoning procedure) added to the sizes of domains relations, over the product of the number of ontologies in the context space with the sizes of knowledge bases entailed using OWL implicit mappings with global view strategy (non-distributed reasoning procedure).

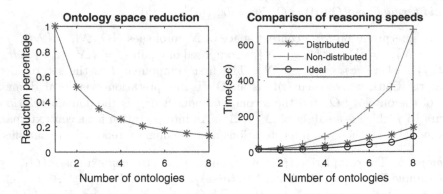

Fig. 1. Ontology space reduction and reasoning speeds

Figure 1 (right) compares the speedup of the distributed reasoning procedure (implemented with Maude and its socket module using context mappings with local view strategy) to the no-distributed reasoning procedure with Pellet (where the OWL implicit mappings with global view strategy are adopted). The time taken by the distributed reasoning procedure is compared to the time taken by the non-distributed reasoning procedure over the number of machines used (this is the ideal speed). We found in all cases, the speedup of distributed reasoning procedure is not far from the ideal speed.

4   Conclusion

This paper contextualizes the OWL ontologies by automatic translation to RL descriptions where the implicit mappings used in OWL with its mechanism of importation are changed to explicit mappings using the context mappings. Scalable and distributed approaches to ontology reasoning are required. The second contribution of this paper is the development with Maude and its socket mechanism of a distributed reasoning system. The DL semantics is extended with relations semantics to deal with the context mappings and make the different connected ontologies operating locally with controlled globalization via contexts.

As perspectives of this work, we will extend the distributed reasoning procedure to cases more complex such as distributed conjunctive query answering and thinking about issues like the tension between how much we should share and globalize (via ontologies) and how much we should localize with limited and totally controlled forms of globalization (via contexts).

References

1. Borgida, A., Serafini, L.: Distributed description logics: assimilating information from peer sources. J. Data Semant. **1**, 153–184 (2003)
2. Bouquet, P., Giunchiglia, F., van Harmelen, F., Serafini, L., Stuckenschmidt, H.: C-OWL: contextualizing ontologies. In: Fensel, D., Sycara, K., Mylopoulos, J. (eds.) ISWC 2003. LNCS, vol. 2870, pp. 164–179. Springer, Heidelberg (2003)
3. Clavel, M., Durán, F., Eker, S., Lincoln, P., Martí-Oliet, N., Meseguer, J., Talcott, C. (eds.): All About Maude - A High-Performance Logical Framework. LNCS, vol. 4350, pp. 1–28. Springer, Heidelberg (2007)
4. Grau, B.C., Parsia, B., Sirin, E.: Working with multiple ontologies on the semantic web. In: McIlraith, S.A., Plexousakis, D., van Harmelen, F. (eds.) ISWC 2004. LNCS, vol. 3298, pp. 620–634. Springer, Heidelberg (2004)
5. Hitzler, P., Krötzsch, M., Parsia, B., Patel-Schneider, P.F., Rudolph, S. (eds.): OWL 2 Web Ontology Language: Primer. W3C (2009)
6. Horrocks, I., Kutz, O., Sattler, U.: The even more irresistible SROIQ. In: Proceedings of the 10th International Conference on Principles of Knowledge Representation and Reasoning (KR 2006). AAAI Press, pp. 57–67 (2006)
7. Horrocks, I., Sattler, U.: A tableau decision procedure for SHOIQ. J. Autom. Reasoning **39**(39–3), 249–276 (2007)
8. Joseph, M., Kuper, G.M., Mossakowski, T., Serafini, L.: Query answering over contextualized RDF/OWL knowledge with forall-existential bridge rules: decidable finite extension classes. Seman. Web **7**(1), 25–61 (2016)
9. Kutz, O., Lutz, C., Wolter, F., Zakharyaschev, M.: E-connections of abstract description systems. Artif. Intell. **156**(1), 1–73 (2004)
10. Lutz, C., Milicic, M.: A tableau algorithm for DLs with concrete domains and GCIs. J. Autom. Reasoning **38**(1–3), 227–259 (2007)
11. Serafini, L., Tamilin, A.: DRAGO: distributed reasoning architecture for the semantic web. In: Gómez-Pérez, A., Euzenat, J. (eds.) ESWC 2005. LNCS, vol. 3532, pp. 361–376. Springer, Heidelberg (2005)

Towards a Formal Validation of ETL Patterns Behaviour

Bruno Oliveira[1], Orlando Belo[2(⊠)], and Nuno Macedo[3]

[1] CIICESI, School of Management and Technology,
Porto Polytechnic, Porto, Portugal
[2] ALGORITMI R&D Centre, University of Minho, Braga, Portugal
obelo@di.uminho.pt
[3] HASLab, INESC TEC, University of Minho, Braga, Portugal

Abstract. The development of ETL systems has been the target of many research efforts to support its development and implementation. In the last few years, we presented a pattern-oriented approach to develop these systems. Basically, patterns are comprised by a set of abstract components that can be configured to enable its instantiation for specific scenarios. Even when using high-level components, the ETL systems are very specific processes that represent complex data requirements and transformation routines. Several operational requirements need to be configured and system correctness is hard to validate, which can result in several implementation problems. In this paper, a set of formal specifications in Alloy is presented to express the structural constraints and behaviour of a slowly changing dimension pattern. Then, specific physical models can be generated based on formal specifications and constraints defined in an Alloy model, helping to ensure the correctness of the configuration provided.

Keywords: Data Warehousing Systems · ETL systems · ETL patterns · Component-reuse · Alloy · ETL systems formal specification

1 Introduction

The use of patterns is a recurrent practice in most software development areas, in which systems are frequently designed based on existing components, taking advantage of previous knowledge and experience. Nowadays, the importance of using reusable practices and the design techniques that promote them is recognized, contributing to higher software quality and to reduce time and money needed to its implementation and maintenance. Additionally, patterns enforce the use of well-proven practices representing knowledge of broadly accepted standards and techniques [16]. The development of ETL (*Extract-Transform-Load*) processes for *Data Warehousing Systems* (DWS) represent a specific software area and a critical component to any DWS that addresses very specific needs [10]. Each DWS implementation serves its own user community linked to a specific set of business and decision-making processes supported by specific data models. Additionally, ETL designers frequently deal with legacy systems that provide limited mechanisms for data extraction, and data inconsistencies resulting from years of business change or evolution. All these require

© Springer International Publishing Switzerland 2016
L. Bellatreche et al. (Eds.): MEDI 2016, LNCS 9893, pp. 156–165, 2016.
DOI: 10.1007/978-3-319-45547-1_13

extreme care and concern from ETL architects and software engineers in its planning, architecture, design, and implementation. Moreover, current commercial tools that support ETL data migration implementation processes provide specialized transformation tasks resulting in very complex processes represented using proprietary notations and implemented according to specific architectures and philosophies. These practices are by nature error-prone and hard to maintain. Since the development of ETL processes shares several development phases and typical problems related to the other types of software, we believe that a pattern oriented approach can be applied through the identification of recurrent procedures or techniques, identifying the cluster of operations needed and abstracting its behaviour to provide its instantiation for specific cases. To support the complexity of the knowledge involved and the application of each pattern to specific contexts, a first approach to formalize ETL patterns is also presented using Alloy [9], a declarative specification language that supports problem structural modelling and validation. Thus, after a brief summary of related work in Sect. 2, we demonstrate in Sect. 3 the feasibility and effectiveness of a pattern-oriented approach for ETL development based on the description and formalization of one of the most common used ETL techniques: the *Slowly Changing Dimension* (SCD) with history maintenance (SCD-H). The operational requirements are identified and the respective structural constraints and behaviour formalized using Alloy. Finally, in Sect. 4, we evaluate the work done so far, pointing out some research guidelines for future work.

2   Related Work

Aiming to reduce ETL design complexity, the ETL modelling has been the subject of intensive research and many approaches to ETL implementation have been proposed to improve the production of detailed documentation and the communication with business and technical users. As far as we know, Köppen [11] firstly presented a pattern-oriented approach to support ETL development, providing a general description for a set of design patterns. The work focuses on important aspects defining patterns for internal composition properties and the relationship between them. However, patterns are represented only at design level, lacking the identification of the main configuration components that could be used to translate them to code. With this work, we intend to go further, encapsulating behaviour inside components that can be reused. In fact, we propose a generator-based reuse approach [5] that uses a generator system. The generator produces a specific instance that can represent the complete system or part of it, leaving physical details to further development phases. For that, we believe that a formal model that describes model constraints and behaviour is needed to support physical generation of ETL processes.

The work presented by other authors should also be referred since represent some important contributions to the area. Vassiliadis and Simitsis proposed a technique for the conceptual, logical and physical modelling of ETL processes [17]. More recently, Akkaoui [4] presented a work based on MDA (*Model-Driven Architecture*) for ETL process development, covering the automatic generation of source code for specific computer platforms using a meta-model based on BPMN (*Business Process Model and Notation*).

The bridge to execution primitives was explored using a model-to-text approach, supporting its execution through some ETL commercial tools. These and other related works [14, 18] revealed very important aspects that were taken into consideration for the approach presented here. However, they fail to provide an integrated approach that focus on the complete ETL lifecycle and to take advantage of work performed in initial development to implementation phases. Additionally, they focus on very granular tasks, resulting in very large and disorganized process, resulting in process inconsistencies and redundancy.

3   ETL Patterns: SCD-H Pattern

Patterns have been used in several software development areas as a way to help developers solve recurring problems, promoting the sharing of experience and knowledge obtained across several areas. Patterns can be viewed as a three-part rule expressing the context, the forces that typically occur, and how the solution [8] resolves the forces [3]. Next, we will identify and formalize a common ETL procedure, namely a SCD-H transformation pattern, which is used to preserve changes in dimensions used to track historical data. A subset of common pattern description based structure [1, 3] is used to describe its internal composition, complemented by a formalization model in Alloy. When a *Data Warehouse* (DW) is updated, some decisions must be considered in order to maintain a consistent view of its data. Any SCD process embodies well-defined policies representing design patterns to support old and new data over time in a DW dimension context. Several types of SCD can be applied [10], each one considering specific scenarios. In this work, a specific strategy of SCD that preserves history using an auxiliary history table is followed. Basically, this approach considers that any dimension integrates two distinct tables: one table to store up-to-date dimension's data and other to store previous record versions. With this strategy all current and historical records are stored with no limitations and with low process complexity, since they are easier to compute than other approaches [15] - in Fig. 1 we present a specific template that can be used to describe a SCD-H pattern.

Audit tables are used in the *Data Staging Area* (DSA) and provide the record for processing to SCD process according to the operation performed in source systems. When records are new, insert operations are triggered to the dimension table as current data, while the deleted records are marked as inactive in target dimension. A more complex process should be initiated for updated records, since the current versions of updated records should be transferred to history table, partially or totally, depending on the dimension table's SCD specification. Depending on the needs, all or some of these operations can be registered in the system's log file, identifying the record, the operation that was performed, the data source origin and temporal data. The quarantine table also plays an important role in a SCD process, since it supports unexpected scenarios that usually compromise processes. Records with structural errors or data entry errors can be redirected to quarantine tables that store all inconsistent records, identifying (at least) the record, the error that occurred and the temporal data associated. These records can be posteriorly analysed by specific procedures or even manually in order to be reintroduced in ETL workflow or deleted, helping to identify important scenarios that can be useful to check ETL integrity.

Name: Slowly changing dimension, with history maintenance (SCD-H).

Classification: Transformation pattern.

Problem: Dimension tables store data that can change slowly over time. In such cases, we need to track these changes to support historical data reporting. How can current and historical data be properly stored?

Context: DWS are built based on the concept of temporal data. The facts stored in fact tables are linked to a specific date in which they occurred, as well as other dimensions that can be also affected by time. Data coming from information sources can be modified to reflect a change in a certain point of time that should be preserved in a specific dimension, in order to maintain the consistency of the data warehouse.

Solution: The SCD process begins when the data that was changed is available for populating the target system. Typically, this data is stored using specific audit tables that keep records composed by the attributes (*Att*) with history maintenance (*SCDAtt*) for a specific dimension table along with the operation (*Operation*) that record was subject, the operation date (*Date*), and the dimension surrogate key (*Skey*): auditData = $(Skey, SCDAtt_1, ..., SCDAtt_n, Operation, Date)$.

Fig. 1. An example of a template for describing a SCD-H pattern

Moreover, log track techniques also have an important role in a SCD-H pattern since they are used to recover the system from unexpected situations. For example, if some critical error happens, the process can restart only from the point when the error occurs, useful mainly when large volumes of data are involved. After processing all records, the audit table will be cleared and the records processed will be loaded into the target dimensional table. In order to support all these structural and operational constraints, we developed a specific model for representing the structure of the pattern (Fig. 2). This model represents a subset of the ETL patterns meta-model for the representation of the SCD structure and all the objects supporting its structure. The SCD class is a specific type of transformation patterns that can be specialized in several types if necessary. We distinguish only two types: one that holds no historical data (data is simply replaced by the new one) and another that keeps the history of the changes occurred in the dimension table. To support the SCD–H pattern, a specific set of metadata should be provided to produce the instances of the patterns. The *DataObject* class represents the several types of data source/target objects that can be used in SCD-H context. The *Audit table* holds data extracted from data sources and respective operation and time data, the *Dimension* that stores current data, the *History* that stores historical data for each record, the *Quarantine* that represents the object that stores noncompliant data, and the *Log* object that stores all operations performed. Each one of these objects will have fields from several types, revealing specific operational characteristics of each data object. For example, the state of each record (to signal active and inactive attributes) is identified using a specific field.

The correspondences between fields of each data source should be defined according to the constraints defined for each mapping: the *auditToQuarantine* relationship represents the mapping between audit table and dimension table, which is

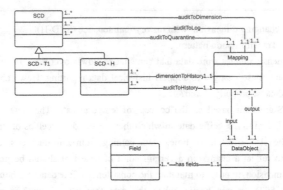

Fig. 2. Class diagram for SCD pattern structure representation

related to the source of data and target dimension, the *auditToQuarantine* that represents the mapping between the dimension table and the quarantine table to store fields that for some reason could not be stored in the target dimension, and the *auditToLog* that represents the relationship between the audit table and the target log object storing the operations performed, including the non-successful ones. The *dimensionToHistory* and *auditToHistory* relationships describe specific features of the SCD-H pattern, representing the mapping between dimension fields to history dimension fields, and audit table fields to history dimension fields, respectively. Although the pattern structure can be described in a straightforward manner using class models like the one presented in Fig. 2, such is not the case for several richer structural constraints that specify the integrity of the pattern. These must be considered not only at the level of the pattern configuration but also by the pattern operational behaviour. To provide a simple and solid specification of a SCD pattern amenable to being automatically analysed, its description was embedded into a formal specification.

Alloy is a lightweight formal specification language, whose Analyser provides support for automatic assertion checking, within a bounded universe, by relying on off-the-shelf constraint solvers. The flexibility and object-oriented flavour of the Alloy language render it well-suited to specify and analyse software design models, addressing both complex structural constraints [2, 7, 12] and behavioural constraints imposed by transformations [6, 13]. An embedding of ETL pattern specifications into Alloy would not only provide a formal specification of their structure and behaviour, but would also allow their fully automatic verification, ensuring that the pattern preserves the consistency of the system. Figure 3 presents an excerpt of the Alloy specification of ETL patterns and related concepts, formalizing the meta-model structure and providing a new degree of detail to the class model presented before in Fig. 2.

The class hierarchy can be easily described using Alloy signatures, introducing sets of elements of a certain type in the model. Abstract signatures are used to describe abstract concepts that should be refined by more specific elements, which is the case of top-level signatures *Field*, *DataObject* and *Pattern*. These abstract signatures can then be specialised through extension into concrete objects, mirroring the hierarchy of the model from Fig. 2. Signatures may contain fields of arbitrary arity, embodying the

```
abstract sig Field{}
sig SKField, ControlField, VariationField, DescriptiveField extends Field{}
sig DateField, OperationField, ErrorField extends ControlField{}

abstract sig DataObject{fields: some Field, keys: some SKField, (...)}
fact dataobject {all o : DataObject | o.keys in o.fields,(...)}

pred consistentDataObject[s:State,o:DataObject] {
 all r1,r2 : o.rows.s |
  (all f : o.keys | f.(r1.values) = f.(r2.values)) => r1 = r2
  (...)
}
sig Mapping {inData: one DataObject, outData: one DataObject, association:
Field -> Field}
fact mapping {
 all m : Mapping | m.association in m.inData.fields -> m.outData.fields
  (...)
}
pred consistentMapping[s:State,m:Mapping] {
  consistentDataObject[s,m.inData]
  consistentDataObject[s,m.outData]
  (...)
}
abstract sig Pattern{}
abstract sig TransformationPattern extends Pattern{}
abstract sig SCD extends TransformationPattern{
  auditToDimension : one Mapping,
  auditToQuarantine: one Mapping,
  auditToLog: one Mapping
}
fact scd { (...) }
sig SCDH extends SCD {dimensionToHistory: one Mapping,
auditToHistory:one Mapping}
fact scdh {all scd : SCD {
    scd.dimensionToHistory.inData in Dimension
  (...)
}
```

Fig. 3. Basic alloy specification to support ETL patterns

associations between the different artefacts of the specification. For instance, similarly to the Fig. 2 representation, data objects represent repositories that are used to read and write data and contain a set of field declarations that is shared by its extensions: each *DataObject* element is related to a non-empty set of *Field* elements (imposed by the keyword some) that represent data fields used to characterise records, and a set of *SKField* elements used to express the SK fields. These can then be restricted by additional constraints through Alloy facts, like the one stating that every *SKField* is selected from the data object Field elements. Signature mapping represents the association between fields from two data sources, establishing the relationship between attributes from two different sources through binary field association. Additional constraints impose, for instance, that a mapping is only valid if it associated fields from the input (*inData*) and the output (*outData*) data sources. Facts represent constraints that are enforced in the system. However, certain constraints should not be enforced but rather preserved by the ETL procedure - this denotes the notion of correctness in the specification. The behaviour of the patterns should then be checked to assess whether they guarantee the consistency of the system. These predicates include properties like the uniqueness of the values in SK fields and the referential integrity between the SK fields of the data sources associated to the mappings. Other relevant signatures, omitted in the figure, are specified in a similar manner, like those regarding the target and historical dimension and their respective constraints, as well as the log and quarantine objects.

The pattern signature is then specialised to represent SCD patterns, containing the expected mappings, like *auditToDimension*, *auditToQuarantine* and *auditToLog*. These fields describe the relationship between the audit object used for the SCD process and the respective target repositories: a dimension object that will receive data from audit table, a quarantine object that holds non-conformed data that was excluded from the dimension object, and a log object that will preserve all operations performed by the audit, dimension and quarantine objects. These mappings enable the preservation of variation, control, surrogate key and data fields between data objects, which are imposed by facts defined over both the SCD and the SCD-H signatures. For instance, for the *dimensionToHistory*, the correspondent mapping is established between a dimension object data as input and a history object data as output. Additionally, several signature facts were used to enforce the correctness of each mapping, i.e., that the mapping associates fields of the same nature. This means that related fields are correctly mapped and that invalid relationships are avoided. A predicate is then defined to embody the notion of consistent SCD. In this case, this amounts for checking whether the mappings of SCD are themselves consistent, as defined above. This property can then be automatically processed by the Alloy Analyser, either to simulate instances that conform to the specification or to check for the correctness of concrete instances. The specification presented in Fig. 3 embodies the static constraints of ETL patterns. However, we are interested in checking the correctness of the process as data is collected from the sources and ETL procedures are executed. In Alloy, dynamic behaviour is encoded through well-established idioms, like the local state idiom followed in this work [9]. Roughly, a new signature State is introduced in the specification, representing different states of the system, modelling the notion of evolving time. Artefacts that are expected to evolve in time are then appended with a State element, denoting their value in each instant of time. In our scenario, only the data contained in each data object are expected to change - the structure of the data objects and the patterns is static. This dynamic version of the specification is presented in Fig. 4, where a *Row* signature was introduced to describe the association between a *Field* and a specific *Value*. Data objects were then extended to contain a dynamic row field representing its data in each instant of time. An additional fact restricts rows to assign values to the fields of the parent data object.

The system evolution is then modelled through declarative predicates that relate two different states. Thus, if the static components of the specification represent the pattern configuration, dynamic components define the pattern behaviour based on those configurations. Figure 4 depicts, as an example, the predicate *addToDimension* that models the behaviour of the pattern insert operation, involving the audit and target dimension objects. Being declarative, these definitions are usually comprised by pre-, post- and frame conditions. In this case, the pre-conditions restrict the operation to be applied only if the surrogate keys of the audit row that will be processed do not exist in the dimension table. Otherwise the update operation should be applied instead. The post-conditions state that the row is removed from the audit table and inserted in the

```
sig State {}
sig Value {}
sig Row {values: Field -> lone Value}
abstract sig DataObject{(...),rows: Row -> State}
fact rows {
    all s : State, o : DataObject, r : o.rows.s | r.values.Value = o.fields
}
pred addToDimension [s,s': State, r,r': Row, scd: SCD] {
    r in scd.auditToDimension.inData.rows.s
    r' not in scd.auditToDimension.outData.rows.s
    scd.auditToDimension.inData.rows.s' =
        scd.auditToDimension.inData.rows.s - r
    scd.auditToDimension.outData.rows.s' =
        scd.auditToDimension.outData.rows.s + r'
    all f : scd.auditToDimension.association.Field |
        f.(r.values) = f.(scd.auditToDimension.association).(r'.values)
    (...)
}

assert addToDimensionCorrect {

    all s: State, s': s.next, scd: SCD, r: Row |

        (consistentSCD[s,scd] and addToDimension[s,s',r,scd]) =>

            consistentSCD[s',scd]
}
```

Fig. 4. Excerpt of the alloy specification for SCD-H pattern for dynamic behaviour simulation

target dimension, preserving the data as defined by the associations of the SCD mappings. The frame conditions state that every other artefact, like the history table, stays unchanged. The two states are represented by the predicate *s* and *s'* parameters - whenever the rows field is annexed with the *s* elements it represents the data in the pre-state, while rows at *s'* represents the data in the post-state. Once these operation predicates are defined, the specification can be automatically analysed by the Alloy Analyser to check whether they preserve the consistency constraints defined above within a bounded universe. These are defined in the assert clause in Fig. 4, which tests whether the execution of the *addToDimension* operation preserves the consistency of the system. The check command effectively instructs the Alloy Analyzer to verify this assertion for a specific scope. It has shown that the three defined operations indeed preserve the specified consistency predicates, providing an increased level of confidence on the correctness of the procedure. Additional constraints and level of detail can be added to the specification to verify more complex properties.

4 Conclusions and Future Work

This paper proposed a pattern-oriented approach that allows for the implementation of ETL processes with a higher level of abstraction. With this pattern-oriented approach, the knowledge and best practices revealed by several works can be put in practice using a set of software patterns that can be applied to the ETL development life cycle: from model representation to its physical implementation primitives. A specific design pattern - SCD-H - was identified along with its skeleton, representing its structure, constraints and behaviour according to specific rules. The presented approach keeps a specific template and instance as separated layers, since users need to provide data about data, i.e., users describe data repositories and its contents in structural terms and a specific generator will generate the respective code based on the primitives previously established and using specific data. The SCD-H pattern can be applied to any ETL scenario. To support this process an excerpt of a formal specification in Alloy was presented, providing an automatic way for analysis and searching for false assertions through the generation of counterexamples. That way, patterns not only become easier to use than in the common granular approach, but can also be easily reused to produce better software, because models can be checked using a powerful simulation engine before its execution. This work is a first attempt to specify formally ETL patterns in Alloy, representing the static and behavioural specifications of a SCD-H pattern. At short term, a more complete Alloy specification for ETL patterns will be developed, particularly in what is concerned to behaviour formalization, assertion checking and exception and error handling scenarios. Additionally, several other patterns need to be formalized to provide a complete package specification for ETL patterns. A complete validation engine is also planned, translating the pattern configuration to Alloy models, allowing the ETL designers to seamlessly and automatically check the consistency of the developed patterns.

Acknowledgments. This work has been supported by COMPETE: POCI-01-0145-FEDER-007043 and FCT – Fundação para a Ciência e Tecnologia within the Project Scope: UID/CEC/00319/2013. Our thanks to Alcino Cunha, from HASLab R&D Centre, for the comments and suggestions he did during the preparation of this paper.

References

1. Van der Aalst, W.M.P., ter Hofstede, A.H.M., Kiepuszewski, B., Barros, A.P.: Workflow patterns. Distrib. Parallel Databases. **14**, 5–51 (2003)
2. Anastasakis, K., Bordbar, B., Georg, G., Ray, I.: On challenges of model transformation from UML to alloy. Softw. Syst. Model. **9**, 69–86 (2010)
3. Appleton, B.: Patterns and Software: Essential Concepts and Terminology. Object Mag. Online, p. 1 (2000)
4. Akkaoui, Z., Zimànyi, E., Mazón, J.-N., Trujillo, J.: A model-driven framework for ETL process development. In: Proceedings of ACM 14th International Workshop Data Warehousing OLAP, pp. 45–52 (2011)
5. Biggerstaff, T.J.: A perspective of generative reuse. Ann. Softw. Eng. **5**, 169–226 (1998)
6. Büttner, F., Egea, M., Cabot, J., Gogolla, M.: Verification of ATL transformations using transformation models and model finders. In: Aoki, T., Taguchi, K. (eds.) ICFEM 2012. LNCS (LNAI and LNBI), vol. 7635, pp. 198–213. Springer, Heidelberg (2012)
7. Cunha, A., Garis, A., Riesco, D.: Translating between alloy specifications and UML class diagrams annotated with OCL. Softw. Syst. Model. **14**, 5–25 (2013)
8. Gabriel, R.P.: Patterns of Software Tales from the Software Community. Architecture, p. 239. Oxford University Press, New York (1996)
9. Jackson, D.: Software Abstractions: Logic, Language, and Analysis. MIT Press, Cambridge (2012)

10. Kimball, R., Caserta, J.: The Data Warehouse ETL Toolkit: Practical Techniques for Extracting, Cleaning, Conforming, and Delivering Data. Wiley, Hoboken (2004)
11. Köppen, V., Brüggemann, B., Berendt, B.: Designing data integration: the ETL pattern approach. Eur. J. Inform. Prof. **XII**, 49–55 (2011)
12. Kuhlmann, M., Gogolla, M.: From UML and OCL to relational logic and back. In: France, R.B., Kazmeier, J., Breu, R., Atkinson, C. (eds.) MODELS 2012. LNCS (LNAI and LNBI), vol. 7590, pp. 415–431. Springer, Heidelberg (2012)
13. Macedo, N., Cunha, A.: Least-change bidirectional model transformation with QVT-R and ATL. Softw. Syst. Model. **15**(3), 783–810 (2016)
14. Muñoz, L., Mazón, J.N., Trujillo, J.: A family of experiments to validate measures for UML activity diagrams of ETL processes in data warehouses. Inf. Softw. Technol. **52**, 1188–1203 (2010)
15. Santos, V., Belo, O.: No need to type slowly changing dimensions. In: Proceedings of IADIS International Conference Information Systems 2011, Avila, Spain, 11–13 March 2011
16. Sommerville, I.: Software Engineering, 7th edn. Addison Wesley, Pearson (2004)
17. Vassiliadis, P., Simitsis, A., Georgantas, P., Terrovitis, M.: A framework for the design of ETL scenarios. In: Eder, J., Missikoff, M. (eds.) CAiSE 2003. LNCS, vol. 2681, pp. 520–535. Springer, Heidelberg (2003)
18. Wilkinson, K., Simitsis, A., Castellanos, M., Dayal, U.: Leveraging business process models for ETL design. In: Parsons, J., Saeki, M., Shoval, P., Woo, C., Wand, Y. (eds.) ER 2010. LNCS (LNAI and LNBI), vol. 6412, pp. 15–30. Springer, Heidelberg (2010)

Building OLAP Cubes from Columnar NoSQL Data Warehouses

Khaled Dehdouh[(✉)]

ERIC Laboratory/University of Lyon 2,
5 avenue Pierre Mendes-France, 69676 Bron Cedex, France
Khaled.Dehdouh@univ-lyon2.fr

Abstract. The work presented in this paper aims to build OLAP cubes from big data warehouses implemented by using the columnar NoSQL model. The use of NoSQL models is motivated by the inability of the relational model, usually used to implement data warehousing, to allow data scalability easily. Indeed, the columnar NoSQL model is suitable for storing and managing massive data, especially for decisional queries. However, the column-oriented NoSQL DBMS do not offer online analysis operators (OLAP). Our main contribution is to define a new cube operator called MC-CUBE (MapReduce Columnar CUBE), which allows building columnar NoSQL cubes by taking into account the no relational and distributed aspects when data warehouses are stored.

Keywords: Data warehouses · Columnar NoSQL model · Big data

1 Introduction

The data warehouse is a database for online analytical processing (OLAP) to aid decision-making. It is designed according to a dimensional modelling which has for objective to observe facts through measures, also called indicators, according to the dimensions that represent the analysis axes. It is often implemented in the relational database management system (RDBMS) [17]. Thanks to the OLAP (On-Line Analytical Processing), the users can create multidimensional representations related to the particular analysis contexts in compliance with the specific needs, according to the criteria which they define, called hypercubes or OLAP cubes. Cube computation produces aggregations that are beyond the limits of the Group by [15]. For example, in the case of calculation of the sum, it computes in a multidimensional way and returns sub-totals and totals for all possible combinations. This involves performance of all aggregations according to all levels of hierarchies of all dimensions. For a cube with three dimensions A, B and C, the performed aggregations relate to the following combinations: (A, B, C), (A, B, ALL), (A, ALL, C), (ALL, B, C), (A, ALL, ALL), (ALL, B, ALL), (ALL, ALL, C), (ALL, ALL, ALL). The (A, B, C) combination corresponds as the lowest (least) aggregate level of the cube, and the rest are considered as the high aggregate levels. The advent of the big data has created new opportunities for researchers to achieve high relevance and impact amid changes and transformations in how we study several science phenomena. Big data has become important as many organizations, both public and private, have been collecting massive amounts of

© Springer International Publishing Switzerland 2016
L. Bellatreche et al. (Eds.): MEDI 2016, LNCS 9893, pp. 166–179, 2016.
DOI: 10.1007/978-3-319-45547-1_14

domain-specific information; i.e.: useful information about issues such as national intelligence, cyber security, fraud detection, marketing, and medical informatics. However, unusual volumes of data become an issue when faced with the limited capacities of traditional systems, especially when data storage is in a distributed environment which requires the use of parallel treatment as MapReduce paradigm [11]. To solve a part of this issue, new models have appeared such as the column oriented NoSQL which gives a data structure more adequate to the massive data warehouses [6]. In the big data warehouses context, a column-oriented NoSQL database system is considered as the storage model which is highly adapted to data warehouses and online analysis [20]. Indeed, the storage of data column by column allows values belonging to the same column to be shared in the same disk space which improves the column access time enormously when the aggregate operations are performed. Furthermore, the no relational aspect that characterizes the NoSQL model when data are stored allows to deploy data easily in a distributed environment. Yet, the cube computation process requires to take into account the data structure which characterizes the columnar NoSQL model and should be adapted to the parallel paradigms to ensure the treatment of distributed data. Unfortunately, column-oriented NoSQL DBMSs do not have OLAP operators.

To solve this problem, we propose a new aggregation operator, called MC-CUBE (MapReduce Columnar CUBE) which allows OLAP cubes to be computed from big data warehouses implemented by using column-oriented NoSQL model. MC-CUBE implements the invisible join, used by the columnar RDBMS [1], in order to compute aggregation from several tables and extend it to take into account all possible aggregations at different levels of granularity of the cube. Furthermore, MC-CUBE uses the MapReduce paradigm to parallelize the treatments of data stored in a distributed environment. We have evaluated the performance of MC-CUBE operator on star schema benchmark (SSB[1]), implemented within the column-oriented NoSQL DBMS HBase[2] using Hadoop[3]. The HBase DBMS and the Hadoop platform were chosen because of their distributed context which was necessary for storing and analyzing big data. The rest of this paper is organized as follows. Section 2 gives a related work. Section 3 introduces basic concepts about columnar NoSQL Data warehouse, and explains the columnar approach for building a data cube. Section 4 introduces the MC-CUBE operator and shows the execution phases through an example. Section 5 shows performance results and exemplifies of MC-CUBE operator when OLAP cubes are performed. Finally Sect. 6 concludes the paper.

2   Related Work

Big data have lead data warehouses towards to distributed environments to store and to analyze the large amount of data. Since the column storage has outperformed the row storage, several research projects based on the columnar relational model have been

---

[1] http://www.cs.umb.edu/~poneil/StarSchemaB.PDF.

[2] https://hbase.apache.org/.

[3] http://hadoop.apache.org/.

commercialized such as InfoBright [21], Brighthouse [22], Vectorwise [23], MonetDB [16], SAP HANA [14], Blink [4], and Vertica [18]. These systems have led legacy RDBMS vendors to add columnar storage options to their existing engines [19]. However, the relational model that is often used for storing data warehouses has shown its limits. Indeed, the use of distributed solutions based on the relational model is as costly as the implementation of the referential integrity constraints (RIC) that ensures the validity of relation between tables in the RDBMS, because the system must continuously ensure that the associated-data are stored in the same node. Furthermore, it is very difficult to respect the ACID (Atomicity, Consistency, Isolation and Durability) properties that characterize the transactional systems with correct consistency when data are stored in distributed environment [7]. Moreover, the variety aspect of data cannot be supported by the relational model. Thus, for analytical purposes, Google developed a massively scalable infrastructure that includes a distributed file system, a column-oriented storage system, a distributed coordination system and parallel execution algorithm based on the paradigm of MapReduce, and opened them to the community in 2004 and 2006, respectively [8]. Regarding the implementation of the big data warehouses within the column-oriented NoSQL model, two approaches are defined [13]. The first one (normalized approach) uses different tables for storing fact and dimension at physical level which requires to achieve the join between tables when aggregation is performed. The second approach (denormalized approach) stores the fact and dimensions into one table, which allows to avoid performing join between tables.

For building OLAP cubes, we would name four relevant works: [2, 9, 10, 12]. Firstly, [2] outlines the possibility of having data in a cloud by using columnar NoSQL DBMS to store data and MapReduce as an agile mechanism to build cubes. However, the cube is built at one level of granularity (least level) and from data warehouse implemented according the denormalized approach. Thus, the authors do not give any indications regarding the computing of the aggregates when the others level of granularities that compose the cube are performed. A similar proposal to build cubes using MapReduce can be found in [12], but in this case the authors just perform the cube at different level of granularity and do not provide a solution for performing join between tables (fact and dimensions) when data warehouses are implemented according the normalized approach. In [10], the different level of granularity that compose the OLAP cube can be computed using the naive method, using a combination of group-by queries and gathering the outputs via the UNION operator. This solution is not suitable for big data warehouses. Indeed, for D dimensions, the execution of 2^D sub-queries to perform the various aggregations, which considerably increase the number of times when the data warehouse is accessed. Consequently, the naive method reduces DBMS performance, particularly when scaling-up. Finally, [9] gives a solution to perform join between tables and performing aggregates from data warehouses implemented according the normalized approach. It consists to integrate software and tools such as Hive and Kylin in the ecosystem used for implementing the data warehouse, and use their cube building operators. However, the use of these tools is limited; because they are row-oriented, and once integrated into column-oriented NoSQL DBMS, they do not allow to take a full effective of the columnar NoSQL DBMS when data are handled.

3 Columnar NoSQL Data Warehouse

In the case of data warehouse implementation by using the columnar NoSQL model, both the dimensions and the fact are stored by column-wise. Each data is stored in the form of a "key/value" pair. When the data belongs to the dimension, the key part is represented by the key of this dimension. By cons, if the data belongs to the fact table, the part key is represented by the key of the fact table. As the dimensions and fact are stored in different tables, the link between them is ensured by the join attributes, where the key contains the key of the fact table and in the value part contains the key of dimension.

3.1 Formalization

Given the columnar NoSQL star data warehouse DW which is composed by the fact table F and dimensions tables $D = \{d_1, d_2, \ldots, d_n\}$. Each dimension table d_j, with $j \in [1, n]$ is composed by a_j^i attributes with $i \in [1, k]$, such as $d_j = \left\{a_j^1, a_j^2, \ldots, a_j^k\right\}$, where k varies from dimension to another. Each dimension attribute value is stored in the form of a "key/value" pair. The key part contains the dimension identifier $d_j.RowKey$ and the value part contains $a_j^i.value$. The fact table, on the other hand, groups together a number of attributes which represent the measures to aggregate $M = \{m_1, m_2, \ldots, m_t\}$. Each measure m_q, with $q \in [1, t]$, is identified by the fact table key ($F.RowKey$, $m_q.value$). Furthermore, F contains the join attributes $F.d_j$, where each one is composed by the fact table identifier and the identifier of dimension table that represent ($F.RowKey$, $d_j.RowKey$). Columnar NoSQL star data warehouse composed of one fact table F and two dimension tables' d_1, d_2 is depicted in Fig. 1.

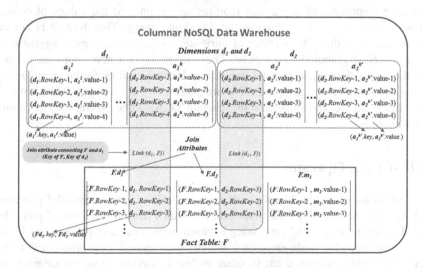

Fig. 1. Columnar NoSQL data warehouse

3.2 Building OLAP Cubes

In General, to generate an OLAP cube compound aggregates of several levels of granularity, it is preferable to calculate the first level of granularity which is the least aggregated and then using it to achieve aggregates of other levels of granularity which are above. This allows to avoid returning to the data warehouse to perform the calculation of aggregates every time, and thus avoids performing the joins between the dimension tables and the fact table, that are considered very expensive in terms of resources and execution time. If the storage of data is row-oriented, each table (dimension or facts) stores data by row (record). Each record stores the column (attribute) values which is a row of the table. Once the column value belonging to a record is accessed, the other values of columns that compose this record do the same. To optimize computing the aggregates of the cube, it is better to compute the most aggregate level from the least aggregate, and then use it to compute the one after, because it contains fewer attributes in the composition of his record. Thus, the underlying idea is to use, for each computing of the aggregates, the level of granularity with the least attributes to calculate the one that comes just after (most aggregated) [5]. For a cube with three dimensions A, B, C for instance, the computing of aggregates is defined according to four levels of granularity. The first represents the least aggregate level (A, B, C). It is used to compute aggregates of others levels of granularity. The transition from one level of granularity to another is carried out sequentially with a downward direction (2 - > 3 - > 4). Thus, the second level of granularity (A, B, ALL), (A, ALL, C), (ALL, B, C) allows to compute the third (A, ALL, ALL), (ALL, B, ALL), (ALL, ALL, C), that can be used to compute the next level (ALL, ALL, ALL). Thus, according to the row-oriented approach, the fourth level of granularity can be obtained only if the third level of granularity has already been performed. This approach, based on the exploitation of least aggregate levels of granularity to perform the most aggregate levels, is effective when the storage environment is row-oriented.

However, in a column-oriented environment, where the data is stored column by column, the computing of aggregates requires access only to the values of columns (dimensions or measures) involved in the decisional query. Therefore, it is not necessary to seek to reduce the number of attributes in order to compute aggregates at different levels of granularity of a cube. Thus, we propose a new approach for computing the cube where the aggregates granularity levels are all performed from a single level, which is the least aggregated. We are positioning in this approach to provide MC-CUBE an aggregation operator to generate OLAP cubes from column-oriented data warehouses.

4 MC-CUBE Operator

MC-CUBE is based on the MapReduce paradigm. This later is a parallel processing model suited to the massive data treatment. It handles data in the form of pairs (key, value). This model of parallel processing is based on two main steps Map and Reduce [11]. In Map step, the node (machine) which is submitted to a problem cuts it in sub-problems and delegates them to other nodes. In Reduce step, the original node reconstructs a solution to the problem which he had been requested for. Since, the fact and dimensions are stored in different tables, the MC-CUBE operator implement in distribute environment the invisible join, which is used by the relational column-oriented to materialize the join between tables (fact and dimensions) and perform the aggregation computing. Recall that, the invisible join uses the positions of the data in the columns to identify data to be aggregated. This allows to process large amounts of data at memory level. To optimize the data cube calculating, the MC-CUBE operator performs first, from the data warehouse, the calculation of aggregates of the lowest level, and then uses it to compute the other levels of aggregation that compose the data cube. This allows the MC-CUBE to avoid returning to data warehouse when higher level aggregates are performed.

4.1   MC-CUBE Operator Execution Phases

MC-CUBE operator performs the cube aggregation in four phases by executing seven MapReduce jobs as follows (Fig. 2).

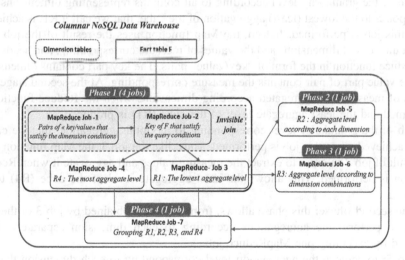

Fig. 2. MC-CUBE operator execution phases

The first phase: this phase allows, from the data warehouse, the aggregations both at the lowest and higher levels of granularity to be produced. It is carried out by executing four MapReduce jobs which two to materialize the join between tables (fact and dimensions), and the two others for achieving calculation of aggregates.

Job 1: the "key/value" pairs of dimensions which will be use to perform the join with the fact table, are identified when this job is performed. At the Map function, the treatments are parallelized in order to apply the query predicates to the respective dimensions. The result is output to the Reduce function which gathered the partial results and provides a set of pairs "key/value" representing the dimension values involved in the join with the fact table. The key part of "key/value" pair contains the value of the dimension and the other part contains the dimension identifier corresponding.

Job 2: this job uses the result of the first, and identifies at the map function level, the values of the primary key of the fact table corresponding to the dimensions' primary keys which satisfied the query predicates are recovered. This allows building a list of "key/value", where the key part contains the primary key of the fact table, and the value part contains a boolean value (0 or 1). This latter shows if the query predicate is satisfied (1) or not (0). For optimization reasons, only the first join attribute at the fact table is scanned, the others are scanned by using the keys that are obtained from the first scan. Indeed, the first scan allows to have the values of the primary key of the fact table that satisfied the predicate's dimension (boolean value corresponding to 1). Thus, from this set of keys that the others join attributes will be checked. This avoids to scan the values of the primary key unnecessary of the fact table and reduces the treatment of the number of "key/value" pairs. The result of the Map function is used by the Reduce function which apply the logical AND on the boolean value belonging to the same key. The set of keys that keeping their boolean value to 1, represents the values of the primary key of the fact table which satisfy all query predicates.

Job 3: the granularity level according to all columns representing dimensions that corresponds to the lowest (least) aggregation of the cube, that we call it R1, is achieved when this job is performed. Indeed, the Map function uses the result of the job 2 to extract the keys of dimensions and the values of measure corresponding, and sends it to the Reduce function in the form of "key/value" pairs. The key part contains dimensions and the value part of pair contains the measure corresponding. At the second stage, the values of measure are aggregated according dimensions when the Reduce function is performed and the least aggregate level of the cube (R1) is produced.

Job 4: the granularity level corresponding to the total aggregation, that we call it R4, is achieved when this job is performed. Thus, like the job 3, the Map function uses the result of job 2 in order to extract the measure values and aggregate it when Reduce function is performed. This allows the most aggregate level of the cube (R4) to be produced.

The second phase: this phase allows, from the result obtained by job 3 of the first phase, to perform the aggregations according to each dimension separately. It is achieved by executing one MapReduce job.

Job 5: to achieve the aggregation level corresponding to each dimension that we call it R2, the result of the job 3 (R1) is used. Recall that the part key of pairs composed the R1 contains the dimensions' identifiers, and the part value contains the corresponding measure. Thus, at the Map function level, each identifier of dimension is extracted with the corresponding measure which produces a pair of "key/value". The key part contains an identifier of dimension, and the part value contains the corresponding measure. For each same dimension identifier (key), the measures (value) are aggregated when the Reduce function is performed.

The third phase: it involves using the result obtained by job 3 of the first phase, to perform the rest of aggregates that compose the cube. It is achieved by executing one MapReduce job, and we call the result of this operation R3.

Job 6: the result of the job 3 (R1) is used when the aggregation corresponding to the combinations of the dimensions that rest for building the cube, is achieved. Thus, at the Map function level, the identifiers of dimension with different combinations are extracted with the corresponding measure which produces in each case a pair of "key/value". The key part contains a combination of dimension identifiers, and the part value contains the corresponding measure. For each same combination of dimensions' identifiers (key), the measures (value) are aggregated when the Reduce function is performed.

The fourth phase: since the aggregates are performed with dimensions' identifiers, this phase replacing these identifiers with the dimensions attributes cited in the query, and gathered it to provide the cube. It is achieved by executing one MapReduce job.

Job 7: this job allows to adapt the results obtained in the previous phases to the query context. Indeed, at the Map function the identifiers of dimensions belonging to the R1, R2, and R3 are changed by the values of dimensions cited in the query. The results of this function are gathered when Reduce function is performed which produce the cube.

In order to set out the jobs that defined the MC-CUBE execution phases, we use in the next section an example.

4.2 Example

We use the Star Schema Benchmark as a data warehouse example in order to set out the different jobs required to perform the compute phases of the cube by using MC-CUBE operator from columnar NoSQL data warehouse. Recall that SSB is a data warehouse which manages line orders according to dimensions, PART, SUPPLIER, CUSTOMER and DATE. It consists of a single fact table called LINEORDER made up of seventeen column to give the information about order, with a composite primary key consisting of the Orderkey and Linenumber attributes, and foreign keys that refer to the dimension tables. In order to provide more detail on MC-CUBE execution phases, we illustrate our explanation with an example. This example computes the sales revenue from products delivered by FRENCH suppliers and for which orders were placed by ITA-LIAN customers in the years 1996 and 1997.

According to the example, the lowest and highest levels of aggregation corresponding respectively to (c.city, s.city, d.year), and (ALL, ALL, ALL) are produced when the first phase is performed. Indeed, the first MapReduce job allows to identify the primary keys of dimensions that satisfied the query conditions. Thus, the Map function allows to obtain the keys of FRENCH suppliers, ITALIEN customers, and 1996 and 1997 years when the query predicates (supplier.Nation = France), (customer. Nation = Italien), and (Year in (1996, 1997)) are applied separately to the respective dimensions SUPPLIERS, CUSTOMERS, and DATE. The output is consolidated and gathered to produce a set of pairs (Nation, Custkey), (Nation, Suppkey), and (Year, Datekey) representing the dimension values that will be used in the join with the fact table Lineorder.

The result of the first job is used by the second job to perform the join between dimensions and the fact table. Indeed, this job aims to identify the key of Lineorder that satisfy all the query conditions at once. Thus, by using the values of Custkey, Suppkey, and Orderdate of dimensions that are obtained by job 1, the join attributes Custkey,

Suppkey, and Orderdate of fact table Lineorder are scanned to find the corresponding
Lineorder key when the Map function is performed. For each dimension key found the
mapper associate to the Lineorder key a boolean value "1", otherwise "0". The output
is a set of pairs of "key/value" where the key contains the Lineorder key and the value
part contains a boolean value. For instance, for Lineorder key = 6, the Map function
produces three pairs (6, 1), (6, 1), and (6, 0) corresponding respectively to the scan of
the join attributes Custkey, Suppkey, and Orderdate. This means, when the Lineorder
key = 6, it satisfies the predicates of CUSTOMER and SUPPLIER dimensions but
does not satisfy the predicate of DATE dimension. Thus, in the Reduce function, the
boolean values belonging to the same key are associated with a "logical AND". The
Lineorder key that keeps the boolean value equal "1" represents the one which satisfies
all query conditions.

The third job uses the output of job 2 (the Lineorder keys satisfy the entire query
predicate) to perform the lowest (least) aggregation of the cube corresponding to
((Custkey, Suppkey, Orderdate), sum(Revenue)). Thus, the Map function uses the keys
obtained by the job 2 in order to select the dimensions identifiers Custkey, Suppkey,
and Orderdate that satisfy all query conditions, and extract the measure values (Revenue) corresponding. The output is a set of pairs of "key/value" where the part of key
contains the identifiers dimensions combination (Custkey, Suppkey, Orderdate) and the
value contains the value of measure (Revenue) corresponding. For each the same key
of the Map function output, the value part is aggregated when de Reduce function is
performed. This operation allows to produce the granularity level corresponding to
((Custkey, Suppkey, Orderdate), Revenue) that we call it R1.

The fourth job uses the output of job 2 to perform the highest (total) aggregation of
the cube corresponding to (ALL, Sum (Revenue)) that we call it R4. Thus, the Map
function uses the Lineorder keys that satisfy the entire query predicate obtained by the
job 2 in order to perform the total aggregation. The output is merged and consolidated
to produce a pairs (ALL, sum(Revenue)) when the Reduce function is performed.

The fifth job uses the output of the third job ((Custkey, Suppkey, Orderdate),
Revenue) to produce the aggregations according to each dimension separately that we
call it R2. Each dimension key is selected separately with the revenue corresponding
when the Map function is performed. The output is used to produce the aggregation of
the sum (revenue) corresponding to (Custkey, ALL, ALL), (ALL, Suppkey, ALL) and
(ALL, ALL, Orderdate) when the Reduce function is performed.

The sixth job uses the output of the third job ((Custkey, Suppkey, Orderdate),
Revenue) to produce the aggregations according to the different dimensions combinations remaining to compose the cube we call the result of this operation R3. For this,
each combination of dimensions keys are selected with the revenue corresponding
when the Map function is performed. The output is used to produce the aggregation of
the sum (revenue) corresponding to (Custkey, Suppkey, ALL), (Custkey, ALL,
Orderdate), and (ALL, Suppkey, Orderdate) when the Reduce function is performed.

The seventh job does not perform any aggregation. It allows to change the identifiers of dimensions that are used with the dimensions attributes cited in the query, and
gathered it to provide the cube. According to our example, at the Map function, the
keys (2, 3, 1) of the Custkey, the keys (1, 2) of the Suppkey, and the keys (01011996,
01121997) are replaced respectively by (Rome, Naples, Milan) of the SUPPLIER

dimension, (Berlin, Munich) of the CUSTOMER dimension, and finally (1996,1997) of the DATE dimension. The output is gathered to produce the OLAP cube when the Reduce function is performed.

5 Implementation and Experiments

In order to implement the MC-CUBE operator in a columnar NoSQL environment using MapReduce, we have put in place a non-relational and distributed storage and processing environment. This environment is based on a private Cloud Computing architecture produced using the Hadoop-2.6.0 and HBase-0.98.8 DBMS, for managing data in a distributed environment. Since HBase DBMS does not have a cube operator to generate the OLAP cubes and compared it to MC-CUBE, we have integrated into this environment HIVE, which is data warehouse software to manage large datasets. Hive provides a SQL like language called HiveQL (Hive Query Language) to query data. HIVE is not column-oriented but, when integrated to HBase allows the data stored in HBase to be handled using HQL and building OLAP cubes [3]. The test environment is a cluster made up of 25 machines (nodes). Each machine has an intel-Core TMi5-3470S CPU@2.90 GHZ processor with 8 GB RAM. These machines operate with the operating system Ubuntu-14.04 and are interconnected by a switched Ethernet 1 Gbps in a local area network. One of these machines is configured to perform the role of Namenode in the HDFS system, the master and the Zookeper[4] of HBase. However, the other machines are configured to be HDFS DataNodes and the HBase RegionServers.

Dataset: we implemented the warehouse benchmark SSB, and we populate it with data samples by using the data generator (SSB-dbgen).

Queries set: we used a set of queries composed by four queries that generate OLAP cubes with a gradually increasing number of dimensions as follow.

Query 1: This is a query allowing a two dimensional OLAP cube to be computed with restrictions on the columns Nation of the CUSTOMER dimension, Nation of the SUPPLIER dimension and Year of the DATE dimension. This query computes the revenue (sum ((Revenue)) at different levels of granularity according to the attributes, City of the CUSTOMER dimension and City of the SUPPLIER dimension.

Query 2: This is a query which allows us to compute the three dimensional OLAP cube with the same restrictions as for the first query. It computes the revenue (sum (Revenue)) at different levels of granularity according to the attributes City of the CUSTOMER dimension, City of the SUPPLIER dimension and Year of the DATE dimension.

Query 3: It is a query allowing a four dimensional OLAP cube to be computed with restrictions on the columns Nation of the CUSTOMER dimension, Nation of the SUPPLIER dimension, Brand1 of the PART dimension and Year of the DATE dimension. It computes the revenue (sum (Revenue)) at different levels of granularity according to the attributes City of the CUSTOMER dimension, City of the SUPPLIER dimension, and Year of the DATE dimension AND Brand1 of the PART dimension.

---

[4] http://hbase.apache.org/0.94/book/zookeeper.html.

Query 4: This is a query which allows us to compute the five dimensional OLAP cube with the same restrictions as for the previous query (query 3). It computes the revenue (sum (Revenue)) at different levels of granularity according to the attributes City of the CUSTOMER dimension, City of the SUPPLIER dimension, and Year and Month of the DATE dimension AND Brand1 of the PART dimension.

To evaluate the performances of the MC-CUBE operator in terms of OLAP cube computation times, we conducted two experiments. The first was to evaluate the MC-CUBE operator by gradually increasing the number of dimensions when computing the OLAP cube. The second evaluates the cube computation time when scaling-up.

5.1   OLAP Cube Computation on a Single-Node Cluster

The objective of this experiment is to empirically evaluate the MC-CUBE operator when faced with variations in the number of dimensions. The comparison between the generation times of OLAP cubes is performed with two to five dimensions on a sample of data comprising 6×10^7 records. The results we obtained are shown in the following Fig. 3.

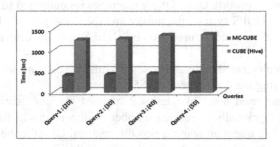

Fig. 3. OLAP cube computations faced with variations in dimensions number.

We observe a slight variation in OLAP cube computation times with the MC-CUBE and CUBE operators when the number of dimensions was increased. However, MC-CUBE shows a better performance than CUBE. Indeed, the CUBE operator records times between 1240 and 1378 s, whereas the MC-CUBE operator records times of between 401 and 456 s. The weakness of the HIVE CUBE operator lies in the strategy used when cube is generated which is similar to CUBE operator of Apache Kylin. Indeed, Hive is row-oriented rather than column-oriented. It uses the metadata of a table that is stored in HBase (column-oriented) and uses relational engine DBMS (row-oriented), which requires building tuples to handle data. Furthermore, Hive CUBE operator uses the vertical approach when the different aggregates that composed the cube are performed. This strategy consists to use the aggregates of the lower level of granularity having the fewest attributes when the aggregates of the above level of granularity are performed. However, MC-CUBE benefits from the column-store, and performs the aggregates of the above levels of granularity, from the one level which is the least aggregated. This allows the MC-CUBE to generate the cube quickly in terms of execution times. From the results obtained, we find that the MC-CUBE operator optimizes the time up to three times when the OLAP cube performed compared with the CUBE operator of HIVE. Thus, it is of interest to evaluate the MC-CUBE behavior when it is scaled up in a distributed environment by varying the number of nodes composing the cluster and the size of the warehouse.

5.2   OLAP Cube Computation on a Multi-node Cluster (Scaling-up)

The purpose of this experiment is to expose the MC-CUBE operator to scaling-up which is the raison of advent of NoSQL data models to store and manage massive data. The experiment involved calculating the execution time for query 2 of Sect. 3-A which computes a three dimensional OLAP cube with three different configurations, with data samples of different sizes (100 GB, 500 GB and 1 TB). The three configurations are a ten-node cluster, an eighteen-node cluster and a twenty-five-node cluster. The results we obtained are shown in the following Fig. 4.

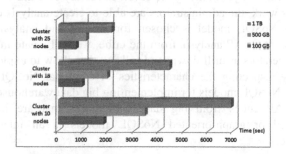

Fig. 4. Result of scalability in a multi-node cluster

We noted that computation times for OLAP cubes of different warehouse sizes decrease as the number of nodes that make up the cluster is increased. It is the 25 nodes cluster which records the best computation times. The difference between the OLAP cube computation times for the different clusters seems more striking for large data warehouses (500 GB and 1 TB) and the benefits of adding nodes to the cluster can be seen as the size of the warehouse increases. For a warehouse size of 100 GB, the increase in the number of nodes reduces the OLAP cube computation time to 1121 s, and for a warehouse size of 1 TB, it reduces the OLAP cube computation time to 4787 s. Thus, the increasing of the number of nodes allows to reduce the time of the cubes computing against the increase of the volume of the data warehouse. Indeed, the HBase DBMS natively adopts data storage and processing system based on the HDFS file and the MapReduce paradigm respectively. The workload, in terms of memory and computation (CPU) as well as storage is distributed across all the machines of the cluster. This presents two advantages: on the one hand, warehouse data storage is physically distributed across the machines (nodes) that make up the cluster. This prevents all tables being subject to a full scan to extract data. Moreover, the OLAP cube computation query is split into sub-processing across all machines of the cluster thus producing sub-results. These sub-results are gathered to produce the final result of the query which in this case corresponds to the OLAP cube. Based on this, it is clear that the MC-CUBE benefits from the addition of the distributed environment of the NoSQL database in computing OLAP cubes.

6 Conclusion

We have proposed in this work MC-CUBE that is an aggregate operator which allows generate OLAP cubes from big data warehouses implemented by using columnar NoSQL model. MC-CUBE takes benefits of column-oriented storage of data when aggregates are performed. In order to take into account the distributed environment for storing data, MC-CUBE uses the MapReduce paradigm to parallelize handling of data and run seven MapReduce jobs to perform the aggregates of different level of granularity that compose the OLAP cube. For materializing the join between facts, and dimensions tables and selecting values that will be used to compute the cube, MC-CUBE performs two jobs among the seven necessary to build the cube.

Thanks to this work, the administrators are able to create analysis contexts (OLAP cubes) when the NoSQL model is chosen for storing and analysis the big data. However, to perform OLAP analysis from the cube, we will create in a short term as perspective, the operators as drill-down, and roll-up, that allow to explore the cube and navigate in it, by respecting the characteristics of columnar NoSQL model. In the context of the use NoSQL models for implementing big data warehouses, we think that building the OLAP cubes from big data warehouses that are implemented via documents-oriented or graph-oriented NoSQL models is an interesting research problem to pursue.

References

1. Abadi, D.J., Madden, S.R., Hachem, N.: Column-stores vs. row-stores: how different are they really? In: Proceedings of the ACM SIGMOD International Conference on Management of Data, pp 967–980. ACM, New York (2008)
2. Abelló, A., Ferrarons, F., Romero, O.: Building cubes with MapReduce. In: ACM International Workshop on Data Warehousing and OLAP, pp. 17–24. ACM, New York (2011)
3. Apache Hive (2014). https://cwiki.apache.org/confluence/display/Hive/HBaseIntegration
4. Barber, R., Bendel, P., Czech, M., Draese, O., Ho, F., Hrle, N., Idreos, S., Kim, M.S., Koeth, O., Lee, J.G.: Business analytics in (a) blink. IEEE Data Eng. Bull. 35(1), 9–14 (2012)
5. Beyer K.S., Ramakrishnan, R.: Bottom-up computation of sparse and Iceberg CUBE. In: Proceedings of ACM SIGMOD International Conference on Management of Data, pp. 359–370. ACM, New York (1999)
6. Bhogal, J., Choksi, I.: Handling big data using NoSQL. In: IEEE International Conference on Advanced Information Networking and Applications Workshops, pp. 393–398. IEEE Computer Society, Washington, D.C. (2015)

7. Cattell, R.: Scalable SQL and NoSQL data stores. SIGMOD Rec. **39**, 12–27 (2011)
8. Chang, F., Dean, J., Ghemawat, S., Hsieh, W.C., Wallach, D.A., Burrows, M., Chandra, T., Fikes, A., Gruber, R.E.: Bigtable: a distributed storage system for structured data. In: Symposium on Operating Systems Design and Implementation, Berkeley, USA, vol. 7, pp. 15–25 (2006)
9. Chavan, V., Phursule, R.N.: Survey paper on big data. Int. J. Comput. Sci. Inf. Technol. **5** (6), 7932–7939 (2014)
10. Chevalier, R., El Malki, M., Kopliku, A., Teste, O., Tournier, R.: Implementation of multidimensional databases in column-oriented NoSQL systems. In: Advances in Databases and Information Systems, Poitiers, France, pp. 79–91 (2015)
11. Dean, J., Ghemawat, S.: MapReduce: simplified data processing on large clusters. In: Proceedings of the 6th Conference on Symposium on Operating Systems Design and Implementation, Berkeley, CA, USA, vol. 6, pp. 137–149 (2014)
12. Dehdouh, K., Bentayeb, F., Boussaïd, O., Kabachi, N.: Columnar NoSQL CUBE: aggregation operator for columnar NoSQL data warehouse. In: IEEE International Conference on Systems, Man, and Cybernetics, San Diego, USA, pp. 3828–3833(2014)
13. Dehdouh, K., Bentayeb, F., Boussaïd, O., Kabachi, N.: Using the column oriented NoSQL model for implementing big data warehouses. In: International Conference on Parallel and Distributed Processing Techniques, Las Vegas, USA, pp. 469–475 (2015)
14. Färber, F., Cha, S.K., Primsch, J., Bornhövd, C., Sigg, S., Lehner, W.: SAP HANA database: data management for modern business applications. SIGMOD Rec. **40**, 45–51 (2012)
15. Gray, J., Chaudhuri, S., Bosworth, A., Layman, A., Reichart, D., Venkatrao, M., Pellow, F., Pirahesh, H.: Data cube: a relational aggregation operator generalizing group-by, cross-tab, and sub-totals. Data Min. Knowl. Discov. **1**, 29–53 (1997)
16. Idreos, S., Groffen, F., Nes, N., Manegold, S., Mullender, S., Kersten, M.: MonetDB: two decades of research in column-oriented database architectures. IEEE Data Eng. Bull. **35**, 40–45 (2012)
17. Imhoff, C., Geiger, J.G., Galemmo, N.: Relational Modeling and Data Warehouse Design. Wiley, New York (2003)
18. Lamb, A., Fuller, M., Varadarajan, R., Tran, N., Vandiver, B., Doshi, L., Bear, C.: The vertica analytic database: C-store 7 years later. Proc. VLDB Endow. **5**(12), 1790–1801 (2012)
19. Larson, P.-Å., Hanson, E.N., Price, S.L.: Columnar storage in SQL server 2012. IEEE Data Eng. Bull. **35**, 15–20 (2012)
20. Rabuzin, K., Modrušan, N.: Business intelligence and column-oriented databases. In: Proceedings of the Central European Conference on Information and Intelligent Systems, Varaždin Croatia, pp. 12–16 (2014)
21. Ślezak, D., Eastwood, V.: Data warehouse technology by infobright. In: Binnig, C., Dageville, B. (eds.) Proceedings of the 2009 ACM SIGMOD International Conference on Management of Data, New York, NY, USA, pp. 841–846 (2009)
22. Ślezak, D., Wróblewski, J., Eastwood, V., Synak, P.: Brighthouse: an analytic data warehouse for ad-hoc queries. Proc. VLDB Endow. **1**, 1337–1345 (2008)
23. Zukowski, M., Wiel, M.V., Boncz, P.: Vectorwise: a vectorized analytical DBMS. In: IEEE 28th International Conference on Data Engineering (ICDE), Washington, pp. 1349–1350 (2012)

On Representing Interval Measures by Means of Functions

Gastón Bakkalian[1,2]([✉]), Christian Koncilia[3], and Robert Wrembel[1]

[1] Poznan University of Technology, Poznań, Poland
gaston.bakkalianlapachian@doctorate.put.poznan.pl,
robert.wrembel@cs.put.poznan.pl
[2] Aalborg University, Aalborg, Denmark
[3] Klagenfurt University, Klagenfurt, Austria
koncilia@isys.uni-klu.ac.at

Abstract. Multiple applications e.g., energy consumption meters, temperature or pressure sensors, generate series of discrete data. Such data have two characteristics, namely: they are naturally ordered by time and are frequently represented as intervals. Most of the research contributions, commercial software, or prototypes either (1) allow to analyze set oriented data, neglecting their order and duration or (2) represent intervals as discrete collection of points stored in tables. In this paper, based on our interval OLAP data model, we propose a method for representing interval data by means of functions and show that it is feasible to aggregate such data along hierarchical dimensions - in an OLAP-like style. To this end, we implemented a micro-prototype using Oracle PL/SQL. Its experimental evaluation showed that the concept is more space efficient and offers better performance than traditional approaches for some classes of analytical queries.

1 Introduction

Ubiquitous devices and applications generate huge amounts of data that are events that last either an instant or a given time period. Events typically have a strict order, thus possess a sequential nature. Sequential data can be categorized either as *time point-based* or *interval-based* [26].

Examples of applications that generate sequential data include: workflow systems, Web logs, RFID devices, public transportation infrastructures, industrial and household sensor networks. In workflow systems, objects arrive to tasks at certain points in time and they are processed within a certain time period. By analyzing workflow log data one is able to discover bottlenecks and idle times. In Web log analysis, especially for e-commerce, one may be interested in knowing the navigation path leading to a product purchase. RFID technology is widely used in supply chain management (e.g., just-in-time delivery). Here, by analyzing sequences of events generated by the RFID devices, one is able to optimize product transportation routes. In advanced public transportation infrastructures [21], passenger tracking records are automatically generated by various devices.

© Springer International Publishing Switzerland 2016
L. Bellatreche et al. (Eds.): MEDI 2016, LNCS 9893, pp. 180–193, 2016.
DOI: 10.1007/978-3-319-45547-1_15

These records can be used for analyzing the most frequently used routes to help discovering route bottlenecks, station bottlenecks, and rush hours in various districts. In industrial sensor networks, numerous sensors supply their data about some physical characteristics, such as vibration, temperature, pressure, and humidity. In household networks, intelligent meters gather data about temperature, thermal, and electrical energy consumed. Based on the chronologically ordered data, patterns of behavior may be discovered. Multiple of these sequential data have a continuous nature with respect to time, such as energy consumption, temperature, or pressure. Such data can be represented by means of intervals. Within a given interval, a measured value can be constant or can fluctuate.

The research approaches, prototypes, and commercial systems mainly represent interval data as discrete collection of points stored in tables, e.g., [1, 10, 13, 17, 21, 28, 30, 33, 36]. Such representations have some drawbacks, i.e., (1) do not allow to find a value between the beginning and end of an interval, (2) can perform worse than alternative approaches, and (3) queries are typically complex. An alternative approach to represent intervals is to use functions. To the best of our knowledge, two such approaches have been proposed so far. In [35] continuous data are represented by function databases. In [27], a model-based database system is proposed. It stores a pool of models to generate approximate answers much faster than getting exact answers. Nonetheless, none of these approaches considers processing interval data represented by functions in an OLAP-like style.

Paper Contribution. In this paper, we show the proof of concept of our interval data model [17]. In this model, intervals are represented as mathematical functions stored in an *interval function table*. If needed, this table can be joined with regular relational tables to fetch descriptive data. When posing queries, to get either values that already exist in the raw data or interpolated data, we set aside the raw data and use directly the mathematical functions. Linear and nonlinear functions may be used in our approach. Moreover, intervals of a variable length may be represented.

As a proof of concept, we implemented the approach in Oracle PL/SQL and evaluated it experimentally using energy consumption data as a use case. The experiments showed that our approach has a better performance (for some classes of queries) than the traditional approaches that represent intervals as discrete collections of points and requires less storage.

Paper Organization. Section 2 outlines related work. Section 3 includes a running example based on energy consumption. Section 4 briefly outlines our interval data model, Sect. 5 presents its implementation, and Sect. 6 shows its experimental evaluation. Section 7 concludes the paper and outlines future work.

2   Related Work

Research related to the work presented in this paper includes: (1) analyzing temporal data, (2) analyzing sequential data, (3) complex event processing,

(4) warehousing sequential data, and (5) function databases. In this section, due to space limit, we only outline these approaches.

Analyzing Temporal Data. Temporal data are stamped with begin and end validity times in order to distinguished versions of data valid within a given time period. This functionality is supported by temporal databases, e.g., [14,16,34] and temporal data warehouses, e.g., [11,25]. Timestamps associated with temporal data at some extent resemble begins and ends of intervals. However, in temporal techniques the focus is on tracking the evolution of data in time and inferring in queries valid data to use within a given time period.

Analyzing Sequential Data. There are a few data models supporting sequential data. Some of them are based on an extended relational data model [28–33] and some - on a dedicated array model [18,37], with dedicated storage and operators for processing sequences.

Complex Event Processing. The approaches in this category focus on analyzing data within a given time window and on discovering patterns in data, e.g., [15,19,20], by means of SQL-like languages.

Warehousing Sequential Data. [21] focuses on data structures and algorithms for searching patterns in sequences. To this end, sequence cuboids are build to materialize answers to the so-called pattern-based aggregate queries. The model was further extended in [9,10] with an algorithm for supporting pattern-based aggregate queries. [12,13] focused on warehousing RFID data in a relational storage. The authors proposed a few techniques for reducing the size of sequential data, for constructing RFID cuboids, and for computing higher level cuboids from the lower level ones. [8] showed a high level overview of another RFID warehouse, without providing details on its internals. [6] presented a dedicated data model for OLAP-like processing sequential data and [5] showed a SQL-like query language implementation, based on this model. In the area of processing interval data, few approaches have been proposed so far [22,23], where a query language is outlined. It is an extension of SQL and the select statement works in a multidimensional data model with measures and hierarchical dimensions.

Commercial and Open-Source Systems. Teradata Aster supports a query language called SQL-MapReduce that includes the nPath clause applied to analyzing sequences [1]. Oracle together with IBM proposed an ANSI SQL standard for finding patterns within sequences stored in tables [24]. To this end, the MATCH_RECOGNIZE clause was defined. It allows to search for patterns, define patterns and pattern variables. From an open-source software, Apache Spark [2] allows to process stream data in order to detect interesting events and patterns. InfluxDB [3] is a dedicated system for processing time series, with an SQL-like language. OpenTSDB [4] is another time series storage, based on HBase. It allows to analyze data by means of a script language.

Function Databases. An alternative approach to storing data is to represent them by mathematical models - implemented as functions. In [35] functions are treated as first class citizens and can be used in queries. The results of function executions are available by a relational interface called function views. In [27], the authors proposed a model-based database system. The system manages models for generating approximate query answers faster than querying original raw data. The models are created from raw data and stored in the database along with the data. Upon receiving a query, the system decides whether to use an adequate model or to query raw data. To this end, the system stores statistics of queries that were executed in the past.

3 Motivation

The motivation of this research comes from mini energy grids that for a few years have been developed in Poland and other European countries. A mini energy grid is used to produce energy for a local community (e.g., a district or a town). It should be self-sufficient, i.e., it should produce an exact amount of energy that would be used by the community, so that energy is neither delivered to nor acquired from a state network. To this end, a thorough measurement of energy produced and consumed by a mini grid is needed. In order to measure energy consumption of a community, every household is equipped with multiple intelligent meters, e.g., thermal energy consumption meter on every radiator and electrical energy consumption on household appliances. In this paper we use thermal energy consumption scenario as a use case.

One technique of measuring thermal energy delivered to a radiator is based on measuring the temperature of the radiator and the temperature of the air in a room. Based on the difference between these two temperatures, the energy is calculated. In this paper we assume that the energy has already been calculated by a smart meter and sent to a database.

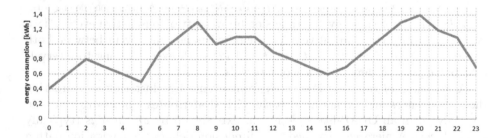

Fig. 1. Energy delivered to a radiator within 24 h

In our setting, energy measurements delivered by a smart meter are called events. For example, Fig. 1 shows a daily consumption of energy by a radiator in a house, assuming that every hour a smart meter delivers a measurement. Event $e_{01:00}$ (at 01:00 am) reported energy usage of 0.6 kWh, event $e_{02:00}$ (at 02:00 am) reported usage of 0.8 kWh. Events $e_{01:00}$ and $e_{02:00}$ constitute an interval,

Table 1. Energy consumption - smart meter data corresponding to Fig. 1

room_num	floor_num	building	city	smart_meter	service_provider	event_time	energy
100	1	Stary Browar	Poznan	SM_1	Polish Energy Group	2016.02.20 00:00:00	0.4
100	1	Stary Browar	Poznan	SM_1	Polish Energy Group	2016.02.20 01:00:00	0.6
100	1	Stary Browar	Poznan	SM_1	Polish Energy Group	2016.02.20 02:00:00	0.8
100	1	Stary Browar	Poznan	SM_1	Polish Energy Group	2016.02.20 03:00:00	0.7
100	1	Stary Browar	Poznan	SM_1	Polish Energy Group	2016.02.20 04:00:00	0.6
100	1	Stary Browar	Poznan	SM_1	Polish Energy Group	2016.02.20 05:00:00	0.5
100	1	Stary Browar	Poznan	SM_1	Polish Energy Group	2016.02.20 06:00:00	0.9
100	1	Stary Browar	Poznan	SM_1	Polish Energy Group	2016.02.20 07:00:00	1.1
100	1	Stary Browar	Poznan	SM_1	Polish Energy Group	2016.02.20 08:00:00	1.3
100	1	Stary Browar	Poznan	SM_1	Polish Energy Group	2016.02.20 09:00:00	1.0
100	1	Stary Browar	Poznan	SM_1	Polish Energy Group	2016.02.20 10:00:00	1.1
100	1	Stary Browar	Poznan	SM_1	Polish Energy Group	2016.02.20 11:00:00	1.1
100	1	Stary Browar	Poznan	SM_1	Polish Energy Group	2016.02.20 12:00:00	0.9
100	1	Stary Browar	Poznan	SM_1	Polish Energy Group	2016.02.20 13:00:00	0.8
100	1	Stary Browar	Poznan	SM_1	Polish Energy Group	2016.02.20 14:00:00	0.7

denoted as i_{01-02}. A sample data reported by the smart meter (corresponding to the chart in Fig. 1 until event $e_{14:00}$) are shown in Table 1.

4   Interval Data Model: I-OLAP

This paper is based on an interval data model, detailed in our previous contribution [17]. The model is based on the following components: *events and its attributes, dimensions, hierarchies, and dimension members, intervals, sequences of intervals*, and *iCubes*, as visualized in Fig. 2.

Events are represented by tuples in the original transactional database. In our running example, the first $e_{00:00}$ is mapped to tuple (cf. Table 1)

$(100, 1,' Stary\ Browar',' Poznan', SM_1,' Polish\ Energy\ Group', 2016.02.2000 : 00 : 00, 0.4)$.

Intervals are defined by the time slot between two consecutive events. Two events e_1 and e_2 are consecutive if: (1) there exists no other event between both events, i.e. $\nexists e_i \in S : e_1.t \leq e_i.t \leq e_2.t$ and (2) both events belong to intervals that belong to the same sequence of intervals.

A *sequence of intervals* is created from events by clustering and ordering them. Sequences and events have distinguished attributes - *measures* that can be analyzed in an OLAP-like style in contexts set up by *dimensions* (typically hierarchical). A hierarchy assigned to a dimension defines the navigation path a user may use to perform roll-up and drill-down operations.

Processing of sequential data is performed by means of *operations* on an *iCube*. The *iCube* consists of sequences of intervals organized by dimensions. Moreover, two types of functions are distinguished in the model, namely: *compute value functions* and *fact creating functions*. The first one is used to derive/estimate values from two given consecutive events, whereas the second one is used to create facts that stem from sequences or intervals but not from events.

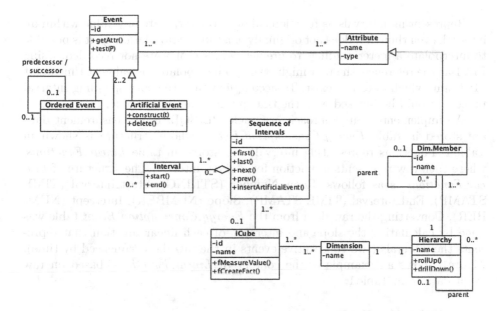

Fig. 2. The I-OLAP metamodel [17]

The well-known operations from traditional data warehouses, i.e., Roll-Up and Drill-Down [7] enable users to analyze data at different levels of granularity. For instance, a user may start analyzing an average energy consumption for the whole building in a given period of time, e.g., an hour. By using the Drill-Down operation, he/she may then switch from level *Building* to level *Floor*, to analyze the average energy consumption of each floor. In our running example, he/she may then switch from level *Floor* to *Room*, to analyze data on the level with the finest granularity of the *Location* dimension. Moreover, he/she could Roll-Up an average energy consumption of rooms, floors, or a building from the finest granularity of the *Time* dimension to a coarser granularity, e.g. from *Minute* to *Hour* and to *Day*.

5   Implementation

The concept of functions plays an essential role in our approach as they represent every single interval, allowing us to reach a comprehensive representation of sequences of intervals, setting aside the raw data. The functions are store in the *Linear_Functions* table. The whole sequences are then represented by a piecewise model, where every row of the *Linear_Functions* table represents a different function, hence, a different interval. Each piece of the model is a continuous function. For simplicity reasons and only as a proof of the concept, in our running example to represent intervals we use linear functions of type $y = ax + b$ (one dependent and one independent variable), but any type of function is allowed in our solution.

Representing intervals as functions allows to interpolate any value within an interval, even though it does not originally exist in the raw data, e.g., it is possible to interpolate a meter readings to predict values that were not recorded. Using Fig. 1 as the reference, the user might want to interpolate the value at time point 01:30 am, which does not exist. To accomplish this, the corresponding interval function would be invoked with the time point as an input value.

We implemented our approach in Oracle PL/SQL. Raw measurement data are stored in table *Energy_Consumption_Event*, whose structure is shown in Table 1. Functions representing intervals are stored in table *Linear_Functions*, where each row represents a function for a given interval. The structure of *Linear_Functions* is as follows: Room_Number (STRING), Start_Interval (TIME STAMP), End_Interval (TIME STAMP), Slope (NUMBER), Intercept (NUMBER). Converting the raw data from the *Energy_Consumption_Event* table was done by calculating the slope and intercept of each linear function that represents the intervals (two consecutive events in the raw data sequenced by time). Figure 3 shows an example of the content of *Linear_Functions*, based on raw event data from Table 1.

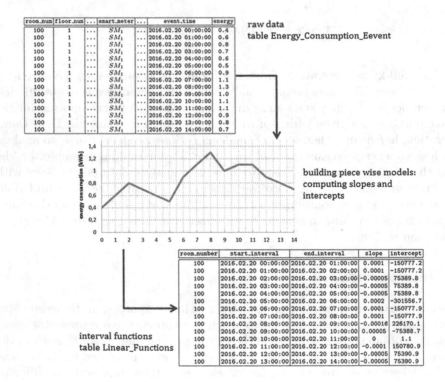

Fig. 3. Interval Function table example

It is important to notice, that each single function that represents an interval, implicitly represents an infinite set of values (measurements) fitting the curve of the function (line in our case), where each measurement is computed for each time point within a given interval. Since it is impossible to output an infinite set of values, in the current implementation when we query a time range (within an interval or including more than one interval), we interpolate the start and end value of each interval covered by the time range, represented by the linear functions, and we use those values to perform the aggregations. It would be part of the future work to develop a mechanism able to establish a closed form representation set by the user, similar to the gridding technique proposed in [35].

6   Experimental Evaluation

6.1   Settings

The **goal of the evaluation** was to compare the functional representation of intervals to its standard row-like representation with respect to: (1) query performance and (2) occupied disk space. To this end, the set of the 6 following **test queries** was defined:

- Q1: Interpolate energy consumption (a value that does not exist in the raw data) at a given time point for a specific office.
- Q2: Aggregate an interpolated total amount of energy consumption (a value that does not exist in the raw data) at a given time point for a given floor, i.e., roll-up energy consumption of each office into energy consumption of a floor.
- Q3: Find an office with the lowest energy consumption within a given time range.
- Q4: Find an office with the lowest average energy consumption within a given time range.
- Q5: For each building find the total energy consumption within a given time range.
- Q6: For each floor find the average energy consumption per office within a given time range.

In each experiment we compared our approach, i.e., representing intervals by means of functions, against three **competitors** - alternative approaches, which we named base lines. The alternative approaches consist in querying directly raw data, as follows:

- *Base Line 1* - it queries the raw data when the energy consumption values are already known. Otherwise, it calculates the slope and intercept of the linear function on the fly (using a PL/SQL function) for a specific time point and then interpolates the value for the time point given.
- *Base Line 2* - it works analogously to *Base Line 1*, but instead of calculating the slope and intercept on the fly, it uses an auxiliary table that stores the data required by the linear function – start and end of the interval represented by the function, and the energy consumption values that belong to them – to calculate and store the slope and the intercept.
- *Base Line 3* - it works analogously to *Base Line 2*, but instead of storing the data in an auxiliary table, it keeps everything in memory.

We tested the elapsed execution times of our implementation and base lines, running queries *Q1–Q6*. *Q3–Q6* analyzed data in two different time windows, i.e., 1 month and 1 year. We used a real-world energy consumption data set[1], where the original records have an interval length of 30 min, but we randomly modified the intervals length to show that our approach is not fixed to intervals of the same length. We used a sample raw data of 400,000 rows. Each test was ran 10 times and the average times with standard deviations are shown in the figures.

The test system was installed on an Intel Core i7 2.40 GHz processor with 8 GB of main memory, running a 64-bit Windows 8.1. The implementation was done in Oracle 12c ES.

6.2 Test Results

The performance of queries *Q1* and *Q2* (interpolating non-existing energy consumption values), is shown in Fig. 4. It can be noticed that our approach (denoted as *Interval Functions*) is much faster than the base line approaches and this is even more noticeable in Q2 (about 70 times faster) where the SUM function was applied. The interval function approach is much faster since it supports a straightforward interpolation, by solely executing the function itself (y = ax + b in this case). Whereas the base line approaches need to first build an approximation model and then apply it to a given query.

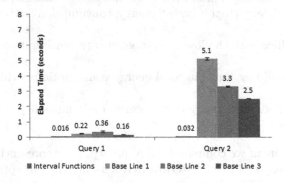

Fig. 4. Performance comparison for *Q1* and *Q2*

The performance characteristics of queries *Q3* and *Q4* (aggregating energy consumption within a given time range) for a time window of 1 month and 1 year are shown in Fig. 5. It reveals that the interval function approach offers better performance than the base line approaches for 1 month time window, although the processing time increased as compared to the performance visualized in Fig. 4. It is because the interval functions have to first compute values along a specific time range (one month in this case) which implies a bigger number of

---

[1] http://publicdata.eu/dataset/home-office-energy-and-water-consumption.

interpolations (not a single time point value) and then the interpolated values are aggregated. Whereas the base line approaches mainly query directly the raw data. Still, representing intervals as functions yields a better performance.

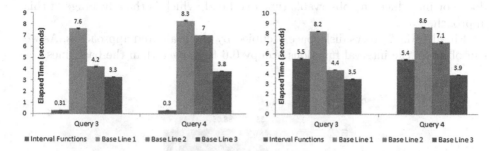

Fig. 5. Query 3 and 4 results (1 month vs 1 year)

As it can also be observed from Fig. 5, within a 1 year time range, the elapsed execution time of all the baselines barely increased, whereas the execution time of the interval functions had a bigger increase. This behavior is caused by a need to interpolate values along an entire year for all offices, while the base lines only needed to scan raw data and aggregate them within a larger number of rows. Nevertheless, we consider this time increase acceptable taking into account that the time range involved is quite big and that the way we represent intervals has the advantage of being more intuitive, interpolation of values is done straight-forward, and the amount of lines of code is considerably reduced. Moreover, the number of interpolations can be reduced by increasing time granularity, thus reducing the computation time. This issue will be investigated in the nearest future.

Figure 6 shows the performance of queries $Q5$ and $Q6$ (rolling-up aggregation of energy consumption within time range).

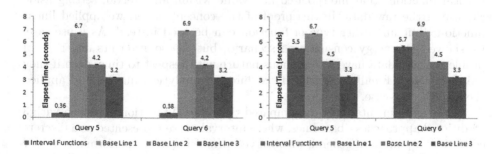

Fig. 6. Query 5 and 6 results (1 month vs 1 year)

The charts show the same type of behavior as for $Q3$ and $Q4$, i.e., elapsed execution times increased for the interval functions with respect to the increase of a time window from 1 month to 1 year. On the contrary, the performance of the base lines remained mainly the same. Since the execution of the roll-up queries with interval functions took approximately the same amount of time as the execution of *Q3* and *Q4*, we can conclude that rolling-up interval functions does not introduce any observable time overhead, which is the advantage of this approach.

Finally, Fig. 7 shows disk space occupied by the evaluated approaches. As we can observe, the interval functions occupy 0.6 less space than the base lines.

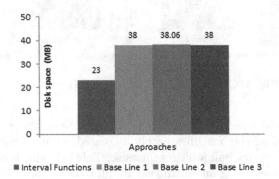

Fig. 7. Storage space comparison

7   Conclusions and Future Work

In this paper, we outlined the implementation of our I-OLAP data model. I-OLAP was designed to represent interval data by means of functions and to aggregate such data in an OLAP-like style. We modeled intervals as mathematical functions that interpolated any value within an interval, setting aside the use of the raw data. In this proof of the concept paper, we applied linear functions, but any other type of function can be used instead. As a use-case, we showed an energy consumption scenario, but the solution fits any type of problem where data have a continuous nature with respect to time, even if they are discretized. Finally, we defined six different analytical queries and applied them to the use-case.

In the experimental part we compared the interval function approach with 3 traditional approaches - base lines, where intervals were represented as a discrete collection of points. In general, we observed promising query performance of our approach. However, in some cases there was a slight time deterioration for 1 year time range with respect to the base lines. Additionally, the interval functions occupy much less space than the base lines.

We argue that representing interval data by means of interval functions has the following advantages:

- a user can query data at time points that do not exist - in this case an interval function interpolates the value;
- a user can predict values in the future - in this case an interval function represents a prediction model;
- for multiple queries including time windows the interval functions offer better performance than the traditional approaches - the performance can further be optimized by selecting right time granules at which the interval functions compute their values;
- queries are more compact and simple as compared to standard queries (not shown in this paper due to space limits);
- it needs much less storage than the traditional approaches - the space usage can further be reduced by defining the interval functions for larger time intervals;
- rolling-up the interval functions along a dimension does not incur any noticeable time overhead.

Future work will focus on:

- incorporating into the model non-linear functions;
- analyzing and developing methods and structures for query optimization and compression techniques, mainly to enhance the performance for large time ranges;
- defining a fully functional SQL-like query language to build interval functions and use them in queries; some examples of queries would include: CREATE INTERVAL FUNCTION MODEL FROM RAW DATA AS TYPE LINEAR AT (TS, TE) or SELECT VALUE FROM INTERVAL FUNCTION MODEL AT (T);
- developing a technique similar to gridding [35] for reducing the number of interval function calls.

Acknowledgement. The research of Gastón Bakkalian has been funded by the European Commission through the "Erasmus Mundus Joint Doctorate Information Technologies for Business Intelligence Doctoral College (IT4BI-DC)". The research of Robert Wrembel has been funded by the Polish National Science Center, grant "Analytical processing and mining of sequential data: models, algorithms, and data structures".

References

1. Aster   nPath.   http://developer.teradata.com/aster/articles/aster-npath-guide. Accessed 15 Jan 2016
2. Big data processing with Apache Spark. http://www.infoq.com/articles/apache-spark-introduction. Accessed 6 Mar 2016
3. InfluxDB - Time Series Data Storage. https://influxdata.com/time-series-platform/influxdb/. Accessed 15 Mar 2016
4. Open TSDB. http://opentsdb.net/index.html. Accessed 15 Mar 2016

5. Bebel, B., Cichowicz, T., Morzy, T., Rytwiński, F., Wrembel, R., Koncilia, C.: Sequential data analytics by means of Seq-SQL language. In: Chen, Q., Hameurlain, A., Toumani, F., Wagner, R., Decker, H. (eds.) DEXA 2015. LNCS, vol. 9261, pp. 416–431. Springer, Heidelberg (2015)
6. Bębel, B., Morzy, M., Morzy, T., Królikowski, Z., Wrembel, R.: OLAP-like analysis of time point-based sequential data. In: Castano, S., Vassiliadis, P., Lakshmanan, L.V.S., Lee, M.L. (eds.) ER 2012 Workshops 2012. LNCS, vol. 7518, pp. 153–161. Springer, Heidelberg (2012)
7. Chaudhuri, S., Dayal, U.: An overview of data warehousing and OLAP technology. ACM SIGMOD Rec. **26**(1), 65–74 (1997)
8. Chawathe, S.S., Krishnamurthy, V., Ramachandran, S., Sarma, S.: Managing RFID data. In: Proceedings of International Conference on Very Large Data Bases, pp. 1189–1195 (2004)
9. Chui, C.K., Kao, B., Lo, E., Cheung, D.: S-OLAP: an olap system for analyzing sequence data. In: Proceedings of ACM SIGMOD International Conference on Management of Data, pp. 1131–1134. ACM (2010)
10. Chui, C.K., Lo, E., Kao, B., Ho, W.-S.: Supporting ranking pattern-based aggregate queries in sequence data cubes. In: Proceedings of ACM Conference on Information and Knowledge Management, pp. 997–1006. ACM (2009)
11. Eder, J., Koncilia, C., Morzy, T.: The COMET metamodel for temporal data warehouses. In: Pidduck, A.B., Mylopoulos, J., Woo, C.C., Ozsu, M.T. (eds.) CAiSE 2002. LNCS, vol. 2348, pp. 83–99. Springer, Heidelberg (2002)
12. Gonzalez, H., Han, J., Li, X.: FlowCube: constructing RFID flowcubes for multi-dimensional analysis of commodity flows. In: Proceedings of International Conference on Very Large Data Bases, pp. 834–845. VLDB Endowment (2006)
13. Gonzalez, H., Han, J., Li, X., Klabjan, D.: Warehousing and analyzing massive RFID data sets. In: Proceedings of International Conference on Data Engineering, p. 83 (2006)
14. Goralwalla, I.A., Tansel, A.U., Ozsu, M.T.: Experimenting with temporal relational databases. In: Proceedings of ACM Conference on Information and Knowledge Management, pp. 296–303 (1995)
15. Han, J., Chen, Y., Dong, G., Pei, J., Wah, B.W., Wang, J., Cai, Y.D.: Stream Cube: an architecture for multi-dimensional analysis of data streams. Distrib. Parallel Databases **18**(2), 173–197 (2005)
16. Jensen, C.S., Lomet, D.B.: Transaction timestamping in (temporal) databases. In: Proceedings of International Conference on Very Large Data Bases, pp. 441–450 (2001)
17. Koncilia, C., Morzy, T., Wrembel, R., Eder, J.: Interval OLAP: analyzing interval data. In: Bellatreche, L., Mohania, M.K. (eds.) DaWaK 2014. LNCS, vol. 8646, pp. 233–244. Springer, Heidelberg (2014)
18. Lerner, A., Shasha, D.: Aquery: query language for ordered data, optimization techniques, and experiments. In: Proceedings of International Conference on Very Large Data Bases, pp. 345–356 (2003)
19. Liu, M., Rundensteiner, E., Greenfield, K., Gupta, C., Wang, S., Ari, I., Mehta, A.: E-Cube: multi-dimensional event sequence analysis using hierarchical pattern query sharing. In: Proceedings of ACM SIGMOD International Conference on Management of Data, pp. 889–900. ACM (2011)
20. Liu, M., Rundensteiner, E.A.: Event sequence processing: new models and optimization techniques. In: Proceedings of SIGMOD PhD Workshop on Innovative Database Research, pp. 7–12 (2010)

21. Lo, E., Kao, B., Ho, W.-S., Lee, S.D., Chui, C.K., Cheung, D.W.: OLAP on sequence data. In: Proceedings of ACM SIGMOD International Conference on Management of Data, pp. 649–660 (2008)

22. Meisen, P., Keng, D., Meisen, T., Recchioni, M., Jeschke, S.: Bitmap-based online analytical processing of time interval data. In: International Conference on Information Technology-New Generations, pp. 20–26 (2015)

23. Meisen, P., Keng, D., Meisen, T., Recchioni, M., Jeschke, S.: TIDAQL: a query language enabling on-line analytical processing of time interval data. In: Proceedings of International Conference on Enterprise Information Systems (2015)

24. Melton, J., (ed.): Working draft database language SQL - part 15: Row pattern recognition (SQL/RPR). ANSI INCITS DM32.2-2011-00005 (2011)

25. Mendelzon, A.O., Vaisman, A.A.: Temporal queries in OLAP. In: Proceedings of International Conference on Very Large Data Bases, pp. 242–253 (2000)

26. Mörchen, F.: Unsupervised pattern mining from symbolic temporal data. SIGKDD Explor. Newsl. 9(1), 41–55 (2007)

27. Perera, K.S., Hahmann, M., Lehner, W., Pedersen, T.B., Thomsen, C.: Modeling large time series for efficient approximate query processing. In: Liu, A., Ishikawa, Y., Qian, T., Nutanong, S., Cheema, M.A. (eds.) DASFAA 2015 Workshops. LNCS, vol. 9052, pp. 190–204. Springer, Heidelberg (2015)

28. Ramakrishnan, R., Donjerkovic, D., Ranganathan, A., Beyer, K.S., Krishnaprasad, M.: SRQL: Sorted relational query language. In: Proceedings of International Conference on Scientific and Statistical Database Management, pp. 84–95 (1998)

29. Sadri, R., Zaniolo, C., Zarkesh, A., Adibi, J.: Optimization of sequence queries in database systems. In: Proceedings of ACM SIGMOD-SIGACT-SIGART Symposium on Principles of Database Systems, pp. 71–81 (2001)

30. Sadri, R., Zaniolo, C., Zarkesh, A., Adibi, J.: Expressing and optimizing sequence queries in database systems. ACM Trans. Database Syst. 29(2), 282–318 (2004)

31. Seshadri, P., Livny, M., Ramakrishnan, R.: Sequence query processing. ACM SIGMOD Rec. 23(2), 430–441 (1994)

32. Seshadri, P., Livny, M., Ramakrishnan, R.: SEQ: a model for sequence databases. In: Proceedings of International Conference on Data Engineering, pp. 232–239 (1995)

33. Seshadri, P., Livny, M., Ramakrishnan, R.: The design and implementation of a sequence database system. In: Proceedings of International Conference on Very Large Data Bases, pp. 99–110 (1996)

34. Snodgrass, R. (ed.): The TSQL2 Temporal Query Language. Kluwer Academic Publishers, Norwell (1995)

35. Thiagarajan, A., Madden, S.: Querying continuous functions in a database system. In: Proceedings of ACM SIGMOD International Conference on Management of Data, pp. 791–804 (2008)

36. Witkowski, A.: Analyze this! Analytical power in SQL, more than you ever dreamt of. Oracle Open World (2012)

37. Zhang, Y., Kersten, M., Manegold, S.: SciQL: array data processing inside an rdbms. In: Proceedings of ACM SIGMOD International Conference on Management of Data, pp. 1049–1052 (2013)

Automated Data Pre-processing
via Meta-learning

Besim Bilalli[1]([✉]), Alberto Abelló[1], Tomàs Aluja-Banet[1], and Robert Wrembel[2]

[1] Universitat Politécnica de Catalunya, Barcelona, Spain
{bbilalli,aabello}@essi.upc.edu, tomas.aluja@upc.edu
[2] Poznan University of Technology, Poznan, Poland
robert.wrembel@cs.put.poznan.pl

Abstract. A data mining algorithm may perform differently on datasets with different characteristics, e.g., it might perform better on a dataset with continuous attributes rather than with categorical attributes, or the other way around. As a matter of fact, a dataset usually needs to be pre-processed. Taking into account all the possible pre-processing operators, there exists a staggeringly large number of alternatives and non-experienced users become overwhelmed. We show that this problem can be addressed by an automated approach, leveraging ideas from meta-learning. Specifically, we consider a wide range of data pre-processing techniques and a set of data mining algorithms. For each data mining algorithm and selected dataset, we are able to predict the transformations that improve the result of the algorithm on the respective dataset. Our approach will help non-expert users to more effectively identify the transformations appropriate to their applications, and hence to achieve improved results.

1   Introduction

Recently, more and more non-experts are using data mining tools to perform data analysis. These users require off the shelf solutions that will assist them throughout the process. The process itself, a.k.a. knowledge discovery, consists of several steps, such as *data selection, data pre-processing, data mining*, and *evaluation* or *interpretation* [5], see Fig. 1. One of the most important steps of this process is the data pre-processing step. Data pre-processing is so important that usually 50–80% of analysis time is spent on it [13]. The reason for this, is that, a properly prepared/pre-processed dataset yields better results. One can apply the best learning algorithm, but if the data is not well-prepared, the algorithm may perform poorly (e.g., bad predictive accuracy) [3].

Now, if the data pre-processing is so important and in addition it needs to be performed by a non-expert user, then a way must be found such that pre-processing becomes easy, i.e., offer assistance to the users in order to perform this step in a successful way.

In this paper, we propose a solution to this problem. We aim at assisting the user by recommending transformations i.e., pre-processing operators, that will

© Springer International Publishing Switzerland 2016
L. Bellatreche et al. (Eds.): MEDI 2016, LNCS 9893, pp. 194–208, 2016.
DOI: 10.1007/978-3-319-45547-1_16

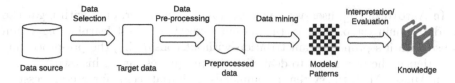

Fig. 1. Data analysis/knowledge discovery process, adapted from [5].

ultimately improve the result of the analysis, that usually happens to be a prediction task. In order to do that, we make use of the concept of *meta-learning*, which consists of two phases, such as learning and predicting. For a given dataset and a selected data mining algorithm we are able to predict transformations that once applied yield an improved algorithm performance (e.g., predictive accuracy).

Contributions. The main contributions of this paper can be summarized as follows:

- We leverage ideas from meta-learning to present a technique for ranking preprocessing transformations depending on their impact on the final result of the data analysis.
- We show the benefits of our approach by implementing a tool that is capable of automatically recommending pre-processing transformations to the user.
- We show experiments that demonstrate the effectiveness and quality of our approach.

The rest of the paper is organized as follows: the related work is discussed in Sect. 2. An overview of data pre-processing, together with its benefits is given in Sect. 3. Our proposed solution is formally defined and a brief look at the implementation prototype is given in Sect. 4. The results of the experimental evaluations are reported in Sect. 5. Finally, Sect. 6 summarizes our work and outlines some future work.

2   Related Work

A lot of research has been conducted in terms of providing user support for different steps of data analysis. The focus however, has usually been on the data mining step, and data pre-processing has generally been overlooked.

Weka [7], an open source tool for data mining, allows users to apply preprocessing algorithms but it does not provide assistance in terms of which one to apply. However, since different data mining algorithms have different requirements regarding the dataset, some pre-processing is applied by default inside some of the algorithms. This pre-processing is usually a simple transformation that does not aim at improving the performance of an algorithm but it aims at transforming the dataset so that it can fit to the data mining algorithm. Furthermore, note that only few algorithm implementations in Weka contain these kind of on the fly transformations.

In AutoWeka [16], user assistance is provided, however, only with regard to the data mining step. That is, the system suggests the best learning algorithm to use with it's proper parametrisation without considering the pre-processing step. Hence, the user needs to deal with the pre-processing on his own.

In AmazonML[1], the system recommends an initial recipe for pre-processing, which is prepared taking into consideration the attributes of the dataset, including the response (i.e., the attribute to be predicted). The recipes provided, however, are pre-formatted instructions for common transformations and do not guarantee improvements of the final result. Hence, they are recommended only because they are applicable to the particular dataset. Whereas, we are interested in performing pre-processing with the only goal of improving the final result of the analysis.

eIDA [9], which is a product of the eLico[2] project, aims to autonomously construct workflows that are combinations of pre-processing and data mining algorithms. In order to do that, the problem of workflow construction is viewed as a planning problem, in which a plan must be built consisting of operators that transform the initial data into models or predictions. In order to find the plans, an exhaustive combination of all applicable transformations with all applicable algorithms is performed. Taking into consideration the number of algorithms (e.g., hundreds in RapidMiner [12], since the project is built on top of Rapid-Miner), the search space of the problem is unfeasible to compute, hence, the optimal solution may not be found. Moreover, in this approach, independent support, exclusively for pre-processing is not provided. As a matter of fact, a "take it all, or leave it" solution is given. In contrast, we focus only on pre-processing, which not only reduces the search space but at the same time allows independent support, hence, the data mining algorithm can be chosen at will.

There exist some other systems [2,8,11], however, they are also focused on providing support for the data mining step only.

3   Overview

3.1   Data Pre-processing

Traditionally, data mining has been performed on transactional data consisting of continuous attributes. The continuous scale of these attributes has enabled the use of conventional statistical methods, such as logistic regression. However, the advances in computational and storage capacity have enabled the accumulation of ordinal, nominal, and binary data, giving rise to datasets of heterogeneous scales. This has induced: (1) advances in the application of data driven methods (e.g., decision trees, artificial neural networks, support vector machines) capable of mining large datasets, (2) challenges in transforming attributes of different scales into mathematically feasible and computationally suitable formats [3]. Indeed, each attribute may require special treatment, such as discretization of

---

[1] https://aws.amazon.com/machine-learning.

[2] http://www.e-lico.eu.

numerical attributes, rescaling of ordinal attributes and encoding of categorical ones. Hence, different transformations may be required.

For the sake of this paper, we consider the transformations shown in Table 1. They are available in the form of open source packages in different data mining tools (e.g., Weka, RapidMiner). We aimed at selecting some of the most important transformations that cover a wide range of data pre-processing tasks, which are distinguished as *data reduction* and *data projection*. *Data reduction* aiming at decreasing the size of the dataset (e.g., instances selection or feature selection) and *data projection*, altering the representation of the data (e.g., mapping continuous values to categories or encoding nominal attributes) [14].

In Table 1, a transformation is described in terms of: (1) the *Technique* it uses, which can be Supervised—the algorithm knows the class of each instance and Unsupervised—the algorithm is not aware of the class, (2) the *Attributes* it uses, which can be Global—applied to all compatible attributes and Local—applied to specific compatible attributes, (3) the *Input Type*, which denotes the compatible attribute type for a given transformation, which can be Continuous— represent measurements on some continuous scale, or Categorical— represent information about some categorical or discrete characteristics, (4) the *Output Type*, which denotes the type of the attribute after the transformation and it can similarly be Continuous or Categorical.

Table 1. List of transformations.

Transformation	Technique	Attributes	Input type	Output type
Discretization	Supervised	Global	Continuous	Categorical
Discretization	Unsupervised	Local	Continuous	Categorical
Nominal to Binary	Supervised	Global	Categorical	Continuous
Nominal to Binary	Unsupervised	Local	Categorical	Continuous
Normalization	Unsupervised	Global	Continuous	Continuous
Standardization	Unsupervised	Local	Continuous	Continuous
Replace Miss. Val.	Unsupervised	Global	Continuous	Continuous
Replace Miss. Val.	Unsupervised	Global	Categorical	Categorical
Principal components	Unsupervised	Global	Continuous	Continuous

3.2 Impact of Pre-processing

In the following we devise a brief example that reveals the importance of data pre-processing for a prediction (e.g., classification) problem. For more in depth analysis of the impact of pre-processing we refer the reader to [3,4].

Let us suppose that a user wants to apply the Logistic algorithm to the Automobile[3] dataset. The summary of Automobile is given in Table 2. This

---

[3] https://archive.ics.uci.edu/ml/support/Automobile.

Table 2. Summary of autos.

Metadata	Value
Instances	205
Attributes	26
Classes	2
Categorical Atts.	11
Continuous Atts.	15
Miss. Values	59

Table 3. Transformations on autos.

Transformation	Attribute	PA
Unsup. Discretiz.	1, 9, 10, 11, 12, 13	0.81
Unsup. Discretiz.	1, 9, 10	0.80
Unsup. Discretiz.	All Cont. Atts.	0.75
Sup. Nom. To Bin.	All Cat. Atts.	0.73
Unsup. Normaliz.	All Cont. Atts.	0.71

dataset specifies autos in terms of their various characteristics like fuel type, aspiration, num-of-doors, engine-size, etc. The response attribute (i.e., class) is *symboling*. *Symboling* is a categorical attribute that indicates the insurance risk rate, and its range is: -3, -2, -1, 0, 1, 2, 3. Value 3 indicates that the auto is risky, -3 that it is pretty safe. The problem is to build a model that will predict the insurance risk rate for a new auto.

Now, if Logistic is applied to the original non-transformed dataset, a predictive accuracy of 0.71 is obtained with a 10 fold cross-validation. Note that for this run the Weka implementation of Logistic with default parametrization is used. On the other hand, if some pre-processing is first performed on Automobile and then the data mining algorithm is applied, the results shown in Table 3 are obtained. In Table 3, the first column denotes the transformation applied, the second denotes the index values of the attributes to which the transformation is applied and the third is the predictive accuracy obtained after the Logistic algorithm is applied on the transformed dataset. Note that for instance, if the transformation Unsupervised Discretization (with default parametrization) is applied to attributes {1,9,10,11,12,13} an improvement of 14 % is obtained in terms of the predictive accuracy. A non-experienced user would not be aware of that. Hence, a proper recommendation of transformations would ease user's task and at the same time it would improve the final result.

4   Our Solution

4.1   Meta-learning for Data Pre-processing

Meta-learning is a general process used for predicting the performance (e.g., predictive accuracy) of an algorithm on a given dataset. It is a method that aims at finding relationships between dataset characteristics and data mining algorithms. However, taking into consideration the above mentioned scenario where a user needs to be provided with some transformations to be applied, meta-learning can also be used to find relationships between transformations and data mining algorithms. That is because transformations by nature modify a dataset, and in turn, the dataset characteristics. As a matter of fact, transformations, through

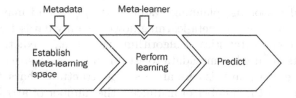

Fig. 2. Tree phases of the ranking process.

the changes they cause in the dataset characteristics, can be indirectly linked to a data mining algorithm. Hence, we can find/learn the relationships between transformations and data mining algorithms. Thus, we use meta-learning to rank transformations according to their capability of improving the final result of the data mining algorithm.

The process of ranking consists of three phases, see Fig. 2. First, a *meta-learning space* is established using metadata consisting of dataset characteristics along with some performance measures for data mining algorithms on those particular datasets, see Table 4. Then, the *meta-learning phase* generates a model (i.e., predictive meta-model) which defines the area of competence of the data mining algorithm [8]. Finally, when a transformed dataset (i.e., a transformation was applied on the dataset) arrives, the metadata are extracted and fed to the predictive meta-model, which predicts the performance of the algorithm—given the characteristics of the transformed dataset, and ultimately provides a ranking of the transformations. This concludes the *prediction* phase.

Table 4. An example (sample) from a meta-learning space. All columns except the last one, denote dataset characteristics. The last column is the predictive accuracy obtained if **Logistic** was applied to the respective dataset. Sign # means "number of".

Name	# Instances	# Atts.	# Miss. Val.	# Cat. Atts.	# Cont. Atts.	PA
autos	205	26	59	11	15	0.71
credit	690	16	9	6	4	0.85
iris	150	5	0	0	4	0.97
vote	435	17	392	16	0	0.96

Two necessary ingredients for performing the aforementioned process are the **metadata** and the **meta-learner**. In the following we give details on each one of them.

4.1.1   Metadata

In our previous work [1], we studied and classified all types of metadata that can be used by systems that intelligently support the user during the process of data analysis. These systems may vary in terms of the methodology they follow (e.g., case based reasoning, planning systems, etc.) [15] and may use different metadata. When it comes to meta-learning however, only dataset characteristics and performance characteristics of algorithms runs (i.e., predictive accuracies) on those datasets are used as metadata to establish the meta-space (see Table 4). Hence briefly, metadata in this case are a set of structural characteristics (e.g., extracted features)—the number of instances, the number of attributes, predictive accuracies of the algorithms runs on datasets, precisions of the algorithms runs on datasets, etc.—that jointly represent the relationships of algorithms with datasets. Different meta-learning systems may use different characteristics of datasets and different performance measures of algorithms runs in the meta-space. The metadata used in our approach is shown in Table 5.

Note that hundreds of metadata could be used and there is no defined methodology to find the set that will yield the best results. Moreover, their extraction might be costly and a tradeoff must be made between the amount of metadata to be used and the accuracy that can be obtained using them in the meta-learning phase.

In order to determine the metadata to be used, we followed an empirical approach. That is, we experimented with different combinations of metadata. Our experiments showed that the metadata in Table 5 give a good tradeoff. Note that they happen to coincide at a rate of 53 % with the metadata used in the literature [2].

In Table 5, we also show the *Importance* of each metadata. The *Importance* coefficients are computed after generating the models in the meta learning phase, and they denote how important a metadata is, for creating the model. The bigger the coefficient, the more important the attribute is. We noticed that some metadata are assigned value 0, that is, they were not used at all by the meta-learner. As a matter of fact, we removed them and recreated the models. Furthermore, in Table 5 column *Modifiable* indicates whether the metadata is modifiable through the transformations we use, shown in Table 1. If metadata are not transformable, we do not use them in the meta-learning phase, because those metadata remain constant and they do not reflect the impact of transformations. Hence finally, in the meta-learning phase we use only the metadata that are indicated with a check mark in the column *Used* in Table 5. Note, also the last row in Table 5, i.e., predictive accuracy, is the metadata we use as the performance measure of the algorithm on a specific dataset. In the meta-learning phase, this metadata is the one that needs to be predicted (i.e., the response). Naturally, columns *Importance* and *Modifiable* are not applicable to it, because this measure is not subject to transformations (e.g., transformations do not modify it directly).

4.1.2   Meta-learner

Having stored an algorithm performance characteristic (i.e., predictive accuracy) and a set of dataset characteristics, the goal is to predict the performance of an algorithm in a transformed dataset. Formally, the problem can be defined as follows. Given algorithm A and a limited number of training data $D = (\mathbf{x}_1, y_1)...(\mathbf{x}_n, y_n)$, the goal is to find a meta learner with optimal/good gen-

Table 5. The list of metadata.

Metadata	Importance	Modifiable	Used
Negative Percentage	0.519947929	No	✗
Class Entropy	0.472033619	No	✗
Majority Class Size	0.366513463	No	✗
Number of Instances	0.327327764	Yes	✓
Positive Percentage	0.24615823	No	✗
Dimensionality	0.147883677	Yes	✓
Minority Class Size	0.144647803	No	✗
Equivalent Number of Attributes	0.140606534	Yes	✓
Number of Features	0.123255813	Yes	✓
Percentage of Numeric Attributes	0.091996975	No	✓
Number of Classes	0.090051421	No	✗
Noise to Signal Ratio	0.089608376	Yes	✓
Mean Kurtosis of Numeric Attributes	0.08734816	Yes	✓
Mean Means of Numeric Attributes	0.071206736	Yes	✓
Mean Std. Dev. of Numeric Attributes	0.056879682	Yes	✓
Mean Mutual Information	0.046159738	Yes	✓
Max. Nominal Att. Distinct Values	0.042945917	Yes	✓
Std. Dev. Nominal Att Distinct Values	0.040555858	Yes	✓
Mean Nominal Att. Distinct Values	0.040086227	Yes	✓
Mean Skewness of Numeric Attributes	0.025735383	Yes	✓
Percentage of Nominal Attributes	0.023476599	Yes	✓
Mean Attribute Entropy	0.021198277	Yes	✓
Percentage of Binary Attributes	0.009063724	Yes	✓
Percentage of Missing Values	0.002302323	Yes	✓
Incomplete Instance Count	0	Yes	✗
Number of Instances With Missing Values	0	Yes	✗
Min. Nominal Att. Distinct Values	0	Yes	✗
Predictive Accuracy	NA	NA	✓

eralization performance. Generalization performance is estimated by splitting D into disjoint training and validation sets $D_{train}^{(i)}$ and $D_{valid}^{(i)}$. We use leave-one-out validation [10], which splits the training data into n partitions $D_{valid}^{(1)}, ..., D_{valid}^{(n)}$, and sets $D_{train}^{(i)} = D \backslash D_{valid}^{(i)}$ for $i = 1, ..., n$. Note that $\mathbf{x} \in x_1, x_2...x_n$ are the dataset characteristics and y_1 is the predictive accuracy of algorithm A run on that particular dataset. Hence, $\mathbf{x}$ and y altogether are the extracted metadata.

The meta-learner we decided to use is a *regression tree*. Trees have many good properties, such as: they perform implicit feature selection, require little effort for data preparation, nonlinear relationships between variables do not affect their performance and they are easy to interpret and explain. Thus, we created a regression tree for each data mining algorithm or more precisely for each classification algorithm.

In particular, the classification algorithms for which we generated regression trees are representative algorithms for all, except three classes of algorithms in Weka. In Weka, the classification algorithms are classified into: *bayes, functions, lazy, rules, trees, meta-methods, multi-instance methods, and ensemble-methods*. We aimed at considering one algorithm for each one of the first five classes, and they are: *Naive Bayes, Logistic, IBk, JRip, and J48* respectively. The last three classes were omitted due to the fact that they are more complex and are not commonly used by non experienced users.

4.2   Solution Prototype

The general architecture of the developed solution prototype is depicted in Fig. 3. The solution's main processes, the **Learning** and **Recommending** are implemented independently of each other. Below we give detailed explanations for each one of them.

4.2.1   Learning Phase

In the previous sections we mentioned that in order to build a model (e.g., predictive meta-model), we must firstly establish the meta-space—denoted as *Learning phase* in Fig. 3. In our context, the meta-space needs to be constructed out of metadata that can be extracted from datasets and from the executions of

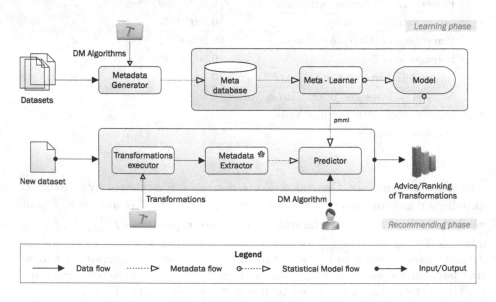

Fig. 3. Solution architecture.

algorithms on those datasets. As a matter of fact, we needed to fetch hundreds of datasets, extract some of their required characteristics, run different algorithms on them and get the predictive accuracies with 10 fold cross validation. Finally, use all of these to feed the *Meta-database*.

In order to do the aforementioned, we first used OpenML [17] to fetch several hundred datasets. Next, from each dataset we extracted the 17 dataset characteristics—highlighted with a check-mark in Table 5. Finally, we executed the classification algorithms (see Sect. 4.1.2), on the datasets, and extracted the predictive accuracy values after evaluating with 10-fold cross validation. For each data mining algorithm, we obtained a meta-dataset that was fed to the *Meta-database*. In Fig. 3, this is represented via the *Metadata creator* module and was developed in Java.

After obtaining the metadata, hence constructing the meta-space, we continued on building the *Models* (or predictive meta-models) through the *Meta-learners*, which in this case are regression trees. We used the R language to construct a tree for each one of the algorithms. Hence, we obtained one model per data mining algorithm. After that, the models were exported to pmml [6] files, and were next fed to the *Predictor* in the recommending phase.

Note that this process is not specifically tailored for datasets from the OpenML repository, but it can work on any collection of datasets. However, the models obtained are expected to slightly change from one collection to another.

4.2.2   Recommending Phase

When a user wants to analyze a dataset, he/she selects an algorithm to be used for the analysis and then the system automatically recommends transformations to be applied, such that the final result is improved. In order to do that, the system first, applies different transformations to the dataset through the *Transformation executor* module. Then, the metadata of the transformed dataset are extracted through the *Metadata extractor* module and they are fed to the *Predictor*, which using the model (pmml) of the respective algorithm (the one selected by the user) predicts the impact of the transformation. Finally, the Transformations are ranked according to their impact on the final result (according to whether they improve the final result). The modules of the *Recommending phase* are entirely developed in Java.

5   Evaluation

We performed an experimental study of the performance that can be achieved by our approach on various algorithms and various datasets. After specifying our experiment environment we evaluate our systems ability to predict the transformations that will improve the final result of the analysis.

5.1   Experimental Setup

Recall that when building the meta-learners, we performed leaf-one-out validation for evaluating them (see Sect. 4.1.2). However, in order to enable a larger number of datasets for performing the experiments, each time we performed the leave-one-out validation we created a tree using the subset of datasets (i.e., withholding the dataset that was left-out). Hence, for each data mining algorithm we created as many trees (meta-learners, meta-models) as datasets were used for training the tree of the respective algorithm. As a matter of fact, in order to perform experiments for an algorithm, we can use the entire set of datasets for testing, only bearing in mind that for each dataset, in the *Predictor*, we use the tree (meta-model) that was built without using that particular dataset.

In our context, an experiment is performed in the following way. We first select a dataset and a data mining algorithm to be used for performing analysis (i.e., classification) on the dataset. Next, our system finds the **impact** of a **set of transformations** on the final result of the analysis.

The **set of transformations**, consists of iteratively applying the transformations shown in Table 1, however each time changing the set of attributes to which the transformation is applied. Note that the transformations which are denoted as `Global` in the table, are applied only once to the set of all compatible attributes (altogether), whereas the transformations, which are denoted as `Local` are applied to: (1) every compatible attribute separately (one by one), and (2) all the set of compatible attributes (altogether).

The **impact**, is the effect of transformations to the final result (i.e., predictive accuracy) of the selected algorithm, and it can be, the *foreseen/predicted impact* and the *real impact*.

The *foreseen/predicted impact* is calculated by applying the set of transformations, as defined above, and subsequently extracting the characteristics (metadata) of the transformed datasets, which are then used for predicting (foreseeing) the performance of the respective algorithm (on the transformed dataset).

The *real* impact is calculated by similarly applying the set of transformations, but then, subsequently applying the respective data mining algorithm for real to the transformed datasets, and hence obtaining the real performance (e.g., predictive accuracy) of the data mining algorithm. In terms of computational complexity, the latter is a costly process, and it is performed only for the sake of evaluating the system (experiments).

The experiments were performed on an Intel Core i5 machine, running at 1.70 GHz with 8 GB of main memory. An experiment for a single algorithm, on average took approximately 4 CPU hours.

5.2   Results for the Improvements Obtained by Transformations

On each run, the system internally categorizes a transformation, into one of the following three categories: *Good*—an improvement of the final result for the respective algorithm is foreseen if the transformation were to be applied, *Bad*—a worsening of the final result for the respective algorithm is foreseen if the transformation were to be applied, or *Neutral*—neither improvement nor worsening is foreseen if the transformation were to be applied. Note that the latter occurs when the transformed dataset remains in the same leaf within the meta-learner (i.e., regression tree) or it moves to another leaf which predicts the

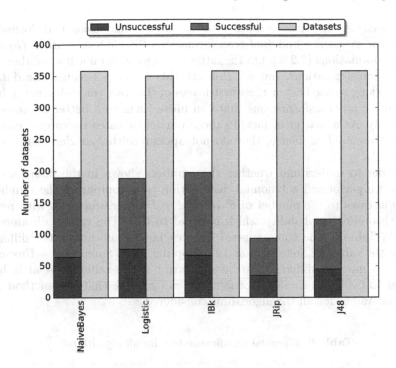

Fig. 4. Successful vs unsuccessful datasets. (Color figure online)

same value (i.e., predictive accuracy). This is a limitation of the regression trees because they contain a discrete number of leaves, and hence a discrete number of possible predictions.

The aim of the experiments is to verify whether the foreseen categorizations are so for real. This, as previously mentioned (though costly) is done by executing the data mining algorithms on the transformed datasets and examining the real impact of the transformations.

In this context, we mark as *Successful*, the cases (i.e., datasets) on which the real average improvement we get from all the transformations categorized as *Good* for a dataset, is greater than the real average improvement we get from the transformations that were categorized as *Bad* for the same dataset. That is, the transformations foreseen as *Good*, "beat" on average the transformations foreseen as *Bad*.

In contrast, we mark as *Unsuccessful*, the cases on which the transformations foreseen as *Good* cannot "beat" on average the transformations foreseen as *Bad*.

In Fig. 4, we show the results obtained. We show the comparison between the number of *Successful* cases—the green bar, and the number of *Unsuccessful* cases—the red bar. In addition, a third bar (i.e., gray) in the figure, denotes the total number of cases (datasets) for which we performed the experiments on each respective algorithm. Note that the sum of *Successful* (green) and *Unsuccessful* (red) cases does not coincide with the total number of datasets (gray).

This is because, for some datasets we either do not find *Good* transformations (54.7 %), or we do not find *Bad* transformations (38.1 %), or neither *Good* nor *Bad* transformations (7.2 %). On the latter cases we could not find neither *Good* nor *Bad* transformations, but for the rest this happens because the datasets already belong to the best or the worst leaves of the trees (meta-learners), hence there can be no transformations that can move them to a better or worse leaf respectively. As a matter of fact, in those particular cases we cannot compare the *Good* versus *Bad*, hence, they do not appear neither as *Successful* nor as *Unsuccessful*.

In order to understand whether the numbers shown in the figure are significant, we performed a binomial distribution test, comparing the number of *Successful* cases to the number of *Successful + Unsuccessful* cases with respect to the theoretical probability which is equal to 0.5. The results obtained are shown in Table 6. The column *p-val* denotes how significant is the difference between the values of Successful and the population of *Successful + Unsuccessful*. We assume the difference to be significant if the value in *p-val* is below or equal to 0.05. As a matter of fact, we can observe that our method gives significant values for all the algorithms considered.

Table 6. Binomial significance test for all algorithms.

Algorithm	Weka class	Successful	Successful+Unsuccessful	p-val
Naive Bayes	Bayes	126	190	1.99359E−06
Logistic	Functions	112	189	0.004326558
IBk	Lazy	131	198	1.57706E−06
JRip	Rules	59	94	0.004773905
J48	Trees	79	124	0.000782367

6 Conclusions and Future Work

In this work, we have shown that the daunting problem of data pre-processing can be alleviated by a practical, automated tool. This is made possible through meta-learning which enables predicting the impact of transformations on the final performance of algorithms on the corresponding datasets, and in turn, allows ranking the transformations according to their impact on the final result.

We built a tool that draws on a range of classification algorithms in Weka and makes it easy for non-experts to perform data pre-processing. An extensive evaluation on hundreds of datasets showed that for a set of algorithms even blindly (e.g., users without any prior knowledge wrt data mining) applying the recommended transformations improves the final result of the algorithm. We believe that this can be a handy tool for experienced users as well, because they can discriminate within the recommended transformations and pick the ones that are potentially more suitable for their problem at hand.

We see several promising avenues for future work. First, some limitations of using regression trees as meta-learners were observed (e.g., many transformations predicted to perform the same, due to the discrete number of leaves), suggesting the investigation of more sophisticated methods (e.g., neural networks). Second, we see potential value in customizing the transformations depending on the class of algorithms (e.g., trees) or even specific algorithms. Finally, we aim at extending the range of the classification algorithms that we have considered so far.

Acknowledgments. This research has been funded by the European Commission through the Erasmus Mundus Joint Doctorate "Information Technologies for Business Intelligence - Doctoral College" (IT4BI-DC).

References

1. Bilalli, B., Abelló, A., Aluja-Banet, T., Wrembel, R.: Towards intelligent data analysis: the metadata challenge. In: IoTBD (2016)
2. Charest, M., et al.: Bridging the gap between data mining and decision support: a case-based reasoning and ontology approach. In: IDA (2008)
3. Crone, S.F., Lessmann, S., Stahlbock, R.: The impact of preprocessing on data mining: an evaluation of classifier sensitivity in direct marketing. Eur. J. Oper. Res. **173**(3), 781–800 (2006)
4. Dasu, T., Johnson, T.: Exploratory Data Mining and Data Cleaning, vol. 479. Wiley, Hoboken (2003)
5. Fayyad, U.M., Piatetsky-Shapiro, G., Smyth, P.: From data mining to knowledge discovery in databases. AI Magazine (1996)
6. Guazzelli, A., Zeller, M., Lin, W.-C., Williams, G., et al.: PMML: an open standard for sharing models. R J. **1**(1), 60–65 (2009)
7. Hall, M., Frank, E., Holmes, G., Pfahringer, B., Reutemann, P., et al.: The weka data mining software: an update. ACM SIGKDD Explor. Newsl. **11**(1), 10–18 (2009)
8. Kalousis, A., Hilario, M.: Model selection via meta-learning: a comparative study. Int. J. Artif. Intell. Tools **10**(4), 525–554 (2001)
9. Kietz, J.-U., Serban, F., Fischer, S., Bernstein, A.: "Semantics Inside!" but let's not tell the data miners: intelligent support for data mining. In: Presutti, V., d'Amato, C., Gandon, F., d'Aquin, M., Staab, S., Tordai, A. (eds.) ESWC 2014. LNCS, vol. 8465, pp. 706–720. Springer, Heidelberg (2014)
10. Kohavi, R.: A study of cross-validation and bootstrap for accuracy estimation and model selection. In: IJCAI (1995)
11. Michie, D., Spiegelhalter, D.J., Taylor, C.C., Campbell, J. (eds.): Machine Learning, Neural and Statistical Classification. Ellis Horwood, Upper Saddle River (1994)
12. Mierswa, I.: Rapid miner. Künstliche Intelligenz (2009)
13. Munson, M.A.: A study on the importance of and time spent on different modeling steps. SIGKDD Explor. Newsl. **13**(2), 65–71 (2012)
14. Pyle, D.: Data Preparation for Data Mining. Morgan Kaufmann, San Francisco (1999)

15. Serban, F., Vanschoren, J., Kietz, J., Bernstein, A.: A survey of intelligent assistants for data analysis. ACM Comput. Surv. **45**(3), 31 (2013)
16. Thornton, C., Hutter, F., Hoos, H.H., et al.: Auto-weka: combined selection and hyperparameter optimization of classification algorithms. In: KDD (2013)
17. Vanschoren, J., van Rijn, J.N., Bischl, B., Torgo, L.: OpenML: networked science in machine learning. ACM SIGKDD Explor. Newsl. **15**(2), 49–60 (2014)

Individual Relocation: A Fuzzy Classification Based Approach

Djellal Asma[1,2(✉)] and Boufaida Zizette[2]

[1] Preparatory School of Economics,
Business and Management Sciences of Constantine, Constantine, Algeria
asmadjellal@gmail.com
[2] LIRE Laboratory, Constantine 2 - Abdelhamid Mehri – University,
Constantine, Algeria
zizette.boufaida@univ-constantine2.dz

Abstract. Like crisp ontologies, the success of fuzzy ones depends on the availability of effective software allowing their exploitation. Thus, serval reasoners for very expressive fuzzy description logics have been implemented. However, in some cases, applications do not require all the reasoners tasks and would benefit from the efficiency of just certain services. To this scope, we focused on the individual classification task to realize fuzzy ontologies. After their classification, individuals may evolve and change their description. To deal with this evolution, we propose, in this paper, a sufficiently clear and complete process for relocating individuals into fuzzy ontologies. This evolution may be the result of an enrichment, an impoverishment, and/or modification of the individual description. The proposed fuzzy relocation process is based on a fuzzy classification algorithm that supports $(\mathcal{Z}\,\mathcal{SHOIN}(\mathcal{D}))$ and allows (i) fuzzy domains, (ii) modified and (iii) weighted concepts.

Keywords: Fuzzy knowledge · Fuzzy logic · Fuzzy ontology · Fuzzy classification · Individual classification · Fuzzy ontology evolution

1 Introduction

Based on fuzzy logic, several approaches have been proposed in order to make possible the representation of vague, imprecise or fuzzy knowledge [9, 11–14]. Moreover, a number of reasoners for very expressive fuzzy description logics (DLs) have been implemented [16], including FiRE [10], FuzzyDL [4] and DeLorean [6]. In fact, the availability of tools and effective software for dealing with fuzzy ontologies guarantee their success. However, in some cases, applications do not require all the reasoners services and would benefit from the efficiency of just certain tasks. To this scope, we have been interested in the individual classification issue.

Classification is the main reasoning mechanism for systems based on class/instance models. It is one of the most powerful and fundamental human inference mechanisms. It maintains the stability of the knowledge base, by attaching each object to its class. However, since we are handling imperfect knowledge, giving exact definitions of class boundaries, for such attachment, seems to be a very difficult, perhaps even impossible,

© Springer International Publishing Switzerland 2016
L. Bellatreche et al. (Eds.): MEDI 2016, LNCS 9893, pp. 209–219, 2016.
DOI: 10.1007/978-3-319-45547-1_17

task. Therefore, we have integrated fuzzy logic with classification to offer a more human-oriented classification by assigning an individual to several fuzzy concepts with different membership degrees which makes the sharp borders between concepts disappear, and then better reflecting reality.

Having these ideas in mind, we have been interested in the individual fuzzy classification problem which consists in connecting new individuals to their most specialized concepts in the fuzzy ontology. After their classification, individuals may evolve and update their knowledge which requires their relocation in the hierarchy. This evolution may be the result of an enrichment, an impoverishment, and/or a modification of the individual knowledge. Ontology evolution aims at maintaining an ontology up to date with respect to changes in the domain. It is a challenging problem [18] and need to be analyzed from different point of views. Thus, the present paper addresses the individual evolution issue by providing an individual relocation process for fuzzy ontologies. The proposed process is based on a fuzzy classification algorithm supporting a fuzzy extension of the well-known DL $\mathcal{SHOIN}(\mathcal{D})$ under Zadeh Semantics ($\mathcal{Z}\,\mathcal{SHOIN}(\mathcal{D})$). It allows (i) fuzzy domains, (ii) modified and (iii) weighted concepts.

The remainder of this paper is organized as follows. Section 2 introduces fuzzy logic and how it is used to handle vague knowledge by means of fuzzy ontology elements. Section 3 outlines a fuzzy realization algorithm for classifying new individuals into such ontologies. An extension of this algorithm, namely, a fuzzy relocation of already classified, but updated, individuals is presented in Sect. 4. Finally, Sect. 5 concludes the paper with ideas for future research.

2 Handling Imperfect Knowledge

Human reasoning is, often based on fuzzy knowledge. To solve his daily problems, human uses knowledge on which he doubts their validity or poorly expressed due to the complexity of the problem. Fuzzy logic was designed to solve the problem of handling vague or imprecise knowledge by allowing their characterization in a gradual way. Zadeh [19], as an extension of Boolean logic, has introduced Fuzzy Logic in the middle 60s, to handle several situations frequently encountered in our daily life where Boolean logic seems to be inappropriate to be used. Indeed, a two-valued modelization is not sufficient for managing fuzzy knowledge, manifested by terms like *tall*, *young*, *hot* and the like, which are quite common in human language.

Just like Boolean logic, fuzzy logic is based on some basic fuzzy operators; complementation, intersection and union operators respectively use negation, t-norm and s-norm functions. In the literature, we can find several definitions to these operators, so that one can form different fuzzy logics. The most widely used one is Zadeh fuzzy logic, known as *Zadeh Semantics* [5]; it is a combination of Gödel conjunction and disjunction ($t_G = \min(a,b)$ *and* $S_G = \max(a,b)$) and Łukasiewicz negation ($N_L(a) = 1 - a$).

Fuzzy ontologies extend classical ones by interpreting concepts and roles as fuzzy sets of individuals and binary relations respectively [1, 2, 7]. In fact, vague notions can be represented by means of fuzzy ontology elements using different constructs [15].

Most importantly, one can use *fuzzy domains* such *High* to represent explicit fuzzy concepts like *HighTemperature* as *HighTemperature* $\equiv$ *temperature* $\sqcap$ $\exists$ *Degree.High*. We can also use *modifiers* such *Very* to represent fuzzy modified concepts like *VeryHighTemperature* as VeryHighTemperature $\equiv$ temperature$\sqcap\exists$ Degree.Very(High). Finally, *weighted concepts* can be used to express the importance of some concepts representing preferences or priorities. These are defined as $C \equiv w\ (C)/w \in [0, 1]$.

3   Fuzzy Ontology Realization: An Individual Fuzzy Classification Based Approach

Ontology representation is, primarily based on two mechanisms: *instantiation* and *classification*. An instance, also called individual, is instantiated, in order, to be, properly classified by matching it with the ontology different concepts. For this matching, two approaches can be distinguished: crisp and fuzzy. In the first case, each matching is dichotomous; that is, the membership degree of an individual to a concept is 1 for inclusion and 0 for exclusion. Such matching requires exact definition of concept boundaries which is a very difficult, perhaps even impossible, task. Unlike crisp classification, the fuzzy one assigns an individual to several fuzzy concepts with different membership degrees expressing how strongly it belongs to each concept. Such classification offers a more human-oriented modelling process by making the crisp boundaries between concepts disappear, which better reflects reality [17].

The instantiation mechanism creates individuals, possibly incomplete ones, by providing the maximum possible of their knowledge. Despite the eventual lake of information, the fuzzy realization process [3], based on a fuzzy classification mechanism, allows the classification of such individuals the lowest possible in the ontology hierarchy graph. The implementation of this process is held according to the following algorithm.

```
Algorithm1. Fuzzy realization algorithm
Input:  H: Fuzzy concepts hierarchy
        A: New individual
Output: Evolved fuzzy ontology: (H realized with A)
Begin
Initialization ( );
C*:= TOP (H);
While (not empty (C*)) do
     Matching (C*, A);
     Marks-Propagation (C*, label, degree);
     C*:= Next-Concept (C*);
End while
  End.
```

After collecting the necessary knowledge about the new individual *A*, the algorithm explores the hierarchy *H* and matches *A* with the current concept C*, starting at the root

TOP. The Matching procedure verifies A's membership in C^* and marks it with a label. To accelerate the classification, the Marks_Propagation procedure propagates marks to different concepts related to C^* without needing to match them with A which reduces future matching. This propagation is based on logical relations between concepts applied under Zadeh Semantics. The next concept for the matching test is chosen by the function Next_Concept. If there is no unmarked concept to be chosen, the function returns *null* which terminates the classification.

This realization is primarily based on a matching mechanism which marks C^* with a label, indicating whether it is *sure, possible* or *impossible* for A. Since there is no full membership in fuzzy ontologies [2], a membership degree is added to the concept's mark. In sum, *Matching* procedure generates one of the following three outputs:

- $\langle C^*, sure, d \rangle$ (means, A is C^* with a truth-value of d): if A is complete and all its attributes values satisfy the constraints of C^*.
- $\langle C^*, impossible, null \rangle$ (means, A is not C^*): if A's value for at least one attribute does not satisfy the constraints in C^*.
- $\langle C^*, possible, null \rangle$ (means, A may be C^*): if A is incomplete and there is no contradiction with C^*.

Calculating the membership degrees depends on the description of each current concept (C^*) which can be a: concept conjunction/disjunction, modified/weighted concept, etc. Based on its description and under Zadeh Semantics, the membership degree is computed according to the following rules:

1. Concept conjunction ($C^* \equiv C1 \sqcap \ldots \sqcap Cn$): Degree($C^*$, A) = min(Degree($C_i$, A))/i = 1n.
2. Concept disjunction ($C^* \equiv C1 \sqcup \ldots \sqcup Cn$): Degree ($C^*$, A) = max (Degree ($C_i$, A))/i = 1...n.
3. Concept negation ($C^* \equiv \neg C$): Degree (C^*, A) = 1 − Degree(C, A).
4. Fuzzy modified concept ($C^* \equiv m(C)$): Degree (C^*, A) = f_m (Degree(C, A))/m is a modifier defined by the function f_m.
5. Fuzzy weighted concept ($C^* \equiv w$ (C)): Degree (C^*, A) = w * Degree(C, A)/$w \in$ [0, 1]
6. Explicit fuzzy concept ($C^* \equiv \exists$ Attribute.Range/Range is a fuzzy domain) Degree (C^*, A) = f_{Range} (A.Attribute). e.g. $\exists$ Age.YoungAge, results to f_{Young} (A.Age).
7. Limited existential quantification ($C^* \equiv \exists R.C$): the function returns the maximum of membership degrees of all individuals (A_i) related by R in C as: Degree(C^*, A) = max(Degree(C, A_i)).
8. Value restriction ($C^* \equiv \forall R.C$): it returns the minimum of membership degrees of all individuals (A_i) related by R in C as Degree(C^*, A) = min(Degree(C, A_i)).
9. Max cardinality ($C^* \equiv \geq n R.C$): the membership is full (1) if the number of all individuals (A_i) related by R in C is greater than or equal to n, otherwise there is no membership (0) in C^*. *If*|Degree (C, A_i) > 0 | > = n *then* Degree (C^*, A) = 1 *else* 0.
10. Min cardinality ($C^* \equiv \leq n R.C$): the membership is full (1) if the number of all individuals (A_i) related by R in C is less than or equal to n, otherwise there is no membership (0) in C^*. *If* |Degree(C, A_i) > 0 | <= n *then* Degree (C^*, A) = 1 *else* 0.

4 Individual Relocation Process for Fuzzy Ontologies

After their classification, individuals may evolve and change their knowledge. Indeed, a person changes age, address or professions. To address this problem, a relocation process must be evoked. Therefore as an extension of the previously presented algorithm, we propose a fuzzy relocation process, in which, already classified, but updated, individuals have to be relocated in the fuzzy ontology. This process allows an individual to migrate from its current belonging concepts to new ones that satisfy its evolved knowledge. This evolution can be the result of an (i) *Enrichment* of incomplete individual by replacing unknown values with concrete ones, (ii) *Modification* of concrete values by new ones, or (iii) *Impoverishment* and removal of concrete values and replacing them with unknown ones.

An already classified individual is represented with two types of knowledge:

- *Belonging concepts:* the list of its most specific (fuzzy) concepts having the mark *sure to some degree*. Formally, it is a set of pairs (concept, degree) as $S_A = \{(C1, d1) \dots (Cn, dn)/\langle Ci, sure, di \rangle$ for $A\}$.
- *Data of the individual*: represented by a set of pairs (attribute, value) as $A = \{(Att1, Val1) \dots (Attn, Valn)\}$. Two cases can be considered:
  - A is a complete individual: $\forall\ (Att_i, Val_i) \in A$, $Val_i \neq$ unknown/$i \in \{1 \dots n\}$.
    A is an incomplete individual: $\exists\ (Att_i, Val_i) \in A/Val_i =$ unknown, $i \in \{1 \dots n\}$.

The fuzzy relocation process is held according to the following algorithm:

Algorithm2: Fuzzy Relocation
Input: Updated individual: A= { (Att₁, Val₁)… (Attₙ, Valₙ) }
         Belonging concepts S_A = { (C1, d1)… (Cn, dn) }.
Output: Evolved S_A.
Begin
  If Impoverishment **then**
    Ascent_Possible (A);   (1)
  Else /* enrichment or modification*/
    For all (inconsistent (Ci) in S_A) **Do**
      Ascent_Impossible (A) ;   (2)
      Marks_Propagation (Ci, impossible, nul) ; (3)
    End for
    Fuzzy-Realization (A);   (4)
  End if

  End.

In the following sections, we will explain the relocation of an updated individual using the proposed algorithm for the following excerpt from of a simple fuzzy ontology of persons as an illustrative example (see Fig. 1).

Person ⊑T

Young   ≡   *Person*   ⊓   ∃ *HasAge.YoungAge*

Adult ≡ Person ⊓ ∃ HasAge.AdultAge

Middle_Age   ≡   *Person*   ⊓ ∃*HasAge.Midd*

Old_Age≡ Person ⊓ ∃HasAge.Old

YoungAge (x) = Left-shoulder (20, 24)

AdultAge(x)=Trapezoidal(23,30,80,90)

Midd (x) = Trapezoidal (23, 25, 45, 50)

Old (x) = Trapezoidal (45, 50, 80, 90)

Considering the following classified individual:

Tom = {(Name, Tom), (Age, 23)...}

Tim = {(Name, Tim), (Age, 46)....}

Tomi = {(Name, Tomi), (Age, 51)....}

S_{Tom} = {(Young, 0.25)}

S_{Tim} = {(Middle_Age, 0.20)}

S_{Tomi} = {(Old_Age, 1)}

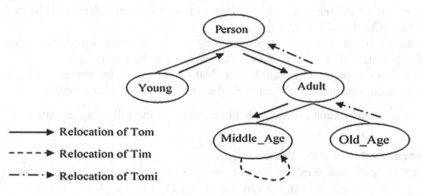

Fig. 1. Relocation of evolved individuals.

4.1   Enrichment and Modification

In these two cases, we have to handle a new data by replacing a concrete or an unknown value. The new data can satisfy the fuzzy ontology constraints which results to a consistent fuzzy ontology as it may be in contradiction with some constraints which generates an inconsistency:

Consistent Fuzzy Ontology. Since there is no contradiction in the fuzzy ontology, all the concepts in S_A must keep their marks as *sure*, but probably with a new membership degree. For instance, consider the individual Tim of our illustrative example, if its age changes to 47 years old, then S_{Tim} evolves to S_{Tim} = {(Middle_Age, 0.40)} (*Cf.* Fig. 1). Moreover, it is possible that the new data allows the individual to migrate from its current belonging concepts to new ones that are more specific. Therefore, for this first case, a simple realization process (Sect. 3) (*Cf. Algorithm2 line 4*) is revived to descend the evolved individual starting at its current belonging concepts in S_A.

Inconsistent Fuzzy Ontology. In this second case, there is an inconsistency in at least one concept in S_A. Consequently, a fuzzy relocation process is invoked to restore the consistency of the evolved fuzzy ontology by migrating the updated individual to its new belonging concepts and then updating the set S_A.

Let *Att* be the modified attribute of the updated individual A, *newVal* its new value and C^* is the current inconsistent belonging concept of A (that is, *newVal* does not satisfy the type of *Att* in C^*). Note that the relocation of A is realized independently in each inconsistent belonging concept in S_A trough the following three steps:

Ascent of the Individual. During this first step, A is raised up in the fuzzy hierarchy, by following the path of its sure super-concepts from C^* until the first concept D^* for which *newVal* satisfies the type of *Att*. It should be noted that *newVal* does not satisfy the constraints of *Att* in all concepts between C^* and D^* (except D^*). Therefore, all these concepts must change their marks from $\langle C_i^*, sure, di \rangle$ to $\langle C_i^*, impossible, null \rangle$. This ascent is realized by the procedure Ascent_Impossible (*Cf. Algorithm2, Line 2*). Giving the illustrative example, *Tom*'s knowledge evolves after his 24th anniversary. Consequently, the fuzzy concept *Young* is no longer consistent since f_{Young} (24) = 0. To restore the ontology consistency, the relocation process raises up *Tom* to the concept *Person* (*Cf.* Fig. 1) which is the first *sure* super-concept. Moreover, *Young* changes its mark from $\langle Young, sure, 0.25 \rangle$ to $\langle Young, impossible, null \rangle$ which generates $S_{Tom} = \{(Person, 1)\}$.

Propagation of the Mark Impossible. The second step consists of propagating the marks change which reduces future ascents and accelerates the relocation process. For this, the procedure Marks-Propagation of the fuzzy realization algorithm (Sect. 3) is invoked (*Cf. Algorithm2, Line 3*). The procedure propagates marks to all concepts related to each inconsistent concept according to the following rules and under Zadeh semantics:

[R.1] If $\langle C^*, sure, d \rangle$ for A, then $\forall D, C^* \equiv D \langle D, sure, d \rangle$ for the same individual.

[R.2] If $\langle C^*, impossible, null \rangle$, then $\forall D, C^* \equiv D \langle D, impossible, null \rangle$.

[R.3] If $\langle C^*, sure, d \rangle$, then $\forall D, C^* \equiv \daleth D \langle D, impossible, null \rangle$.

[R.4] If $\langle C^*, impossible, null \rangle)$, then $\forall D, C^* \equiv \daleth D \langle D, sure, d \rangle / d = Get\_degree (D, A)$.

[R.5] If $\langle C^*, sure, d \rangle, \forall D, C^* \sqsubseteq D$, then $\langle D, sure, \geq d \rangle$.

[R.6] If $\langle C^*, impossible, null \rangle, \forall D, D \sqsubseteq C^*$, then $\langle D, impossible, null \rangle$.

[R.7] If $\langle C^*, possible, null \rangle, \forall D, D \sqsubseteq C^*$, then $\langle D, label, null \rangle / label \notin \{sure\}$.

[R.8] If $\langle C^*, sure, d \rangle, \forall D, D \equiv m(C^*)$, then $\langle D, sure, f_m (d) \rangle$.

[R.9] If $\langle C^*, sure, d \rangle, \forall D, D \equiv w (C^*)$, then $\langle D, sure, w*d \rangle$.

  Supposition1. D is defined by a concept conjunction as $D \equiv C^* \sqcap C1 \sqcap ... \sqcap Cn$.

[R.10] If $\langle C^*, impossible, null \rangle$, then $\langle D, impossible, null \rangle$.

[R.11] If $\langle Ci, sure, di \rangle$, and $\langle C^*, sure, d \rangle$, then $\langle D, sure, deg \rangle / deg = min(d, di) / i = 1 ... n$.

[R.12] If $\langle D, impossible, null \rangle, \langle C^*, sure, di \rangle$ and $\exists j \in \{1...n\} \langle Cj, "", "" \rangle$ (Cj is unmarked), $\forall i \in \{1 ... n\} / i \neq j \langle Ci, sure, di \rangle$, then $\langle Cj, impossible, null \rangle$.

Supposition2. D is defined by a concept disjunction as $D \equiv C* \sqcup C1 \sqcup ... \sqcup Cn$.

[R.13] If $\langle C*, Sure, d \rangle$, then $\langle D, Sure, deg \rangle / deg = \max (d, di)/i = 1 ... n$.

[R.14] If $\langle Ci, impossible, null \rangle$ and $\langle C*, impossible, null \rangle$, then $\langle D, impossible, null \rangle$.

[R.15] If $\langle D, sure, d \rangle$, $\langle C*, impossible, null \rangle$ and $\exists j \in \{1...n\} \langle Cj, "", "" \rangle$, $\forall i \in \{1... n\}/i \neq j \langle Ci, impossible, null \rangle$, then $\langle Cj, sure, d \rangle$.

Recall our evolved individual Tom, after the mark change of *Young* to *impossible;* we can apply [R.4] to mark *Adult* as *sure.* Indeed, these are two opposite fuzzy concepts, since they are defined based on two complementary fuzzy concrete domains (*YoungAge* and *AdultAge*). Thus, *Adult* will be marked $\langle Adult, sure, f_{Adult} (24) \rangle$ which results to $S_{Tom} = \{(Adult, 0.14)\}$ (*Cf.* Fig. 1).

Descent of the Individual. The consistency of the fuzzy ontology has been restored by raising up *A* to its first consistent concept D*. Hence, the last step of the fuzzy relocation process consists of the descent of *A* to its new belonging concepts. Indeed, *newVal* can satisfy other concepts that are more specific than D*. Then, the fuzzy realization algorithm (Sect. 3) is evoked starting at D* (*Cf. Algorithm2, Line* 4). To complete the relocation of Tom from our earlier example, the fuzzy realization algorithm will descent it to the fuzzy concept *Middle_Age* since $f_{Middel\_Age} (24) = 0.5$. However, it does not satisfy *Old_Age.* Thus, S_{Tom} will change to $S_{Tom} = \{(Middel\_Age, 0.5)\}$ (*Cf.* Fig. 1).

During the ascent of *A*, the procedure *Ascent_Impossible* must match *newVal* with the type of *Att* defined in every super-concept between C* and D*. This type-verification is quite similar to the *Matching* procedure of the fuzzy realization algorithm, except that Ascent_Impossible is not as complicated as Matching. Indeed, during the classification of a new individual, *Matching* must verify if the individual data satisfies the constraints of all attributes defined in each concept. Unlike *Matching*, *Ascent_Impossible* verifies the satisfaction of just one attribute which causes of the relocation.

4.2 Impoverishment

An impoverished individual is an updated individual who has been evolved to an unknown value. For instance, after the classification of Tomi, from our illustrative example, as a fully *Old Age* person (degree = 1), we noticed that it is not his correct age. Consequently, until we obtain the correct information, we must change Tomi's Age value (51) with the value "unknown". This type of evolution does not affect the ontology consistency. Indeed, even with this update, the evolved individual still satisfies the constraints of its belonging concepts. However, it will contains, instead of a concrete value, an unknown one which results to an incomplete individual.

To handle this change, the fuzzy ontology must evolve and the impoverished individual *A* must raise up, by following the path of its super-concepts, from each belonging concept in S_A until the first sure super-concept in which there is no specification of *Att*. All these super-concepts (which specify *Att*) must change their mark from *sure to some degree* to *possible*. The ascent of *A* is realized by the procedure *Ascent_Possible* (*Cf. Algorithm2, Line 1*). Unlike the enrichment/modification, in the case of an individual impoverishment, once the ascent is complete, no further descent is possible. Indeed, there is no concrete *NewVal* to be matched with more specific concepts. Consequently, the first super-concept for which there is no specification for *Att* will be the belonging concept of *A*. In the case of our impoverished individual Tomi, it must raise up to the atomic concept *Person*, while *Old_Age* and *Adult* will change from *sure* to *possible* concepts for Tomi which results to $S_{Tomi} = \{(Person, 1)\}$ (*Cf.* Fig. 1).

It should be noted that, *Ascent_Possible* raise up the impoverished individual to its first sure super-concept like *Ascent_Impossible*. However, there is a difference between these two procedures. Indeed, the first one attaches the updated individual to the first super-concept which does not specify the attribute *Att*, while the second one attaches it to the first concept for which the *NewVal* satisfies *Att*.

Discussion. Fuzzy ontologies are designed to solve the problem of handling vague and fuzzy knowledge. However, this problem does not arise while relocating an impoverished individual. In fact, while removing an attribute value, the individual must be attached to the first super-concept for which there is no specification for this attribute. Consequently, no membership is to be computed, neither fuzzy nor crisp. However, during the relocation of an enriched/modified individual, the problem of fuzzy knowledge slightly arises when comparing the new attribute value with its range. If the updated attribute is a fuzzy one, the range is defined by means of a fuzzy domain. Therefore, to identify the first consistent super-concept, we have to compute a partial membership in this fuzzy domain. However, in the case of a crisp attribute, the consistent super-concept is identified by a type verification which is a crisp comparison.

Relocating an updated individual into a fuzzy ontology refers to fuzzy ontology evolution, a topic which is rarely discussed in the literature. Indeed, ever since the development of ontologies, especially from large text corpuses, became a well-understood problem, reconstruction is always preferred to an evolutionary process [8]. Unlike crisp ontologies, relocating an updated individual into a fuzzy ontology is preferred to a new realization process. Indeed, the relocation process is not as complicated as a new realization one. In fact, during the realization process, all attributes of the individual are enriched and we have to match all their values with the ontology concepts. Therefore, to identify the individual belonging concepts we have to match each attribute value with its type, defined in every (fuzzy) concept. Unlike the realization process, during the relocation process we have to manage just one attribute (the one who causes the relocation). Consequently, a fuzzy relocation process is preferred to a new fuzzy reconstruction. Fuzzy ontology evolution is a challenging problem [18], and need to be further studied. To this scope, we have addressed the individual fuzzy classification issue by proposing fuzzy realization and relocation processes for fuzzy ontologies.

5 Conclusion

In our work, we have been interested in the classification reasoning mechanism applied on fuzzy ontologies for realizing them with new individuals. After their classification, individuals may evolve and change their knowledge. This evolution may be the result of an enrichment, modification or/and impoverishment of the individual knowledge. Data changes for already classified individuals imply their relocation in the fuzzy ontology. For this issue, we have proposed an extension of the individual fuzzy realization algorithm, namely an individual relocation process. Based on a fuzzy classification mechanism, it can relocate already classified, but updated, individuals into fuzzy ontologies. As future work, we would like to extend the proposed process so that it will not be limited to Zadeh semantics, but to be more flexible by supporting more fuzzy logics, for instance Łukasiewicz, Gödel or Product logics.

References

1. Alexopoulos, P., Wallace, M., Kafentzis, K., Askounis, D.: IKARUS-onto: a methodology to develop fuzzy ontologies from crisp ones. Knowl. Inf. Syst. **32**(3), 667–695 (2012)
2. Asma, D., Zizette, B.: Conceptualisation d'une Ontologie Floue. In: 9eme Colloque sur l'Optimisation et les Systèmes d'Information, Tlemcen, Algeria, pp. 62–73 (2012)
3. Asma, D., Zizette, B.: Fuzzy ontology evolution: classification of a new individual. J. Emerg. Technol. Web Intell. **6**(1), 9–14 (2014)
4. Bobillo, F., Straccia, U.: The fuzzy ontology reasoner fuzzyDL. Knowl.-Based Syst. **95**, 12–34 (2016)
5. Bobillo, F., Straccia, U.: Fuzzy ontology representation using OWL 2. Int. J. Approximate Reasoning **52**(7), 1073–1094 (2011)
6. Bobillo, F., Straccia, U.: General concept inclusion absorptions for fuzzy description logics: a first step. In: Description Logics, pp. 513–525 (2013)
7. Ghorbel, H., Bahri, A., Bouaziz, R.: Fuzzy protégé for fuzzy ontology models. In: 11th International Protégé Conference (IPC 2009), Academic Medical Center, University of Amsterdam, Amsterdam, Netherlands (2009)
8. Scharrenbach, T., Bernstein, A.: On the evolution of ontologies using probabilistic description logics. In: The First ESWC Workshop on Inductive Reasoning and Machine Learning on the Semantic Web (2009)
9. Simou, N., Mailis, T.P., Stoilos, G., Stamou, G.B.: Optimization techniques for fuzzy description logics. In: Description Logics (2010)
10. Stoilos, G., Simou, N., Stamou, G., Kollias, S.: Uncertainty and the semantic web: intelligent systems. IEEE Intell. Syst. **21**(5), 84–87 (2006)
11. Stoilos, G., Stamou, G., Pan, J.Z.: Fuzzy extensions of OWL: logical properties and reduction to fuzzy description logics. Int. J. Approximate Reasoning **51**(6), 656–679 (2010)
12. Straccia, U.: A fuzzy description logic for the semantic web. Capturing Intell. **1**, 73–90 (2006)
13. Straccia, U.: Description Logics with Fuzzy Concrete Domains. arXiv preprint arXiv:1207.1410 (2012)
14. Straccia, U.: Foundations of Fuzzy Logic and Semantic Web Languages. CRC Press, Boca Raton (2013)

15. Straccia, U.: All about fuzzy description logics and applications. In: Faber, W., Paschke, A. (eds.) Reasoning Web 2015. LNCS, vol. 9203, pp. 1–31. Springer, Heidelberg (2015)

16. Tsatsou, D., Dasiopoulou, S., Kompatsiaris, I., Mezaris, V.: LiFR: a lightweight fuzzy DL reasoner. In: Presutti, V., Blomqvist, E., Troncy, R., Sack, H., Papadakis, I., Tordai, A. (eds.) ESWC Satellite Events 2014. LNCS, vol. 8798, pp. 263–267. Springer, Heidelberg (2014)

17. Werro, N.: Fuzzy Classification of Online Customers. Springer, Heidelberg (2015). ISBN 3319159690 9783319159690

18. Zablith, F., Antoniou, G., d'Aquin, M., Flouris, G., Kondylakis, H., Motta, E., Sabou, M.: Ontology evolution: a process-centric survey. Knowl. Eng. Rev. **30**(01), 45–75 (2015)

19. Zadeh, L.A.: Fuzzy sets. Inf. Control **8**(3), 338–353 (1965). doi:10.1016/S0019-9958(65) 90241-X

Incremental Approach for Detecting Arbitrary and Embedded Cluster Structures

Keshab Nath[1], Swarup Roy[1,2](✉), and Sukumar Nandi[2]

[1] North-Eastern Hill University, Shillong, India
keshabnath@live.com, swarup@nehu.ac.in
[2] Indian Institute of Technology, Guwahati, India
sukumar@iitg.ernet.in

Abstract. In this paper, we present a new incremental clustering approach (InDEC) capable of detecting arbitrary cluster structures. Cluster may contain embedded structures. Available methods do not address this important issue in the context of continuously growing databases. A density variation concept is used to detect embedded clusters that may occurs after successive updation of database. Unlike popular methods which use distance measure, we use a new affinity score to decide the proximity of a new object with the clusters. We use both synthetic and real datasets to evaluate the performance of our proposed method. Experimental result reveals that proposed method is effective in detecting arbitrary and embedded clusters in dynamic scenario.

Keywords: Incremental clustering · Arbitrary cluster structure · Embedded cluster · Density variation

1 Introduction

Clustering data is a well-known problem that has been extensively studied and applied successfully in wide range of real life applications. Clustering is used to organize collection of data into homogeneous groups [1] by exploring the inter-relationship among collections of data in an unsupervised way without having any prior knowledge about the possible category of data. Traditional clustering considers dataset as static and is available for analysis beforehand. A large number of real life databases such as daily transaction databases, Medical databases and biological databases etc. are non-static in nature and growing with respect to time. With the rapid growth of data generation sources in different domains extended the importance of clustering even further. In terms of memory storage, computational time complexity, it is impractical to store the whole dataset in to memory and process them at the same time. Time variant data generation may alter the overall distribution of a cluster and leads to formation or shrinking of clusters. Traditional clustering approaches are limited in handling incremental data. It cannot assign a new data point in to the existing cluster without rerunning the algorithm to the updated dataset. These necessities motivate researchers towards incremental clustering, where data points are clustered

© Springer International Publishing Switzerland 2016
L. Bellatreche et al. (Eds.): MEDI 2016, LNCS 9893, pp. 220–233, 2016.
DOI: 10.1007/978-3-319-45547-1_18

immediately with the arrival of data. While performing incremental clustering, the qualitative aspects of the clusters should be preserved. Moreover, they
should perform no re-computation or at least limited number of re-computations
of existing data.

A number of methods are proposed to cluster incremental data. Several clustering approaches require number of clusters as input a priori which is not well
suited for incremental data. At the same time a good incremental clustering
should able to detect clusters of different shapes and sizes. It is observed that
clusters are not only arbitrary in shape and distribution; they may be intrinsic
or embedded in nature [2], where one cluster is embedded inside another cluster.

In this paper we present an incremental clustering method, which is capable
to detect both arbitrary and embedded cluster structures. Instead of using classical distance or similarity measures for capturing inter-relationship between the
data objects, we compute an affinity membership of an object with the existing
clusters. To detect variation in density inside a cluster, occurs due to the continuous updation the cluster, we use a new parametric approach based on degree
distribution of the objects within the cluster. We evaluate the performance of
the proposed method in the light of four synthetic and real datasets and compare
its effectiveness with well know density based clustering methods, DBSCAN and
OPTICS. Experimentally we show the superiority of the proposed method in
detecting arbitrary and intrinsic clusters in incremental data.

We organize our paper as follows. In Sect. 2 we discuss about incremental
clustering and some related works. The proposed approach for incremental clustering is presented in Sect. 3 and the performance evaluation of the proposed
model is reported in Sect. 4. Finally, in Sect. 5 the paper is summarized with
concluding remarks.

2 Incremental Clustering Approaches

Incremental clustering is a special case of traditional clustering where input data
is evolved continuously with time. It is a challenging task in comparison to clustering static data, where entire dataset is available before analysis. However,
unlike static data clustering, dynamic data clusters change in structure and distribution overtime very rapidly. Interestingly, incremental clustering is one of
the solutions for handling big data issue [3] related to managing data velocity.
Static clustering methods compute similarity among all pair of data objects from
the given dataset. Next, it applies optimization to minimize inter-cluster similarity and maximize intra-cluster similarity among the clusters. Mathematically,
clustering method is a mapping function and can be defined as follows.

Definition 1 (Static Clustering). *Given a database $D = \{x_1, x_2, \cdots, x_n\}$ of
objects, the static clustering problem is to define a mapping $f : D \rightarrow \{1, .., k\}$
where each x_i is assigned to cluster C_j. Cluster C_j contains those objects that
are precisely mapped to it (for $\forall j = 1, \cdots, k$).*

Any effective clustering algorithm must decide the parameter k, i.e. required number of clusters automatically without having prior knowledge of k. However, the total number of data objects to be grouped by static clustering is known a priori. On the contrary, in case of incremental clustering the number of data objects (n) is unknown beforehand and appears continuously over time.

Definition 2 (Incremental Clustering). *Given an incremental database* $D = \{x_1, x_2, \cdots, x_n\}$ *of objects, the incremental clustering problem is to define a mapping* $f : D \rightarrow \{1, \cdots, k\}$ *where each* x_i *is assigned to cluster* $C_i(t)$ *with respect to time* t. *Cluster* $C_i(t)$ *contains those objects that are mapped to it (for* $\forall j = 1, \cdots, k$) *at time* t. *At time* $t + 1$, *any cluster* $C_i(t + 1)$ *may contain object* $x_p \in C_j(t)$ *and* $C_j(t + 1) = C_j(t) - x_p$.

In case of incremental clustering movement of data objects among different clusters is possible. Ideally, clustering outcome produced by any incremental clustering approach should not deviate largely from the outcome produced by applying static data clustering on the same set of data. The main issue of incremental clustering is that it is sensitive to incoming data points ordering. For last few decades a number of methods have been proposed to address the issue of clustering incremental data. *Ester et al.* [4] proposed an incremental DBSCAN algorithm for dynamic datasets. The idea behind this algorithm is that after certain time if there is a addition/removal of new data points occur, the density connection of the clusters gets affected. The result yields by incremental DBSCAN are same with original DBSCAN algorithm. *Jun-Song Fu et al.* [5] present an incremental clustering algorithm based on OPTICS. They have modified the original algorithm parameters such as *Minpts* and ϵ and they have introduce a new parameter called distance, which is nothing but the replacement of reachability distance. In this method they have also proposed a method which automatically generate clusters from cluster-ordering structure based on user's needs. Authors claimed that Incremental Clustering Algorithm (ICA) is more suitable for dynamic datasets than traditional OPTICS algorithm. The main advantage of this ICA is that no parameters are needed to preset. So it becomes helpful for those user who does not have prior knowledge of that dataset. The main limitation of this algorithm is that it need to scan the whole dataset every time and secondly it condensed the data structure and due to this process some details of the dataset are lost. *Tao et al.* [6] proposed a single pass incremental clustering algorithm for relational dataset. *Ahmad M. Bakr et al.* [7] proposed an enhanced version of incremental DBSCAN algorithm. The main idea of this algorithm is to reduce the search space to partitions rather than processing the whole dataset. According to this research work the proposed algorithm produced better result in large dataset with high dimensions compared to related incremental clustering algorithms. *S. Asharaf et al.* [8] proposed an incremental clustering algorithm which is based on rough set theory concept for interval dataset. The main advantage of this method is that it is scalable, because clusters are generated in a single scan, secondly it store only the min and max vectors for its operation and it is robust to outliers.

Majority of the incremental clustering techniques adopt density based clustering for clustering arbitrary cluster structures from incremental data. Existing methods are effective in detecting arbitrary shape clusters without having prior knowledge of number of clusters. It has been observed that clusters exhibits embedded patterns and may contain one cluster inside another. Available methods fail to address the issue effectively. Moreover, they use traditional similarity measure to compute proximity of an incoming data objects with the existing clusters. Such measures in its original form are inadequate to detect appropriate membership of a new object towards a cluster. Next, we introduce a new incremental approach to detect clusters of arbitrary and embedded in nature. Our approach handles data dynamism by automatically deciding the need of new cluster or merging of existing clusters with respect to time.

3 A New Density Based Incremental Clustering

Density based approaches are effective in detecting arbitrary shaped clusters in presence of noise. They produce results without considering number of required clusters as input. Like any traditional clustering techniques, their performances are also heavily depended on suitable similarity measures. The same limitation is also persists in their extended version for handling incremental data. In this work, we calculate affinity score of a newly arrived object with the existing clusters.

3.1 Calculating Cluster Membership

We introduce here a new but simple way to calculate proximity of an object with respect to existing clusters instead of using any distance measure directly. An object is assigned to a group where the affinity score is maximum. Affinity score of an object x_j to a cluster C_i can be given as follows.

Definition 3 (Cluster Affinity Score). *Given a cluster C_i and a new data object x_j, whose degree of belongingness to cluster C_i can be calculated as the ratio between number of neighbours of $x_j \in C_i$ and size of cluster C_i ($|C_i|$).*

$$Affinity(x_j, C_i) = \frac{\sum_{k=1}^{|C_i|} \delta(x_j, y_k)}{|C_i|}. \tag{1}$$

Given any suitable distance measure $dist(.,.)$ and a user defined threshold θ, $\delta(x, y)$ can be calculated as:

$$\delta(x, y) = \begin{cases} 1, & if\ dist(x, y) < \theta \\ 0, & otherwise, \end{cases} \tag{2}$$

where, y is the neighbour of x if distance between x and y is within θ.

3.2   Clustering Incremental Data

We treat each incoming object independently for clustering. Initially, it starts with zero cluster. In our approach initial seed cluster is not necessary to start the incremental clustering process. With the arrival of first object x_1, a new cluster C_1 is formed with x_1. We use above affinity score to assign any new object into the cluster with maximum affinity. we form a new cluster if there is no matching clusters. On every insertion of a data in a cluster may lead to following situations.

– Concentration or intra density of the cluster may alter over time.
– Successive updation of a cluster may bring two clusters close to each other to form a single cluster.

We handle the above situation while clustering in following ways.

3.3   Detecting Density Variation

To detect density variation in a cluster, we define a cluster as *density function* with respect to degree distribution of the nodes in a cluster. We represent each cluster of m objects with a dynamic cluster feature vector $CF_{C_i} = \{\delta_1, \delta_2, \cdots, \delta_m\}$. δ_j is the sum of θ nearest neighbour of an object $x_j \in C_i$ and can be calculated using Eq. (2). On insertion of each new element in C_i, CF_{C_i} is updated accordingly. Effected δ_j ($\forall j \in CF_{C_i}$) is incremented if object x_j is within the θ nearest neighbour of newly inserted object x_k. Accordingly the CF_{C_i} is updated to accommodate δ_k for the new object x_k.

Continuous updation of a cluster may generate new dense regions within a cluster forming intrinsic or embedded cluster structures. We detect a density variation in a cluster CF_{C_i} at time $t+1$ if significant change happens in the area under the density curve. Given feature vector $CF_{C_i}^{t+1}$ at time $(t+1)$, the density variation occurs if following inequality satisfy.

$$\mu(CF_{C_i}^{t+1}) > max(CF_{C_i}^{t+1}) - \xi \times \sigma(CF_{C_i}^t) \tag{3}$$

where, ξ is the curve spread factor and μ and σ are the mean and standard deviation of the feature vector of C_i respectively and can be calculated as

$$\mu(CF_{C_i}) = \frac{1}{|C_i|} \sum_{i=1}^{|C_i|} \delta_i \tag{4}$$

$$\sigma(CF_{C_i}) = \sqrt{\frac{1}{|C_i|} \sum_{i=1}^{|C_i|} (\delta_i - \mu(CF_{C_i}))^2} \tag{5}$$

For any convex or non-convex shaped clusters it usually follows a normal degree distributions. The objects in the core are highly connected and connectivity become sparse as it move towards the boundary. We consider such ideal case to demonstrate the validity of our way to detect density variation. To illustrate the fact we consider two clusters, one at time t with sparse degree distribution and second curve is based on incremental data at time $(t+1)$ with the addition of embedded structure. The curves are shown in Fig. 1. We try to detect variation in density with the change in the curve spread or area. This can be achieved by considering the change in mean and standard deviation of the curve. For example, let us assume a degree distribution for a sparse cluster is $t = \{1, 1, 2, 8, 9, 7, 6, 3, 2, 2\}$ and $t+1 = \{2, 3, 4, 8, 8, 10, 13, 13, 15, 15, 14, 13, 12, 8, 6, 4, 4, 4, 3, 2\}$. We calculate μ^t and σ^t for our first curve at time t with $\mu^t = 4.1$ and $\sigma^t = 4.07$. The μ^{t+1} is 6.5 and σ^{t+1} is 4.66 is calculated for the degree distribution of the incremental data. If the δ_{max}^{t+1} (maximum degree)for the second distribution is 15 and $\xi = 1.9$, the inequality given in Eq. (3) holds because of density variation occurs at $(t+1)$.

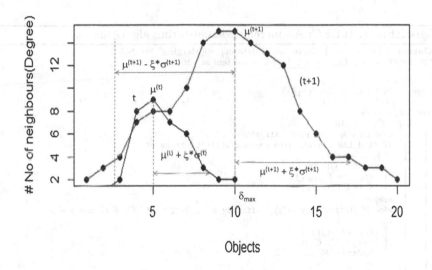

Fig. 1. Illustration of density variation in the density curve at t and t+1 time

On variation in density of the cluster C_i we start the re-clustering to detect embedded cluster. Interestingly, to perform re-clustering it requires only CF_{C_i} and the adjacency matrix created by Eq. (2). No need to store the entire dataset for performing incremental updation of clusters.

3.4   Merging Clusters

Given two clusters C_i and C_j, we merge the clusters if insertion of a new object x_k acts as linking factor between C_i and C_j. In other words, if x_k become linking factor, forwhich x_k having significant number of shared neighbours in both the clusters. This can be detected easily by comparing the affinity score of x_k with respect to both the clusters. We merge them if affinity score difference is very small i.e. $|Affinity(x_k, C_i) - Affinity(x_k, C_j)| < \tau$.

3.5   InDEC: The Algorithm

Stepwise representation of our proposed method for detecting arbitrary and embedded cluster in incremental data, *InDEC* (Incremental Density based Embedded Clustering), is given in Algorithm 1. InDEC initialize cluster set C with a cluster C_i containing first data object x_1. For any other incoming object x_i it is assigned to the cluster C_j with highest affinity. If the affinity score of x_i with clusters C_j and any other cluster C_p is similar to each other, we consider x_i as a intermediate object between the two clusters sharing significant number of nearest neighbours. We merge C_j and C_p to form a single cluster. Otherwise, a new cluster C_{new} is created with the object x_i. We update the cluster feature vector of $CF_{C_{new}}$ or CF_{C_j} as per requirement.

Algorithm 1. InDEC: An incremental clustering algorithm

Data: D $=\{x_1, x_2, \cdots\}$ (Incremental dataset); τ (Merging threshold)
Result: C $= \{C_1, C_2, \cdots, C_m\}$ (Set of clusters at time t)

```
1  Initialize C = {φ};
2  Create Cluster Cᵢ = Cᵢ ∪{x₁};
3  D = D- {x₁}; C = C ∪ Cᵢ;
4  for ∀xᵢ ∈ D do
5      for ∀Cⱼ ∈ C do
6          Compute k = arg maxⱼ{Affinity(xᵢ, Cⱼ)};
           // find the cluster with maximum affinity score of xᵢ
7          if (k = φ) then
8              Create Cluster C_new;
9              C_new = C_new ∪ xᵢ ;
10             C = C ∪ C_new;
11         end
12         else if (|Affinity(xᵢ, Cⱼ) − Affinity(xᵢ, Cₚ)| < τ)// ∀Cₚ ∈ C and j ≠ p
13         then
14             Cⱼ = Cⱼ ∪{xᵢ};
15             Merge (Cⱼ, Cₚ);
16             Update CF_Cⱼ;
17             C = C − {Cₚ};
18         end
19         else
20             Cⱼ = Cⱼ ∪{xᵢ};
21             Update CF_Cⱼ;
22         end
23     end
24  end
25  Return(C) ;
```

To detect intrinsic clusters, InDEC explore the density variation in a cluster at time $(t + 1)$ in comparison to cluster density distribution at time t. We perform embedded cluster with a time interval instead of online. Set of updated cluster feature vectors CF is enough to represent the clusters. Hence, we do not require original datasets to be stored in the memory. This makes the approach memory efficient. Each cluster feature vector CF_{C_i} is verified to detect any density variation, in turn checking for any embedded cluster formation. We start the process by taking the object with highest neighbours (degree). In line 3 of Algorithm 2 we are checking density variation using Eq. (3). Before forming a

---

Algorithm 2. Embedded Clustering

Data: CF $=\{CF_{C_1}, CF_{C_2}, \cdots CF_{C_m}\}$ (Set of Cluster Feature Vectors at time t+1)
Result: C (Set of clusters at time t+1)

1 **for** $\forall CF_{C_i} \in$ CF **do**
2   Compute $\arg\max_j\{\delta_j \in CF_{C_i}\}$;
     // find the maximum degree node in C_i
3   **if** $\mu(CF_{C_i}) > (\delta_j - \xi * \sigma^t(CF_{C_i}))$ // Checking Density variation
4   **then**
5   **if** $\delta_j > (\mu(CF_{C_i}) + \sigma^{(t+1)}(CF_{C_i}))$ // to check minimum neighbour of x_j
6   *to form new cluster* **then**
7   Create Cluster C_{new};
8           $C_{new} = C_{new} \bigcup x_j$;
9   **for** $\forall x_k \in Neighbours_\theta(x_j)$ // Expanding the neighbour of x_j
10   **do**
11   **if** $\delta_k > (\delta_j - \xi * \sigma^{(t+1)}(CF_{C_i}))$ **then**
12                $C_{new} = C_{new} \bigcup x_k$;
13   ExpandCluster (x_k);
14   **end**
15   **end**
16   **end**
17   **end**
18   Update $CF_{C_{new}}$;
19   Update CF_{C_i};
20   C = C $\bigcup C_{new}$;
21 **end**
22 Return(C) ;

---

new embedded cluster C_{new} within C_j we first check the eligibility of x_j to form a new cluster (line 5). x_j should have minimum number of neighbours to form a new cluster. We decide minimum neighbours by comparing with a threshold $(\mu(CF_{C_i}) + \sigma^{(t+1)}(CF_{C_i}))$, i.e. mean and standard deviation of current cluster degree distribution. Next, we expand the neighbours of x_j to detect the embedded cluster. The cluster expansion module is given in Algorithm 3.

Algorithm 3. ExpandCluster (x_k)

---

for $\forall x_p \in Neighbours_\theta(x_k)$ // Expanding the neighbour of x_k
do
   if $\delta_p > (\delta_j - \xi * \sigma^{(t+1)}(CF_{C_i}))$ **then**
      $C_{new} = C_{new} \bigcup x_p$;
      ExpandCluster (x_p);
   end
end

---

4 Performance Evaluation

To evaluate performance of our proposed method we use both synthetic and real datasets. We consider four synthetic and four real datasets for testing. We compare our results with two well known density based clustering methods, DBSCAN and OPTICS. This is performed with a justification that incremental clustering must produce results at par with the results generated by any static clustering. Pearson correlation is used to compute affinity score of an object with a cluster for real datasets.

4.1   Dataset Used

Point dataset helps in visual interpretation and assessment of quality of clusters produced by any clustering algorithm. We generate four such point datasets with embedded and arbitrary cluster structures. The arbitrary structure datasets Arda1 and Arda2 have 178 and 184 patterns with embedded structure. The spiral dataset (Arda4) have 398 pattern distributions with two spiral clusters. The datasets are shown in Figs. 2 and 3.

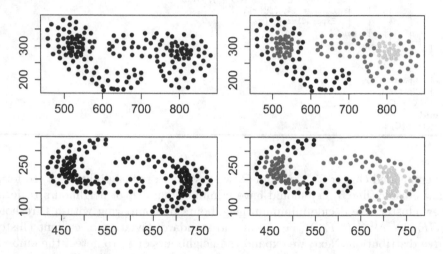

Fig. 2. InDEC output on dataset Arda1 (top) & Arda2 (bottom)

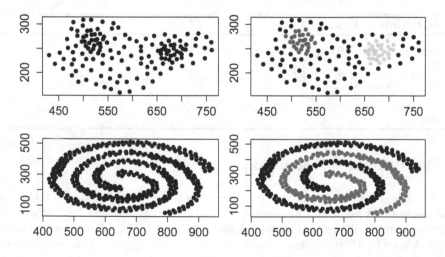

Fig. 3. InDEC output on dataset Arda3 (top) & Arda4 (bottom)

Table 1. Dataset used in experiments

Type	Dataset	Pattern#	Attributes
Synthetic	Arda1	178	2
	Arda2	184	2
	Arda3	144	2
	Spiral	398	2
Real-World	Iris	150	4
	Wine	178	13
	Ecoli	336	8
	Shuttle	58000	9

Four multi-dimensional real-world datasets from the UCI machine repository[1] is used for experimentation. A brief description of the datasets used in our experiment is given in Table 1.

4.2 Experimental Results

The InDEC algorithm is implemented in R language and run in Windows 7 environment having machine configuration 2 GB RAM and 2.10 GHz. For our all experiments we achieve better performance with $\xi = 1.9$. However, we suggest possible range of values for $\xi = [1.9, 3]$. Superior performances of InDEC in detecting embedded and arbitrary clusters can easily be evident from the

Table 2. Qualitative Assessment of InDEC for Real Datasets

Dataset	Method	Dunn	Silhouette	Connectivity	Davies-Bouldin
Iris	InDEC	**0.3389**	**0.6863**	**10.9135**	**0.4488**
	DBSCAN	0.2019	0.3249	11.1892	0.7898
	OPTICS	0.3187	0.2963	10.9634	0.7349
Wine	InDEC	**0.3784**	**0.3945**	**12.9024**	0.4214
	DBSCAN	0.3161	0.3359	12.9147	**0.4123**
	OPTICS	0.3417	0.3276	13.9340	0.5798
Ecoli	InDEC	**0.4569**	**0.6068**	**10.5678**	**0.39675**
	DBSCAN	0.3957	0.4391	12.6275	0.8479
	OPTICS	0.3521	0.3706	11.4720	0.8142
Shuttle	InDEC	**0.3762**	**0.3674**	14.9783	0.5784
	DBSCAN	0.3312	0.3194	**12.0861**	0.6509
	OPTICS	0.3049	0.3250	13.7842	**0.5428**

---

[1] http://archive.ics.uci.edu/ml/datasets.html.

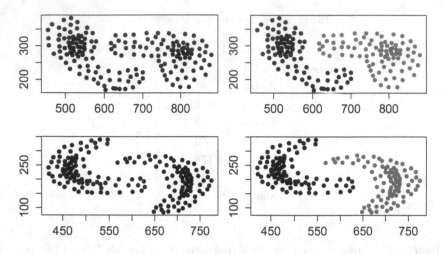

Fig. 4. DBSCAN output on dataset Arda1 (top) & Arda2 (bottom)

results, on all the synthetic data, given in Figs. 2 and 3 (shown in left side of the figure in black color). It can be clearly observed that InDEC outperform DBSCAN and OPTICS in detecting arbitrary and embedded clusters. Incase of real datasets, we use various statistical validity index for determining the effectiveness of InDEC and compare its performance with DBSCAN and OPTICS. For all our experiments we use $\epsilon = 5$ and *Minpoint* $= 3$ required for DBSCAN and OPTICS.

Dunn validity index measures the compactness and separation. A higher *Dunn* index indicates better clustering. The *Silhouette* index range from -1 to 1.

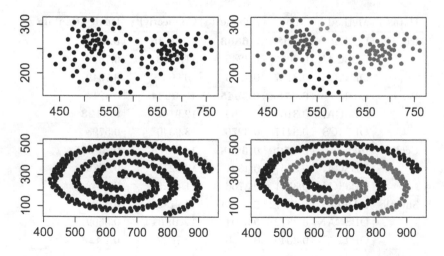

Fig. 5. DBSCAN output on dataset Arda3 (top) & Arda4 (bottom)

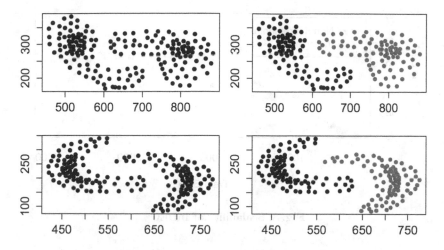

Fig. 6. OPTICS output on dataset Arda1 (top) & Arda2 (bottom)

High *Silhouette* value indicates that the objects is well matched to its own cluster. *Connectivity* index range from zero to ∞ and should be minimized. *Davies-Bouldin*(DB) index attempts to identify compact and well separated clusters. The smallest DB value is considered the best. Table 2 represents the qualitative assessments of InDEC based on various validity measures. Best performing scores, in each validity criterias, are highligted in the table. From the results it is clearly evident that InDEC performs better than DBSCAN and OPTICS with respect to various validity measures (Table 2).

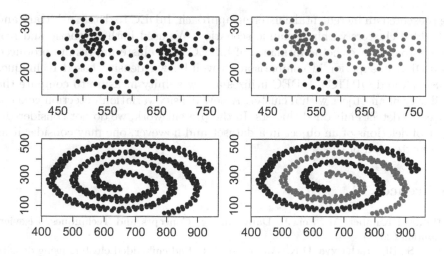

Fig. 7. OPTICS output on dataset Arda3 (top) & Arda4 (bottom)

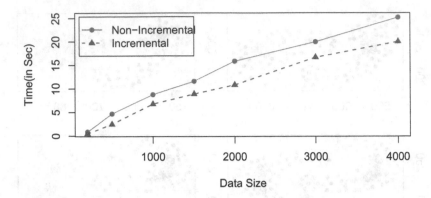

Fig. 8. Scalability of InDEC

To measure the scalability of InDEC, we use synthetic data. In first case (Non-incremental), we gradually increase the size of the data up to 4000 and report the total time requirements in seconds for different sizes by re-running our method with varying data sizes from the scratch. While in other case we consider data is incremental and report the time taken after specific interval and arrival of data of different sizes. Unlike first case we input the entire data (maximum size) incrementally. The execution time of InDEC with varying data size is presented in Fig. 8. Results reported gives a clear indication that InDEC is scalable with respect to data size.

5 Conclusion

We presented an incremental clustering approach, InDEC to detect arbitrary and embedded clusters within dynamic scenarios. We used both synthetic and real datsets to evaluate the performance of InDEC. The clustering results produced by InDEC is superior in comparison to well-known density based techniques DBSCAN and OPTICS. InDEC utilizes a new affinity measure to compute the similarity of an object with a cluster. A new density variation detection concept is used to detect embedded clusters. In the present work, we do not consider the effect of deletions of an object in a dataset and however, one may consider it as future extension of this work.

References

1. Han, J., Kamber, M., Pei, J.: Data Mining: Concepts and Techniques. Elsevier, London (2011)
2. Roy, S., Bhattacharyya, D.K.: An approach to find embedded clusters using density based techniques. In: Chakraborty, G. (ed.) ICDCIT 2005. LNCS, vol. 3816, pp. 523–535. Springer, Heidelberg (2005)

3. Fahad, A., Alshatri, N., Tari, Z., Alamri, A., Khalil, I., Zomaya, A.Y., Foufou, S., Bouras, A.: A survey of clustering algorithms for big data: taxonomy and empirical analysis. IEEE Trans. Emerg. Top. Comput. **2**(3), 267–279 (2014)
4. Ester, M., Kriegel, H.P., Sander, J., Wimmer, M., Xu, X.: Incremental clustering for mining in a data warehousing environment. In: VLDB, vol. 98, pp. 323–333 (1998)
5. Fu, J.S., Liu, Y., Chao, H.C.: ICA: an incremental clustering algorithm based on optics. Wirel. Pers. Commun. **84**(3), 2151–2170 (2015)
6. Li, T., Anand, S.S.: Hirel: an incremental clustering algorithm for relational datasets. In: Eighth IEEE International Conference on Data Mining, ICDM 2008, pp. 887–892. IEEE (2008)
7. Bakr, A.M., Ghanem, N.M., Ismail, M.A.: Efficient incremental density-based algorithm for clustering large datasets. Alexandria Eng. J. **54**(4), 1147–1154 (2015)
8. Asharaf, S., Murty, M.N., Shevade, S.K.: Rough set based incremental clustering of interval data. Pattern Recogn. Lett. **27**(6), 515–519 (2006)

Annotation of Engineering Models by References to Domain Ontologies

Kahina Hacid[✉] and Yamine Ait-Ameur

Université de Toulouse, INP,
IRIT Institut de Recherche en Informatique de Toulouse,
Toulouse, France
{kahina.hacid,yamine}@enseeiht.fr

Abstract. Complex engineering systems execute within different contexts and domains. The heterogeneity induced by these contexts is usually implicitly handled in the development cycle of such systems. We claim that reducing this heterogeneity can be achieved by handling explicitly the knowledge mined from these domains and contexts. Verification and validation activities are improved due to the expression and verification of new constraints and properties directly extracted from the context and domains associated to the models. In this paper, we advocate the use of domain ontologies to express both domain and context knowledge. We propose to enrich design models that describe complex information systems, with domain knowledge, expressed by ontologies, provided by their context of use. This enrichment is achieved by annotation of the design models by references to ontologies. Three annotation mechanisms are proposed. The resulting annotated models are checked to validate the new minded domain properties. We have experimented this approach in a model driven engineering (MDE) development setting.

Keywords: Design models · Ontologies · Annotation · Model engineering

1 Introduction

In general, during system development, the knowledge provided by the engineering domain is not explicitly taken into account in the different models that result from this development. The system development process leads to the production of several heterogeneous models corresponding to different views or analyses of the same system. In this context, the most important heterogeneity factor, in addition to the one due to the use of different modelling languages, is related to information, knowledge and assumptions of the domain (the environment and context of execution of the systems) that are not explicitly formalised and therefore not used in the models of these systems. One of the reasons is the absence of such domain knowledge in the modelling language. The developer has to handle this information in the development process. It may happen that the assumptions made by the developers are contradictory due to an implicit consideration of domain knowledge. Indeed, although systems are developed according

© Springer International Publishing Switzerland 2016
L. Bellatreche et al. (Eds.): MEDI 2016, LNCS 9893, pp. 234–244, 2016.
DOI: 10.1007/978-3-319-45547-1_19

to development standards and good practices, a large part of the knowledge required to the interpretation and validation of these models of systems remain implicit. This situation may raise several insufficiencies and drawbacks during system verification and validation activities. More precisely, a system assumed to be sound after verification and validation may loose some of its properties if information related to its domain, context and environment are integrated to the model. Indeed, general knowledge information expressed as properties may be no longer valid in the developed model. For example, the addition of two variables X and Y, occurring in a design model, may not be valid if domain information states that X is measured in *meters* and Y in *miles*, although the modelling language allows such addition. The objective of our work is to propose a sound and operationalised approach to strengthen design models with domain knowledge resources carried out by the engineering domain associated to the designed models. We consider that on the one hand, ontologies are good candidates for describing and making explicit such knowledge [1], and on the other, annotation of model resources by references to ontologies makes it possible to handle domain knowledge in design models. More precisely, to reach this objective, we propose a solution involving in a first step the use of ontologies to clarify and formalise the domain knowledge. As a second step, annotation mechanisms are defined and set up to link both design models and ontologies. It becomes possible to express and verify new properties of the enriched design models. This paper is structured as follows. Section 2 recalls basic definitions of domain ontologies. Section 3 presents the NoseGear case study [2] illustrating the work developed in this paper. Our approach for strengthening models through an annotation based method, the developed annotation mechanisms and details of the implementation on the basis of a model driven engineering (MDE) approach are presented in Sect. 4. Application of the proposed approach to the case study is given in Sect. 5. Finally, Sect. 6 overviews different approaches promoting annotation and semantic enrichment of models. A conclusion ends this paper and identifies some research directions.

2   Domain Ontologies as Models for Domain Knowledge

Gruber defines an ontology as *an explicit specification of a conceptualisation* [3]. In our work, a domain ontology is considered as a *formal and consensual dictionary of categories and properties of entities of a domain and the relationships that hold among them* [4]. In this definition, entity represents any concept belonging to the studied domain. The term dictionary emphasises that any entity and any kind of domain relationship described in the domain ontology may be referenced directly, for any purpose and from any context, independently of other entities or relationships, by a symbol (URI i.e. unique resource identifier). Ontology design requires to express a set of basic concepts related to structure (class, relationships, etc.), description (properties, attributes, etc.) and behaviour (derivation expression, labelled transitions systems, etc.). An ontology modelling language is required to describe such ontologies. Several ontology modelling languages have been developed so far. OWL [5], PLIB [6,7], RDFS [8] are some examples of such languages. These languages describe ontology entities using different modelling artefacts like hierarchies, properties, relationships, instances and individuals, constraints, etc. According to [4], a domain ontology is a domain conceptualisation that obeys to the three fundamental criteria: being formal, consensual and offering references capabilities.

Formal. An ontology is a conceptualization based on a formal theory to check consistency properties and to perform some automatic reasoning over concepts.

Consensual. An ontology is a conceptualization agreed upon by a community larger than the members involved in one particular application development (one design model). Ontology standards are good supports for such agreements.

Capability to be referenced. Each ontological concept is associated with an URI. References to this concept become possible, using this identifier, from any environment, independently of the ontology where this concept was defined. In this paper, we do not address the ontology design process, we suppose that ontologies already exist. This section is voluntarily made concise. The literature related to ontology engineering is full of definitions, approaches, work, tools, etc.

3   The NoseGear Case Study

The NoseGear [2] is a sub-component of the landing gear of an airplane. The objective of the case study addressed in this paper is to estimate the speed of a grounded airplane. Speed is estimated by measuring the time taken by the NoseGear wheel to achieve a turn. An interruption is triggered each time a round is completed. This interruption increments two counters: a counter which calculates the number of turns the wheel made, and another recording the current time value. Then, a function operates to calculate the speed of the plane from the recorded values of both counters. The complete description of the NoseGear case study is given in [2]. This case study involves several independent views of the same system (physical, computing, etc.). We assume that multiple ontologies are used to express knowledge and properties associated to each view. Since these views relate to the same engineering area, *implicit* relationships may exist between the different views and therefore between the related ontologies. Through this case study, our goal is, first, to identify and to formalise these implicit relations existing between ontologies. Then, we use them to link multiple system components of the NoseGear design model. *Constraints* are used to express invariants defining properties mined from different ontologies.

4   Our Approach

4.1   Methodology

We propose a stepwise methodology to establish a formal explicit link between these two models. Figure 1 shows the overall schema of the approach involving four steps. Concepts, properties and constraints of the studied domain are represented and formalised within a knowledge model (domain ontologies) at step 1. Specific design models are defined at step 2. At step 3, relationships between design model entities and the corresponding knowledge concepts are identified. Three different kinds of relationships can be set up, they are discussed in Sect. 4.2. Finally, at step 4, the annotated model is analysed to determine whether the constraints associated to the knowledge domain, carried out by the annotations, can be expressed in the new enriched design model. More details about the developed approach can be found in [9].

4.2 Model Annotation: Three Cases

Relations, formalized as model annotations, are established between design model entities and ontology concepts. Three annotation mechanisms are identified.

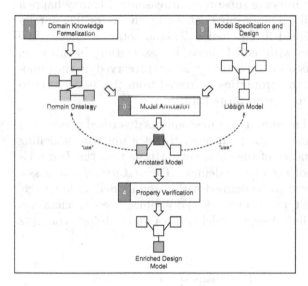

Fig. 1. A four steps methodology for handling domain knowledge in design models.

Annotation by inheritance. (Figure 2(a)) is defined by the *Is_a* relationship (subsumption relationship [10]). In this case, a concept of the ontology subsumes an entity of the design model. The mapping relationship is the subsumption (is_a). Properties, attributes, rules and constraints that apply to the ontological concept are also applicable to the design model entity. This annotation maintains the ontological reasoning and preserves it at the design model level. This relationship is usually set up in an a priori setting where the ontology is designed before the design models are defined.

Annotation by partial inheritance. (Figure 2(b)) is defined by the *Is_case_of* relationship. It is also a subsumption relationship. It defines a partial inheritance [10]. This relation behaves like the *Is_a* relationship, except that it does not require the inheritance of all the ontological properties. In fact, only some of the relevant properties and constraints of the ontology class are imported. The annotation mechanism is in charge of selecting which properties and constraints are imported. The main advantage of this approach is flexibility, it can be set up in any situation (a priori and a posteriori).

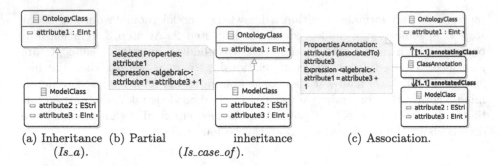

(a) Inheritance   (b) Partial   inheritance   (c) Association.
     (*Is_a*).   (*Is_case_of*).

Fig. 2. Annotations mechanisms.

Annotation by association. (Figure 2(c)) *Is_a* and *Is_case_of* relationships are based on relationships that preserve subsumption reasoning. It may happen that an annotation needs specific relationships defined by the users. These relationships are themselves described in ontologies. This annotation enables the connection of ontological classes with model classes by association. In this case, subsumption reasoning contained in the ontology is not preserved at the annotated design model level. But, the properties borrowed from the association to the design model can be used to express properties.

Annotation meta-models. The annotation mechanisms described above need to be described in the modelling language in order to get a uniform modelling setting (here UML). A consequence of the choice of UML, is that the *Is_a* relationship is built-in and does not need to be defined. The *Is_Case_of* and *Association* annotation relations need to be defined within the modelling language. Two meta-models (one for each type of annotation) describing these mechanisms are introduced (Fig. 3). They link design model entities and ontology concepts at the meta-model level.

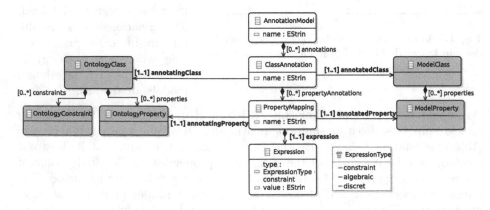

Fig. 3. Annotation by *Association* meta-model.

AnnotationModel: the entry point of the annotation models.
ClassAnnotation: an association of ontology concepts and design model classes.
PropertyMapping: relations between properties of design model and of ontology.
Expression: algebraic expressions to compose properties (constraint, derivation).

4.3   Properties Expression and Verification

The last step of the approach analyses the obtained annotated design models. The annotation process leads to the enrichment of the original design model with new relations, properties, constraints and rules. Ontological properties and classes are considered to be available (or expressible) in the enriched model if they have been explicitly selected or linked to model properties during the annotation process (third step of Fig. 1). It may happen that these relations, properties and constraints could not be expressed at the design model level and thus not valuable at instantiation level due to the absence of attributes to express them or of the values of these attributes (instances). These constraints become meaningless. At this level, an analysis of the obtained annotated model is necessary after an annotation by *Is_Case_Of* or by *association* because these two types of annotation offer the possibility of having only some ontological properties in the enriched design model. The annotation by *Is_a* does not suffer from this drawback since all ontological constraints in the design model can be expressed (all the properties of the annotating ontological classes are inherited in the design model). The proposed analysis procedure is depicted on Fig. 4. The process begins by selecting an annotated class in the model and analyse it to retrieve the ontological class that annotates it. Each constraint of the annotating class is then analysed to decide if it is expressible in the model. The expressible constraints are integrated into the model, the other ones are discarded.

```
 BEGIN
     For (an annotated model)
     begin
        Select a new annotated class;
        Select the corresponding onology class;
        For (all ontology class constraints)
        begin
           Select a new constraint;
           if (constraint is expressible in the design model) then
              Integrate to the domain model;
           else
              Add an error message;
           endif;
        end;
     end;
 END;
```

Fig. 4. Algorithm of the verification process.

5   Application to the NoseGear Case Study

5.1   Step 1. a Domain Ontolgy

Figure 5 depicts the ontology used to annotate the NoseGear design model. It is composed of two parts defining specific modelled domain knowledge: an avionic ontology *PlaneOntology* and a devices ontology *DevicesOntology* composed of classes and properties. *Constraints* are defined on the ontology model *Ontology* (Fig. 5).

Constraints. We present two *constraints*: N_{max} and F_{CPU}. They express implicit relations that may exist between different views of the NoseGear models (e.g. computation and physical views). Formalized within ontologies, these *constraints* describe implicit links between domain ontologies. They link the components of the design model after making explicit the knowledge in the model.

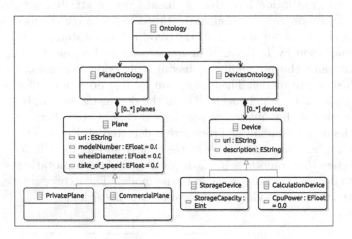

Fig. 5. Overview of the ontology of the NoseGear.

N_{max} **of the wheel.** This *constraint* determines the optimal memory size *StorageCapacity*) of the landing gear's lap counter (*StorageDevice* in the ontology). We calculate the maximum number of laps (N_{max}) that can be made by the wheel on the take off track. N_{max} is obtained by dividing the maximum distance that can be travelled (i.e. length of the take off track) by the distance travelled in one turn (circumference of the wheel). $N_{max} = D_{max}/C_{wheel}$ is obtained.

The maximum memory size of the laps counter can then be deduced by bounding N_{max}: $2^{k-1} \leqslant N_{max} \leqslant 2^k$, k being the number of bits needed to represent N_{max}. As a consequence, we have been able to exploit the topology knowledge to determine the optimal size of the register encoding the N_{max} value.

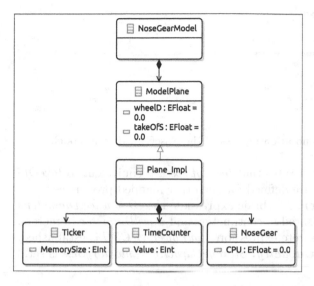

Fig. 6. Overview of the NoseGear design model.

$\mathbf{F}_{CPU}$. The second *constraint* determines which kind of CPU processor (the CPU frequency $\mathbf{F}_{CPU}$) is needed to support calculations related to the number of laps of the NoseGear wheel. To be responsive, the CPU frequency must be adjusted to be able to detect at best every lap of the wheel. It involves having at least a rising edge clock whenever a complete lap is done. The following relationship: $\mathbf{F}_{CPU}$ = $take\_of\_speed / \mathbf{C}_{wheel}$ is obtained. Here, cinematic theory specifies the required frequency of a calculator.

These two *constraints* are defined in the presented ontologies. They help to explicit existing relations between different knowledge domains of the NoseGear model.

5.2   Step 2. Design Models

The design model of the *NoseGear* describes a simple architecture of an aircraft. An overview of the Ecore model is given in Fig. 6. Note that the NoseGear architecture is usually represented by several models, each one describing a specific view. These models are not given here due to space limitation but may be obtained from [11]). The NoseGear model is defined by the abstract system *ModelPlane*. *Plane_Impl* implements the Plane system. It is composed of the *Nosegear* (calculator to detect and calculate the number of laps the wheel makes), the *Ticker* (the counter to store the value of the number of laps) and *TimeCounter* (the time counter).

5.3   Step 3. Annotation Process

In Fig. 7, *annotation by association* is established between *Plane* ontological class and *ModelPlane* of the model using *ClassAnnotation* (bullet 1). Annotations are also established between *StorageDevice* and *Ticker* and between *Calculation-Device* and *NoseGear*. A correspondence is established between *take_of_speed* of the ontology and *takeOfS* of the model using *PropertyAnnotation* (bullet 2). Correspondences are also established between: *wheelD* and *wheelDiameter*, *CpuPower* property of the ontological *CalculationDevice* and *CPU* property of *NoseGear*, and finally, between *StorageCapacity* property of *StorageDevice* and *memorySize* property of the *Ticker* model.

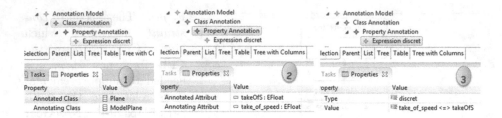

Fig. 7. Overview of the annotation process of the NoseGear design model.

A *discrete* typed expression states that *take_of_speed* is equivalent to *takeOfS* (bullet 3). Other expressions are defined for the other mapped properties.
wheelD and wheelDiameter. Algebraic expression *wheelD = wheelDiameter* ∗ 100 is defined. *wheelD* is measured in centimeters and *wheelDiameter* in meters.
Cpu and CpuPower. A discrete expression *CpuPower ⟺ CPU* is established.
memorySize and StorageCapacity. *StorageCapacity ⟺ memorySize* is set.

5.4   Step 4: Property Verification

The *verification* step consists in analysing the obtained annotated NoseGear design model. A constraint analysis is trigged according to the algorithm of Fig. 4. This analysis shows that the ontological *constraints* N_{max} and F_{CPU} linking different views of the system are expressible within the enriched model. Indeed, all the ontological properties they are related to are retrieved within the NoseGear model. Thus, they are included in the final NoseGear design model to ease the plane speed computation.

6   Related Work

Many researchers studied the issue of semantic enrichment of models. [12] proposed informal annotations for business models in an interoperability context. Annotations are classified according to their type (decoration, linking, instance identification etc.), their content and artefacts models. In [13], the authors propose an annotation method which promotes mapping UML class's attributes with domain ontology concepts. It shows the corresponding relations with a markup language and UML itself. [14], presented a semantic annotation method allowing the annotation of templates, process model fragments and modelling languages. General Process Ontology (GPO) is used as a reference in the ontology modelling process. [15] propose a semantic annotation framework for the management of heterogeneous process models according to four perspectives: basic description of process models (profile annotation), process's modelling languages (meta-model annotation), process model (model annotation) and purposes of process models (annotation goal). In [16], a reasoning phase is based on the output of the annotation phase. Reasoning rules produce inference results: (1) suggestion of semantic annotation, (2) detection of inconsistencies between semantic annotations and (3) conflict identification in annotated objects.

Compared to our work, the approaches cited above, propose informal and restrictive annotations to improve the common understanding of models and to address interoperability issues. They do not deal with the formal correctness of models with respect to domain properties and constraints.

7   Conclusion and Future Work

The work achieved in this paper starts from the general observation that domain knowledge related properties are not handled nor formalised during the system development. It focuses on making explicit domain knowledge. It shows how the integration of domain knowledge in design models handles the expression and the verification of new properties and constraints that emerge from the explicit expression of domain specific knowledge. In order to allow such properties expression and verification, we proposed an incremental model oriented approach to enrich and strengthen design models thanks to references to domain knowledge resources. This stepwise approach is based on model engineering techniques and is composed of four steps. First, ontologies are set up in order to make explicit and formalise domain knowledge using concepts like classes, properties, constraints, relations etc. To get a uniform model for all the resources involved in our approach, we have characterised these ontologies using a meta-model. Then, as a second step, we have defined and used annotations to explicitly establish a link between the domain ontologies and the design models. Three types of annotations have been defined for this purpose: annotation *by inheritance Is_a*, annotation by *partial inheritance Case_of* and annotation by *association*. Finally, the last step checks if the ontological constraints can be expressed and interpreted within the annotated design model before they can be integrated to the final enriched design model obtained after annotation. A prototype implementing this approach has been built on top of the EMF Eclipse platform. This approach has been developed as part of the IMPEX-ANR project [17] and has been deployed within formal methods based on refinement and proof using the Event-B method. It has been applied to several case studies of the engineering domain [9].

Several other research directions to pursue our work can be envisaged. First, we are interested in promoting our approach to handle, during the annotation process of design models, instances of ontologies. Design models could be annotated by both classes and instances of an ontology. Then, the capability to annotate behavioural resources in design models (like state-transition systems, events, etc.) is another open issue. Finally, we are interested in moving forward towards the formalisation of an ontological language in an upper level within a formal context based on proof using Event-B [18] theories.

References

1. Aït Ameur, Y., Méry, D.: Making explicit domain knowledge in formal system development. Sci. Comput. Program. **121**, 100–127 (2016)
2. The NoseGear Case Study. http://www.cl.cam.ac.uk/mjcg/FMStandardsWork shop/NoseGear.html
3. Grube: toward principles for the design of ontologies used for knowledge sharing (1993)
4. Jean, S., Pierra, G., Aït Ameur, Y.: Domain ontologies: a database-oriented analysis. In: Filipe, J., Cordeiro, J., Pedrosa, V. (eds.) WEBIST 2005/2006, LNBIP, vol. 1, pp. 238–257 (2006)
5. Ontology web language. http://www.w3.org/2001/sw/wiki/OWL
6. ISO: Parts library - part 42: Description methodology: Methodology for structuring parts families, ISO ISO13584-42 (1998)
7. ISO: Parts library - part 25: Logical resource: Logical model of supplier library with aggregate values and explicit content, ISO ISO13584-25 (2004)
8. RDF Schema. http://www.w3.org/TR/rdf-schema/
9. Hacid, K., Aït Ameur, Y.: Strengthening MDE and formal design models by references to domain ontologies, a model annotation based approach. In: ISOLA (2016, to appear)
10. Jean, S.: OntoQL, an exploitation language for ontology-based databases, Theses (2007)
11. The NoseGear Case Study. http://www.cl.cam.ac.uk/mjcg/FMStandardsWork shop/sampleCode.pdf
12. Boudjlida, N., Panetto, H.: Annotation of enterprise models for interoperability purposes. In: IWAISE, April 2008
13. Wang, Y., Li, H.: Adding semantic annotation to UML class diagram. In: ICCASM (2010)
14. Lin, Y., Strasunskas, D.: Ontology-based semantic annotation of process templates for reuse. In: CAiSE (2005)
15. Lin, Y., Strasunskas, D., Hakkarainen, S., Krogstie, J., Solvberg, A.: Semantic annotation framework to manage semantic heterogeneity of process models. In: CAiSE (2006)
16. Carvalho, V.A., Almeida, J.P.A., Guizzardi, G.: Using reference domain ontologies to define the real-world semantics of domain-specific languages. In: CAiSE (2014)
17. Consortium: Formal models for ontologies, Technical report (2015)
18. Abrial, J.R.: Modeling in Event-B - System and Software Engineering. Cambridge University Press, New York (2010)

Unifying Warehoused Data with Linked Open Data: A Conceptual Modeling Solution

Franck Ravat and Jiefu Song[✉]

IRIT - Université Toulouse I Capitole,
2 Rue Du Doyen Gabriel Marty, 31042 Toulouse Cedex 09, France
{ravat, song}@irit.fr

Abstract. Linked Open Data (LOD) become one of the most important sources of information allowing enhancing business analyses based on warehoused data with external data. However, Data Warehouses (DWs) do not directly cooperate with LOD datasets due to the differences between data models. In this paper, we describe a conceptual multidimensional model, named *Unified Cube*, which is generic enough to include both warehoused data and LOD. *Unified Cube*s provide a comprehensive representation of useful data and, more importantly, support well-informed decisions by including multiple data sources in one analysis. To demonstrate the feasibility of our proposal, we present an implementation framework for building *Unified Cube*s based on DWs and LOD datasets.

Keywords: Data Warehouse · Linked Open Data · Unified Conceptual Model

1 Introduction

In today's highly dynamic business context, decision-makers should access internal and external sources to obtain an overall perspective over an organization [2]. *Data Warehouses* (DWs) have been widely used as internal sources to support online, interactive analyses, while *Linked Open Data* (LOD)[1] have become one of the most important external information sources allowing enhancing business analyses on a web scale [12]. However, warehoused data and LOD follow different models in each domain, which makes it difficult to analyze both types of data in a unified way. Moreover, dispersion of related data in different schemas results in repetitive searches for relevant information in different sources, which reduces the efficiency of analysis.

Motivating Example. In a company selling home appliances, a decision-maker looks up in an internal R-OLAP DW to assess the performance of sales staff. The DW relates to an analysis subject (i.e. fact), named *Sales Analysis*, which contains a set of numeric indicators (i.e. measures), namely *unit price* and *quantity*. Each measure can be computed according to three analysis axes (i.e. dimensions): *salesman*, *product* and *time* (cf. Fig. 1(a)). The R-OLAP DW alone does not provide enough information to support effective and well-informed decisions. The decision-maker must search for

---

[1] http://linkeddata.org.

© Springer International Publishing Switzerland 2016
L. Bellatreche et al. (Eds.): MEDI 2016, LNCS 9893, pp. 245–259, 2016.
DOI: 10.1007/978-3-319-45547-1_20

additional information to obtain other complementary perspectives over the sales activities. Since the sales of some home appliances (e.g., heaters) are strongly influenced by the climate changes, the decision-maker browses in an online dataset denoted LOD1 revealing the *monthly* average temperature according to *countries*. The LOD are published in RDF *Data Cube Vocabulary* (QB)[2] format, which is the current W3C standard to publish multidimensional statistical data. Moreover, since retail sales may compete with the company's promotions in the same catchment area, the decision-maker consults another online dataset denoted LOD2 about the outlet prices offered by rival retailers. The LOD2 dataset is published in QB4OLAP, it involves the *retail price* for a *class* (i.e., type) of merchandise offered by a retailers' *shop*. Extracts of the LOD datasets in tabular form are available in Fig. 1(b) and (c).

Without a comprehensive representation of related data, analyses involving several sources are carried out in a sequential way. Decision-makers must explore all data sources one after another before obtaining an overall vision on an analysis subject. Carrying out such analyses is inefficient and difficult, because all schemas do not include the same information at the same analytical granularities: (a) the same analysis axes present in different sources may include different analytical granularities, e.g., for the temporal analysis axis, the source ROLAP contains three analytical granularities *Year-Month-Date*, whereas the sources LOD1 only includes one analytical granularity *YearMonth*; (b) the same data may have different labels in different sources e.g., *heater* is labeled as products' *type* in the source ROLAP and merchandises' *class* in the source LOD2; (c) a same analytical granularity may group several attributes from heterogeneous sources, e.g., since the decision-maker indicates each salesman's team competes with the retailers in one catchment area (cf. Fig. 1(d)), the attribute named *Team* from ROLAP and the one named *CatchmentArea* from LOD2 refer actually to the same analytical granularity; (d) an analytical granularity from one source may belong to a broader one from a different source, e.g., the decision-maker specifies that several salesman's teams are in charge of the sales in one country (cf. Fig. 1(d)), therefore the analytical granularity about *team* from ROLAP can be aggregated into the one related to *country* from LOD1; (e) some indicators from different sources can be analyzed together starting from certain analytical granularities, e.g., Fig. 2 shows a dashboard including related measures sharing common analytical granularities. This dashboard allows better illustrating the sales' *quantity* is highly influenced by the price: higher sales *quantity* of a *type* of product is due to the lower *unit price* compared to the *retail price* in the *same catchment area*.

Contribution. Our aim is to make full use of all relevant data in a decision-making context. To this end, we provide decision-makers with a unified view of both warehoused data and multidimensional LOD. To facilitate decision-making, the unified view should include in a single schema all the indicators along with all available analysis axes as well as all the attributes and hierarchies (coming from the heterogeneous sources). The unified view should be independent of the modeling solutions of the data sources. In the previous example, a unified view would enable decision-makers to more easily build the dashboard shown in Fig. 2.

---

[2] http://www.w3.org/TR/vocab-data-cube.

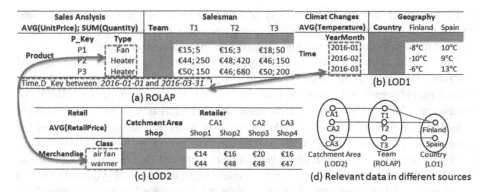

Fig. 1. Extracts of a ROLAP DW and two LOD datasets.

Measures from ROLAP	Measure from LOD2	Attribute from LOD2		
Sales	AVG(UnitPrice); SUM(Quantity); AVG(RetailPrice)	Team[Catchment Area]	Participant		
			T1[CA1]	T2[CA2]	T3[CA3]
	Type [Class]				
Product	Fan		€15; 5; €15	€16; 3; €20	€18; 50; €16
	Heater		€47; 400; €46	€47; 1100; €50	€48; 350; €47
Time.D_Key between 2016-01-01 and 2016-03-31					
Attribute from R-OLAP					

Fig. 2. A dashboard built on a unified view.

In this paper, we describe a generic modeling solution for both warehoused data and multidimensional LOD. First, we discuss related work about a unified representation compatible with warehoused data and LOD (cf. Sect. 2). Second, we present the conceptual definitions and graphical notations of *Unified Cubes* (cf. Sect. 3). At last, we describe an implementation framework for *Unified Cubes* (cf. Sect. 4).

2 Related Work

The classical method of analyzing data from multiple sources consists of combining data from several fact tables according to *conformed* dimensions under a DW Bus Architecture [6]. It has very limited practical utility since all dimensions must share the same structure and content across different sources. To overcome this drawback, many state-of-art papers [1, 2, 7] draw a roadmap enabling unified analyses to be carried out based on all kinds of dimensions. A key step towards such analyses consists of a generic multidimensional representation which is compatible with both warehoused data and LOD. Two approaches can be identified from the existing work.

The first approach aims at reusing classical DW models. The work [3, 9, 11] proposes mechanisms to *Extract, Transform* and *Load* (ETL) LOD into a local DW. However, warehousing real-time LOD in a stationary data repository is hardly practical [5]. According to the authors of [4], this approach is not recommended, since it collides with the distributed nature and the high volatility of LOD. In terms of analytical uses, the first approach only supports offline analyses of warehoused data with preprocessed LOD, which makes it difficult to guarantee the high freshness of the obtained information.

The second approach aims at publishing LOD according to a multidimensional structure. The RDF *Data Cube Vocabulary* (QB) is the current W3C standard to publish multidimensional statistical data. In [4], the authors propose the QB4OLAP vocabulary which adds more multidimensional characteristics to QB, like multiple analytical granularities within multiple aggregation paths and the specification of the aggregation functions associated to a measure. [8] proposes IGOLAP vocabulary allowing representing the correlation relationships between two different dimensions. QB, QB4OLAP and IGOLAP are logical models expressed in RDF vocabularies. No conceptual model independent of specific modeling languages has been proposed.

In this paper, we propose a generic multidimensional model which provides a uniform vision of both warehoused data and relevant multidimensional LOD. Unlike approaches involving ETL processes which collide with the dynamic nature of data, our unified data model supports on-the-fly analyses of data in the sources.

3   The *Unified Cube* Model

Unified Cubes provide a single, comprehensive representation of data from one or multiple sources. Within a *Unified Cube*, data are organized according to analysis axes (i.e., *dimensions*) and an analysis subject (i.e., fact). Concepts about *Unified Cubes* will be presented in the following sections.

3.1   Unified Cube

In a *Unified Cube*, a dimension is a union of relevant analytical granularities from several sources concerning the same analysis axis, while the fact includes all measures concerning the analysis subject. Each measure from one source may only be summarizable with regards to the set of analytical granularities from the same source. A generalization of the *dimension-measure* relationship is needed to associate subset of analytical granularities within a dimension with a measure in a *Unified Cube*.

Definition 1. A *Unified Cube* is a n-dimensional finite space describing a fact with some dimensions. A *Unified Cube* is denoted as UC=$\{F; \mathcal{D}; \mathcal{LM}\}$, where

- F is a *fact* containing a set of *measures*;
- $\mathcal{D}=\{D_1;\ldots; D_n\}$ is a finite set of *dimensions*;
- $\mathcal{LM}: 2^{\mathcal{L}^1_{\setminus l_p} \times \ldots \times \mathcal{L}^n_{\setminus l_q}} \to m_e$ is a *level-measure* mapping which associates a subset of summarizable analytical granularities (i.e., *levels*) to a measure m_e of the fact, such as $\forall i \in [1..n]$, $\mathcal{L}^i_{\setminus l_s}$ ($l_s \in \mathcal{L}^i$) corresponds to a subset of levels on the dimension D_i ($D_i \in \mathcal{D}$) which starts from the level l_s.

We propose a graphical notation of *Unified Cubes* based on the *fact-dimension* model with minor modifications (cf. Fig. 3). The graphical notation aims at facilitating data exploitation at the schema level for non-expert users. For readability purposes, concepts involving data instances are not included in the graphical notation.

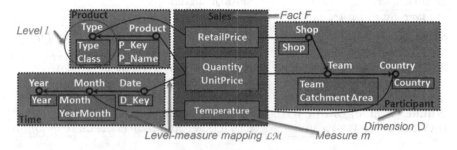

Fig. 3. Graphical notation of *Unified Cubes*.

Example. Figure 3 shows a *Unified Cube* which is built upon the warehoused data and the two LOD datasets in the motivating example. It contains three dimensions $D = \{D_{Participant}, D_{Time}, D_{Product}\}$. Each measure is associated to its related levels. For the sake of simplicity, in the graphical notation the *level-measure* mappings are represented only between the lowest levels of sub-dimension and related measures. i.e., LM:

$$\{\{L^{Product}_{\backslash l_{Type}}; \ L^{Participant}\} \rightarrow \{m_{RetailPrice}\}; \ \{L^{Product}; \ L^{Participant}_{\backslash l_{Team}} \ L^{Time}\} \rightarrow \{m_{Qunatity}; \ m_{Unit-}$$

$$Price\}; \ \{L^{Time}_{\backslash l_{Month}}; \ L^{Participant}_{\backslash l_{Country}}\} \rightarrow \{mTemperature\}\}.$$

3.2 Analysis Subject: Fact

A fact models an analysis subject composed of a set of *measures*. Since the fact of a *Unified Cube* may include measures from DWs and LOD datasets, we should explicitly indicate how the values of a measure can be accessed from data sources.

Definition 2. A *Fact* corresponds to an analysis subject composed of a set of *measures*. A fact is denoted as $F = \{n^F; \mathcal{M}^F\}$ where

- n^F is the name of the fact;
- $\mathcal{M}^F = \{m_1; \dots; m_p\}$ is a finite set of numeric indicators called *measures*. Each measure m_e ($m_e \in \mathcal{M}^F$) is a pair $\langle n^{m_e}, E^{m_e} \rangle$, where n^{m_e} is the name of the measure, E^{m_e} is an *extraction formula* defined through query algebra (e.g., *relational* algebra and *SPARQL* algebra[3]).

Remark. *Extraction formulae* enable on-the-fly querying of measures' values during analyses. The algebraic representation of *extraction formula* makes sure its compatibility with specific implementation environments of data source. Note that although the *SPARQL* algebra is not yet a W3C standard, it has already been integrated within several RDF querying framework. Each algebraic SPARQL expression is translated into one SPARQL query which is generic enough to work with all types of LOD datasets. Table 1 shows the algebraic form of commonly used SPARQL queries.

Table 1. SPARQL queries and their algebraic representation

SPARQL query	SPARQL algebra
SELECT * WHERE {?s ?p ?o}	(BGP (TRIPLE ?s ?p ?o))
SELECT ?s ?p WHERE {?s ?p ?o}	(PROJECT(?s ?p) (BGP (TRIPLE ?s ?p ?o)))
SELECT ?o1 ?o2 WHERE{?s ?p ?o1. FILTER (?o1 < 5) OPTIONAL {?s ?p2 ?o2. FILTER (?o2 > 10)}}	(PROJECT(?o1 ?o2) (FILTER (< ?o1 5) (LEFTJOIN(BGP (TRIPLE ?s ?p ?o1)) (BGP (TRIPLE ?s ?p2 ?o2)) (> ?o2 10))))
SELECT ?s (COUNT(?o) as ?nb) WHERE {?s ?p ?o} GROUP BY ?s HAVING (COUNT(?o) > 10)	(PROJECT(?s ?nb) (FILTER (> ?.0 10) (EXTEND((?nb ?.0)) (GROUP (?s) ((?.0 (COUNT ?o))) (BGP (TRIPLE ?s ?p ?o))))))

Example. The fact named *Sales* contains four measures, namely $m_{RetailPrice}$, $m_{Quantity}$, $m_{UnitPrice}$ and $m_{Temperature}$. The measure $m_{Quantity}$ has an *extraction formula* $E^{m_{Quantity}} =_{P\_Key,D\_Key,Team} F_{sum}(SalesAnalysis.Quantity)$. The *extraction formula* of the measure $m_{RetailPrice}$ is defined upon SPARQL algebra, such as:

$E^{m_{RetailPrice}}$ = (project (?retailer ?merchandise ?avgPrice)
    (extend ((?avgPrice ?.0)) (group (?retailer ?merchandise) ((?.0 (avg ?Prive)))
    (bgp (triple ?ob qb:dataSet eg:RETAIL) (triple ?ob eg:M_RETAILPRICE ?Price)
        (triple ?ob eg:MERCHANDISE ?merchandise)(triple ?ob eg:RETAILER ?retailer)))))

3.3 Analysis Axis: Dimension

A dimension may include a single analytical granularity (e.g., dimensions in a QB dataset) or multiple analytical granularities. If several analytical granularities are defined, we can find one or several aggregation paths (i.e. hierarchies). Two hierarchies from different sources do not always share a common lowest analytical granularities. Therefore, we remove the constraint of unique root level in the following definition.

Definition 3. A *dimension* corresponds to a one-dimensional space regrouping the analytical granularities related to an analysis axis. A dimension is denoted as $D_i=\{n^{D_i}; \mathcal{L}^{D_i}; \preccurlyeq^{D_i}\}$, where:

- n^{D_i} is the dimension name;
- $\mathcal{L}^{D_i}=\{l_1;...; l_k\}$ is a set of levels characterizing the dimension, each level models a distinct analytical granularity;
- $\preccurlyeq^{D_i}$ is a reflexive *binary* relation which associates a level l_a ($l_a \in \mathcal{L}^{D_i}$) with its parent level l_b ($l_b \in \mathcal{L}^{D_i}$), such as $l_a \preccurlyeq^{D_i} l_b$. The reflexivity means each level can be seen as a parent level of itself, i.e., $\forall l_c \in \mathcal{L}^{D_i}, l_c \preccurlyeq^{D_i} l_c$.

Example. We identify a dimension named *Participant* which groups all analytical granularities related to the participants of the sales activities (i.e., *salesmen* of the organization and their rival *retailers*). The dimension $D_{Participant}$ includes three levels, such as $L^{Participant} = \{l_{Shop}; l_{Team}; l_{Country}\}$. The *binary* relation $\preccurlyeq^{Participant}$ reveals the aggregation paths (i.e., hierarchies) such as $l_{Shop} \preccurlyeq^{Participant} l_{Team} \preccurlyeq^{Participant} l_{Country}$.

Our definition of dimension is generic enough to model a non-hierarchical dimension as well. A non-hierarchical dimension (e.g. D_{QB}) is defined with only one level (e.g., $L^{QB} = \{l_1\}$) including all the attributes of the dimension.

Without the constraint of unique root level (i.e., $\exists_{=1} l_p \in L^{D_i}, \forall l_q \in L^{D_i}: l_p \preccurlyeq^{D_i} l_q{}^3$), a dimension may start at any level. This is an important property of a dimension regrouping levels from multiple sources, since the measures from one source may only be analyzed according to a subset of levels coming from the same source. We define a *sub-dimension* as a part of dimension along which a measure can be summarized.

Definition 4. A *sub-dimension* of D_i, denoted $D_{i \backslash l_s} = \{n^{D_i \backslash s}; \mathcal{L}^{D_i \backslash s}; \preccurlyeq^{D_i}\}$, corresponds to the part of the dimension D_i starting with the level l_s, where

- $n^{D_i \backslash s}$ is the name of the sub-dimension;
- $\mathcal{L}^{D_i}{}_{\backslash l_s}$ is the subset of levels, $\mathcal{L}^{D_i}{}_{\backslash l_s} \subseteq \mathcal{L}^{D_i}, \forall l_i \in \mathcal{L}^{D_i}{}_{\backslash l_s}, l_s \preccurlyeq^{D_i} l_i$;
- $\preccurlyeq^{D_i}$ is the same binary relation of the one on the dimension D_i.

Example. A sub-dimension of the dimension named *Time* may be $D_{Time \backslash l_{Month}}$ named *Time-Month* with $L_{Time \backslash l_{Month}} = \{l_{Month}; l_{Year}\}$, which represent the subpart of the dimension D_{Time} that measure from the LOD1 dataset can be calculated along.

3.4   Analytical Granularity: Level

A level includes a set of attributes describing a distinct analytical granularity. We present the definition of a level which (a) indicates the source of each attribute, (b) manages heterogeneous representations of attribute instances referring to the same concepts and (c) implements the *binary* relation at the attribute instance level.

---

[3] $\exists_{=1}$ represents the *unique existential quantification* meaning "there exists only one.

> **Definition 5.** A *level* represents a distinct analytical granularity on a dimension. A level is denoted as l_d= $\{n^{l_d};\, A^{l_d};\, C^{l_d};\, R^{l_d}_c\}$, where:
> - n^{l_d} is the name of level;
> - $A^{l_d} = \{a_1;\ldots;\, a_e\}$ is a finite set of *attributes*. Each attribute a_x ($a_x \in A^{l_d}$) is a pair $\langle n^{a_x}, E^{a_x}\rangle$, where n^{a_x} is the name of the attribute and E^{a_x} is an *extraction formula* indicating the instances of a_x. The domain of an attribute is denoted as $dom(a_x)$.
> - $C^{l_d}:\, dom(a_x) \rightarrow 2^{dom(a_y)}$ ($a_x \in A^{l_d}$, $a_y \in A^{l_d} \backslash a_x$) is a symmetric *correlative* mapping which associates an attribute a_x with its related ones at the same level.
> - $R^{l_d}_c:\, 2^{dom(a_y)} \rightarrow dom(a_z)$ ($a_x \in A^{l_d}$, $a_z \in A^{l_e}$ and $l_d \preccurlyeq l_e$.) is a *rollup* mapping implementing the *binary* relation between two levels. It connects the instances of child attributes with the instances of a parent attribute at an adjacent level.

Example. The level l_{Team} on the dimension $D_{\text{Participant}}$ contains a finite set of attributes $A^{l_{\text{Team}}} = \{a_{\text{Team}};\, a_{\text{CatchmentArea}}\}$ from the ROLAP DW and the LOD2 dataset. To indicate attribute instances in data sources, two *extraction formulae* are defined within the level l_{Team}: $E^{a_{\text{Team}}} = \pi_{\text{Team}}(\text{SalesAnalysis.Salesman})$ is associated to the attribute a_{Team}, while the attribute $a_{\text{CatchmentArea}}$ is connected with an *extraction formula*:

```
EaCatchmentArea= (distinct (project (?CAName)
            (bgp (triple ?ob qb:dataSet eg:RETAIL) (triple ?ob eg:RETAILER ?retailer)
                (triple ?retailer skos:broader ?CA) (triple ?CA qb4o:inLevel eg:CATCHMENTAREA)
                (triple ?CA rdfs:label ?CAName)))))
```

The *correlative* mapping $C^{l_{\text{Team}}}$ associates the instances of the attribute a_{Team} to its related instances of the attribute $a_{\text{CatchmentArea}}$, e.g., $C^{l_{\text{Team}}}$: $\{\{T1\} \rightarrow \{CA1\};\, \{T2\} \rightarrow \{CA2\};\, \{T3\} \rightarrow \{CA3\}\}$. The *rollup* mapping $R^{l_{\text{Team}}}$ aggregates the instances of a_{Team} and $a_{\text{CatchmentArea}}$ at the level l_{Team} to the ones of a_{Country} at the level l_{Country}, such as: $R^{l_{\text{Team}}}$: $\{\{\{T1;\, CA1\};\, \{T2;\, CA2\}\} \rightarrow \{\text{Finland}\};\, \{T3;\, CA3\} \rightarrow \{\text{Spain}\}\}$.

4   Implementation of *Unified Cubes*

In this section, we present an implementation framework for *Unified Cubes*. By building a *Unified Cube* based on the ROLAP DW and the two LOD datasets of the motivating example, we show the feasibility of our proposal.

4.1   Architecture

The implementation framework aims at enabling unified analyses of data from DWs and multidimensional LOD sources. Two modules are defined within the framework, namely *Schema* and *Instance* (cf. Fig. 4). The first module named *Schema* aims at revealing the internal structure of data from multiple sources. It includes a non-materialized *Unified Cube* schema with a set of extraction formulae allowing querying sources on-the-fly. The second module, named *Instance*, is devoted to managing related attribute instances scattered in different sources. It contains (a) a toolkit identifying the *correlative* and *rollup* relations between attribute instances and (b) a set of tables of correspondences materializing the identified relations.

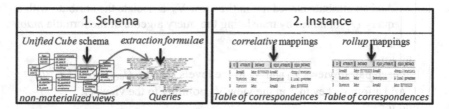

Fig. 4. Implementation framework for *Unified Cubes*

4.2   *Schema* Module

The implementation of a conceptual *Unified Cube* schema can take several forms. Due to the wide use of relational databases in current information management, in this paper we focus on one implementation alternative based on relational views.

Within our framework, the *Schema* module hosts (a) a set of non-materialized views implementing the components of a schema of *Unified Cube* and (b) a set of queries implementing the *extraction formulae* of attribute and measure. Specifically, each dimension is transformed into a set of views. Each view represents a level with a synthetic primary key and the set of attributes of the level. The *extraction formula* of each attribute is translated into an executable query to indicate how attribute instances can be accessed from sources. For a pair of views implementing two levels associated together through a *binary* relation, the view of the lower level includes a foreign key pointing to the view of the higher level. The fact is also implemented with a set of views: each one regroups a set of measures sharing the same sub-dimensions. A set of foreign keys pointing to the starting levels of the related sub-dimensions is included in each view of fact. We propose the following algorithm to automate the implementation of *Unified Cube* schema.

Algorithm. *Unified Cube Schema Implementation*

Input: A *Unified Cube*={F; $\mathcal{D}$, $\mathcal{LM}$}.

Output: A set of non-materialized views implementing the *Unified Cube* schema

Begin

1. For each dimension $D_i \in \mathcal{D}$
2. $\quad$ For each level $l_d \in \mathcal{L}^{D_i}$
3. $\quad\quad$ Create a view V_d named n^{l_d} with a key id^{V_d};
    $\quad\quad$ For each attribute $a_x \in \mathcal{A}^{l_d}$
4. $\quad\quad\quad$ Add an attribute named n^{a_x} in the view V_d, associate the attribute with a
    $\quad\quad\quad$ query Q_{a_x} obtained by translating the query algebra of the formula map^{a_x};
5. $\quad\quad$ End for
6. $\quad$ End for
7. $\quad$ For each pair of views V_d and V_e of the levels l_d and l_e ($l_d, l_e \in \mathcal{L}^{D_i} \wedge l_d \preccurlyeq^{D_i} l_e$)
8. $\quad\quad$ Add a foreign key id^{V_e} in the view V_d pointing to the view V_e;
9. $\quad$ End for
10. End for
11. For each subset of measures $\mathcal{M}_{sub} \subseteq \mathcal{M}^F$ sharing the same related levels, such as
    $\forall m_e \in \mathcal{M}_{sub}, \exists \mathcal{L}^r_{V_h} \times ... \times \mathcal{L}^t_{V_k} \subseteq \mathcal{L}^1 \times ... \times \mathcal{L}^n$, $\mathcal{LM}$: $\mathcal{L}^r_{V_h} \times ... \times \mathcal{L}^t_{V_k} \rightarrow m_e$ (r,t∈[1..n]∧r≤t)
12. $\quad$ Create a view V_{sub};
13. $\quad$ Add a measure named n^{m_e} ($m_e \in \mathcal{M}_{sub}$) in V_{sub}, associate the measure with a
    $\quad$ query Q_{m_e} obtained by translating the query algebra of the formula map^{m_e};
14. $\quad$ For each set of levels $\mathcal{L}^s_{V_j}$ ($\mathcal{L}^s_{V_j} \subseteq \mathcal{L}^r_{V_h} \times ... \times \mathcal{L}^t_{V_k}$) of the subdimension $D^s_{V_j}$
15. $\quad\quad$ Add a foreign key id^{V_j} in V_{sub} pointing to the view V_j of the level l_j;
16. $\quad$ End for
17. End for

End

4.3 *Instance* Module

Related data are scattered in multiple sources and represented according to different modeling vocabularies. The framework must provide methods identifying related data from DWs and/or LOD datasets. Once identified, related warehoused data and LOD should be kept in a generic, coherent environment to avoid repetitive relevance processing during analyses. To this end, the *Instance* module (a) pre-processes related attribute instances involved in *correlative* and *rollup* mappings before analyses and (b) materializes related data in tables of correspondences for future uses. At the beginning of an analysis process, the framework verifies the last changed date of each source to determine if materialized data in the *Instance* module should be updated.

Step I: Identifying the Relevance Between Data. In the context of *Unified Cubes*, the relevance between data from multiple sources can be divided into two types, namely *direct* relevance and *deductive* relevance. *Direct* relevance exists between two attribute instances which are already associated together in sources (e.g., the *correlative* mapping between the instances of a_{P_Key} and those of a_{P_Name} from ROLAP). *Deductive* relevance, on the other hand, is identified by using some processing methods. The *Instance* module contains a toolkit implementing some most effective methods to facilitate the identification of related data involved a *Unified Cube*. We describe three categories of processing methods that can be potentially included in the *Instance* module to identify related attribute instances.

Automatic Processing Methods for Correlative Mappings. We identify two methods allowing automatically computing the *deductive* relevance between attribute instances involved in a *correlative* mapping. The first approach is applicable for data from different LOD datasets. It is based on an intermediate ontology with a comprehensive coverage of the common concepts in two LOD datasets (i.e., containing enough matches between equivalent entities). The second approach aims at identifying relevant instances sharing similar labels (e.g., a product's *type* from the ROLAP DW and a merchandise's class from the LOD2 dataset). This approach consists of calculating the *string-based* similarity $\bar{\sigma}$ of two related attribute instances s_1 and s_2, such as $\bar{\sigma}(s_1, s_2) \in$ [0..1]. Several amelioration techniques can help improving the obtained similarity, such as case normalization (e.g., converting s_1 and s_2 to lowercase) and synonym matching (e.g., using an external thesaurus to associate "heater" with its synonym "warmer").

Automatic Processing Methods for Rollup Mappings. The DW domain mainly focuses on the multidimensional structure of data (i.e. schema), the *rollup* mappings between attributes from DWs do not need additional processing methods, since they can be directly derived by referring to the multidimensional schema of data source. In the domain of LOD, a dataset, especially real-world QB datasets, often only includes independent data instances without an explicitly defined schema. Discovering the *rollup* mapping in previously unknown LOD datasetsis not a trivial task. The existence of various proposals in the scientific literature, such as some computer-assisted approaches presented in [5], shows there is no *one-size-fits-all* method for identifying *child-parent* relations between all types of LOD. The implementation framework should only include methods applicable to the hosted *Unified Cube*. With regard to the running example, we implement an automatic reasoning method based on existing *correlative* and/or direct *rollup* mappings. This approach is particularly useful to deduce the *rollup* mapping between an attribute from DWs and another one from LOD dataset, such as: let $a_{iDW}, a_{iLOD} \in A^{l_i}$, $a_{jDW}, a_{jLOD} \in A^{l_j}$ $(l_i \leqslant l_j)$: $(C^{l_i}: dom(a_{iDW}) \rightarrow dom(a_{iLOD})) \wedge (R^{l_i}: dom(a_{iLOD}) \rightarrow dom(a_{jLOD})) \Rightarrow \exists R^{l_i}: dom(a_{iDW}) \rightarrow dom(a_{jLOD})$, $(R^{l_i}: dom(a_{iLOD}) \rightarrow dom(a_{jLOD})) \wedge (C^{l_j}: dom(a_{jLOD}) \rightarrow dom(a_{jDW})) \Rightarrow \exists R^{l_i}: dom(a_{iLOD}) \rightarrow dom(a_{jDW})$.

Semi-automatic Processing Methods for Correlative Mappings and Rollup Mappings. Besides the automatic approaches, some semi-automatic approaches should also be adapted, especially for the relevance between attribute instances which holds only in a specific analysis context (e.g., the *correlative* mapping between a_{Team} and $a_{CatchmentArea}$ in Fig. 1(d) is valid only if a *catchment area* of retailer attracts the same clientele of a salesman's *team*). In this case, decision-makers should explicitly describe the correspondences between relevant attributes instances. Then the system checks the local and overall validity of *correlative* and *rollup* mappings in a *Unified Cube*. Due to limited space, more details can be found in our previous work [10].

Step II: Materializing Relevant Data. *Direct* relevance between attributes is already embedded in the sources thus does not need to be materialized in the *Instance* module. *Deductive* relevance between data, on the other hand, is identified after applying appropriate processing methods. To avoid repetitive relevance processing during analyses, *correlative* mappings and *rollup* mappings involving *deductive* relevance are materialized in tables of correspondences (cf. Fig. 5): the table of correspondences implementing the *correlative* mappings associates the instances (i.e., *instance*) of an attribute (i.e., *attribute*) to the related ones (i.e., *cor_ins*) of a correlative attribute (i.e., *cor_att*) within the same level, while the table of correspondences materializing the *rollup* mappings connects a set of instances (i.e., *child_ins*) of a child attribute (i.e., *child_att*) with a corresponding instance (i.e., *parent_ins*) of a parent attribute (i.e., *parent_att*).

ID	ATTRIBUTE	INSTANCE	COR_ATT	COR_INS
1	CatchmentArea	CA1	Team	T1
2	CatchmentArea	CA2	Team	T2
3	CatchmentArea	CA3	Team	T3

ID	CHILD_ATT	CHILD_INS	PARENT_ATT	PARENT_INS
1	Team	T1	Country	Finland
2	Team	T2	Country	Finland
3	Team	T3	Country	Spain

(a) Materialized *correlative* mappings   (b) Materialized *rollup* mappings

Fig. 5. Extract of tables of correspondences

4.4 Experimental Assessments

The experimental assessments aim at showing the feasibility of our proposal. Specifically, the internal structure of data from DWs and LOD datasets should be correctly managed by the *Schema* module, while related data from different sources must be identified and materialized within the *Instance* module within a reasonable time.

Protocol. The data sources are hosted in a Microsoft Windows 7 work stations (Interl (R) i7-4510U 2 GHz CPU, 8 GB RAM, SSD 500 GB disk). Each source is populated with a reasonable amount of synthetic data to avoid timeout during the experimental assessments: the ROLAP contains about 18 million pre-aggregated data in the fact table, while the LOD1 and LOD2 datasets respectively include 7240 and 840 observation (cf. Table 2).

Table 2. Data collection

Source	Dimensions
ROLAP	40 teams × 40 products (20 types) × 7300 days (360 months, 20 years)
LOD1	20 countries ×360 months
LOD2	40 shops (20 catchment area) ×20 merchandise classes

Schema **module.** We firstly implement the schema of the *Unified Cube* and the *extraction formulae* in the *Schema* module. After applying the algorithm described in Sect. 4.2, we obtain (a) 8 views implementing the dimensions, (b) 3 views implementing the fact and (c) 16 queries translated from *extraction formulae (Fig. 6).*

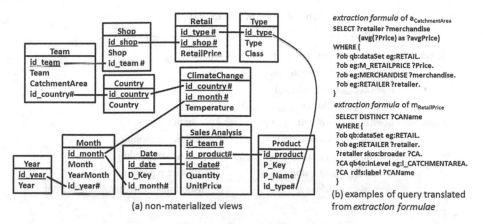

extraction formula of $a_{CatchmentArea}$
SELECT ?retailer ?merchandise
    (avg(?Price) as ?avgPrice)
WHERE [
  ?ob qb:dataSet eg:RETAIL.
  ?ob eg:M_RETAILPRICE ?Price.
  ?ob eg:MERCHANDISE ?merchandise.
  ?ob eg:RETAILER ?retailer.
}

extraction formula of $m_{RetailPrice}$
SELECT DISTINCT ?CAName
WHERE {
  ?ob qb:dataSet eg:RETAIL.
  ?ob eg:RETAILER ?retailer.
  ?retailer skos:broader ?CA.
  ?CA qb4o:inLevel eg:l_CATCHMENTAREA.
  ?CA rdfs:label ?CAName
}

(b) examples of query translated
from extraction formulae

(a) non-materialized views

Fig. 6. Content of the *Schema* module after implementation

The non-materialized *Unified Cube* schema along with extraction queries enables on-the-fly analyses of warehoused data and LOD to be carried out in a unified way. Details and examples of such analyses are presented in our previous work [10].

Instance module

Identifying Relevant Data. As shown in Table 3, four *correlative* mappings are identified. The *correlative* mapping between a_{P_Key} and a_{P_Name} are obtained by directly referring to the ROLAP DW, while the other *correlative* mappings require additional processing methods.

Table 3. List of *correlative* mappings

Type	Mapping	Processing method
direct	$dom(a_{P\_Key}) \rightarrow dom(a_{P\_Name})$	n/a
deductive	$dom(a_{Type}) \rightarrow dom(a_{Class})$	Automatic: *string-based* similarity
	$dom(a_{Type}) \rightarrow dom(a_{CatchmentArea})$	Semi-automatic: declarative operator
	$dom(a_{Month}) \rightarrow dom(a_{YearMont})$	Automatic: *string-based* similarity

Table 4 shows the *rollup* mappings in the implemented *Unified Cube*. To identify relevant data involved in *rollup* mappings, we firstly search for *child-parent* relations embedded in data sources. Four *rollup* mappings are found by directly referring to the ROLAP DW and the LOD2 dataset which both have a well-defined multidimensional schema. The other five *rollup* mappings involving *deductive* relevance are obtained by (a) executing the declarative operator which associates relevant data together according to users' needs and (b) using reasoning techniques based on existing *rollup* mappings and *correlative* mappings.

Remark. Reasoning is an important means to identify *rollup* mappings in a *Unified Cube*, especially for two attributes from different sources without intermediate onto-logical resource. For instance, the *rollup* mapping $R^{l_{Shop}}$: $dom(a_{Shop}) \rightarrow dom(a_{Team})$ is

Table 4. List of *rollup* mappings

Type	Mapping	Processing methods
direct	$dom(a_{P\_Key}) \rightarrow dom(a_{Type})$	n/a
	$dom(a_{D\_Key}) \rightarrow dom(a_{Month})$	n/a
	$dom(a_{Month}) \rightarrow dom(a_{Year})$	n/a
	$dom(a_{Shop}) \rightarrow dom(a_{CatchmentArea})$	n/a
deductive	$dom(a_{P\_Key}) \rightarrow dom(a_{Class})$	Automatic: reasoning
	$dom(a_{Shop}) \rightarrow dom(a_{Team})$	Automatic: reasoning
	$dom(a_{CatchmentArea}) \rightarrow dom(a_{Country})$	Automatic: reasoning
	$dom(a_{YearMonth}) \rightarrow dom(a_{Year})$	Automatic: reasoning
	$dom(a_{Team}) \rightarrow dom(a_{Country})$	Semi-automatic: declarative operator

obtained by referring to the *rollup* mapping $R^{l_{Shop}}$: $dom(a_{Shop}) \rightarrow dom(a_{CatchmentArea})$ and the *correlative* mapping $C^{l_{Team}}$: $dom(a_{Team}) \rightarrow dom(a_{CatchmentArea})$.

Without any optimization technique (e.g., parallel computing), defining all *deductive* mappings takes about 200 s. The execution time remains reasonable in consideration of the laptop-level configuration of the working station.

Materializing Relevant Data. Deductive *correlative* mappings and *rollup* mappings are materialized in the *Instance* module. After the implementation, we obtain two tables of correspondences containing 400 tuples and 480 tuples for *correlative* mappings and *rollup* mappings respectively. Comparing to the large volume of data in the sources (cf. Table 2), a *Unified Cube* only materializes a relatively small amount of data from different sources. Advantage of the partial materialization is twofold: it (a) avoids repetitive computing of *deductive* relevance during analyses and (b) minimizes the cost of updating the materialized data at the beginning of an analysis process.

5   Conclusion

Our aim is to make full use of all relevant data to support effective and well-informed decisions. To this end, we define a generic conceptual multidimensional model, named *Unified Cube*, which includes data coming from DW and LOD domains.

A *Unified Cube* organizes data coming from different sources according to analysis axes (i.e., *dimensions*) and an analysis subject (i.e., *fact*). A dimension is composed of levels which are associated together through a reflexive *binary* relation. The definition of dimension is generic enough to model several aggregation paths (i.e., *hierarchies*) sharing no common lowest level as well as a non-hierarchical dimension composed of only one level. A level groups a set of attributes from multiple sources. Each attribute is associated with an extraction formula, so that attribute instances that can be directly obtained from data sources are not materialized in a *Unified Cube*. *Correlative* mappings are defined between related attributes, while *rollup* mappings manage *child-parent* relations among attributes. A fact represents the analysis subject containing numeric indicators (i.e., *measures*). Through a *level-measure* mapping, a measure can be associated with its related dimensions starting from any level. We also propose an implementation framework compatible with *Unified Cubes*. By describing how a *Unified Cube* is built from the DW and the LOD datasets of the motivating example, we show the feasibility of our proposal.

In the future, we intend to build *Unified Cubes* from other LOD formats (e.g. RDF) that do not necessarily have a multidimensional structure. The scalability of the proposed implementation framework and the precision of the obtained mapping will also be studied with real-world data. A more long-term objective is to study the influences of the materialization of source data over analysis efficiency in *Unified Cubes*.

References

1. Abelló, A., Darmont, J., Etcheverry, L., Golfarelli, M., Mazón, J.-N., Naumann, F., Pedersen, T., Rizzi, S.B., Trujillo, J., Vassiliadis, P., Vossen, G.: Fusion cubes: towards self-service business intelligence. Int. J. Data Warehous. Min **9**, 66–88 (2013)
2. Abelló, A., Romero, O., Pedersen, T.B., Berlanga, R., Nebot, V., Aramburu, M.J., Simitsis, A.: Using semantic web technologies for exploratory OLAP: a survey. IEEE Trans. Knowl. Data Eng. **27**, 571–588 (2015)
3. Deb Nath, R.P., Hose, K., Pedersen, T.B.: Towards a Programmable Semantic Extract-Transform-Load Framework for Semantic Data Warehouses, pp. 15–24. ACM Press, New York (2015)
4. Etcheverry, L., Vaisman, A., Zimányi, E.: Modeling and querying data warehouses on the semantic web using QB4OLAP. In: Bellatreche, L., Mohania, M.K. (eds.) DaWaK 2014. LNCS, vol. 8646, pp. 45–56. Springer, Heidelberg (2014)
5. Ibragimov, D., Hose, K., Pedersen, T.B., Zimányi, E.: Towards Exploratory OLAP over Linked Open Data–A Case Study. HangZhou, pp 1–18 (2014)
6. Kimball, R.: The Data Warehouse Lifecycle Toolkit: Expert Methods for Designing, Developing, and Deploying Data Warehouses. Wiley, New York (1998)
7. Laborie, S., Ravat, F., Song, J., Teste, O.: Combining business intelligence with semantic web: overview and challenges. Inform. Organ. Syst. Inf. Decis. INFORSID, 2015 (2015)
8. Matei, A., Chao, K.-M., Godwin, N.: OLAP for multidimensional semantic web databases. Enabling Real-Time Business Intelligence, pp. 81–96. Springer, Heidelberg (2015)
9. Nebot, V., Berlanga, R., Pérez, J.M., Aramburu, M.J., Pedersen, T.B.: Multidimensional integrated ontologies: a framework for designing semantic data warehouses. In: Spaccapietra, S., Zimányi, E., Song, I.-Y. (eds.) Journal on Data Semantics XIII. LNCS, vol. 5530, pp. 1–36. Springer, Heidelberg (2009)
10. Ravat, F., Song, J., Teste, O.: Designing multidimensional cubes from warehoused data and linked open data. In: IEEE International Conference Research Challenges in Information Science Grenoble, France, pp. 171–182 (2016)
11. Romero, O., Abelló, A.: Automating multidimensional design from ontologies. In: International Workshop Data Warehouse OLAP, pp. 1–8. ACM Press (2007)
12. Zorrilla, M.E., Mazón, J.-N., Ferrández, Ó., Garrigós, I., Daniel, F., Trujillo, J.: Business Intelligence Applications and the Web: Models Systems and Technologies. IGI Global, Hershey (2012)

Correct-by-Construction Evolution of Realisable Conversation Protocols

Sarah Benyagoub[1], Meriem Ouederni[2(✉)], Neeraj Kumar Singh[2],
and Yamine Ait-Ameur[2]

[1] University of Mostaganem, Mostaganem, Algeria
benyagoub.sarah@univ-mosta.dz
[2] IRIT-INP of Toulouse, Toulouse, France
{meriem.ouederni,neeraje,yamine}@enseeiht.fr

Abstract. Distributed software systems are often built by composing independent and autonomous peers with cross-organisational interaction and no centralised control. These peers can be administrated and executed by geographically distributed and autonomous companies. In a top-down design of distributed software systems, the peers' interaction is often described by a global specification called Conversation Protocol (CP) and one have to check its realisability *i.e.*, whether there exists a set of peers implementing this CP. In dynamic environments, CP needs to be updated *wrt.* new environment changes and end-user interaction requirements. This paper tackles CP evolution such that its realisability must be preserved. We define some evolution patterns and prove that they ensure the realisability. We also show how our proposal can be supported by existing methods and tools based on refinement and theorem proving, using the event-B langage and RODIN development tools.

Keywords: System evolution · Realisability · Conversation protocols · Formal verification · Proof and refinement · Correct-by-construction method · Event-B

1 Introduction

In a top-down design of distributed software, the system interaction is usually modelled as a set of conversations, *i.e.* the allowed sequences of sent messages. Such a model is called conversation protocol (CP) [1] and describes the whole distributed system as a unique entity. Considering a CP, one must check whether there exists a set of peers where their composition generates the same sequences of send messages as specified by the CP. This issue characterises the realisability problem. Several recent work has tackled the CP realisability in order to avoid errors such as deadlocks or no-respect of messaging order specified in a CP.

In this paper, we take the realisability challenge one step forward: we study the correct evolution of realisable CPs. In fact, these specify cross-organisational interactions with no centralised control between peers which can be administrated and executed by geographically distributed and autonomous companies.

© Springer International Publishing Switzerland 2016
L. Bellatreche et al. (Eds.): MEDI 2016, LNCS 9893, pp. 260–273, 2016.
DOI: 10.1007/978-3-319-45547-1_21

In this setting, system interaction and the corresponding CP need to be updated continuously over time in order to cope with new environment changes and end-user requirements. However, changing CP might result in knock-on effects on its realisability. Hence, verifying the correctness of CP evolution to ensure realisability preservation must also be run continuously.

In our work, we rely on the necessary and sufficient conditions defined in [2] for CP realisability, considering asynchronously communication throughout FIFO buffers with no restriction on their buffer sizes. This work solves the realisability issue for a subclass of asynchronously communicating peers, namely, the synchronisable systems, i.e., systems composed of interacting peers behave equally by applying synchronous or asynchronous communication. A CP is realisable if there exists a set of peers implementing that CP, i.e., they send messages to each other in the same order as in the CP, and such that their composition is synchronisable. In [2], the full checking of CP realisability applies the following steps: (i) peer projection from CP; (ii) checking synchronisability; and (iii) checking equivalence between CP and its distributed system.

Regarding the literature, existing work such as [3–5] give some solutions for system evolution. In [3,4], the authors propagate the choreography updates into communicating peers. Roohi et al. [5] focus on system reconfiguration meaning that a CP has been updated into CP' by checking whether a set of traces that has been executed in CP can be performed again in CP'. This reconfiguration can be better applied for run-time system to ensure execution consistency. All these approaches do not consider realisability preservation.

There exist other research approaches which can be applied as a posteriori evolution checking. The approaches suggest solutions every time the realisability check fails. For example, existing work on enforcing CP realisability, such as the one given in [6] and recently on CP repairability [7] can be used to ensure the realisability of an already updated CP.

Our statement is different than existing work and it is as follows: an evolution is allowed if it does not violate the CP realisability. By doing so, we suggest a priori verification approach of CP evolution. Instead of running the full realisability checking as described previously and detailed in Sect. 2, our proposal consists in performing partial verification uniquely at the CP level in order to answer the question if there *still* exists a set of peers implementing the updated CP. In this work, we consider the evolution at the CP level and we study its realisability effect on the distributed peers. The main issue is considering that system specifications may change over time (*e.g.*, service upgrade or degrade by adding and/or removing either exchanging messages or interacting peers). So, how can we ensure realisability preservation? To answer these questions, we formally describe the systems using Labelled Transition Systems (LTSs). We identify a set of behavioural properties sufficient to assert that the CP evolution due to the application of each evolution operator and their composition is correct. For this purpose, we define a set of patterns of correct evolution and we suggest a naive method to prove that these patterns preserve CP realisability.

The remainder of this paper is structured as follows: Sect. 2 introduces the background on which our proposal relies. Section 3 presents a *correct-by-construction* checking of CP realisability. In Sect. 4, we suggest some evolution operators and an algebra. Section 5 illustrates our contribution through an illustrative example. Section 6 presents our tool support. Section 7 overviews related work. Finally, Sect. 8 concludes our work with some future perspectives.

2   Background

This section presents the main definitions for CP realisability. We use Labeled Transition Systems (LTSs) for modelling CP and peers. This behavioural model defines the order of sent messages in a CP. At the peers level, the LTS can be computed by projection from CP and they describe the order in which those peers execute their send and receive actions. Lastly, we define synchronisable systems, and we present the realisability condition considering asynchronous communication.

Definition 1 (Peer). *A peer is an LTS* $\mathcal{P} = (S, s^0, \Sigma, T)$ *where S is a finite set of states, $s^0 \in S$ is the initial state, $\Sigma = \Sigma^! \cup \Sigma^? \cup \{\tau\}$ is a finite alphabet partitioned into a set of send messages, receive messages, and the internal action, and $T \subseteq S \times \Sigma \times S$ is a transition relation.*

We write $m!$ for a send message $m \in \Sigma^!$ and $m?$ for a receive message $m \in \Sigma^?$. We use the symbol τ (tau in figures) for representing internal activities. A transition is represented as $s \xrightarrow{l} s'$ where $l \in \Sigma$ and $\{s, s'\} \subseteq S$.

Example 1. The right side of Fig. 1 shows an example of three peers modelled as LTSs.

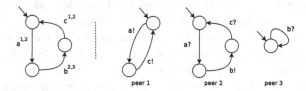

Fig. 1. CP (left side), Peers (right side)

Definition 2 (Conversation Protocol: CP). *A conversation protocol CP for a set of peers $\{\mathcal{P}_1, \ldots, \mathcal{P}_n\}$ is an LTS $CP = \langle S_{CP}, s^0_{CP}, L_{CP}, T_{CP} \rangle$ where S_{CP} is a finite set of states and $s^0_{CP} \in S_{CP}$ is the initial state; L_{CP} is a set of labels where a label $l \in L_{CP}$ is denoted $m^{\mathcal{P}_i, \mathcal{P}_j}$ such that $\mathcal{P}_i$ and $\mathcal{P}_j$ are the sending and receiving peers, respectively, $\mathcal{P}_i \neq \mathcal{P}_j$, and m is a message on which those peers interact; finally, $T_{CP} \subseteq S_{CP} \times L_{CP} \times S_{CP}$ is the transition relation. We require that each message has a unique sender and receiver: $\forall (\mathcal{P}_i, m, \mathcal{P}_j), (\mathcal{P}'_i, m', \mathcal{P}'_j) \in L_{CP} : m = m' \implies \mathcal{P}_i = \mathcal{P}'_i \wedge \mathcal{P}_j = \mathcal{P}'_j$.*

In the remainder of this paper, we denote a transition $t \in T_{CP}$ as $s \xrightarrow{m^{\mathcal{P}_i, \mathcal{P}_j}} s'$ where s and s' are source and target states and $m^{\mathcal{P}_i, \mathcal{P}_j}$ is the transition label.

Example 2. The left side of Fig. 1 shows an example of CP modelled as LTS.

Definition 3 (Projection). *Peer LTSs $\mathcal{P}_i =< S_i, s_i^0, \Sigma_i, T_i >$ are obtained by replacing in $CP =< S_{CP}, s_{CP}^0, L_{CP}, T_{CP} >$ each label $(\mathcal{P}_j, m, \mathcal{P}_k) \in L_{CP}$ with $m!$ if $j = i$ with $m?$ if $k = i$ and with τ (internal action) otherwise; and finally removing the τ-transitions by applying standard minimisation algorithms [8].*

Example 3. Notice that the peers on Fig. 1 are obtained by projection from the CP shown on left side of the same Figure.

Synchronous System. Here, an interaction occurs between two peers if both agree on a synchronisation label, *i.e.*, if one peer is in a state in which a message can be sent, then another peer must be in a state where the same message can be received. The peers can however evolve independently from the others through internals actions.

Definition 4 (Synchronous System). *Given a set of peers $\{\mathcal{P}_1, \ldots, \mathcal{P}_n\}$ with $\mathcal{P}_i = (S_i, s_i^0, \Sigma_i, T_i)$, the synchronous system $(\mathcal{P}_1 \mid \ldots \mid \mathcal{P}_n)$ is the LTS (S, s^0, Σ, T) where:*

- $S = S_1 \times \ldots \times S_n$
- $s^0 \in S$ *such that* $s^0 = (s_1^0, \ldots, s_n^0)$
- $\Sigma = \cup_i \Sigma_i$
- $T \subseteq S \times \Sigma \times S$, *and for* $s = (s_1, \ldots, s_n) \in S$ *and* $s' = (s_1', \ldots, s_n') \in S$ *interact* $s \xrightarrow{m} s' \in T$ *if* $\exists i, j \in \{1, \ldots, n\} : m \in \Sigma_i^! \cap \Sigma_j^?$ *where* $\exists s_i \xrightarrow{m!} s_i' \in T_i$, *and* $s_j \xrightarrow{m?} s_j' \in T_j$ *such that* $\forall k \in \{1, \ldots, n\}, k \neq i \wedge k \neq j \rightarrow s_k' = s_k$

Asynchronous System. Here, the peers communicate with each other through FIFO buffers. Each peer $\mathcal{P}_i$ is equipped with a (possibly) unbounded message buffer Q_i. A peer can either send a message $m \in \Sigma^!$ to the tail of the receiver buffer Q_j at any state where this send message is available, read a message $m \in \Sigma^?$ from its buffer Q_i if the message is available at the buffer head, or evolve independently through an internal action. Since reading from the buffer is not considered as an observable action, it is encoded as an internal action in the asynchronous system.

Definition 5 (Asynchronous Composition). *Given a set of peers $\{\mathcal{P}_1, \ldots, \mathcal{P}_n\}$ with $\mathcal{P}_i = (S_i, s_i^0, \Sigma_i, T_i)$, and Q_i being its associated buffer, the asynchronous composition $((\mathcal{P}_1, Q_1) \mid\mid \ldots \mid\mid (\mathcal{P}_n, Q_n))$ is the labeled transition system $LTS_a = (S_a, s_a^0, \Sigma_a, T_a)$ where:*

1. $S_a \subseteq S_1 \times Q_1 \times \ldots \times S_n \times Q_n$ *where* $\forall i \in \{1, \ldots, n\}$, $Q_i \subseteq (\Sigma_i^?)*$
2. $s_a^0 \in S_a$ *such that* $s_a^0 = (s_1^0, \epsilon, \ldots, s_n^0, \epsilon)$ *(where ϵ denotes an empty buffer)*
3. $\Sigma_a = \cup_i \Sigma_i$

4. $T_a \subseteq S_a \times \Sigma_a \times S_a$, and for $s = (s_1, Q_1, \ldots, s_n, Q_n) \in S_a$ and $s' = (s'_1, Q'_1, \ldots s'_n, Q'_n) \in S_a$

   send $s \xrightarrow{m!} s' \in T_a$ if $\exists i, j \in \{1, \ldots, n\}$ where $i \neq j : m \in \Sigma^!_i \cap \Sigma^?_j$, (i) $s_i \xrightarrow{m!} s'_i \in T_i$, (ii) $Q'_j = Q_j m$, (iii) $\forall k \in \{1, \ldots, n\} : k \neq j \Rightarrow Q'_k = Q_k$, and (iv) $\forall k \in \{1, \ldots, n\} : k \neq i \Rightarrow s'_k = s_k$

   consume $s \xrightarrow{\tau} s' \in T_a$ if $\exists i \in \{1, \ldots, n\} : m \in \Sigma^?_i$, (i) $s_i \xrightarrow{m?} s'_i \in T_i$, (ii) $mQ'_i = Q_i$, (iii) $\forall k \in \{1, \ldots, n\} : k \neq i \Rightarrow Q'_k = Q_k$, and (iv) $\forall k \in \{1, \ldots, n\} : k \neq i \Rightarrow s'_k = s_k$

   internal $s \xrightarrow{\tau} s' \in T_a$ if $\exists i \in \{1, \ldots, n\}$, (i) $s_i \xrightarrow{\tau} s'_i \in T_i$, (ii) $\forall k \in \{1, \ldots, n\} : Q'_k = Q_k$, and (iii) $\forall k \in \{1, \ldots, n\} : k \neq i \Rightarrow s'_k = s_k$

Synchronisability. A system built over a set of peers $\{\mathcal{P}_1, \ldots, \mathcal{P}_n\}$ is synchronisable [2], when both synchronous and asynchronous compositions obtained by application of Definitions 4 and 5, respectively, are equivalent. The equivalence holds if and only if the order of sending messages is the same. This relation is referred to as language equivalence and it is formalised in [2].

Well-formedness. The realisability condition on which we rely requires that the asynchronous system must be well-formed. It consists in checking whenever the i-th peer buffer Q_i is non-empty, the system can eventually move to a state where Q_i is empty. It has been shown in [2] that for every synchronisable set of peers, if the peers are deterministic, i.e., for every state, the possible send messages are unique, well-formedness holds.

Definition 6 (Realisability). *A conversation protocol CP is realisable, denoted R(CP), if and only if (i) the peers computed by projection from this protocol are synchronisable, (ii) the asynchronous system resulting from the peer composition is well-formed, and (iii) the synchronous version of the distributed system $\{\mathcal{P}_1, \ldots, \mathcal{P}_n\}$ is equivalent to CP.*

3   *Correct-by-Construction* **Realisability**

In order to check the realisability condition given in Definition 6, we rely on a stepwise *correct-by-construction* approach to build asynchronous distributed systems [9]. We apply several refinement steps where the sufficient and necessary realisability conditions must be preserved in each step. Notice that these conditions are described using invariants. The first refinement returns peer behaviours obtained by synchronous projection. The previously computed system is then refined into its asynchronous version using unbounded FIFO buffers. We prove, thanks to invariant preservation, that a sequence of exchanged messages is preserved at each refinement step. By doing so, this method gives a formalised proof of an algorithm for a priori realisability checking and such a method scales up to any number of peers communicating with each other.

In this section, we define only the abstract model of CP to show feasibility and scalibilty of our proposed approach. To define the static properties of the system, we declare three sets: *SET_LTS* - a set of Labeled Transition Systems, *STATES* - a set states and *MESSAGES* - a set of exchanged messages. A set of required additional properties related to these sets is given using axioms (*axm*1-*axm*6). An enumerated set is declared in *axm*7. A set of constants is declared in order to specify the required behaviour of the system. These constants are: *LTS_STATES* a relation between LTS and their states, *INITIAL_STATES* - a set of initial states, *FINAL_STATES* - a set of final states, *EXCHANGED_MESSAGES* - a set of exchanged messages, *ETIQ* - a set of edges relating two LTS states, *TRANSITIONS* - a set of transitions, *S_Next-_States* - a next synchronous state and *A_Next_States* - a next asynchronous state. Additional properties are defined using other axioms.

```
axm1 : SET_LTS ≠ ∅
axm2 : finite(SET_LTS) ∧ card(SET_LTS) ≥ 2
axm3 : STATES ≠ ∅
axm4 : finite(STATES) ∧ card(STATES) ≥ 2
axm5 : MESSAGES ≠ ∅
axm6 : finite(MESSAGES) ∧ card(MESSAGES) ≥ 1
axm7 : partition(ACTIONS, {Send}, {Receive}, {Internal})
axm8 : LTS_STATES ∈ SET_LTS ↔ STATES
...
axm10 . INITIAL_STATES ∈ SET_LTS ↔ STATES
...
axm15 : FINAL_STATES ∈ SET_LTS ↔ STATES
axm16 : EXCHANGED_MESSAGES ∈ SET_LTS ↔ MESSAGES
...
axm21 : ETIQ ⊆ ACTIONS × MESSAGES × SET_LTS
...
axm23 : TRANSITIONS ∈ (STATES × ETIQ) ↠ STATES
...
axm29 : S_Next_States ∈ ℙ(TRANSITIONS) × ℙ(SET_LTS × STATES) ↠ ℙ(SET_LTS × STATES)
axm30 : A_Next_States ∈ ℙ(TRANSITIONS) × ℙ(SET_LTS × STATES) ×
        ℙ(SET_LTS × MESSAGES × ℕ) ↠ ℙ(SET_LTS × STATES)
```

Abstract model describes CP behaviour abstractly that contains only initialisation of communication, progress, internal actions and reset. To model the dynamic behaviour, we declare a list of variables using invariants (*inv*1-*inv*4). These variables are: *Conversation* - a sequence that records a set of exchanged messages in the conversation, *Index* - a message exchange order, *lts* - a subset of *LTS_SET*, and *transitions* - a subset of *TRANSITIONS*.

```
inv1 : Conversation ∈ SET_LTS × MESSAGES × SET_LTS ↔ ℕ
inv2 : Index ∈ ℕ
inv3 : lts ⊆ SET_LTS
inv4 : transitions ⊆ TRANSITIONS
```

Initially, we define three events *Interact*, *Internal* and *Reset*. The *Initialisation* event is a default event that initialises initial state of the system, for example, this event sets the conversation to the empty set. The next *Interact* event shows the progress of CP by sending and receiving actions. In this event, the first guard shows the type of given parameters, and the next two guards states the required conditions according to Definition 2. The actions (*act*1 and *act*2) of the this event are used to update the message sequencer *Conversation* and the message index order *Index*. The next *Internal* event is used to model the internal actions (*τ*) and the last *Reset* event is used to reset the conversation.

```
EVENT Initialisation ≜
  ...
EVENT Interact ≜
  ANY lts_source, lts_destination, message
  WHERE
    grd1 : lts_source ∈ lts ∧ lts_destination ∈ lts ∧ message ∈ MESSAGES
    grd2 : ∃send_st_src, send_st_dest·send_st_src ∈ STATES ∧ send_st_dest ∈ STATES∧
           (((send_st_src ↦ (Send ↦ message ↦ lts_destination)) ↦ send_st_dest) ∈ transitions)
    grd3 : ∃receive_st_src, receive_st_dest·receive_st_src ∈ STATES ∧ receive_st_dest ∈ STATES∧
           (((receive_st_src ↦ (Receive ↦ message ↦ lts_source)) ↦ receive_st_dest) ∈ transitions)
  THEN
    act1 : Conversation := Conversation ∪ {((lts_source ↦ message ↦ lts_destination) ↦ Index}
    act2 : Index := Index + 1
  END
EVENT Internal ≜
  ...
EVENT Reset ≜
  ...
```

The refinement models of the abstract events presents synchronous and asynchronous behaviour of CP, which are not presented here due to page limitations.

4 *Correct-by-Construction* Evolution

4.1 Behavioural Properties

In order to check the realisability of a CP that has been updated, we must ensure that the resulting LTS does not violate the realisability condition. We define in the following some properties which enable us to check the realisability preservation after evolution.

Branches Related Properties.

Property 1 (Non-Deterministic Choice). Given a $CP = < S_{CP}, s^0_{CP}, L_{CP}, T_{CP} >$, a state $s_{CP} \in S_{CP}$ is a non-deterministic branching state if: $\exists \{s_{CP} \xrightarrow{m^{P_i, P_j}} s'_{CP}, s_{CP} \xrightarrow{m^{P_i, P_j}} s''_{CP}\} \subseteq T_{CP}$ such that $s'_{CP} \neq s''_{CP}$.

We define in the following divergent choice (also called non-local branching choice in the literature). It differs from process divergence definition [10].

Property 2 (Divergent-Choice). Given a $CP = < S_{CP}, s^0_{CP}, L_{CP}, T_{CP} >$, a state $s_{CP} \in S_{CP}$ is a divergent branching state if: $\exists \{s_{CP} \xrightarrow{m^{P_i, P_j}} s'_{CP}, s_{CP} \xrightarrow{m'^{P_j, P_i}} s''_{CP}\} \subseteq T_{CP}$ such that $s'_{CP} \neq s''_{CP}$, and $m \neq m'$.

Sequences Related Properties. Given a CP, there is at least two partitions of peers where no interaction between both partitions exists.

Property 3 (Independent Sequences). Given a $CP = < S_{CP}, s^0_{CP}, L_{CP}, T_{CP} >$, a transition sequence $s_{CP} \xrightarrow{m^{P_i, P_j}} s'_{CP} \ldots s''_{CP} \xrightarrow{m'^{P_k, P_q}} s'''_{CP}$, where "..." denotes a trace of transitions leading from state s'_{CP} to state s''_{CP} and such that all transitions are in T_{CP}, is called independent sequence if $\{P_i, P_j\} \cap \{P_k, P_q\} = \varnothing$.

The following property enables us to detect traces in a CP which lead to non-local emission choices made by two different peers in the distributed system. To avoid this situation, every peer that joins the conversation at an intermediate state (*i.e.*, different than the initial state) must be receiver the first time it appears in a CP. Otherwise, if a peer is sending a message m at an intermediate state, then this peer must appear as receiver in its last interaction before sending m.

Property 4 (Divergent Sequences). Given a $CP =< S_{CP}, s^0_{CP}, L_{CP}, T_{CP} >$, there exists a transition sequence $s^0_{CP} \xrightarrow{m^{P_i, P_j}} \ldots s'_{CP} \xrightarrow{m'^{P_k, P_q}} s''_{CP}$ where all transitions are in T_{CP} such that:

– for every sender peer P_t involved in a transition before state s'_{CP}, $t \neq k$, or

– there exists at least a transition $s_{CP} \xrightarrow{m^{P_k, P_t}} s'''_{CP} \in T_{CP}$ such that:
  • s'_{CP} is reachable from s_{CP}, and
  • there is no transition in $s_{CP} \xrightarrow{m^{P_k, P_t}} s'''_{CP} \ldots s'_{CP} \xrightarrow{m'^{P_k, P_q}} s''_{CP}$ where P_k is a receiver peer.

4.2 Evolution Patterns

CP evolution stands for two possible tasks, namely, adding and/or removing either messages and/or interacting peers. We define here how CP realisability can be preserved by applying some evolution patterns presented in the following.

Operators. We introduce two operators denoted as $\otimes_{(+, s_{CP})}$ and $\otimes_{(\gg, s_{CP})}$ for branching and sequential composition, respectively, at a state s_{CP} in CP. We also assume other operators not presented here for lack of space, namely, $\otimes_{(\|, s_{CP})}$ for parallel composition, and $\otimes_{(\circlearrowleft, s_{CP})}$ for looping composition. The operator $\otimes_{(\|, s_{CP})}$ generates at a state s_{CP} all the interleaved behaviour of a set of transitions such that every generated branch must satisfy sequence related properties. The operator $\otimes_{(\circlearrowleft, s_{CP})}$ enables us to add self-loop of the form $s \xrightarrow{m^{P_i, P_j}} s$ where $i \neq j$ and such that sequence related properties must be preserved.

Remark 1. The application of an operator $\otimes_{(op, s_{CP})}(CP, CP')$ assumes that the initial state of CP' is fused with the state s_{CP}.

Definition 7. $\otimes_{(\gg, s_{CP})}$ *Given a* $CP =< S_{CP}, s^0_{CP}, L_{CP}, T_{CP} >$, *a* $CP' =< S_{CP'}, s^0_{CP'}, L_{CP'}, T_{CP'} >$ *and a state* $s_{CP} \in S_{CP}$, *the sequential composition* $\otimes_{(\gg, s_{CP})}(CP, CP')$ *means that* CP *must be executed before* CP' *such that Properties 3 and 4 do not hold.*

Definition 8. $\otimes_{(+, s_{CP})}$ *Given a* $CP =< S_{CP}, s^0_{CP}, L_{CP}, T_{CP} >$, *a set* $\{CP'_i\}$, $i = 1..n$ *such that* $CP'_i =< S_{CP'_i}, s^0_{CP'_i}, L_{CP'_i}, T_{CP'_i} >$ *and a state* $s_{CP} \in S_{CP}$, *the branching composition* $\otimes_{(+, s_{CP})}(CP, \{CP'_1, \ldots, CP'_n\})$ *means that there is a choice at* s_{CP} *between the remaining behaviour of* CP *(i.e., starting from* s_{CP}*) and all* CP'_i *such that:*

– *Properties 1 and 2 do not hold at the state s_{CP}, and*
– $\forall CP'_i$, $\otimes_{(\gg, s_{CP})}(CP, CP'_i)$ *holds*

An Algebra of Operators. We introduce in Listing 1.1 a CP algebra the evolution such that realisability is preserved. We refer to a state s^f as final if there is no outgoing transition at that state. We denote ECP as a CP that evolutes over time while preserving realisability. The expression ECP^+ stands for one or more ECP. We refer to a basic CP as $ECP_b = s \xrightarrow{\mathcal{P}_i, m, \mathcal{P}_j} s'$.

$$ECP :: = ECP_b \mid ECP \; op \; ECP_b{}^+$$

$$ECP_b :: = s \xrightarrow{\mathcal{P}_i, m, \mathcal{P}_j} s' \mid \varnothing$$

$$op :: = \otimes_{(+, s^f)} \mid \otimes_{(\gg, s^f)} \mid \otimes_{(\|, s^f)} \mid \otimes_{(\circlearrowleft, s^f)}$$

Listing 1.1. CP Evolution Grammar

4.3 About Correctness

In this section, we discuss the method we have used to check the correctness of the operators definitions and their composition introduced in Sect. 4.2 i.e. check how these operators preserve the realisability condition while building a CP by composing these operators. To do so, we rely on the global approach developed in [9]. The approach of [9] uses the Event-B method and refinement to produce the asynchronous projection of a CP. An abstract model corresponding to the CP description, is first refined to obtain the synchronous projection, and a second refinement produces the asynchronous projection from the synchronous one. The developed approach is a *correct-by-construction* approach, it relies on the Event-B method. The given sufficient and necessary realisability conditions borrowed from [2] are used to prove the correctness of these refinements.

In the context of CP evolution, we proceed as follows to ensure realisability preservation. We prove that each ECP_{bi} is realisable using the approach of [9]. Then, after each application of the composition operator, we apply the approach of [9] until the whole ECP correctness is checked. Another approach consists in checking the correctness of the whole ECP once for all using the approach of [9].

Note that the proposed verification procedure is a naive one. It requires to check the ECP each time an evolution operator is applied. Our intention in a future work, is to propose to check the sufficient conditions for realisability defined in Sects. 4.1 and 4.2. There is no need to re-check the whole ECP.

5 Two Illustrative Examples

This section, we first give an illustration of CP evolution using a simple example. Then, we give a more complex example to better illustrate the evolution operators introduced in this paper.

5.1 A First Example

The first example concerns the sequence and choice evolution operators. An initial CPs and a possible evolution of this CP are shown on Figs. 2a and b, respectively. To illustrate the evolution from one CP to the other one, the added behaviour is presented with dashed transitions on Fig. 2b.

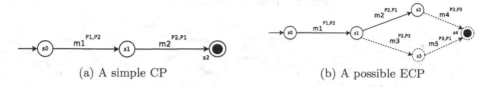

(a) A simple CP   (b) A possible ECP

Fig. 2. An evolution example of CP

Valid Evolution. In this example, the evolution preserves realisability. it produces an ECP by application of the evolution operators identified in (Listing 1.1) as follows. First, we identify below five basic CPs.

$$CP_{b0} = s0 \xrightarrow{m_1^{P1,P2}} s1$$

$$CP_{b1} = s1 \xrightarrow{m_2^{P3,P1}} s2$$

$$CP_{b2} = s1 \xrightarrow{m_3^{P2,P3}} s3$$

$$CP_{b3} = s2 \xrightarrow{m_4^{P2,P3}} s4$$

$$CP_{b4} = s3 \xrightarrow{m_5^{P3,P1}} s4$$

By applying the evolution operators on the basic CPs, we then obtain the following definition of the CP depicted on Fig. 2b:

$ECP = \otimes_{(\gg,s3)}(\otimes_{(\gg,s2)}(\otimes_{(+,s1)}(CP_{b0}, \{CP_{b1}, CP_{b2}\}), CP_{b3}), CP_{b4})$ Notice that the conditions defined in Sects. 4.1 and 4.2 each operator application hold for the *ECP* expression.

5.2 A More Complex Example

For illustration purposes we specify the use of an application in the cloud. This system involves four peers: a client (cl), a Web interface (int), a software application (appli), and a database (db). We show first a conversation protocol (Fig. 3a) describing the requirements that the designer expects from the composition-to-be. The conversation protocol starts with a login interaction (connect) between the client and the interface, followed by the access request (access) triggered by the client. This request can be repeated as far as necessary. Finally, the client decides to logout from the interface (logout)

Invalid Evolution. We show on Fig. 4a an updated version of the CP given on Fig. 3a describing the new requirements that the designer expects from the

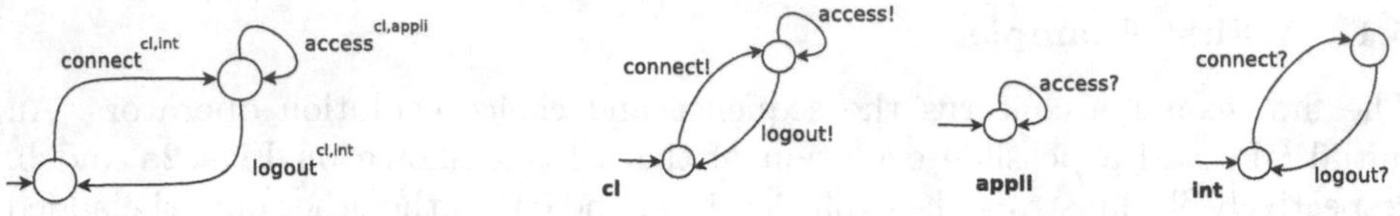

(a) A realisable CP   (b) Peers Projection

Fig. 3. CP and its projection

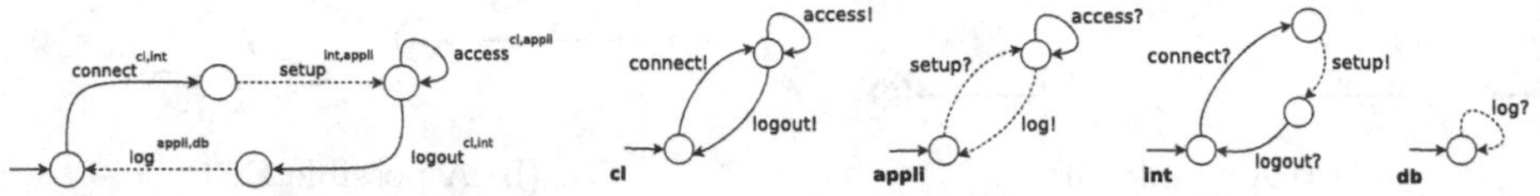

(a) A non correct CP Evolution   (b) Peers Projection

Fig. 4. ECP and its projection

composition-to-be. The conversation protocol starts with a login interaction (connect) between the client and the interface, followed by the setup of the application triggered by the interface (setup). Then, the client can access and use the application as far as necessary (access). Finally, the client decides to logout from the interface (logout) and the application stores some information (start/end time, used resources, etc.) into a database (log).

Figure 4b shows the four peers obtained by projection. This set of peers seems to respect the behaviour specified in the conversation protocol, yet this is difficult to be sure using only visual analysis, even for such a simple example. In addition, as the *CP* involves looping behaviour, it is hard to know whether the resulting distributed system is bounded and finite, which would allow its formal analysis using existing verification techniques. Actually, this set of peers is not synchronisable (and therefore not realisable), because the trace of send messages "connect, access" is present in the 1-bounded asynchronous system, but is not present in the synchronous system. Synchronous communication enforces the sequence "connect, setup, access" as specified in the *CP*, whereas in the asynchronous system peer cl can send connect! and access! in sequence.

This kind of evolution resulting in non realisable CP can be avoided using our method with no need of CP projection as done in [6]. Starting from the initial state of CP that is shown on Fig. 3a and using the algebra given in Listing 1.1, there is no way to generate the interaction sequence "connect, setup, access" because adding "access" interaction violates Property 4.

6 Tool Support

Event-B [11,12] is a modelling method based on set-theory that enables to model a system by supporting a *correct by construction* approach, which allows to design a complex system using stepwise refinement by introducing the required system behaviour and desired functionalities in a new refinement step.

Each refinement step is verified by generated proof obligations corresponding to an abstract model and new refined behaviour. The stepwise modelling process finally leads to a concrete implementation of a system. In the Event-B language, *context* and *machine* are two important components, which describe static behaviour and dynamic behaviour, respectively. The static properties can be described using *carrier sets, enumerated sets, constants, theorems* and *axioms*, while a machine can be described using *variables, invariants, events* and *theorems*. To characterise the dynamic behaviour of a system, a list of events can be used to modify state variables by providing appropriate guards. In order to preserve the desired behaviour of a system, we defined a list of safety properties using invariants and theorems. Moreover, to introduce the convergence properties in the model, we can use *variant* clause in a machine. In a refinement step, an event can be refined by (1) keeping the events as it is; (2) splitting the event into several new events (3) strengthening the guards and actions (to make nondeterministic to deterministic). However, a new refinement level also allows to introduce a new event by modifying the new state variables.

The Rodin platform, java based integrated development environment (IDE) for Event-B, is set of tools to support model development, refinement, proof assistance, code generation and model animation. Due to page limitations, we have not presented a detailed introduction to Event-B. There are numerous publications and books available for an introduction to Event-B and related refinement strategies [11,12].

7 Related Work

Dynamic reconfiguration [13] is an interesting topic that play an important role for designing and developing a class of systems, such as distributed systems, graph transformation, software adaptation and meta modelling. Leite et al. [14] cover a survey on web service evolution, including various techniques and tools. In our work, we focus on the evolution of conversation protocols, and in this section, we describe existing work related to the evolution of CP. Roohi et al. [5] proposed a method to check CP reconfigurability by defining two different CPs, an initial CP and a new CP', and two sets of peers PS and PS'. These peers are obtained by projection of both CPs. A given trace t of CP consists in the history of the current execution. If the trace t can be executed in the reconfiguration peers (generated from CP'), the reconfiguration can take place.

Wombacher et al. [15] use the annotated Finite State Automata (aFSA) to describe the formal model of web service interaction using choreography. This approach preserves changes between updated choreography and the corresponding orchestration, in which the changes are made through adding and/or removing sequences of messages from the distributed peers. The proposed solution is implemented using DYCHOR framework, which requires human validation. A control evolution method, where propagating the changes into one peer requires to check its effect on other partner peers, is proposed in [3,16], which also use DYCHOR framework for implementation.

The evolution that might arise at the peers side is reported in [17,18], in which the authors propagate the change from one peer to other partners. Fdhila et al. [18] study the Business Process Management (BPM) and Service Oriented Architecture (SOA) to describe service choreographies using tree-based model considering some changes like delete, update, replace and insert for behavioural fragments.

A new programming language DIOC, free from deadlocks and races by construction, is defined for distributed applications [17]. The semantic of this language relies on labelled transition systems. The given approach enables to update the fragment of codes of distributed peers. In addition, it can be used at choreography level where code blocks can be updated dynamically and these code blocks must be tagged when describing the choreography. The run-time evolution and the required solution is discussed in [5,17,19].

Börger et al. [20] propose the semantics of concurrent Abstract State Machine (ASM), which overcome the problems of Gurevich's distributed ASM runs and generalise Lamport's sequentially consistent runs. The proposed semantics can also be used for designing the CPs in order to handle the concurrent scenarios.

To the best of our knowledge, this work is a pioneer in applying a *correct by construction* approach to model and verify the evolution of CP to guarantee that the realisability is preserved. Moreover, in our proposed solution, we have no restriction on the application domain, and we can use formal modelling techniques for designing, verification, and implementation of different distributed systems, *e.g.* web services, concurrent systems, Cyber Physical Systems, etc. Our result also applies for asynchronous systems as far as these systems are synchronisable without restricting the buffer size.

8   Conclusion and Perspectives

This paper presentes a preliminary solution for correct evolution of distributed systems for which their interaction is described with a conversation protocol. We proposed a language which enables one to incrementally design distributed systems that can be updated over time such that their realisability is preserved while applying evolution operators. Our naive method is used to prove that these operators preserve CP realisability. Finally, we illustrated our contribution using real-world example. As a main perspective of this work, we are extending the static model of [9] to support CP evolution. We aim at implementing the set of operators based on *correct-by-construction* method using Event-B.

References

1. Bultan, T.: Modeling interactions of web software. In: Proceedings of WWV 2006, pp. 45–52. IEEE(2006)
2. Basu, S., Bultan, T., Ouederni, M.: Deciding choreography realizability. In: Proceedings of POPL 2012, pp. 191–202. ACM (2012)

3. Rinderle, S., Wombacher, A., Reichert, M.: On the controlled evolution of process choreographies. In: Proceedings of ICDE 2006, pp. 124–124. IEEE (2006)
4. Ryu, S.H., Casati, F., Skogsrud, H., Benatallah, B., Saint-Paul, R.: Supporting the dynamic evolution of web service protocols in service-oriented architectures. ACM Trans. Web (TWEB) **2**(2), 13 (2008)
5. Roohi, N., Salaün, G.: Realizability and dynamic reconfiguration of chor specifications. Informatica (Slovenia) **35**(1), 39–49 (2011)
6. Güdemann, M., Salaün, G., Ouederni, M.: Counterexample guided synthesis of monitors for realizability enforcement. In: Chakraborty, S., Mukund, M. (eds.) ATVA 2012. LNCS, vol. 7561, pp. 238–253. Springer, Heidelberg (2012)
7. Basu, S., Bultan, T.: Automated choreography repair. In: Stevens, P., et al. (eds.) FASE 2016. LNCS, vol. 9633, pp. 13–30. Springer, Heidelberg (2016). doi:10.1007/978-3-662-49665-7_2
8. Hopcroft, J.E., Ullman, J.D.: Introduction to Automata Theory. Languages and Computation. Addison Wesley, Reading (1979)
9. Farah, Z., Ait-Ameur, Y., Ouederni, M., Tari, K.: A correct-by-construction model for asynchronously communicating systems. Int. J. Softw. Tools Technol. Transfer 1–21 (2016)
10. Ben-Abdallah, H., Leue, S.: Syntactic detection of process divergence and non-local choice in message sequence charts. In: Brinksma, E. (ed.) TACAS 1997. LNCS, vol. 1217, pp. 259–274. Springer, Heidelberg (1997)
11. Abrial, J.R.: Modeling in Event-B: System and Software Engineering, 1st edn. Cambridge University Press, New York (2010)
12. Project RODIN: Rigorous Open Development Environment for Complex Systems (2004). http://rodin-b-sharp.sourceforge.net/
13. Medvidovic, N.: ADLs and dynamic Architecture Changes. In: Proceedings of SIGSOFT 1996 Workshops, pp. 24–27. ACM (1996)
14. Leite, L.A., Oliva, G.A., Nogueira, G.M., Gerosa, M.A., Kon, F., Milojicic, D.S.: A Systematic Literature Review of Service Choreography Adaptation. SOCA **7**(3), 199–216 (2013)
15. Wombacher, A.: Alignment of choreography changes in BPEL processes. In: Proceedings of SCC 2009. pp. 1–8. IEEE (2009)
16. Rinderle, S., Wombacher, A., Reichert, M.: Evolution of process choreographies in DYCHOR. In: Meersman, R., Tari, Z. (eds.) OTM 2006. LNCS, vol. 4275, pp. 273–290. Springer, Heidelberg (2006)
17. Dalla Preda, M., Gabbrielli, M., Giallorenzo, S., Lanese, I., Mauro, J.: Dynamic choreographies. In: Holvoet, T., Viroli, M. (eds.) Coordination Models and Languages. LNCS, vol. 9037, pp. 67–82. Springer, Heidelberg (2015)
18. Fdhila, W., Indiono, C., Rinderle-Ma, S., Reichert, M.: Dealing with change in process choreographies: design and implementation of propagation algorithms. Inf. Syst. **49**, 1–24 (2015)
19. Jureta, I.J., Faulkner, S., Thiran, P.: Dynamic requirements specification for adaptable and open service-oriented systems. In: Krämer, B.J., Lin, K.-J., Narasimhan, P. (eds.) ICSOC 2007. LNCS, vol. 4749, pp. 270–282. Springer, Heidelberg (2007)
20. Börger, E., Schewe, K.D.: Concurrent abstract state machines. Acta Informatica 1–24 (2015)

White-Box Modernization of Legacy Applications

Kelly Garcés[1]([✉]), Rubby Casallas[1], Camilo Álvarez[1], Edgar Sandoval[1], Alejandro Salamanca[2], Fabián Melo[2], and Juan Manuel Soto[2]

[1] School of Engineering, Department of Systems and Computing Engineering, Universidad de Los Andes, Bogota D.C., Colombia
{kj.garces971,rcasalla,c.alvarez956,ed.sandoval1644}@uniandes.edu.co
[2] Asesoftware Ltda., Bogota D.C., Colombia
{asalaman,fmelo,jsoto}@asesoftware.com
http://www.uniandes.edu.co/
http://www.asesoftware.com/

Abstract. Software modernization consists of transforming legacy applications into modern technologies, mainly to minimize maintenance costs. This transformation often produces a new application that is a poor copy of the legacy due to the degradation of quality attributes, for example. This paper presents a white-box transformation approach that changes the application architecture and the technological stack without losing business value and quality attributes. This approach obtains a technology agnostic model from the original sources, such a model facilitates the architecture configuration before performing the actual transformation of the application into the new technology. The architecture for the new application can be configured considering aspects such as data access, quality attributes, and process. We evaluate our approach through an industrial case study, the gist of which is the transformation of Oracle Forms applications—where the presentation layer is highly coupled to the data access layer—to Java technologies.

Keywords: Industrial case study · Model-driven techniques · Oracle forms · Multi-tier architecture · Configuration · Quality attributes

1 Introduction

Oracle Forms appeared towards the end of the 1980 s and provides a rapid application development environment plus a run-time environment. The architecture of Oracle Forms applications is client/server—where the presentation layer is highly coupled to the data access layer. A basic Forms application consists of forms accessed via a menu and, in most cases, these forms have items that can be mapped to database tables. Most of the database behaviour (read/write/update/delete) is pre-defined in Forms, thus avoiding the need to write too many lines of code. Forms applications are present in many sectors. The results of a

© Springer International Publishing Switzerland 2016
L. Bellatreche et al. (Eds.): MEDI 2016, LNCS 9893, pp. 274–287, 2016.
DOI: 10.1007/978-3-319-45547-1_22

survey carried out by the Oracle User Group Community Focused On Education (ODTUG) in 2009, indicate that 40 percent of 581 respondents (application developers) use Oracle Forms.

Both, the companies using Oracle Forms and the companies using other legacy technologies, such as Cobol, AS400, RPG, Power Builder, etc. face the following challenges: high maintenance costs, difficulty to find experts, fear that the vendor stops supporting the technology, non-fulfillment of functional requirements and quality attributes.

To cope with these challenges, companies "modernize the legacy" by *understanding* and *transforming* software assets to maintain a large part of their business value [5]. Our previous work [4] targets the understanding step. In that work, we proposed a set of views that help to understand the original application and to delimit the modernization scope.

Whereas our previous work focused on the as-is legacy architecture understanding, this paper addresses the transformation step. That is, how to configure the as-is to obtain a to-be that is valid in the target technology, and generate the corresponding code. The transformation step can be performed in thirteen ways, according to the OMG [14]. The Language/Platform migration is the most widely applied transformation in related work. It aims to move systems from one language environment and platform to another. This scenario does not involve any functional or data redesign beyond that, which is essential for platform migration.

This work deals with the problem of manually performing Language/Platform migration. The problem arose as a result of rewriting excerpts of legacy code from scratch—or even worst, of copying and pasting existing excerpts from one place to another—despite their similarity. Also, developers have to switch from the modern IDE to the legacy IDE in order to solve their questions related to the legacy implementation details. Moreover, rewriting and switching are time consuming and error-prone.

We have studied commercial tools and research works that deal with this problem (see Sect. 5), and, therefore, are able to conclude that their output code is difficult to maintain and evolve because they mostly apply a black-box transformation approach [16]. The following are the drawbacks of black-box transformation: (1) Lack of information, which may hamper the proper execution of the application on a modern platform; (2) Analyses to discover dead code that the developer would want to avoid in the new application are rarely performed; (3) The ability to modify the user interface appears very late in the transformation life cycle (i.e., once the code has already been generated); (4) Means to see the transformation progress are uncommon in most of the related work.

These drawbacks have motivated our proposal, which is a white-box transformation process that focuses on the understanding of the legacy application, but put in the terms of a *technology agnostic model* (see Sect. 3). Our work targets stakeholder developers, so that they can use this model to configure the target architecture in the early steps of the process, and indicate the transformation progress. Even though it is likely that developers modify the modern code in our approach in order to complete the implementation of functionalities, the approach reduces the modifications to be made at a code level because they can configure many aspects of the architecture at a model level. The latter favors maintainability because most of the generated code follows default design patterns and standards. We count the following among the aspects that can be configured: *data access, quality attributes (maintainability, usability, and security), and configuration progress.* We demonstrate the applicability of our approach by transforming Oracle Forms applications into a multi-tier architecture (see Sect. 2). The evaluation (see Sect. 4) covers a proof of concept and a pilot study. In particular, the pilot study demonstrates that developers that use the white-box method have a better productivity than that of developers that use a manual method. It is worth noting that these developers are not Oracle Forms experts. We have built an editor (see Sect. 3.3) on top of the technology agnostic model to ease the configuration. Model-driven techniques leverage the whole process and the construction of the editor. Finally, Sect. 6 concludes the paper and outlines future work.

2   Oracle Forms Case Study

The case study comes from the "Forms Modernization" project, which involved academic and industrial partners. The project arose as a result of some problems faced by Asesoftware, a Colombian software company that offers modernization services to its clients, including the migration of Oracle Forms applications to modern platforms.

2.1   Oracle Forms Concepts and Modernization Scope

We present the main concepts of an Oracle Forms application below:

- *Form*: A Form is a collection of objects and code, which includes windows, items, triggers, etc.
- *Blocks*: Represent logical containers for grouping related items into a function unit to store, display and manipulate records of database tables. Programmers configure blocks depending on the number of tables from which they want to manipulate the form: (1) The way to display a single database table in a form is to create a block. This results in a *master form*. (2) The way to display two tables that share a master-detail relationship (i.e., "One to Many" relationship) is through two blocks. Oracle Forms guarantees that the detail block will display only records that are associated with the current record in the master block. This results in a *master/detail form*.
- *Item*: Items display information to users and enable them to interact with the application. Item objects include the following types: button, check box, display item, among others.
- *Trigger*: A trigger object is associated to an event. It represents a named PL/SQL function or procedure that is written in a form, block or item.
- *Menu*: Is displayed as a collection of menu names appearing horizontally under the application window title. There is a drop-down list of commands under each menu name. Each command can represent a submenu or an action.

In the context of the Forms Modernization project, we automate the transformation of master and master/detail forms. Given a form, we are able to generate: (1) The corresponding graphical interface (except the layout); (2) The logic to read/write/update/delete records of database tables; (3) The scaffolding code that (i) Interconnects a given field with the PL/SQL logic that "looks up" data when the application runs; (ii) Calls logic embedded in triggers. In both cases, the transformation of PL/SQL code to modern language is the responsibility of the developer. To avoid switching from the modern IDE to the legacy IDE, this code is embedded as comments into places of the new application where it makes sense to have this logic.

2.2   Architecture and Target Technologies

We defined a multi-tiered architecture for the "Forms Modernization" project. The transformation takes Oracle Forms code as input and produces a modernized application as output that implements this architecture in Java technology. We describe the multi-tiered architecture and technologies below:

- *The presentation tier* represents the front-end of the system. It transfers the user request to the Business logic tier for processing and retrieves the result from there and displays it on the screen. (Java Primefaces)
- *The business logic tier* houses all the major data processing functionalities of the system. It interconnects the presentation tier with the persistence tier. The Business logic tier fetches the results and send them to the user. (EJB, Enterprise Java Beans)
- *The persistence tier* provides the abstraction for database access and thus separates it from other tiers. (JPA, Java Persistence API)

3   Leveraging Target Architecture Configuration

Figure 1 summarizes the overall transformation process, which consists of the following steps: The first step obtains a technology specific model from the legacy code. The second step transforms this model into a technology agnostic model. In contrast to the former model—which is verbose and technology specific—, the latter model conforms to a metamodel, the concepts of which matter in the target architecture. The steps three to six can be performed in an incremental manner. In each iteration, the developer can configure how to transform a set of legacy artifacts (third step), and generate, complete, and test corresponding new code (fourth to sixth steps), until satisfying the scope of a given modernization project.

This section is devoted to the third and main step (i.e., Configuration of target architecture) of our transformation process. In a nutshell, the step consists of completing the information needed in the new application. We classify this information into the following concerns: *data access, quality attributes, and configuration process*. We do believe that the configuration process is applicable to any modernization project, regardless of the source/target technologies.

This section is structured as follows: Firstly, for each concern, we present a list of issues in the context of Oracle Forms applications. Secondly, we propose the technology agnostic metamodel where its concepts represent the concerns and the target architecture. Finally, we elaborate on the graphical editor that eases the configuration.

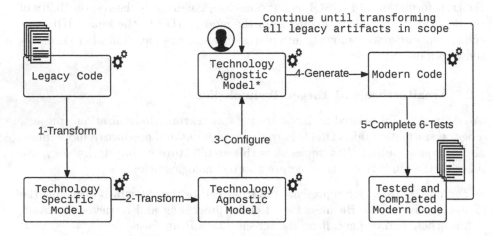

Fig. 1. White-box transformation process.

3.1 Architecture Configuration Concerns

Data Access. This concern involves identifying data access information—needed in the modern application—that is missing at a persistence or application level.

Primary Keys. Legacy database may lack information, which hampers straightforward data access in the modern application. For example, primary keys can be optional in Oracle Forms (instead of using unique indexes) but mandatory in JPA.

Referential Integrity. In a master/detail form, the relationship between two blocks is established through a join condition that might be missed. In that case, developers must provide the information and the transformation must verify that foreign keys are valid.

Quality Attributes. This concern involves determining the quality attributes that matter in modernized applications. We identified the three following quality attributes in the case study:

Maintainability. Oracle Forms IDE provides developers with very few means to detect dead code (e.g., forms that are not called from menu-items). As a consequence, when applying black-box migration, it is possible to obtain garbage in the modernized application. This gives rise to the need to inform developers about these facts in order for them to make the decision of discarding this part of the code for the sake of easing the maintainability of the modern code.

Usability. Besides adopting leading edge technologies, modernization may have the purpose of changing how the application looks like. Developers may want to specify that in the new application, instead of in the legacy, so that, the transformation must provide with the means to: (1) Introduce/delete/modify graphical components to display the information that actually matters in the modernized application. (2) Restructure the menu to help users find the options they are looking for.

Security. Complementing the aforementioned, sometimes useful information is missing in the application layer but present in the database. For example, in Oracle Forms applications, it is common to store security information (e.g., roles and their relation to menu items) in the database. Given that guarantying database access or authorization is crucial, a way to have this information in the target application is necessary.

Configuration Process. This concern involves indicating the progress of the configuration of the aforementioned aspects to members of the modernization project. Since Forms applications may have medium/large size, it is possible to allocate several developers to the modernization project. In each iteration, developers configure the mentioned aspects for a set of forms, and then launch the generation step. It is possible that developers may want to answer the following question: how many screens assigned to them are ready or waiting for configuration?

3.2   Technology Agnostic Metamodel

Figure 2 presents the classes of the metamodel. We have used geometrical figures in the upper-right corner of the classes and a background color to spell out how the classes are related to tiers of the target architecture and the configuration concerns (see Figure legend). Note that some classes help generate artifacts from several tiers of the architecture (e.g., Entity) or leverage different configuration concerns (e.g., Migration Status). Each of these classes is explained below:

- *Application* is the root element of the metamodel. It describes the new application, which consists of menu items, screens, entities, and roles.
- *Menu Item* represents an option available in a menu. A given menu item can display a screen to the user according to the user's role.
- *Role* categorizes the users authorized to access a given screen.
- *Screen* allows the users to request for CRUD operations. It consists of a set of data containers.
- *Data Container* allows multiple data definitions to be contained within a single region of a screen.

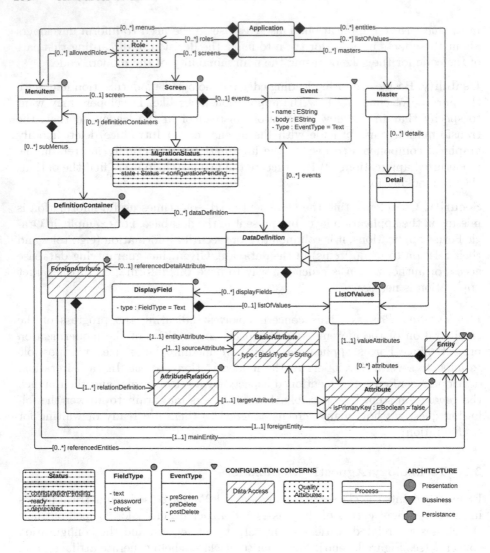

Fig. 2. Simplified version of the technology agnostic metamodel.

- *Data Definition* is an abstract class that represents a grouping of fields to manipulate and display entity attributes.
- *Display Field* specifies a graphical component that displays the data associated to an entity attribute.
- *Master* extends the data definition class and its displayed fields belong to a parent entity.
- *Detail* extends the data definition class and its displayed fields belong to a child entity subordinated to a master. Multiple details can be associated to the same master.

- *Entity* represents elements that are persistent in the legacy database. Each element consists of a set of attributes.
- *Attribute* defines a specific characteristic of an entity. There are two kinds of attributes: basic and foreign.
- *Basic Attribute* specifies a part of an entity.
- *Foreign Attribute* is an attribute that belongs to a given entity and serves as proxy for basic attributes of other entities via attribute relations.
- *Attribute Relation* connects foreign attributes to basic attributes that form the primary key of an entity.
- *List of Values* means that the data populating a display field is the result of a query.
- *Event* contains a set of statements that are executed automatically at run time before/after an action of screen displaying or data manipulation.
- *Migration Status* indicates the configuration status (i.e., configuration pending, ready or deprecated) of a screen.

3.3 Technology Agnostic Metamodel Editor

We have built an editor—on top of the Technology Agnostic Metamodel—that allows developers to configure the target architecture. Below, we present this editor's main functionalities and spell out how they support the configuration of the concerns. For illustration purposes, we include some screenshots (see Fig. 3a and b) that show how the technology agnostic model for the *Conciso* application (introduced in Sect. 4.1) is displayed by the editor.

Menu Structure Definition. If the legacy application owns *.mmb* files, then the editor displays its menu items. For example, as shown in Fig. 3a, the *Conciso* menu items are: *ZONAS, CUENTAS,* etc. In the absence of *.mmb* files, this section is going to appear empty, in which case, the developer can create menu items and associate screens to them from scratch. In any case, the developer can restructure the menu by using drag and drop tools. This functionality targets the usability concern.

Screen Classification. The editor classifies the screens into five categories that allow the developer to easily figure out the screens that are included in a given configuration/validity status (see Fig. 3a): (1) *Configuration pending screens*: lists the screens that lack a basic configuration, that is, name, primary/foreign keys for associated entities, and roles. (2) *Unassigned to menu screens*: groups the screens that are not associated to any menu item. It is important to warn the developer about this fact because, otherwise, the final user would not be able to reach the functionalities of these screens from the modern graphical interface. (3) *Ready screens*: presents the screens whose basic configuration is ready. (4) *Deprecated screens*: groups the screens marked as deprecated by the developer. These screens will not be transformed. (5) *Invalid screens*: lists the screens that are out of the modernization scope, that is, the screens that are not master or master/detail. The first category addresses the data access and security concerns.

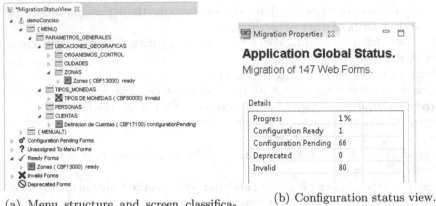

(a) Menu structure and screen classification.

(b) Configuration status view.

Fig. 3. Three functionalities of the technology agnostic metamodel editor.

The second and fourth categories point to the maintainability concern. The third category targets the process concern. Finally, the fifth category enforces compliance to the modernization scope.

Application Configuration Status View. The developer has access to this view from the root element of the editor. The view (see Fig. 3b) summarizes the configuration progress of the application screens, the number of screens in the status ready, configuration pending, deprecated, and invalid. Therefore, this view targets the process concern. To obtain the percentage, we divide the number of ready screens with the result of subtracting the number of deprecated screens from the total number of screens.

Additional Functionalities. The editor also allows the developer to: (1) Change the status of a set of screens via a pop-up menu. This functionality targets the process concern; (2) Validate whether the basic configuration of a given screen has been set; (3) Edit any element of the technology agnostic model via pop-up windows. Common editions include: setting of primary/foreign keys (related to the data access concern), setting of roles (related to the security concern) and introduction/deletion/modification of display fields (related to the usability concern); (4) Open a given form in the Oracle Forms IDE. The first and second functionalities point to the process concern. In turn, the third functionality addresses the usability concern.

4   Evaluation

The evaluation had two parts: a proof of concept and a pilot study. Asesoftware provided five applications that were taken as the dataset to perform the proof of concept. We applied the first and second steps of the transformation process to these applications, namely *Bolivar, Sitri, Maestro, Servibanca,* and *Conciso.* The applications are related to treasury, banking and insurance sectors. In contrast to the proof of concept, the whole transformation process was carried out in the pilot study. In particular, the generation (i.e., the fourth step of the process) was oriented towards Java code. The pilot's main purpose was to compare the productivity of developers who manually transformed legacy with that of developers who used our transformation process.

4.1 Proof of Concept

As a result of applying the first and second steps of the transformation process to the mentioned five applications, we obtained a technology agnostic model for each of them. From each model, we calculated four metrics that are shown in Fig. 4. The metrics are related to the screens that are needed for data access configuration (i.e., primary/foreign keys) and the screens classified by the editor (i.e., invalid screens and screens with unassigned menu). These metrics are percentages related to the total number of screens contained in a given application, this number is between parenthesis next to the application name in the Figure legend. The percentages demonstrate the need for configuration to ensure that the transformation has the basic information to generate an application that is functional. The *Maestro's* percentages show that this application needs a lower effort for basic configuration compared with required for the rest of applications. The reason to this, is that *Maestro* is the most recent developed application among the five applications of our dataset. Therefore, *Maestro's* developers followed design practices similar to those of the target architecture such as the primary key definition, for example.

4.2 Pilot Study

Goal. Our study is aimed at analyzing two methods for Oracle Forms application transformation: "manual" and "(semi)automated through the white-box method", for the purpose of comparison with respect to their productivity from the perspective of practitioners in Asesoftware. We addressed the following research question in this study: **RQ1**: Is the developer productivity significantly different among methods, regardless of the particular form being modernized?

Subjects. The initial group of subjects were 4 developers from Asesoftware. These developers were divided into 2 teams, namely "Manual Team" and "White-box Method Team". The sample comprised 4 men, of whom 50 % were Senior Java developers (at least 5 years of professional experience) and 50 % Junior Java developers (between 0–2 years of professional experience). Each team comprised 1 senior and 1 junior developer. By the time the experiment took place, the subjects received training in the relevant technologies. Such a training consisted of 8 h of training in Oracle Forms, 4 h in the target architecture and 14 h in the white-box method. Two forms were transformed by each team. The selected

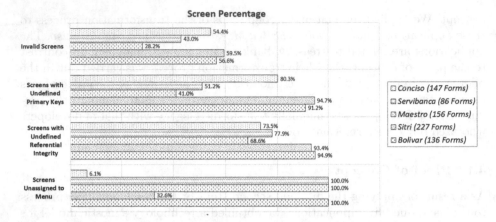

Fig. 4. Metrics obtained from the technology agnostic model of the applications in the dataset.

forms were part of the *Bolivar* application used in the proof of concept. The forms have a different complexity, which depends on the number of items. Therefore, *low complexity* means that a given form has less than ten items, and, *high complexity* means more than twenty. The rationale behind the forms selection is that the customer pointed out as part of their business core. The forms functionality included CRUD operations associated to co-insurers (low complexity form) and loan conditions (high-complexity form). Whereas the junior developer modernized the low complexity form, the senior developer modernized the high complexity one. Developers were scheduled to work on these two forms during three weeks. We strictly defined that both teams had to keep the target architecture. This way, it was possible to standardize to a certain point the modernized code that had to be developed and facilitate its measurement. In order to convert the forms, the Manual Team followed Asesoftware's initial method, which consisted of a code-centric transformation from scratch. The other team, in turn, followed the white-box transformation process assisted by the editor.

Results. Figure 5 shows the time used by the teams to transform the selected forms into modern code. The time spent by the "White-box Method Team" (i.e., 18.1 and 41.5 h for low and high complexity forms, respectively) covers all the steps of the transformation process, where steps one, two, four and six are automated and steps three and five are manual. In the third step, developers configured the basic information (i.e., data access and security) to generate functional code. In the fifth step, developers manually transformed the code of triggers from the comments embedded in the modern application. In contrast, the time spent by the "Manual Team" (i.e., 31.4 and 82.4 h for low and high complexity forms, respectively) encompasses the manual transformation of each form. The development time of the high-complexity form is higher than that of the low-complexity form because the number of items in the former is almost twice the number in the latter.

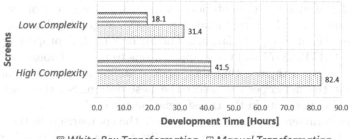

Fig. 5. Development time of the developers for each method and form.

Interpretation of Results. The time shown in Fig. 5 serves as existing empirical evidence to answer **RQ1**: Developers are significantly more productive (environ 40 %) when following the white-box transformation than the manual transformation. This result is independent of the particular form to which the transformation is applied. In addition, the result shows that the developers that used the white-box method had a good productivity regardless of their Oracle Forms experience.

5 Related Work

In a nutshell, we classify the reviewed approaches (except by [12]) in the black-box transformation category because they generate applications that conform to a default architecture instead of letting the user decide about it. Therefore, the users only specify their decisions over the generated code. In contrast, we provide the means to make decisions in the early steps of transformation by using a model and an editor. Similar to us, [12] has a model representing the application in an agnostic way; however, the paper does not report any high-level abstraction means to make decisions based on such a model, which our approach does make possible via the editor. Below, we present more details regarding related work.

We compare our approach to four research works [1,2,7,12], we selected these works because they aim at transforming legacy applications (there the presentation layer is highly coupled to the data layer) to modern platforms. Similarly to [2,12], our approach migrates Oracle Forms applications to modern technologies. Both, [2] and our approach, migrate the Oracle Forms code that performs CRUD operations on database tables. Whilst [2] achieves the PL/SQL migration because of the similarity existing between Oracle Forms and the target technology, this part is out of our scope. The only thing our approach does in that sense is to embed the PL/SQL into the modernized application as commented code. When comparing [12] to our approach, we found that [12] focuses on the migration of the presentation layer structure of any form (thus taking care of the distribution/position of graphical components on the window). In contrast, our method migrates the presentation/logic/persistence layers of two kinds of forms (i.e., master and master/detail forms), where graphical components are put in a fixed layout (i.e., flow layout). The authors of [1,7] propose approaches to migrate FORTRAN-77 and C++ applications to new technologies. The common aspect between them is that they present different options of modernized code, so that the developer can select the best option. So, these works allow decision making very late in the transformation life cycle.

From the commercial perspective, we limit the comparison to the tools that transform Oracle Forms applications. Usually, the transformation is offered as a service (such as in [10]) or as a standalone platform ready to be used by the developer (i.e., [6,9,15]). Some of the tools transform Oracle Forms to an in-house technology such as ADF or APEX (i.e., [8,15].). Others have a completely different target technology such as .Net or Java (i.e., [3,8,11,13,15]. All commercial options are inside the category of Language/Platform migration with the multi-tier style as the most common target architecture.

6   Conclusion and Future Work

This paper presented a white-box process to transform legacy applications to modern technologies/platforms. This approach has been transferred to a Colombian software company that had many years of experience in the manual migration of Oracle Forms applications to Java and .Net. Taking into account the findings of the pilot study, the company has decided to create a new modernization service based on the approach and the editor. Looking at the market, they have identified the need for addressing the variability of Oracle Forms versions (i.e., 6i, 9i, 10i, 11i) and new target technologies (i.e., .Net). The approach can be adapted to take into account the variability because the technology agnostic metamodel serves as a pivot that facilitates the transformation. In particular, we are currently implementing the transformation to migrate to the .Net platform. Furthermore, we are working on providing design pattern variability in the target architecture.

In addition, we wish to extend the set of available metrics, so that they serve as an input to decide whether modernization makes sense. As a result of metrics analysis, the project manager or the client may decide that keeping the legacy application is cheaper than transforming it to modern technologies.

References

1. Achee, B.L., Carver, D.L.: Creating object-oriented designs from legacy FORTRAN code. J. Syst. Softw. **39**(2), 179–194 (1997)
2. Andrade, L.F., Gouveia, J., Antunes, M., El-Ramly, M., Koutsoukos, G.: Forms2Net - migrating oracle forms to microsoft.NET. In: Lämmel, R., Saraiva, J., Visser, J. (eds.) GTTSE 2005. LNCS, vol. 4143, pp. 261–277. Springer, Heidelberg (2006)
3. Technologies, C.: Oracle Forms to Java, April 2016. http://www.composertechnologies.com/

4. Garces, K., Sandoval, E., Casallas, R., Alvarez, C., Salamanca, A., Pinto, S., Melo, F.: Aiming towards modernization: visualization to assist structural understanding of oracle forms applications. In: ICSEA 2015, Tenth International Conference on Software Engineering Advances, pp. 86–95. IARIA (2015)
5. Izquierdo, J., Molina, J.: An architecture-driven modernization tool for calculating metrics. IEEE Softw. **27**(4), 37–43 (2010)
6. Systems, K.: Migration services, April 2016. http://www.kumaran.com/
7. Lau, T.C., Lu, J., Mylopoulos, J., Kontogiannis, K.: The migration of multi-tier e-commerce applications to an enterprise Java environment. Inform. Syst. Front. **5**(2), 149–160 (2003)
8. Oracle: Oracle JHeadstart 12c for ADF, April 2016. http://www.oracle.com/technetwork/developer-tools/jheadstart/
9. Pitss: PITSS.CON overview, April 2016. https://www.pitss.com/
10. QAFE: Solutions, April 2016. http://qafe.com/
11. RENAPS: ORMIT-ADF Version 12c Oracle Forms to Oracle ADF Migration Tool April 2016. https://www.renaps.com/
12. Sanchez-Ramon, O., Sanchez-Cuadrado, J., Garcia-Molina, J.: Model-driven reverse engineering of legacy graphical user interfaces. Autom. Softw. Eng. **21**(2), 147–186 (2014)
13. TURBO Enterprise: Forms conversion, April 2016. http://www.turbo-enterprise.com
14. Ulrich, W., Newcomb, P.: Information Systems Transformation: Architecture-Driven Modernization Case Studies. Morgan Kaufmann Publishers Inc., San Francisco (2010)
15. VGO Software: Client-server modernization - from oracle forms to Java, April 2016. http://www.vgosoftware.com/
16. Weiderman, N., Northrop, L., Smith, D., Tilley, S., Wallnau, K.: Implications of distributed object technology for reengineering , Technical report, Software Engineering Institute Carnegie Mellon University (1997)

Exploring Quality-Aware Architectural Transformations at Run-Time: The ENIA Case

Javier Criado[1]([⊠]), Silverio Martínez-Fernández[2], David Ameller[2],
Luis Iribarne[1], and Nicolás Padilla[1]

[1] Applied Computing Group, University of Almería, Almería, Spain
{javi.criado,luis.iribarne,npadilla}@ual.es
[2] GESSI Research Group, Universitat Politècnica de Catalunya, Barcelona, Spain
{smartinez,dameller}@essi.upc.edu

Abstract. Adapting software systems at run-time is a key issue, especially when these systems consist of components used as intermediary for human-computer interaction. In this sense, model transformation techniques have a widespread acceptance as a mechanism for adapting and evolving the software architecture of such systems. However, existing model transformations often focus on functional requirements, and quality attributes are only manually considered after the transformations are done. This paper aims to improve the quality of adaptations and evolutions in component-based software systems by taking into account quality attributes within the model transformation process. To this end, we present a quality-aware transformation process using software architecture metrics to select among many alternative model transformations. Such metrics evaluate the quality attributes of an architecture. We validate the presented quality-aware transformation process in ENIA, a geographic information system whose user interfaces are based on coarse-grained components and need to be adapted at run-time.

Keywords: Quality-driven model transformation · Component-based software · Architecture configuration · Architecture metrics

1 Introduction

Many today's software systems need to be adapted at run-time. Well-known examples are component-based software systems for human-computer interaction, whose User Interfaces (UI) need to be modified or reconfigured at run-time depending on user preferences, interactions, system requirements, or other evolution needs. For instance, this type of software is offered by dashboard UIs, such as Netvibes[1], Geckoboard[2], or Cyfe[3] applications.

Previous studies have shown that model transformation is a good approach to adapt the component-based architectures [10]. Existing transformation processes

---

[1] Netvibes – https://www.netvibes.com/.
[2] Geckoboard – https://www.geckoboard.com/.
[3] Cyfe – http://www.cyfe.com/.

© Springer International Publishing Switzerland 2016
L. Bellatreche et al. (Eds.): MEDI 2016, LNCS 9893, pp. 288–302, 2016.
DOI: 10.1007/978-3-319-45547-1_23

focus on the functionalities of systems, giving less importance to the Quality Attributes (QA). However, adapting the software architecture of a system without considering the QAs at run-time can negatively affect its quality. For instance, if one UI is adapted by only considering its functionalities, such UI may have a less flexible interaction (*e.g.*, complex UI with a greater number of components) or worse maintainability (*e.g.*, costly evolution from introducing unnecessary dependencies among components) than if we consider QAs at run-time. Actually, some QAs (*e.g.*, availability or performance) can only be measured only at run-time since off-line circumstances provide an estimation and not a real value.

The goal of this paper is to study whether model transformations can be improved by considering QAs at run-time. To this end, we present a QA-aware transformation approach to adapt component-based software systems by measuring the quality of different transformation alternatives. Then, we validate the suitability of such QA-aware transformation approach in two scenarios for the ENIA (ENviromental Information Agent) software. ENIA is a GIS (Geographic Information System) whose UIs are based on coarse-grained components and adapted at run-time depending on user preferences, interactions, system requirements, or other evolution needs [1]. Nevertheless, the approach can be applied to other applications offering their functionality as a mashup or a dashboard.

To accomplish this goal, we formulated the following research question: "*Do model transformations improve their quality by considering QAs at run-time in the ENIA case?*". To measure QAs at run-time, we propose a set of software architecture metrics. We use these metrics to evaluate various alternative architectures (each one obtained by executing a different transformation). As a result, we decide which is the best transformation based on the considered QAs.

The paper is structured as follows. Section 2 introduces a background about adapting component-based systems by model transformation. Section 3 presents a QA-aware model transformation approach. Section 4 exemplifies the approach in the ENIA case. Finally, Sect. 5 ends up with conclusions and future work.

2   Background

In this section we include the required background for contextualizing the presented approach of quality-aware architectural transformations at run-time.

Adapting Component-Based Software Systems. Component-based systems are a type of software which facilitates the execution of adaptation and evolution operations. In this sense, well-known mechanisms of *Component-Based Software Engineering* (CBSE), such as modularization, encapsulation and reuse, favor the development of self-adaptive systems [17].

This software paradigm allows us to manage the components as black-boxes by describing their syntax, semantic, and properties through formal specifications, as in the case of COTS components [6]. Thus, a component can be replaced by other element that matches its specification. Consequently, an architecture can be modified by replacing the parts which need to be adapted.

Model Transformation and Software Architecture Evolution. Model transformation is a common approach to adapt the component-based architecture of software systems [10]. In this context, *Model-Based Engineering* (MBE) techniques facilitate the development of software architectures, defining them (including the structure, components' specifications, and run-time interaction) by models. Moreover, manipulating architecture models at run-time allows us to generate different alternatives based on the same definition [4].

Depending on the model transformation nature (*e.g.*, vertical, horizontal, endogenous, and exogenous) and within the context of software architectures, it is possible to develop refactoring transformations for obtaining different software alternatives. Our goal is to modify the transformation schema proposed in [10] for generating more than one alternative and consider quality information to select the best transformation.

Quality Attributes in Model Transformation. Existing model transformation processes focus on the functionalities of systems, giving less importance to the QA, also known as non-functional requirements or *-ilities* [3]. A notable exception are the guidelines for quality-driven model transformations [12], in which quality is introduced early on the design of the transformation process, avoiding quality evaluation as a separate activity once a model has been transformed. A more recent work presented a model transformation framework designed to automate the selection and composition of competing architectural model transformations [14]. However, up to our knowledge, there is a lack of support to select among alternative architectural transformations considering software architecture metrics at run-time.

Some approaches enable the annotation of model transformations [9] and can be applied for describing QAs in transformation rules. Other proposals extend existing languages with the aim of expressing alternatives and their impact to quality properties at design time [18]. Furthermore, not all QAs share the same importance while adapting or evolving software systems. A recent literature review shows that self-adaptation is primarily used to improve performance, reliability, and flexibility [20]. In this context, an important challenge is to find software architecture metrics that measure quality attributes. The awareness of this problem by the software engineering community is increasing and even dedicated events have been organized [16]. For instance, *dependency structure matrix* metric has been used to measure maintainability [7,15]. Another examples are the number of components, connections, symbols, and interfaces to measure architectural understandability [19,22]. In the next section, we use these metrics and propose others to measure the relevant QAs in adaptive systems.

3   QA-aware Model Transformation Approach

This section presents a QA-aware transformation approach to adapt and evolve software systems by measuring the quality of different transformation alternatives. Such QA-aware transformation approach consists of three steps:

(1) Asking the relevant QAs and constraints to developers, architects, and experts in the application domain.
(2) Measuring QAs and constraints at run-time.
(3) Ranking iso-functional alternative software architectures of the model transformation by considering the relevant QAs and constraints at run-time. With this ranking, the software architecture with the best values in architecture metrics is selected.

Next subsections describe the aforementioned steps respectively, which are also depicted in Fig. 1. Once the last step is carried out and the transformation alternatives have been ranked, the transformation with the best value is executed for adapting the software architecture.

3.1   Step 1: Relevant QAs and Constraints

Depending on a system's targeted goals and architecturally-significant QAs (*e.g.*, improve its flexibility, maximize the modifiability, minimize the cost, or optimize the execution performance), architectural design decisions can be oriented in different ways. Therefore, decisions about the construction of software architectures, such as component selection, may differ from each other by considering them. For this reason, the first step of the approach is to gather the architecturally-significant QAs as part of the rationale to make such decisions.

This step requires two inputs: stakeholders who know the system's targeted QAs, and a quality model to help the stakeholders to reason about QAs (*e.g.*, ISO/IEC 25010 standard [13]). To gather the architecturally-significant QAs, stakeholders can either conduct a focus group, or directly set them in the settings of an admin interface of the model transformation process. The output of this step is the set of relevant QAs and constraints for the adaptive software system.

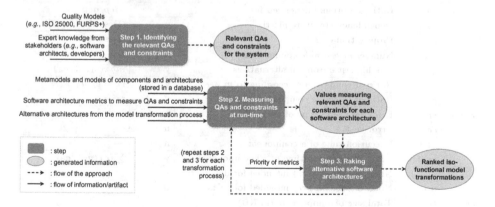

Fig. 1. Steps of the QA-based trasformation approach

3.2 Step 2: Measuring QAs and Constraints at Run-Time

Once the set of relevant QAs and constraints are elicited, the goal of the second step is to find specific software architecture metrics to measure QAs. This enables to quantitatively evaluate several alternative software architectures, since the QA satisfaction of these alternative architectures is measured at run-time. The metrics presented here are focused on our particular domain of component-based systems, but they can be adapted according to the needs.

This step requires three inputs: the set of alternative software architectures (generated by the default model transformation process), a set of metrics to measure QAs and constraints (see Table 1 for QAs and Table 2 for constraints), and the specification of the components to feed the metrics at run-time (stored in the metamodel [8,10]). It is important to emphasize that Tables 1 and 2 show metrics elicited and validated by an expert in the domain architecture of component-based systems, but they may be adapted to the needs of other domains. Table 1 shows simple metrics for important QAs in adaptive systems: performance,

Table 1. Example of software architecture metrics to measure QAs

QA	Metric	Description	Derived	Expression
m	c	Number of components	n	—
	pro	Number of provided interfaces	n	—
	req	Number of required interfaces	n	—
	$\overline{pro}$	Average number of provided interfaces	y	pro/c
	σ_{pro}^2	Variance of provided interfaces	y	$\sum_{i=1}^{c}(pro_i - \overline{pro})^2/c$
	$hpro$	Homogenization of provided interfaces	y	$1 - \sigma_{pro}^2$
	$mdep$	Number of mandatory dependencies	n	—
	$odep$	Number of optional dependencies	n	—
	dep	Total number of dependencies	y	$mdep + odep$
	$rmdep$	Ratio of mandatory dependencies	y	$mdep/dep$
	$rodep$	Ratio of optional dependencies	y	$odep/dep$
	dsm	Dependency structure matrix	y	(Described in [7])
	pc	Propagation cost	y	(Described in [7])
f	r	Number of resizable components	n	—
	m	The highest c from all alternatives	y	$max(c_1, ..., c_n)$
	rc	Ratio of components according to m	y	$rc = c/m$
	rr	Ratio of resizable components	y	$rr = r/c$
r/a	er	Error rate (and type of error)	n	—
	ec	Error cost	n	—
p	$extm$	Execution time of a component	n	—
	$rextm$	Ratio of execution time of all components	y	$\sum(extm_i)/c$
t	$ndiag$	Num. of ops. (in pro) intended for diagnostics	n	—
	$ntest$	Num. of ops. (in pro) intended for tests	n	—
cr	$tsize$	Total size of components (in KB)	n	—
	$avgsize$	Ratio of components' sizes (in KB)	y	$tsize/c$
QAs:	m: modifiability – f: flexibility – r/a: reliability/analizability			
	p: performance – t: testability – cr: consumed resources			

Table 2. Example of metrics to measure constraints

Metric	Description	Derived	Expression
c	Number of components	n	—
pro	Number of provided interfaces	n	—
req	Number of required interfaces	n	—
$tsize$	Total size of components (in KB)	n	—
$avgsize$	Ratio of components' sizes (in KB)	y	$tsize/c$
t	Component technology	n	—
st	No. of components sharing the same technology	n	—
ht	Homogenization among components' technologies	y	$max(st/c)$
p	Component provider	n	—
sp	No. of components sharing the same provider	n	—
hp	Homogenization among components' providers	y	$max(sp/c)$
$type$	Component type	n	—
$stype$	No. of components sharing the same type	n	—
$htype$	Homogenization among components' types	y	$max(stype/c)$

reliability, flexibility [20], and a few more among other important metrics that we used in the ENIA study (modifiability, testability and consumed resource). These QAs are meaningful at run-time in our case study as it is described in Sect. 4. Simple and realistic metrics allow easier adoption in industry [15]. Also, the proposed metrics are just an indicator of a QA, and their improvement must not be seen as a complete satisfaction of any QA. The output of this step is a set of quantitative values measuring the targeted QAs and constraints supporting the selection of the best transformation.

3.3 Step 3: Ordering Alternative Software Architectures

In our approach, we first generate the various possible architectures by applying alternative transformation processes, and then we assess the quality of each architecture. After computing at run-time the corresponding metrics to measure the QAs and constraints, it becomes necessary to rank the alternative software architectures considering the relevant QAs and constraints. Thus, the goal of the third step is to select the "best" software architecture. Consequently, the operation responsible for obtaining this architecture, *i.e.*, the corresponding model transformation, is selected as the best alternative.

This step requires one input: the priority of the architecturally-significant QAs and constraints. This order of importance can be established by system's developers or by users for describing their own priorities. In all cases, it must be specified before the adaptation process starts and could be subsequently modified at run-time to vary this priority. The output is a ranked list of iso-functional model transformation. Finally, the model transformation with the best software architecture is performed. The second and third steps of the approach can be performed at run-time if the number of relevant QAs and alternative architectures to be analyzed is delimited in order to guarantee a proper execution.

4   Application of the QA-aware Transformation Approach

In order to demonstrate the feasibility of the QA-aware transformation process, this section applies it to a particular case of software architectures: mashup UIs [11, 21]. Next subsection respectively show the context of ENIA (mashup UIs), two scenarios at ENIA in which the approach was used, and discussions about how the approach improved the model transformation process.

4.1   The Model Transformation Adaptive Context of ENIA

We addressed this research work focusing on component-based software systems for human-computer interaction. More specifically, we validated the approach presented in Sect. 3 by using the scenario of ENIA UIs, which are used for managing a GIS through coarse-grained components implemented as widgets. Some examples of these components are maps for showing geographic layers, visual charts for representing datasets, or social widgets for enabling the communication with other GIS entities and the community.

ENIA UIs development highlighted the different alternatives that exist when a new architecture is constructed, whether it is determined at design time or it is generated dynamically at run-time. Moreover, such alternatives may be equally valid depending on the quality factors that are taken into account for its construction. For this reason, a quality-aware transformation approach is addressed. Hence, ENIA has been chosen as our test scenario, since the UIs offered by this system are represented and managed as architectures of coarse-grained components. Each component in ENIA architectures contains the required functionality to perform a task by itself or using its dependencies with other components (*e.g.*, a geographical information map, an e-mail manager, a report generator, or a visual chart of datasets). Furthermore, UIs in ENIA are reconfigured at run-time with the aim of adapting their structure to the user interactions, profile preferences, context changes and pro-active system decisions. Since UIs are represented by models, this adaptation process is based on model-to-model (M2M) transformations of component-based architectures (see [10] for further details).

Model transformations in charge of adapting ENIA's UIs are not preset. On the contrary, these operations are dynamically built depending on the initial UI, context information and available transformation rules. In this sense, it is possible to build different transformation operations for the same inputs. In our previous work [10] we proposed a transformation scoring mechanism that allows us to generate only one possible transformation which ensures the functional resolution of the architecture, taking also into account some extra-functional restrictions. In the present paper, we analyze the possibility of incorporating additional quality information into the adaptation process to improve its behavior.

As the Step 1 of the approach indicates, the relevant QAs that should be considered for constructing and adapting the UIs have been discussed for the ENIA scenario. This work is focused on the highest priorities of ENIA, the *modifiability* attribute of the *product quality model* and the *flexibility* attribute of the *quality in use model* of the ISO/IEC 25010 standard, the *total size* of the UI, the homogenization of the *components' providers*, and the homogenization of the *components' types*. These QAs and constraints have been selected because, from the stakeholders' perspective, ENIA UIs must be reconfigurable and provide a friendly interaction by accomplishing the following objectives:

- UI components must encapsulate the required functionality to resolve a domain task but their size must match the coarse-grained concept.
- UIs with a greater number of simple components are preferred over UIs with a lower number of complex components gathering more functionality.
- UIs must be elastic and flexible with the aim of allowing the modification of their structure and visual representation.
- Users can reconfigure and customize their interfaces, e.g., resizing the component displayed in the interface, changing its position, adding new components, and removing existing ones.
- The time for loading the UIs must be the minimum possible.
- UIs with an homogeneous representation are better managed and more understandable by users, generating less confusion for the interaction.

Next, we present two scenarios in the context of ENIA. In the first scenario, we analyzed four metrics related to modifiability and flexibility QAs. Metrics to measure modifiability, flexibility, analyzability, performance, testability and consumed resources are shown in Table 1. In the second scenario, we applied three constraints related to the aforementioned objectives. Metrics to measure constraints are shown in Table 2. Both scenarios share components related to the GIS domain: a map (M) for displaying geographical information layers, a component showing the messages of a social network account (T), a layer list for selecting the information to be displayed on the map (LL), and a legend for visualizing the correspondence of the displayed layers (L). Furthermore, the number of the component name represents different alternatives of the same component type. For example, $M1$, $M2$ and $M3$ are different alternatives of the map component type (M). It is important to remark that we are not representing the identifier of the instance and therefore an architecture can contain elements with the same component name, but these are different component instances.

4.2 Scenario 1: Considering Modifiability and Flexibility

This scenario focuses on two QAs from Step 1, flexibility and modifiability, and following Step 2 applies four corresponding metrics from Table 1: (rc, rr, $hpro$ and pc). These metrics will help to select the best transformation process in charge of adapting a UI from ENIA system based on those QAs. Assuming an initial UI as the one shown in Fig. 2 with four components (map, twitter, legend and layer list), a transformation process for incorporating a session component must be performed. Furthermore, the twitter component must be replaced by a new element of the same type which must be connected to the session component for using its information in the social network account.

We address the use of the following four metrics as worthy information to determine the quality of the resulting architecture and consequently the quality of the transformation process in charge of adapting the UI:

(a) rc for flexibility – The number of components must be maximized because the more pieces constitute a UI, the more reconfiguration and modification operations can be performed on its architecture.

(b) rr for flexibility – The number of resizable components must be maximized since this property favors the flexibility of a UI due to it allows the modification of the components' sizes.

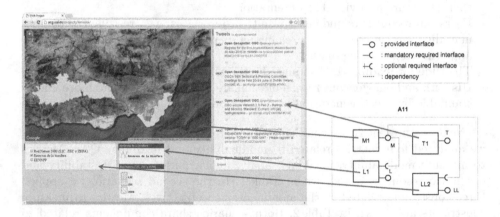

Fig. 2. Initial UI and its architecture

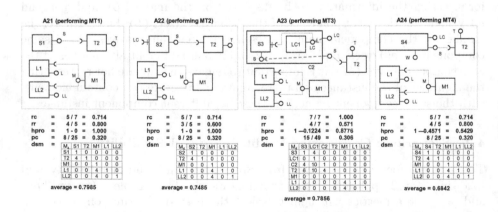

Fig. 3. Transformation alternatives using four example QAs' metrics

(c) *hpro* for modifiability – The homogenization of the distribution of provided interfaces must be maximized because this property avoids the imbalance in the functionality which is offered by each component and fosters the modifiability of the architecture.

(d) *pc* for modifiability – The propagation cost must be minimized due to indirect dependencies between components of an architecture affect the modifiability in a negative manner.

Figure 3 shows the four transformation alternatives that can be obtained from the initial UI represented by $A11$. The architecture $A21$ incorporates a session component $S1$, replaces the previous twitter by $T2$ and connects both elements. $A22$ is similar to $A21$ but the session component $S2$ has an optional required interface for querying geo-localization information. The alternative $A23$ gathers a session component $S3$ and a geo-localization component $LC1$ in a container $C2$. In the case of the last alternative, the component $S4$ in $A24$ provides some geo-localization and weather information apart from the session functional interface.

In order to select the best model transformation alternative among $MT1$, $MT2$, $MT3$ and $MT4$, the bottom of Fig. 3 depicts the values of the metrics calculated for $A21$, $A22$, $A23$ and $A24$. Note that components $M1$, $T2$, $L1$, $C2$, $S1$ and $S4$ are resizable, and components $LL2$, $S2$, $S3$, and $LC1$ cannot be resized. Moreover, delegation of interfaces is considered as a dependency, similar to the connections between required and provided interfaces.

Focusing only on *rc*, the architecture $A23$ has the best value because it owns the maximum number of components among all the alternatives. In the case of *rr*, architectures $A21$ and $A24$ are the best alternatives since both gathers four resizable components among the five possible. Architectures $A21$ and $A22$ have the best value for the *hpro* metric because each component provides one functional interface. On the contrary, the distribution of provided interfaces in $A24$ is the worst possible alternative. With regard to the propagation cost, *pc*, the architecture $A23$ is the best alternative, as shown in the values obtained from dependency structure matrices (DSMs). We normalized *pc* value with respect to the rest of metrics with the expression $npc = 1 - pc$.

Finally, we applied Step 3 to select the best alternative by calculating the average of the four metrics. Therefore, the resulting values for $A21$, $A22$, $A23$ and $A24$ are 0.7985, 0.7485, 0.7856 and 0.6842, respectively. Consequently, we can follow this strategy to select $T1$ as the best transformation process that can be performed to (1) adapt the UI and also (2) get the best value for QAs considered in the transformation. Figure 4 shows the graphical representation of the UI described by the architecture $A21$.

4.3   Scenario 2: Considering Components' Size, Provider, and Type

Continuing with the UI represented by $A21$ in the scenario 1, the next transformation process is intended to incorporate a new map into the workspace. Since the presence of the new map may generate confusion about what is the relationship between the layer list, the legend and the two maps, the components in the

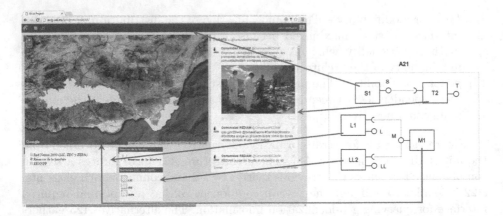

Fig. 4. Transformed UI in scenario 1 and its architecture

initial UI must be restructured accordingly. Figure 5 shows the three alternatives that can be reached from $A21$. The architecture $A31$ replaces the previous map $M1$ by $M2$ and uses $C3$ for containing it. In addition, $C3$ also contains previous $LL2$ and $L2$ components. The new map is resolved with an $M1$ component. The second alternative, $A32$, replaces the initial map $M1$ by $M3$, a map which includes the layer list and legend functionality. The new map is $M1$ type. The alternative $A33$ includes the same replacement of $A31$ but, in this case, the new map is $M2$ type and it is contained in a $C3$ component.

In this transformation process, we want to show that the approach could be used not only for QAs, but also for constraints. In this case, we consider three constraints from Step 1 as drivers to chose a valid alternative for the stakeholders. As a part of Step 2, the metrics used to measure the constraints are:

(a) *tsize* for components' size constraints – The total size of components must be minimized and architectures with a value over 5MB will be rejected. Thus, we try to improve the response time of the browser by reducing the payload of the web components that must be initialized in the UI.

(b) *hp* for components' provider constraints – The homogenization among components' providers must be maximized because, in this scenario, UIs with similar representation are preferred over components with heterogeneous representations. The use of the same provider does not guarantee the pursued homogenization, but the possibilities are greater if the entity providing the components is the same.

(c) *htype* for components' type constraints – The homogenization among components' types must be maximized because it is important to offer the maximum degree of consistency in the structure and representation of the UI's components. Therefore, components of the same type offer their functionality in the same manner.

Regarding the alternatives of Fig. 5, each architecture accomplishes the best value for a different metric. In the case of *tsize*, the value of 925 MB from $A32$

is the best alternative. Focusing on *hp*, the best alternative is the architecture *A*31 because it gathers four components (*M*1, *M*2, *L*2 and *LL*2) from the same provider among the total of seven. With respect to *htype*, the best alternative is *A*33, because it contains four components (*M*2 * 2 and *C*3 * 2) having elements of the same type in the architecture. Therefore model transformation *MT*4 is chosen in the case of prioritize *hp*, whereas *MT*5 and *MT*6 are selected if *tsize* and *htype* are prioritized, respectively.

4.4 Discussion About Using the Approach in ENIA

Answering the research question stated in Sect. 1, we can say that considering QAs at run-time has improved the modifiability and flexibility of generated architectures by model transformations in the ENIA case.

The main advantage of using metrics related to QAs and constraints in ENIA is the incorporation of quality information in the process of selecting the best transformation operation that can be applied in UI adaptation. This allows us to use additional information (to functional interfaces) for solving the transformation process. In this sense, if these metrics are not applied, the transformation can generate architectures which may result in some drawbacks for the present use or future modifications.

For example, looking at the first scenario (see Fig. 3), it is possible to obtain *A*22 as a solution instead of *A*21. In this case, we are 'loosing' the capability of having a session component which can be resized. On the contrary, using our approach we are able to offer 'resizability' of the components through the maximization of the *rr* metric. If we do not give the maximum priority to *rr* but we take it into account in the adaptation, at least the transformation at run-time will be enriched to improve the flexibility of generated UIs.

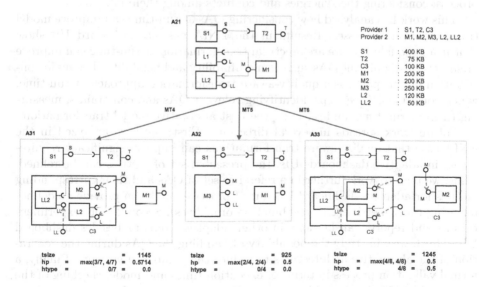

Fig. 5. Transformation alternatives using three example constraints

With regard to the future modifications, let us suppose that in the scenario 2 none of the metrics are applied and consequently, the generated transformation is equivalent to $T5$ and the resulting architecture is $A32$. In this case, if the next adaptation step is aimed to remove the capability of selecting the layers to be displayed on the map (*i.e.*, LL provided interface), we faced two options: (1) the component $M3$ must be modified for hiding this interface and disabling its functionality, or (2) the component $M3$ must be replaced by other map which does not include this functionality, such as $M1$ or $M2$. In both options, we have to perform additional operations compared to those required in the case of starting the adaptation from the architectures $A31$ or $A33$, scenario in which we only should remove the component $LL2$.

Apart from these advantages, nothing is free in software engineering, and the performance of the QA-aware model transformation approach is an important trade-off that must be noted. Performance is related to the computation time necessary to (a) build each transformation alternative, (b) execute them obtaining the resulting architecture, and (c) measure each architecture to decide which transformation alternative is the best in terms of the quality information. The cost of these three execution times must be incorporated to the evaluation of the adaptation process described in [10] and, consequently, may not be possible to evaluate a large number of alternatives at run-time, having to limit the number of architectures evaluated to satisfy performance requirements.

5   Conclusions and Future Work

It is well accepted in the software architecture community that QAs are the most important drivers of architecture design [2]. Therefore, QAs should guide the selection of alternative software architectures from a model transformation process, considering the synergies and conflicts among them [5].

This work has analyzed how considering QAs at run-time can improve model transformation processes. Results in the ENIA case, a dashboard UI, show that using a quality-aware architectural transformation at run-time can improve architectural-significant QAs such as modifiability and flexibility. The main contribution of this paper is a quality-aware transformation approach at run-time, which consists of three steps: identifying relevant QAs and constraints, measuring them at run-time, and selecting the best alternative model transformation.

Future work spreads in several directions. First, once we analyzed in the ENIA case that quality-aware transformations can improve significant requirements in adaptive dashboards UIs, the presented set of metrics can be refined. Thus, we plan to work further in a reference set of QAs and their corresponding metrics for adaptive dashboard UIs out of practice, and then provide guidelines for using those metrics (*e.g.*, combination of metrics). Second, more experimentations and reports can be done in other adaptive domains besides dashboard UIs. Third, we will study the possibility of handling the QAs during the generation of the alternative architectures to reduce the number of variants. Finally, a formal validation process in terms of execution times and model checking of the generated architectures could improve the proposed approach.

Acknowledgments. This work was funded by the Spanish MINECO and the Andalusian Government under TIN2013-41576-R and P10-TIC-6114 projects.

References

1. ACG: ENIA Poject - Development of an intelligent web agent of environmental information. http://acg.ual.es/projects/enia/
2. Ameller, D., Ayala, C., Cabot, J., Franch, X.: Non-functional requirements in architectural decision making. IEEE Softw. **30**(2), 61–67 (2013)
3. Ameller, D., Franch, X., Cabot, J.: Dealing with non-functional requirements in model-driven development. In: RE 2010, pp. 189–198. IEEE (2010)
4. Bencomo, N., Blair, G.: Using architecture models to support the generation and operation of component-based adaptive systems. In: Cheng, B.H.C., de Lemos, R., Giese, H., Inverardi, P., Magee, J. (eds.) Software Engineering for Self-Adaptive Systems. LNCS, vol. 5525, pp. 183–200. Springer, Heidelberg (2009)
5. Boehm, B.: Architecture-based quality attribute synergies and conflicts. In: SAM 2015, pp. 29–34. IEEE Press (2015)
6. Carney, D., Leng, F.: What do you mean by COTS? Finally, a useful answer. IEEE Softw. **17**(2), 83–86 (2000)
7. Carriere, J., Kazman, R., Ozkaya, I.: A cost-benefit framework for making architectural decisions in a business context. In: ICSE 2010, pp. 149–157. IEEE (2010)
8. Criado, J., Iribarne, L., Padilla, N., Ayala, R.: Semantic matching of components at run time in distributed environments. In: Ciuciu, I., et al. (eds.) OTM 2015 Workshops. LNCS, vol. 9416, pp. 431–441. Springer, Heidelberg (2015). doi:10. 1007/978-3-319-26138-6_46
9. Criado, J., Martínez, S., Iribarne, L., Cabot, J.: Enabling the reuse of stored model transformations through annotations. In: Kolovos, D., Wimmer, M. (eds.) ICMT 2015. LNCS, vol. 9152, pp. 43–58. Springer, Heidelberg (2015)
10. Criado, J., Rodríguez-Gracia, D., Iribarne, L., Padilla, N.: Toward the adaptation of component-based architectures by model transformation: behind smart user interfaces. Softw. Pract. Exp. **45**(12), 1677–1718 (2015)
11. Daniel, F., Matera, M.: Mashups - Concepts Models and Architectures. Springer, Heidelberg (2014)
12. Insfran, E., Gonzalez-Huerta, J., Abrahão, S.: Design guidelines for the development of quality-driven model transformations. In: Petriu, D.C., Rouquette, N., Haugen, Ø. (eds.) MODELS 2010, Part II. LNCS, vol. 6395, pp. 288–302. Springer, Heidelberg (2010)
13. ISO/IEC: ISO/IEC 25000. Systems and software engineering - Systems and software Quality Requirements and Evaluation (SQuaRE) - Guide to SQuaRE (2014)
14. Loniewsli, G., Borde, E., Blouin, D., Insfran, E.: An automated approach for architectural model transformations. In: Escalona, M.J., Aragón, G., Linger, H., Lang, M., Barry, C., Schneider, C. (eds.) Information System Development: Improving Enterprise Communication, pp. 295–306. Springer, Switzerland (2014)
15. Martínez-Fernández, S., Ayala, C.P., Franch, X., Marques, H.M.: REARM: a reuse-based economic model for software reference architectures. In: Favaro, J., Morisio, M. (eds.) ICSR 2013. LNCS, vol. 7925, pp. 97–112. Springer, Heidelberg (2013)
16. Ozkaya, I., Nord, R.L., Koziolek, H., Avgeriou, P.: Second international workshop on software architecture and metrics. In: ICSE 2015, pp. 999–1000. IEEE Press (2015)

17. Salehie, M., Tahvildari, L.: Self-adaptive software: landscape and research challenges. ACM Trans. Auton. Adapt. Syst. **4**(2), 14:1–14:42 (2009)
18. Solberg, A., Oldevik, J., Aagedal, J.Ø.: A framework for QoS-aware model transformation, using a pattern-based approach. In: Meersman, R. (ed.) OTM 2004. LNCS, vol. 3291, pp. 1190–1207. Springer, Heidelberg (2004)
19. Stevanetic, S., Javed, M.A., Zdun, U.: Empirical evaluation of the understandability of architectural component diagrams. In: WICSA 2014 Companion, pp. 4:1–4:8. ACM, New York (2014)
20. Weyns, D., Ahmad, T.: Claims and evidence for architecture-based self-adaptation: a systematic literature review. In: Drira, K. (ed.) ECSA 2013. LNCS, vol. 7957, pp. 249–265. Springer, Heidelberg (2013)
21. Yu, J., Benatallah, B., Casati, F., Daniel, F.: Understanding mashup development. IEEE Internet Comput. **12**(5), 44–52 (2008)
22. Zimmermann, O.: Metrics for architectural synthesis and evaluation: requirements and compilation by viewpoint: an industrial experience report. In: SAM 2015, pp. 8–14. IEEE Press (2015)

A Credibility and Classification-Based Approach for Opinion Analysis in Social Networks

Lobna Azaza[1(✉)], Fatima Zohra Ennaji[2], Zakaria Maamar[3],
Abdelaziz El Fazziki[2], Marinette Savonnet[1], Mohamed Sadgal[2], Eric Leclercq[1],
Idir Amine Amarouche[4], and Djamal Benslimane[5]

[1] LE2I Laboratory, Dijon University, Dijon, France
Lobna.Azaza@u-bourgogne.fr
[2] LISI Laboratory, University of Marrakech, Marrakesh, Morocco
[3] Zayed University, Dubai, United Arab Emirates
[4] USTHB, Algiers, Algeria
[5] LIRIS Laboratory, University Claude Bernard Lyon 1, Villeurbanne, France

Abstract. There is an ongoing interest in examining users' experiences made available through social media. Unfortunately these experiences like reviews on products and/or services are sometimes conflicting and thus, do not help develop a concise opinion on these products and/or services. This paper presents a multi-stage approach that extracts and consolidates reviews after addressing specific issues such as user multi-identity and user limited credibility. A system along with a set of experiments demonstrate the feasibility of the approach.

Keywords: Social media · Reputation · Credibility · Opinion · Multi-identity

1 Introduction

The democratization of the Internet and social media has sustained the growth of different areas ranging from education and health to trade and entertainment. Nowadays users are "flooded" with a huge volume of content that needs to be filtered so that it can be used properly. Relying on others' opinions seems offering good solutions to certain challenges of this democratization. In this context, sentiment analysis has become an important research topic. Advanced techniques and systems should be of a great value to those who need to collect and analyze opinions posted on the Web with focus on social networks. However, with the abundance of social content, reputation surfaces as a decisive element in identifying the most relevant opinions, and hence developing reputable sources of information over time. Opinions collected from social networks can be "polluted" by users in different ways. Owing to the large number of opinion sources, determining whether these opinions are subjective or not (objective) remains hard [1]. Unfortunately, analyzing collected data is not an easy task due to the fact that they are hugely different from traditional data that we are familiar with. This contrast is illustrated not only at the level of the extracted data size, but also at the level of its noisiness and formlessness.

© Springer International Publishing Switzerland 2016
L. Bellatreche et al. (Eds.): MEDI 2016, LNCS 9893, pp. 303–316, 2016.
DOI: 10.1007/978-3-319-45547-1_24

1.1   Challenges

This paper tackles two specific challenges: **opinion refinement** in term of collection and **opinion analysis** in term of content.

Opinions collected from social networks can be "biased". Some users have malicious behaviors while others provide subjective feedback. The objective is to either promote or degrade the reputation of a product/service sometimes purposely. For instance, users can evaluate the same products several times from different accounts or use different identifiers so they do not reveal their real identities [2–4,10]. This leads into redundant and/or inconsistent opinions. Users can also provide opinions about products/services that they have not even self-experienced. In fact they rely on social friends' opinions [8] and sometimes word-of-mouth. Taking into account opinions without user credibility has a serious impact on product or service reputation. Hence, while assessing reputation based on opinions, we should first deal with users who have multiple identifiers and second define credibility of users who express opinions.

An opinion is a judgment, a viewpoint, or a statement about matters commonly considered to be subjective. Thus, opinion mining paradigm is the fact of performing a sentiment analysis (i.e. opinions extraction) from heterogeneous and large amounts of data (Big Data). Several constraints need to be taken into account while extracting an opinion from sentences that are written by humans: spam and fake detection (may occur when a user misleads peers by posting reviews that contain false positive or malicious negative opinions) bipolar words (some words can have a negative and positive meaning like dark soul versus dark chocolate), and negation (using negation words like "not" and "nor" along with certain prefixes/suffixes like "un-", "dis-", and "-less").

1.2   Contributions

We tackle the above challenges by proposing an approach that extracts an entity (e.g., product and service) reputation from social networks. Our contributions are manifold including: (i) a model for opinions refinement by detecting virtual users who refer to the same user and calculating users credibility; (ii) a model for analyzing the refined opinions; and (iii) a validation through experiments. This is based on random data generation and a variation of different criteria considered in the detection of the true users.

The rest of the paper is organized as follows. Section 2 discusses briefly some related work. Section 3 is dedicated to the proposed approach including opinions refinement as a first step to clean collected data and opinion analysis as a second step. In Sect. 4, we present some experimental results of the proposed system followed by some concluding remarks and future-work perspectives in Sect. 5.

2   Related Work

This section discusses opinion refinement and then opinion analysis. Both are deemed necessary in any exercise of tapping into the opportunities of social media.

2.1 Opinion Refinement

Due to the dynamic and open nature of the Web, discovering same users with multiple identities is a concern. This concern is tackled in the literature and different solutions are proposed such as string based, stylometric-based, time profile-based, and social network-based. These solutions aim to compare different identities to measure to what extent they refer or not to the same real user. Unfortunately the experimental results of these solutions [2] are not satisfactory because they do not offer techniques combination in user comparison. Multi-identifier detection is also discussed in [3] and an approach is proposed, it relies on supervised learning to determine whether a document is written by a certain author. In [4], multi-identifier users are identified based on a model of communication exchange in a public forum. Hung-Ching et al. observe that posts of multi-identifier users are not as frequent as those from single-identifier users [4]. These users' posts are correlated and spread out over time. The proposed solution detects the identifiers whose posts display such statistical anomalies and identify them as coming from multi-identifier users. In [10] Arjun et al. treat multi identifiers as spammers, model "spamicity" as latent and allows exploiting various observed behavioral footprints of users. The intuition is that opinion spammers have different behavioral distributions than non-spammers.

Opinion diversity is also important when filtering opinions. The TIDY system [6] allows sources diversity by aggregating similar sources into a single virtual source. Such aggregation is based on similarity metrics and learning techniques. Meanwhile, Truth Finder system uses similarity metrics between sources to choose those that are less similar, and therefore the most representative of all evaluators [11]. Other approaches like [8] focus on source diversity to minimize dependency between sources and the influence that they have on each other. A diversified source reduces the number of samples and improves the ability to correctly distinguish facts from rumors.

Some approaches consider the evaluator's credibility through various types of information to estimate the expertise relative to the subject of study. In fact, the credibility of evaluators is simply associated with their expertise [12]. Others argue that a user's credibility must be based on evaluating opinions. Users are credible if peers find their opinions reliable. In [7], authors proposed algorithms for a continuous update of the evaluations. It is based on a model that discriminates high-reputation reviewers from low-reputation reviewers.

2.2 Opinions Analysis

Broadly, each company use two main sources of data (internal and external sources). Both internal (e.g. customer feedback collected from emails and call centers) and external sources (e.g. Web) contains opinionated documents. Opinions classification aims to evaluate the mood expressed about a particular product or service.

Different solutions have been proposed in order to extract the polarity of the opinionated data, they can be categorized into two main approaches. Knowledge based approach [23] that searches the words occurrences of the documents. It relies on a predefined dictionary viewed as a set of words with positive or negative sentiment orientations.

The second approach [24] is based on supervised learning techniques. It aims to train a statistical classifier on pre-labeled texts and use it to predict the sentiment orientation of new texts. In [14], a sentiment model, in which too models were created in order to capture sentiment information and to predict sales performance. In [15], reviews were used to rank products and merchants using a statistic and heuristic based models for estimating its true quality.

3   Proposed Approach

Figure 1 illustrates the proposed approach for opinion collection from online social networks along with the refinement of these opinions based on user credibility. Our approach includes:

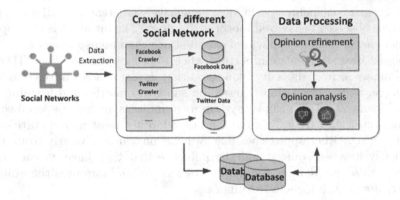

Fig. 1. The proposed approach architecture

- A data Extraction module: its goal is to extract the important and valuable data from the different social networks.
- An opinion refinement module: it aims to eliminates the unvaluable data from those extracted. To do so, two main tasks are performed: (i) detecting virtual users who refer to the same user using different criteria including email addresses, profile names, opinion publication dates, and friends' lists. We rely on Hierarchical Agglomerative Clustering (HAC) [13] to establish the uniqueness of users. (ii) assessing user credibility that takes into account their behaviors, the consistency of opinions, and influence of the virtual environment on users.
- An opinion analysis module: it allow to analyze the refined reviews in order to get the general opinion about the targeted product/service. This model includes a subjectivity and a polarity classification.

3.1 Data Extraction

Data collection refers to all the methods that aims to gather data from online social networks in order to provide an input data source for the system. But, the way how this task is accomplished depends especially on the source (Facebook, Twitter, blogs, etc.) and how the information are represented on the web.

The results obtained from the execution are used to build the social network, and stored into the Hadoop Distributed File System (HDFS), from where they can be consulted, acquired or even reprocessed with another Hadoop application.

3.2 Opinion Refinement

The aims of refining and filtering opinions is to improve their quality prior to carrying out any processing like product reputation (Fig. 2). The opinion filtering module contains three components The multi-identifier detection component establishes the identifiers of the same user. Afterwards, the opinion data representation component eliminates redundant opinions to produce a heterogeneous graph that connects users, products, evaluation sites, and evaluations together. Finally, the credibility component assigns credibility scores to users by exploiting the principles of opinion consistency and user inter-evaluation and inter-influence. After each step of the process, the user profile database is updated with new credibility scores.

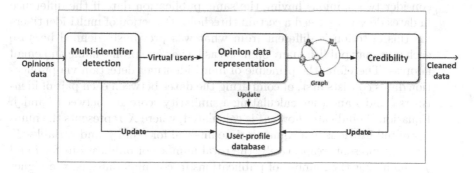

Fig. 2. Opinions refinement

A. Multi-identifier Detection. It is known that users in social networks sign-up in different accounts for different reasons such as malicious behaviors so they evaluate the same product many times and/or evaluate the same product from different Web sites. Hence, detecting virtual users who refer to the same person is critical to avoid redundant opinions.

Detection Criteria. In our approach, we propose a multi-identifier detection model using the following criteria:

- E-mail address. Users, especially non malicious, generally sign-up in accounts in different social Web sites using the same e-mail address.

- Profile name. Assuming the non-malicious behavior of users, they generally provide the same profile name for different social Web sites. In [5], Muniba et al. focus on finding similarities in profile names based on orthographic variations to detect multi-identifiers. In [2] Fredrik et al. use of Jaro-Winkler distance to compare profile names.
- Opinion publication dates. Users tend to post evaluations from different login within a short time period [2]. The Euclidean distance has been used to calculate how similar two identifiers of publication dates are.
- Friend list. It represents the list of followers or friends connected with a certain user. Users mostly have similar friend lists in different social networks [2].

Description of the Multi-identifiers Detection Model. A multi-criteria detection of multiple identifiers aims to generate classes of identifiers. Each class represents identifiers that probably correspond to the same user. The aforementioned criteria, taken alone, produce different classifications. Two identifiers can belong to the same user according to one criterion and to different users according to another :

1. In order to detect multi-identifiers using email-address/profile name criterion, we create a class for all the identifiers sharing the same email (respectively, profile name). The number of classes generated by each criterion is not the same, neither the population of classes is.
2. Detection of multi-Identifiers with opinion publication date criterion. We consider two opinions having the same publication date if the difference in dates does not exceed a certain threshold. Detection of multi-identifiers via this criterion is different from what was previously defined because each user may publish many opinions as he has one profile name and email address. Therefore, the principle of multi-identifier detection via publication dates consists first, of comparing the dates between each pair of identifiers i and j and then calculating a similarity score ω_{ij} between i and j. Equation (1) indicates how ω_{ij} is calculated, where X represents the number of publications in a common time interval for i and j, and variables P_i and P_j represent, respectively, the total number of publications for i and j. The higher the number of publications in common dates is, the higher the probability that the two identifiers are from the same user.

$$\omega_{ij} = \frac{2X}{|P_i + P_j|} \quad 0 \leq \omega_{ij} \leq 1 \tag{1}$$

The set of similarity scores between couples of identifiers is represented in a similarity matrix (Fig. 3a). This matrix is then used via techniques of HAC to generate classes of similar identifiers (Fig. 3b) HAC is automatic and used in data analysis from a set of individuals. Its purpose is to classify individuals with similar behaviors by a similarity criterion defined in advance. The most similar individuals will be put together in homogeneous groups. The classification is agglomerative; it starts from a situation where all individuals are put alone in one class; and is hierarchical, it produces classes increasingly large.

	Id$_1$	Id$_2$	Id$_3$	...	Id$_n$
Id$_1$	1	ω12	ω13		ω1n
Id$_2$	ω21	1	ω23		ω2n
Id$_3$	ω31	ω32	1		ω3n
⋮					⋮
Id$_n$	ωn1	ωn2	ωn3	...	1

(a) Similarity matrix

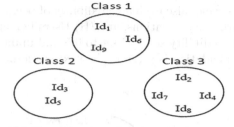

(b) Example of similar identifiers classes

Fig. 3. Identifier classification

3. Detection of multi-Identifiers using friend-list criterion is similar to publication date criterion. Indeed, each identifier can have many friends.
4. Multi-criteria detection of multi-identifiers. Simultaneous use of different criteria produces four different classifications of identifiers. The current step is to use the four classifications to produce ultimately only one using HAC. It assumes that a measure of similarity between individuals exists. A similarity matrix is then created with the combination of the proposed criteria. The similarity computation within the different criteria is calculated as per Eq. (2); the Boolean function $Crit_n$ verifies whether i and j refers to the same user according to each criterion in which case it returns 1, otherwise it returns 0. a, b, c and d correspond to the respective weights given to criteria. These weights can be chosen by experts of the studied domain (e.g. politics, cars...).

$$Similarity_{ij} = a \times Crit_1(i,j) + b \times Crit_2(i,j) \qquad (2)$$
$$+ c \times Crit_3(i,j) + d \times Crit_4(i,j)$$
$$a, b, c, d \in [0,1], \ a+b+c+d = 1$$

B. Opinion Data Representation. The detection of multi-identifiers has an important impact on opinion data representation. By opinion we mean data related to users, sites of evaluations, products and services, and last but not least evaluations. In this step, we aggregate all identifiers in the same class into a single virtual user. This creates a virtual user that is assigned to non-identical evaluations. Redundant evaluations are deleted (correspond to having the same evaluation of the same product on different sites from the same user in a given period of time). After that, opinion data are represented in a graph. The idea of heterogeneous graph was proposed in [9]. However the authors do not represent the evaluators as an interconnected network, which doesn't help in visualizing relations between users. Figure 4 represents the proposed graph. Edges between nodes represent relationships connecting them. Examples of relations are: (A) Users evaluate products, (B) Products are displayed on websites, (C) A user is connected with other users, (D) Evaluations are displayed on websites, (E) A user can also evaluate credibility of peers, (F) Products are evaluated, (G) Users provide evaluations, and (H) Users belong to different Web sites. Each user has a credibility score C set to 0.5 and updated throughout the evaluation process. Calculation is given in the next section.

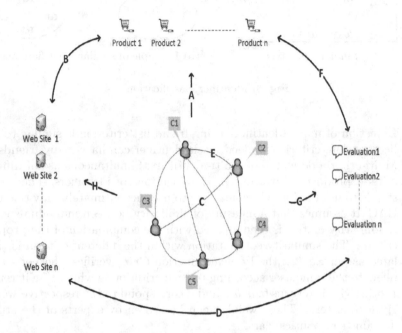

Fig. 4. Graph of opinion data

C. Credibility. Interactions over a social graph help calculate user's credibility score. Three features are observable in the relationships presented in the graph of Fig. 3:

1. Inter-evaluation: Since users establish the credibility of peers, a user is credible if other users refer to him credible [7]. Thus, the credibility score of User U_i is calculated as follows, where $Numbre_{Ev}$ is the total number of evaluations about U_i, $Scale_{sup}$ is the upper limit of the scale considered (e.g., 5 for a scale of 1 to 5).

$$Score_{Ev}(U_i) = \frac{\sum Evaluations}{Number_{Ev}} \times Scale_{sup} \qquad (3)$$

2. Influence: peers can influence a user's opinion. A user is likely to be influenced by another if they share the same evaluation about the same product. This can be direct or indirect through mutual friends. We consider a user as credible if he is not influenced by other users [8].

Therefore, the credibility score of U_i is expressed as follows where x and y denote the direct and indirect influences, respectively. x and y take 1 when the influence they represent exist, otherwise 0. α and β are weights assigned to direct and indirect influence respectively.

$$Score_{Inf}(U_i) = \frac{(\alpha x + \beta y)}{(x + y)} \quad \alpha < \beta \quad and \quad x, y \in 0, 1 \tag{4}$$

A user is consistent if he maintains "almost" the same evaluation for the same product over a certain period of time. The credibility score of U_i is performed as follows where Max_{Ev} is the maximal value of evaluation, Min_{Ev} is the minimal value of evaluations and $Scale_{sup}$ is the upper limit of the scale considered.

$$Score_{Cons}(U_i) = 1 - \frac{Max_{Ev} - Min_{Ev}}{Scale_{Sup}} \tag{5}$$

3. Computation of user credibility. The final credibility of a user is calculated as follows:

$$Credibility(U_i) = \frac{Score_{Ev}(U_i) + Score_{Inf}(U_i) + Score_{Cons}(U_i)}{3} \tag{6}$$

3.3 Opinion Analysis

The data analysis stage, aims to analyze all the filtered reviews that are obtained in the opinion filtering stage. The reviews are divided into sentences so that a sentiment and subjectivity classification can be done to figure out if the review is objective or subjective. In the latter case (the review is subjective), a polarity classification is performed to determine whether the review holds a positive or a negative opinion about the targeted product. A user can publish several reviews about the same product. Thus, an average of the different polarities is linked to the reviews' owner. Figure 5 illustrates the proposed analysis process.

Subjectivity Classification. Subjective and opinionated sentences are not the same although the latter are often a subset of the former. But such classification is required to determine whether a certain opinion is subjective or objective. We call this step as subjectivity classification. We can classify textual expressions into two types: objective expressions and subjective expression to determine the opinionated sentences.

We are concerned with analyzing subjective reviews that describe peoples sentiments, appraisals, and/or feelings. We consider the whole review as a basic information unit, classify the reviews as opinionated and not opinionated (subjectivity classification), and then to pick up the sentiment expressions that reveal the users opinion about the target product. For this purpose, there are some tools that support sentiment classification such as SentiGem[1],

---

[1] Sentigem BETA sentiment analysis API http://sentigem.com/.

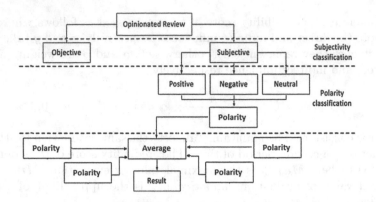

Fig. 5. Data analysis process

SentiStrenght[2] and SentiWordNet[3]. Among these tools this latter is a lexical resource for opinion mining. It assigns for each word several synonyms called synsets. Each synset is associated with three scores: objective, positive and negative score for the different terms in the synset. The subjectivity of each synset is then evaluated as shown in Eq. 7:

$$Sub(t) = \frac{\sum_{s\in t}(neg(s)+pos(s))}{|t|} \qquad t = \{s_1, ..., s_n\} \tag{7}$$

In which s_i represents a synset and t the word found in the review. To evaluate the subjectivity of a review, we use Eq. (8) in which $|\{t \cap t|t \in d, t \in SWN\}|$ means the total number of terms found in the review belonging to SWN:

$$Sub(t) = \frac{\sum_{t\in r} Sub(t)}{|\{t \cap t'| \in d, t' \in SWN\}|} \tag{8}$$

Polarity Classification. Building upon subjectivity classification step, we apply the polarity classification, aka as sentence-level sentiment classification. We would like to classify opinionated text (subjective sentences) into three groups: positive, neutral, and negative.

Sentiment analysis was the subject of several studies. Its objective is to detect the authors feelings. To achieve our goal, a classification and quantification of the collected sentences is made using SentiWordNet (classifying words in three groups: negative, positive, and neutral. This choice was made based on the fact that SentiWordNet proposes also a subjectivity classification by offering an objective score in addition of the polarity scores.

---

[2] SentiStrenght http://sentistrength.wlv.ac.uk/.
[3] SentiWordNet http://sentiwordnet.isti.cnr.it/.

4   System Development

For demonstration purposes, we selected Twitter as a data set and compared the results of three different car brands as keywords: Product 1, Product 2 and Product 3.

4.1   Data Extraction

The system collects the data from Twitter using Twitter4J (twitter4j.org). The reviews containing the keyword such as Product 1, #Product1, and #Product_1 are extracted in addition of the user's details like profile name, e-mail address, friends/followers, etc. So at the end of the process, we were able to collect approximately 5000 tweets published by more than 600 users for each product.

4.2   Opinion Filtering

The results of the experiments are presented in Fig. 6 where the filter criteria are taken individually and then combined. We could read (i) a decrease in the multi-identifier detection accuracy when the number of users increases, (ii) that separate use of criterion gives low accuracy compared to criteria combination, and (iii) that email address criterion taken separately always works better than the rest of criteria with an accuracy of 53 % for 100 users. Indeed, the accuracy decreases as the number of users increases but remains stable at 36 % for 1000 users. This is obvious as email address is generally accessed and used by the same user. The use of publication-date criterion alone is insignificant and accuracy does not exceed 10 % regardless of the number of users.

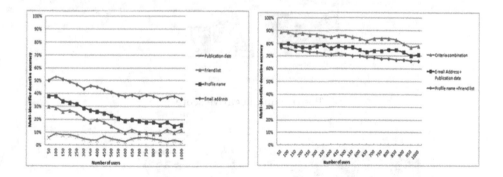

Fig. 6. Separate criteria use versus criteria combination use

The four criteria combination accuracy reaches 88 % for 100 users and gives an accuracy above 80 % for up to 900 users. It decreases slowly as the number of users increases and stabilizes at 78 % for 1000 users. The combination of e-mail address and publication date criteria on one hand and profile name and friend list on the other hand gives better results than criteria taken alone and accuracy stabilizes between 65 % and 70 % for 1000 users. We also notice that the use of publication-date criterion in combination with e-mail address becomes meaningful as the use e-mail address alone gives an accuracy results between 36 % and 53 % and reaches 78 % in combination with publication-date. As expected, the results presented indicate that criteria combination pays off in term of multi-identifier detection accuracy.

4.3 Opinion Analysis

Having a cleaned database is always useful while analyzing social data since it can improve the final results. So, after building the network and filtering and cleaning the data, we can finally perform data analysis. The sentence-level sentiment classification detects the polarity of subjective sentences (subjectivity and polarity classification). Figure 7(a) illustrates the experimental results for the three products. We note that the most important area is always occupied by neutral reviews. This is due to the large number of tweets that contain sales proposals in addition of the real neutral opinions.

To overcome this issue, we choose to neglect the neutral opinion of each product, then recalculate positive and negative opinions. As a result, each product has two scores, positive and negative, noted respectively as S_p(Product) and S_n(Product). The following formula was used to calculate the final score: S(Product) = S_p(Product) − S_n(Product) As we can notice in Fig. 7(b), that Product 2 took the first place then in the second and the third place came respectively Product 1 and −3.

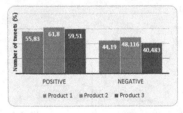

(a) Positive and negative score

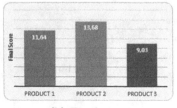

(b) Final score

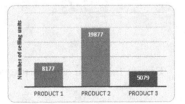

(c) Number of units sold in January 2016

Fig. 7. Experiment results versus real world results

4.4 Discussions

Our proposed approach extracts, filters, cleans, and analyzes the gathered social data from online social networks. To attest its effectiveness, a comparison was made between our result with the number of selling units in January 2016 (Fig. 7(c)). We notice that the ranking was respected either in real world (Product 2, Product 1, ad then Product 3), and that leads us to conclude that our system has reached its goal and did predict the product reputation, since there is a relationship between the product reputation and the number of selling units.

5 Conclusion

There are no doubts that today's customers extensively rely on social media to raise their voices, share their experiences, and convey their opinions. Web sites supporting customers contain valuable details that should be processed. In this paper, we presented an approach for extracting and consolidating customers' opinions so that enterprises understand better their customers needs, requirements, and concerns. The approach relies on Hierarchical Agglomerative Clustering to filter opinions that could be related to virtual and malicious users. It also relies on a credibility model to measure to what extent an expressed opinion is true. The feasibility of the approach in terms of effectiveness and accuracy was demonstrated through a set of experiments. Interesting perspectives emerge to further strengthen the approach. We would like to develop some formal models for representing and reason over uncertain opinions that could result from the vagueness of some words and the user credibility computation as well.

References

1. Liu, B.: Sentiment analysis and subjectivity. In: Handbook of Natural Language Processing, vol 2, pp. 627–666 (2010)
2. Fredrik, J., Lisa, K., Amendra, S.: Detecting multiple aliases in social media. In: Proceedings of the 2013 IEE/ACM International Conference on Advances in Social Networks Analysis and Mining, pp. 1004–101, New York, USA (2013)
3. Tieyun, Q., Bing, L.: Identifying multiple userids of the same author. In: EMNL, pp. 18–21, USA, October 2013
4. Hung-Ching, C., Mark, G., Malik, M.I.: Identifying multi-ID users in open forums. In: Second Symposium on Intelligence and Security Informatics, USA, 10–11 June 2004
5. Muniba, S., Nasrullah, M., Uffe, K.W.: Extended approximate string matching algorithms to detect name aliases. In: 2011 IEEE International Conference on Intelligence and Security Informatics (ISI), pp. 216–219, Beijing, 10–12 July 2011
6. Anthony, E., Timothy, J.N., Murat, S., Chatschik, B., Mudhakar, S.: TIDY: a trust-based approach to information fusion through diversity. In: 2013 IEEE 16th International Conference Information Fusion (FUSION), pp. 1188–1195, Istanbul, 9–12 July 2013
7. Ku, Y.-C., Wei, C.-P., Hsiao, H.-W.: To whom should I listen? finding reputable reviewers in opinion-sharing communities. Decis. Support Syst. **55**(3), 534–542 (2012)

8. Md. Yusuf, S.U., Md. Tanvir, A., Hieu, L., Tarek, A., Boleslaw, S., Tommy, N.: On diversifying source selection in social sensing. In: 9th International Conference on Networked Sensing Systems, INSS 2012, pp. 1–8, Belgium, 11–14 June 2012 (2012)

9. Guan, W., Sihong, X., Bing, L., Philip, S.Y.: Review graph based online store review spammer detection. In: ICDM 2011 Proceedings of the 2011 IEE International Conference on Data Mining, pp. 1242–1247, Washington, USA (2011)

10. Arjun, M., Abhinav, K., Bing, L., Junhui, W., Meichun, H., Malu, C., Riddhiman, G.: Spotting opinion spammers using behavioral footprints. In: KDD 2013 Proceedings of the 19th ACM SIGKDD International Conference on Knowledge Discovery and Data Mining, pp. 632–640, NY, USA (2013)

11. Xin, L.D., Laure, B.E., Divesh, S.: Integrating conflicting data: the role of source dependence. In: VLDB Conference, pp. 550–661, August 2009

12. Tracy, R., Robert, W.: An algorithm for automated rating of reviewers. In: Proceedings of the First ACM/IEEE-CS Joint Conference on Digital libraries (JCDL), pp. 381–387, NY, USA (2001)

13. William, H.E.D., Herbert, E.: Efcient algorithms for agglomerative hierarchical clustering methods. J. Classif. 1(1), 7–24 (1984)

14. Liu, Y., Huang, X., An, A., Yu, X., Huang, J.: ARSA: a sentiment-aware model for predicting sales performance using blogs. In: Proceedings of the 30th Annual International ACM SIGIR Conference on Research and Development in Information Retrieval, pp. 607–614 (2007)

15. McGlohon, M., Glance, N., Reiter, Z.: Star quality.: aggregating reviews to rank products and merchants. Wall Str. J. 114–121 (2010)

16. Yano, T., Smith, N.A.: Whats worthy of comment.? content and comment volume in political blogs. In: Fourth International AAAI Conference on Weblogs and Social Media (2010)

17. Asur, S., Huberman, B.: Predicting the future with social media. In: 2010 IEEE/WIC/ACM International Conference on Web Intelligence and Intelligent Agent Technology (WI-IAT), vol. 1, pp. 492–499 (2010)

18. Joshi, M., Das, D., Gimpel, K., Smith, A.N.: Movie reviews and revenues: an experiment in text regression. In: The 2010 Annual Conference of the North American Chapter of the Association for Computational Linguistics Human Language Technologies, pp. 293–296 (2010)

19. Sadikov, E., Parameswaran, A., Venetis, P.: Blogs as predictors of movie success. In: Third International AAAI Conference on Weblogs and Social Media, pp. 304–307 (2009)

20. Bollen, J., Mao, H., Zeng, X.: Twitter mood predicts the stock market. J. Comput. Sci. 2, 18 (2011)

21. Qingxi, P., Ming, Z.: Detecting spam review through sentiment analysis. J. Softw. 9(8), 2065–2072 (2014)

22. Lucie, F., Eugen, R., Daniel, P.: Analysing domain suitability of a sentiment lexicon by identifying distributionally bipolar words. In: Proceedings of the Workshop on Computational Approaches to Subjectivity, Sentiment and Social Media Analysis, EMNLP (2015)

23. Turney, P.: Thumbs up or thumbs down? semantic orientation applied to unsupervised classification of reviews. In: Proceedings of the 40th Annual Meeting of the Association of Computational Linguistics (ACL 2002), pp. 417–424 (2002)

24. Pang, B., Lee, L.: A sentimental education: sentiment analysis using subjectivity summarization based on minimum cuts. In: Proceedings of ACL (2004)

Engineering Applications Over Social and Open Data with Domain-Specific Languages

Ángel Mora Segura[✉] and Juan de Lara

Modelling and Software Engineering Group, Universidad Autónoma de Madrid,
Madrid, Spain
{Angel.MoraS,Juan.deLara}@uam.es

Abstract. There is a current trend among governments and organizations to make all sort of information (like budgets, demographic or economic data) public. The information released in this way is called *Open Data*. Many institutions promote the creation of innovative applications using the data they have released, e.g., in combination with social networks, but only highly skilled engineers can accomplish this task.

Our goal is to facilitate the construction of applications using open data and social networks as communication platform. For this purpose, we propose a family of domain-specific languages directed to automate the different tasks involved, like describing the structure and semantics of the heterogeneous data sets, the patterns to be sought in social network messages, the information to be extracted from static and dynamic data and the messages (over social networks) that the system needs to produce. We have built an extensible working prototype, which allows adding new open data formats and support for different social networks.

Keywords: Open data · Social networks · MDE · DSLs

1 Introduction

There is currently a trend by different kinds of entities (governmental, foundations and companies) to offer in an open way all sorts of information, like economic, demographic, legal, scientific or service data. Typically, such data are offered as *open data*, which can be freely used and distributed [10]. However, it is not enough to deploy it, but it needs to have a format and description useful for consumers, as well as some degree of interconnection amongst the different resources in which it is presented. Unfortunately, in practice, open data are frequently published "as is" (raw data), and with heterogeneous formats like CSV, Excel, PDF, or accessible via API queries. This heterogeneity makes difficult the systematic engineering of applications making use of them.

Á. Mora Segura – Work supported by the Ministry of Education of Spain (FPU grant FPU13/02698), the Spanish MINECO (TIN2014-52129-R) and the R&D programme of the Madrid Region (S2013/ICE-3006).

© Springer International Publishing Switzerland 2016
L. Bellatreche et al. (Eds.): MEDI 2016, LNCS 9893, pp. 317–331, 2016.
DOI: 10.1007/978-3-319-45547-1_25

In the governmental context, the open data movement is directed to offer higher levels of transparency to citizens, and it is common for institutions to promote the creation of innovative applications that use their data (e.g., through hackatons and contests). Sadly enough, despite having been marked as highly desirable[1], the active involvement of citizens in such activities (by providing data themselves, or creating customized applications) is still scarce. One reason is that only highly qualified technical personnel is able to create and supply valuable open data sources and applications, since this involves highly complex tasks. These include the identification and monitoring of data sources, their cleansing and semantic tagging, their publication and incorporation to public repositories, the integration of data sources, their interlinking and visualization, and the implementation of an application that uses them in an effective way. Our final goal is to lower the barrier to the creation of this kind of applications.

Our proposal to tackle this problem is based on Model-Driven Engineering (MDE) [15]. In particular, we propose a Domain-Specific Language (DSL), named DataDSL, to describe the syntax and semantics of open data. It permits describing heterogeneous data (coming from different sources, formats and domains) in a unified way. The language has facilities to discover and make explicit the underlying schemas of data sets and link such schemas to different domains.

We show the integration of DataDSL within *EagleData*[2], an MDE framework for the high-level description and automated synthesis of applications over social networks [13]. Hence, DataDSL provides open data resources as one more input among the ones *EagleData* supports. *EagleData* comprises two further DSLs: PatternDSL for describing patterns to be sought on messages in social networks (like Twitter), and RuleDSL for describing rules to be triggered upon the reception of messages matching the given patterns. We demonstrate the approach with an example consisting in a service to show a user-requested bus line route in a map. The interaction with the system is performed via Twitter, and the data set is retrieved from the Spanish open data repository[3].

Paper Organization. Sect. 2 motivates our approach, describing current challenges. Section 3 overviews our approach and introduces a running example. Section 4 presents DataDSL. Section 5 shows its integration with *EagleData*. Section 6 describes tool support. Section 7 analyses related work and Sect. 8 concludes.

2   Motivation

Over the last years, web data has become more organized and detailed, i.e., more semantic, and it is common nowadays to find technologies that aim to gather, organize, represent and query web information. Moreover, the data-based web

---

[1] https://www.w3.org/2012/06/pmod/report.

[2] http://miso.es/tools/EagleData.html.

[3] http://datos.gob.es.

is no longer static, but fed by a non-stop streaming of information coming from a vast load of files, databases, sensor devices and social media. Specifically, the Semantic Web[4] provides an infrastructure for defining, integrating, sharing and reusing web data according to its meaning and significance. Together with the Semantic Web, a series of technologies have emerged – like RDF, SPARQL or OWL – enabling applications to query the data or use common vocabularies [4]. However, even though standardization has arrived to Semantic Web via *Linked Data* [2], most data made available to citizens do not follow these guidelines, being most frequently presented in an unstructured way or under private formats.

As an example, the Lod Cloud project[5] holds a series of data sets published by contributors, organisations and others. It provides a trustful measurement of how accessible are these sets, using a rating system known as the *5-star* model[6]. This defines a 5-step incremental path to publish data from *available online* (1 star), *structured* (2 stars), with *non-proprietary formats* (3 stars), with *links* (4 stars) and based on *Linked Data* technologies (5 stars).

As Fig. 1 shows, many of the published data sets do not obtain more than 3 stars, meaning that the majority uses non-proprietary formats. Hence, it might be stated that the Semantic Web orthodoxy is still not sufficiently established, probably because companies and distributors find it easier to publish their data in common formats like CSV or JSON, rather than the ones that Linked Data suggests (namely RDF).

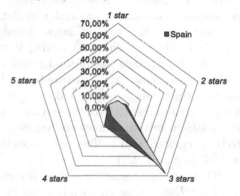

Fig. 1. Status of Lod data sets.

An analysis of the Spanish open data portal evidences the wide variety of formats used, revealing up to 55 different ones, like CSV (16 %), HTML (10,6 %), JSON (10,4 %), XML (9,7 %), ASCII (9,3 %), XLS (6,8 %), and PDF (6,8 %). These formats often lack a semantic description of their content, which is one of the main challenges of this work. Hence, in practice, *Linked Data* formats are not the first choice for open data, probably because most of these data sources are aimed to be read both by developers and non-expert users, and, despite being a very complete standard, human readability is not amongst *Linked Data* features.

Therefore, since expecting a scenario in which public administration achieves acceptable levels in the 5-star model is highly idealistic, it is necessary to have a sound way of giving semantics to open data sets, independently of the chosen format for their representation.

---

[4] https://www.w3.org/standards/.
[5] http://lod-cloud.net/.
[6] http://5stardata.info/.

Our aim is not only to make sense of open data, but also enabling their active use in social applications. For this purpose, we will integrate open data descriptions with *EagleData*. This is a tool for building simple applications over social networks, like Twitter. This way, the content of open data sources will be accessible through social networks.

3   Overview and Running Example

Our challenge is to build a framework that lightens the developement of applications combining open data, social network data, and faciliating human interaction with them. Figure 2 shows the typical process, whose steps are automated by *EagleData* or by the social network of choice (*Twitter* in this case).

The process starts with a certain organism releasing some open data. The developer is to become familiar with these data, performing data *cleansing* if needed [11] (label 1). Ideally, an explicit description of the data structure and its semantics would be produced. Our DataDSL language permits describing such structure and the tooling helps discovering the underlying data schema and linking it with existing data descriptions (see Sects. 4.1 and 4.2). Then, a platform-specific data structure has to be created to store the items (label 2), and the open data sets are parsed and instances of those structures created. If data from several sources are handled, they need to be integrated. Our tooling automates this process as well (see Sect. 4.3).

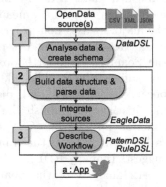

Fig. 2. Creating social apps over open data.

Then, an app using these data is created (label 3). *EaglaData* relies on social networks, and provides two DSLs (see Sect. 5). PatternDSL permits describing patterns to be sought in social network messages. RuleDSL enables the description of actions to be performed upon the reception of social messages, like querying data (e.g., received in previous messages, or in open data sources), and sending messages. The final app uses Twitter as front-end to interact with the open data. Many users are already familiar with social networks, so their use presents and advantage with respect to learning a new *app*.

Running Example. We would like to create an application to visualise the route of a given bus line, so that users can see the closest stop to their current position. The city of Santander (Spain) has made available the static data of the stop positions and bus lines at the open data Spanish portal, in CSV format (see an excerpt in Fig. 3). In the file, the bus line names have been abbreviated to *A* and *B*. In the data set, there is a row per stop and bus line, so that if both lines share a stop (e.g., *Camarreal 109*), there are two rows representing that stop: one for line A, and another for line B.

Taking advantage of the widespread use of Twitter, and that it especially favours interaction via mobile devices, our application expects a user tweet or

```
56; Camarreal 109;          A; Calle; Camarreal;  109; 43.44625; -3.87072;
61; Campogiro 23;           A; Calle; Campogiro;  23;  43.45044; -3.85070;
63; Campogiro 5;            A; Calle; Campogiro;  5;   43.45017; -3.85127;
64; Cajo 17;                B; Calle; Cajo;       17;  43.45405; -3.83708;
80; Parque Doctor Morales;  A; Calle; Cajo;       1;   43.45496; -3.83419;
88; Camarreal 109;          B; Calle; Camarreal;  109; 43.44625; -3.87072;
```

Fig. 3. Excerpt from an Open Data file in CSV format

direct message indicating the line to visualize, search the bus line number in the data set, and build a Google Maps URL that opens a map with the complete bus line route. The resulting URL is sent back to the user as a direct message.

4   DataDSL: A DSL to Describe Heterogeneous Open Data

As we have seen, the main issue with open data is the heterogeneity of formats and the frequent lack of explicit semantics. Hence, in order to treat all these data uniformly, a means to describe their underlying schema is needed. Ideally, these means should allow processing the sources automatically, so that such data can be queried and combined, also with data coming from dynamic sources, like social networks. The solution needs to be extensible, because we would like developers to be able to increase it with support for other new formats.

Several established languages exist in different technological spaces to describe the structure of data. For example, in MDE, one resorts to meta-modelling languages like MOF or Ecore [14]; in grammarware, EBNF grammars are used; while in ontology engineers use languages like OWL [4]. However, none of these languages offer native support for the following requirements: (i) being format independent, but allow to add format dependent options describing the pecularities of certain formats (e.g., the separator or the indication of a header in CSV files), (ii) extensibility mechanisms to add new formats and a set of options for these. While one could somehow encode this information in the mentioned languages (e.g., as annotations in Ecore meta-models), it is more convenient to develop a DSL offering this support in a native way.

4.1   Language Syntax and Semantics

DataDSL is a textual DSL that allows describing the semantics of data in heterogeneous formats. On the one hand it allows building format-independent, reusable descriptions called *fragments*. On the other, it supports format-specific descriptions for concrete data sources, called *data descriptions*. These may reuse fragments, and are typically enriched with options of the particular data format.

Listing 1 shows a DataDSL model with some fragments. Fragments are organized in packages (lines 1–21 and 22–40), which can be annotated (lines 1, 22 and 23) with their application domain. A fragment contains fields, which may declare a cardinality interval, and whose type may be primitive (e.g., source in fragment Line in line 6), an enumeration or another fragment. Fields can be declared key (e.g., id in line 5) to convey that the value is unique. Key fields are used in formats with no native support for references, to uniquely identify the referenced elements. For example, if fragments Line and Stop are reused to describe the content of a CSV file, then the stops reference (line 10) would be serialized as a list of stopIDs. Fragments can be reused to build other fragments, through an extension mechanism similar to inheritance, where a fragment can extend zero or more fragments.

DataDSL supports a large number of primitive data types, like Boolean, Lat (for latitude), Long (for longitude) and String. When using data types, especially within data descriptions, it is possible to indicate the specific serialization of their allowed values. In some specific file, a Boolean may be serialized as true and false, while in others as t and f, or 1 and 0. Hence, fields with primitive type may declare lists of options in parenthesis. Lines 18 and 19 declare the minimum and maximum value for the latitude and longitude. To allow reuse, a refined data type (i.e., a data type with options) can be declared explicitly and given a name. For example, line 3 declares Id as a refinement of Int, where the allowed values have 3 digits as a maximum. As a special case, Strings can be refined by means of options, but also patterns can be specified. For example, PostalCode in lines 26–29 is a refinement of String made of two parts. The first (the city) is made of two digits, and the second (the district) has three.

```
1  @transport                                       22  @city
2  package BusLine{                                 23  @geo
3    datatype Id : Int (minLen = 1, maxLen = 3)     24  package Address{
4    fragment Line{                                 25    enumeration AddrKind{"Calle","Avenida","Paseo"}
5      key Id id                                    26    datatype PostalCode : String {
6      String source                                27      Digits[2] city
7      String destination                           28      Digits[3] district
8      GeoPoint sourcePoint (null ="")              29    }
9      GeoPoint destinationPoint (null = "")        30    fragment Address{
10     Stop[*] stops                                31      AddressPoint addressPoint
11   }                                              32      String others
12   fragment Stop{                                 33      PostalCode postalcode
13     key Int stopID                               34    }
14     String name                                  35    fragment AddressPoint{
15     GeoPoint stopPoint                           36      AddrKind kind
16   }                                              37      String name
17   fragment GeoPoint{                             38      Int number
18     Lat latit (min = −90.0, max = 90.0)          39    }
19     Long longit (min = −180.0, max = 180.0)      40  }
20   }
21 }
```

Listing 1: Some DataDSL fragments for the running example.

The purpose of fragments is to describe knowledge of a domain in a reusable, format-independent way. Instead, data descriptions describe a particular data source, in a particular format. As an example, Listing 2 shows a description for the example CSV of Fig. 3. Such description reuses different fragments and definitions in Listing 1.

```
 1  import BusLine.*
 2  import Address.*
 3  description "CSV" SantanderCityBus{
 4     Id lineId
 5     AddressPoint address
 6     Stop stop
 7  } (
 8     language={"es-ES"},
 9     separator={";"},
10     order={stop.stopID, stop.name, lineId, address.addressPoint, stop.stopPoint}
11  )
```

Listing 2. Describing the CSV in Fig. 3 reusing fragments.

A data description declares its format, which is CSV in the listing (line 3). DataDSL is an *extensible DSL*, where different format handlers (e.g., for CSV, JSON, XML) can be included. As we will see later, each handler is in charge of parsing the data sources of the given format into a common representation, and to provide support for a number of configuration options. Just like fields, data descriptions may include options, specified in parenthesis after their definition (lines 8–10 in the listing). Options for a description may be general (applicable to any format and provided by default by DataDSL) or specific for the given format. The listing declares that the data within the CSV file is in Spanish (line 8) using the general option language. In addition, the CSV format handler contributes with three options: separator (the separator character of fields in the file, ";" in the example), header (whether there is a header row, false by default), and order (to indicate the specific order in which the components of the description will appear in the file). None of the options is mandatory. In particular, if no order is specified, the order in which the fields are listed is taken. If order is specified, and some field of the description is not listed, it is ignored.

An excerpt of DataDSL's meta-model is shown in Fig. 4. It can be observed that both Framents and DataDescriptions are defined through Nodes (i.e., fields). These can be of primitive type (PrimitiveNode), fragment type (FragmentNode) or composite. In the latter case, they may have an enumeration or refined type. Nodes may have Options, some of which are shown in the OptionKey enum. DataDescriptions can have either general or specific options. The former are predefined in DataDSL, while interpreting the later is done through the specific format handler. Finally, the language distinguishes between DataTypeRefinements and StringRefinements, because the later can specify a structure for the string (class Substring).

4.2 Inferring Semantics from Data Sets

Because we intend to minimize the developer's workload, each format handler can contribute an algorithm for inferring the structure of a particular data set, and make it explicit as a DataDSL model. Then, such inferred schema can be refined by the user, or refactored for the reuse of available fragments. It is to notice that both XML and JSON permit the availability of external descriptions of the data, like *DTD (Document Type Definition)* or *JSON Schema*[7]. With them,

---

[7] http://json-schema.org/.

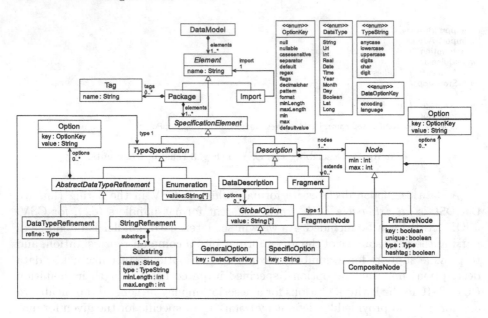

Fig. 4. Simplified meta-model excerpt of DataDSL.

it is easy to convert every element into its proper representation in DataDSL. Unfortunately, neither XML nor JSON force the use of these schemas, and hence it is common to find data sets with no description of their structure. In that case, the process is left to heuristics and user intervention, just like with CSV. Generically, the schema inferring algorithms work in four phases:

1. **Check file readability.** In a first step, conformance to the given format is checked. Thus, we approach an early pre-processing of the input file by removing unexpected characters and literals and by warning the user if the open data source does not meet the format's serialization schema.
2. **Data source structure detection.** Having a valid file to process, we create the structure of the DataDescription to generate. By analysing its components, we infer a correspondence to an instance of our DataDSL meta-model. In this step, we merely identify each component, without assigning them a Type.
3. **Data type inference.** By default, we set primitive types as String if they are not explicitly specified (as it happens with DTD). Then, we look over each primitive value from the input file (e.g., we check CSV column values) for finding out whether we can assign the corresponding Node a more specific primitive type. If, for instance, we discover a column that is entirely filled by integers, then we can set that node type to Int. Additional heuristics to refine the primitive type can also be applied. For example, for CSV, we check the column name against predefined sets of keywords, to suggest whether a column is a key, or represent the Latitude and Longitude of some place if two columns are in the same time in the range of a latitude and longitude values. The compatible types are presented in order from more specific (e.g.,

Lat) to more general (e.g., Real). To give the algorithm some control about mixed values we provide a list of probabilistic rates based on how much values match with the type discovered. Nodes may have options, and so we suggest values for them. For example, for PrimitiveNode we suggest the minimum and maximum values for numbers and the null value for strings (if allowed).

Running Example. With *EagleData* we provide a wizard to import files and discover the value types. In the running example the system automatically produces the description in Listing 3 (where field names have been renamed). Enumerations (like the in in line 1) are generated if the number of different strings values is below a certain configurable threshold. For the example, the algorithm suggests two enums (AddressKind and Line). Once inferred, the user may change the description, and *EagleData* checks if the corresponding source is still conformant to the description.

```
1  enumeration AddressKind {"Calle", "Avenida"}
2  enumeration Line {"A","B"}
3  description CSV SantanderCityBus{
4    Int id (min − 56, max − 88)
5    String idStop (null − "")
6    Line line
7    AddressKind addressKind
8    String addressName (null − "")
9    Int addressNum (min = 1, max = 109)
10   Lat latPoint (minDouble = 43,44625, maxDouble = 43 45496)
11   Long longPoint (minDouble − −3.03419, maxDouble − −3.87072)
12  }("delimiter" − ";")
```

Listing 3. Automatically inferred data source description.

4.3 Handling the Heterogeneity of Formats

As we will see in Sect. 6, *EagleData* provides a series of (Eclipse) extension points to add support for more formats. In order to enable a uniform access to heterogeneous data, we use a common meta-model, shown in Fig. 5. The idea is to provide mappings for different static data sources to this common model. This meta-model has the structure of a Table that can be used to represent tabular data [6]. Cells of the table can be either ContentCell or TableCell which means the cell contains a subtable instead of a string value. This way, *EagleData* assumes that every data provided by format extensions will consist of a group of Tables.

	CSV	XML	JSON
Table	Resource	Document	JSONObject
Row	Record	Node	JSONArray
ContentCell.content	Cell	Content	JSONObject.value
TableCell.table	n/a	Node.array	JSONArray.value

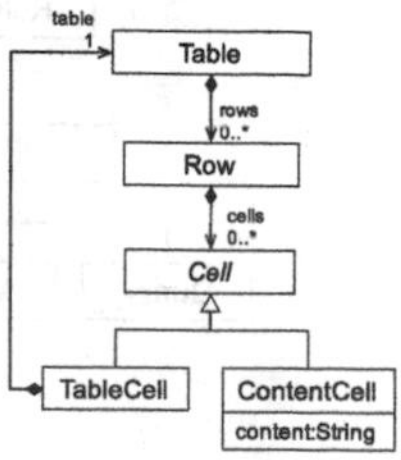

Fig. 5. Mapping data modelling technologies to EagleData's data model.

We provide three basic extensions for the resolution of static data injection: CSV, XML and JSON since they are the top choices when it comes to representing open data. The table shows how those three technologies can be mapped to our common meta-model. Our design is extensible, as it facilitates the integration of new technologies. We will elaborate on the extensibility mechanisms in Sect. 5.

5   Integration with *EagleData*

Once we have assured that our system is able to work with the structure of a certain open data set, the developer needs to have a means to implement the actual behaviour of an open data application. Our previous work [13] introduced a framework called *EagleData* for describing simple applications over Twitter by detecting patterns on messages (with a DSL called PatternDSL) and for performing rule-based actions (with the RulesDSL language), like sending a *message*. In order to benefit from the high use of social networks nowadays, we consider very interesting to be able to integrate open data sets with data coming from social networks. For the example, we use Twitter, but similar to the different open data formats, *EagleData* provides an extension mechanism for adding support for additional social networks.

The execution scheme of an *EagleData* application consists in a loop that observes tweets mentioning a given account. A number of patterns (described using PatternDSL) are sought in those tweets, and the matching of any such pattern may trigger associated rules (defined using RuleDSL). The rules may perform actions, like generating tweets or private messages. These generated messages may contain information found both in the social network messages or in the open data sets. Because most of the information that users post in social networks does not follow a prearranged structure, *EagleData* provides facilities for detecting written language patterns. These patterns are the only information that the final user needs for using an *EagleData* application, although this does not necessarily imply the use of keywords or pre-defined hashtags, but following a flexible conceptual structure the application provider shall ensure that the user knows in advance. Other information, like geoposition, is intrinsically available with the tweets themselves as metadata.

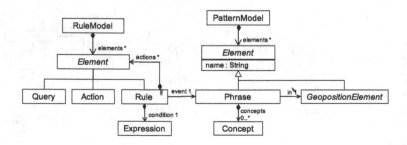

Fig. 6. Simplified meta-model excerpt of PatternDSL and RuleDSL.

Figure 6 shows a very simplified meta-model. The concept *Phrase* represents the largest information unit a social network message can possibly hold. When a message matches a defined pattern, its associated rules are triggered. These rules follow an event-condition-action structure, which means that rules are evaluated whenever a mentioning tweet is received (event), and executed whenever the message matches a given pattern (the *condition*, referenced with the keyword on). For execution, rules may include a series of actions (starting with the keyword do). Currently, we support element-query and message-reply rules. In the action block, static data coming from open data sets can be combined with dynamic social network: both are uniformly available as variables in the domain. See [13] for further details.

Running Example. Listing 4 shows an example of a simple pattern definition in line 1, which serves as the input user interface to our running example, expecting the bus line the user needs to know about. Any other character in the tweet is ignored. If multiple occurrences of a single concept are found, only the first one is considered. The pattern is named MessageLine, and is made of a string "Line" followed by the line id. This id is declared elsewhere as being either A or B. Patterns can also make use of synonyms for words (we use the Wordnet data base [8]) and perform approximate match (e.g., matching an expression where some vowels are missing). Whenever our running application receives a tweet matching the pattern from a user, the query addresses takes place (lines 5–6), which returns a list of the addresses of the queried bus line stops. The query result can be reused for the reply action, started by compose. The language supports string interpolation (line 8), which permits inserting the elements of lists using separators, or perform replacements. The message is sent back to the originator of the tweet.

```
1  phrase MessageLine ("Line", id)
2
3  on MessageLine
4  do
5      addresses:
6        select latPoint, longPoint where MessageLine.id = SantanderCityBus.id
7      compose
8        "https://www.google.com/maps/dir/@{addresses.latPoint,addresses.longPoint}[separator='/']"
```

Listing 4. Rule composing a message with a map of the stops for a given line.

6 Architecture and Tool Support

In this section we introduce an extended version of the prototype created for [13], now called *EagleData*. The tool is based on Eclipse. A schema of the *EagleData* architecture is shown in Fig. 7. *EagleData* is made of a Core component, which provides support for the schema discovery and data injection into the common internal representation. The Core component provides two extension points to support for additional data format handlers. The UI component provides Eclipse views and wizards for performing the queries using the three languages.

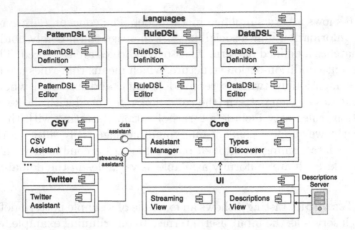

Fig. 7. Architecture of the proposal.

The framework supports the inference of DataDSL descriptions from data sets. Figure 8 shows the wizard providing the assistance for refining the induced types. Datatypes and enumerations are discovered based on the values saved in the concrete data sources. The tool is able to generate template queries and rules based on the underlying open data set structure. Hence, once the DataDSL model is ready (label 2), we can invoke the generator of patterns and rules, with which a user is enabled to obtain an application in just a few minutes. The tool counts with a set of views to check the fragments and datatypes saved on the open repository, and the tweets that match with the patterns (label 3). The tool is available at http://miso.es/tools/EagleData.html. The web page contains videos showing the tool in action to define simple applications over open data sets.

7   Related Work

Some data pre-processing tasks in our framework have similarities with Extract-Transform-Load (ETL) approaches, especially from data warehouses [7]. Many commercial and open source tools exists nowadays supporting ETL processes, like Pentaho's PDI/Kettle[8], and data/API integration technologies like MuleSoft[9] also offer ETL support. Solutions such as CKAN[10] seems to be more complete, offering stream management for publishing and discovering datasets.

However, the purpose of those systems is different from ours. The goal of DataDSL is to describe the structure of existing data sets, both in format independent (through fragments) and format-dependent ways (through data sources). Then, both types of descriptions can be linked, and so the information in heteregeneous data sets can be related in such way. This approach is normally not

---

[8] http://goo.gl/G41Vaa.

[9] http://mulesoft.com.

[10] http://ckan.org/.

Fig. 8. Type refinement wizard and DataDSL editor

followed in ETL, whose goal is moving data from some source data sets into a relational or multi-dimensional data base. Instead, DataDSL serves to describe and relate existing data sets.

DataDSL is a meta-modelling language especially tailored to describe open data. There exist well established meta-modelling languages, like the Meta-Object Facility (MOF) [9], and widely used frameworks like the Eclipse Modelling Framework (EMF) [14]. We refrained to use such approaches and opted instead for a customized language with native support for elements like format specification; fragments and data sources; and the possibility to add options, to be interpreted by the plugins supporting the specific formats. While this might be emulated in MOF/EMF e.g., by using annotations, native support for all these features yields a more natural syntax. Previously to build DataDSL, we also experimented with multi-level modelling technologies, like MetaDepth [12]. While it provided enhanced flexibility (by e.g., enabling the placement of more general fragments at higher meta-levels), it also lacked the useful mentioned primitives that DataDSL has. Moreover, it was not integrated with a framework to build social network applications. The need (raised by open data) to describe textual, tabular data is evidenced by the recent W3C recommendation [6]. While we aim at interperate with such recommendation, the goal is also to be *extensible* to arbitrary formats, including XML and even APIs.

Many works have tackled the problem of inferring schemas from data in different formats. For example, in [5] the authors propose an approach for discovering schemas (meta-models) from JSON data, and in [1] the authors propose an algorithm to obtain a concise DTD from XML data. We took ideas from [5] for our JSON support. As our framework is open, new formats can be added, and therefore algorithms for schema induction can be incorporated into EagleData.

BPM4People[11] extends BPMN enabling to model complex data flow, coming from a social domain, and [3] extends WebML to incorporate social primitives, permitting cross-platform operations for several social networks. While these are more general languages, our DSL approach aims to be much lighter, and specifically target to make accessible open data through social networks.

Hence, altogether, our work is novel with respect to existing works, combining a DSL for data description of heterogeneous open data sets, with DSLs for the description of applications over social networks, to automate the generation of open data applications.

8   Conclusions and Future Work

In this paper we have presented DataDSL, a DSL to describe the structure of heterogeneous *open data* sets. The DSL is integrated within *EagleData*, an MDE framework to create applications over social networks. We have presented a working prototype and a running example consisting in a service to obtain a map-based representation of a bus line, with interaction via Twitter.

While we have used DataDSL to describe static open data, we will tackle its integration with open APIs. Hence, with DataDSL the underlying data schema can be described in the style of [5], and options can be used to describe the available operations of the API. We are currently working in providing *EagleData* with visualization outputs, and also automating the process of mapping data source descriptions to fragments. Our goal is to be able to define programs and services on fragments, that would become reusable to particular data sources when the fragments are reused. To simplify even more the development of open data applications, we will build higher-level DSLs specially targeted for end-users, whose execution will rely on our *EagleData* framework and its three DSLs.

References

1. Bex, G.J., Neven, F., Schwentick, T., Tuyls, K.: Inference of concise DTDs from XML data. In: VLDB, pp. 115–126. ACM (2006)
2. Bizer, C., Heath, T., Berners-Lee, T.: Linked data - the story so far. Int. J. Semant. Web Inf. Syst.(IJSWIS) **5**(3), 1–22 (2009)
3. Brambilla, M., Mauri, A.: Model-driven development of social network enabled applications with WebML and social primitives. In: Grossniklaus, M., Wimmer, M. (eds.) ICWE Workshops 2012. LNCS, vol. 7703, pp. 41–55. Springer, Heidelberg (2012)
4. Hitzler, P., Krotzsch, M., Rudolph, S.: Foundations of Semantic Web Technologies. CRC Press, New York (2010)
5. Cánovas Izquierdo, J.L., Cabot, J.: Discovering implicit schemas in JSON data. In: Daniel, F., Dolog, P., Li, Q. (eds.) ICWE 2013. LNCS, vol. 7977, pp. 68–83. Springer, Heidelberg (2013)
6. Jeni Tennison, G.K., Herman, I.: Model for Tabular Data and Metadata on the Web (2015). https://www.w3.org/TR/tabular-data-model/

---

[11] http://bpm4people.webratio.com/.

7. Kimball, R.: The Data Warehouse ETL Toolkit: Practical Techniques for Building Dimensional Data Warehouses. Wiley, New York (1996)
8. Miller, G.A.: Wordnet: a lexical database for English. CACM **38**(11), 39–41 (1995)
9. OMG: MOF 2.5 (2015). http://www.omg.org/spec/MOF/2.5/
10. Open Data Commons. http://opendatacommons.org/
11. Rahm, E., Do, H.H.: Data cleaning: problems and current approaches. IEEE Data Eng. Bull. **23**(4), 3–13 (2000)
12. Segura, A.M., de Lara, J., Cuadrado, J.S.: ODaaS: towards the model-driven engineering of open data applications as data services. In EDOC 2014, pp. 335–339. IEEE Computer Society (2014)
13. Segura, A.M., de Lara, J., Cuadrado, J.S.: Rapid development of interactive applications based on online social networks. In: Benatallah, B., Bestavros, A., Manolopoulos, Y., Vakali, A., Zhang, Y. (eds.) WISE 2014, Part II. LNCS, vol. 8787, pp. 505–520. Springer, Heidelberg (2014)
14. Steinberg, D., Budinsky, F., Paternostro, M., Merks, E.: EMF: Eclipse Modeling Framework. Addison-Wesley, Reading (2008)
15. Völter, M., Stahl, T.: Model-Driven Software Development. Wiley, Chichester (2006)

Towards Culture-Sensitive Extensions of CRISs: Gender-Based Researcher Evaluation

Miloš Savić[✉], Mirjana Ivanović, Miloš Radovanović, and Bojana Dimić Surla

Faculty of Sciences, Department of Mathematics and Informatics,
University of Novi Sad, Trg Dositeja Obradovića 4, 21000 Novi Sad, Serbia
{svc,mira,radacha,bdimic}@dmi.uns.ac.rs

Abstract. Current research information systems (CRISs) offer great opportunities for extraction of useful and actionable knowledge based on various data analysis techniques. However, many of these opportunities have not been explored in depth, especially in culture-sensitive areas such as gender-based evaluation of researchers. In this paper, we present GERBER, a methodology and accompanying tool for performing gender-based analysis of CRIS data. The tool enables the extraction of co-authorship networks, computation of various author metrics, and statistical comparison of male and female researchers. Functionality of GERBER is demonstrated on data extracted from the CRIS of the University of Novi Sad (UNS). We also present a plan to integrate GERBER into CRIS UNS in order to facilitate continuous gender-based researcher evaluation. Experiences obtained during such integration will enable us to propose more general methodological guidelines and APIs for culture-sensitive extensions of CRIS systems and standards.

Keywords: Research information systems · Culture-sensitive extensions · Gender-based evaluation

1 Introduction

Measuring gender differences in research and teaching productivity has been a topic of interest for researchers and decision makers for many decades [17]. The basic generalization found in the literature is that male faculty outperform female faculty [5,8] (for a more comprehensive list, please see [17] and references therein). However, more recent studies have shown that this is by no means due to some inherent superiority of one gender over the other. Xie and Shauman [34] conducted four large, nationally representative, cross-sectional surveys spanning several decades, observing that differences in research productivity declined over the period 1969–1993. Similarly, Gander [17] concludes that, although analysis of data at first glance supports the generalization, further scrutiny reveals that patterns of employment and distribution of funding are actually the main causes of the observed differences in productivity. Once the analysis is adjusted, it is revealed that female faculty have significant research productivity [17].

© Springer International Publishing Switzerland 2016
L. Bellatreche et al. (Eds.): MEDI 2016, LNCS 9893, pp. 332–345, 2016.
DOI: 10.1007/978-3-319-45547-1_26

Current research information systems (CRISs) contain scientific production data and thus offer great opportunities for research evaluation. One such information system for storing and managing data about scientific research activity at the University of Novi Sad (UNS), Serbia – CRIS UNS was developed following the recommendations of the non-profit organisation euroCRIS [12]. CRIS UNS provides a comprehensive list of publications of researchers affiliated to UNS and enables automated evaluation of individual UNS researchers and institutions. In this paper we present GERBER (*GEndeR-Based Evaluation of Researchers*) – a methodology and an accompanying tool to perform gender-based analysis of data exported from CRIS UNS. The main functionalities provided by the tool are: (1) extraction of a co-authorship network that represents collaborations between authors contained in exported data, (2) computation of various metrics that reflect productivity, competency, collaborativity and social importance of individual researchers and (3) statistical comparison of male and female researchers based on non-parametric statistical tests. To demonstrate applicability of the tool we performed gender-based evaluation of researchers employed at UNS-PMF – University of Novi Sad Faculty of Sciences.

The rest of the paper is structured as follows. The overview of related research works is given in Sect. 2. Section 3 outlines the data preparation methods for gender-based analysis of researchers. The following section describes the proposed methodology for gender-based researcher evaluation and the accompanying GERBER tool. The analysis conducted using GERBER is presented in Sect. 5. Integration of analytical tools into the CRIS UNS system is discussed in Sect. 6. In the last section we give the conclusions and directions for future work.

2   Related Work

In this section we will review relevant related work comprising of studies of gender differences in scientific productivity (Sect. 2.1) and give the background of the CRIS UNS information system for storing and managing data about scientific research (Sect. 2.2).

2.1   Scientometric Analysis of Gender in Research

The comprehensive multi-decade study by Xie and Shauman [34], besides observing the decline of gender differences in research productivity, also correlates gender productivity differences with gender differences in personal characteristics, structural positions, and marital status, implying that gender differences in research productivity stem from gender differences in structural locations, and as such respond to the secular improvement of women's position in science.

Contemporary data in the field of social science shows that not only did gender differences disappear in the younger generations of researchers, but that if some differences exist, it is the young female researchers that outperform their male peers [2]. In educational psychology, on the other hand, although females are gaining ground in terms of primary and secondary article authorship and journal editorial board membership, this increase does not keep pace with the male-female ratio in organizational memberships [15]. Also, in the industrial and organizational psychology there are significant gender differences with respect to publication output and career courses [21].

In the domains of science, engineering and technology, the trends are also varying, with the overall impression that participation and performance of women improved in recent times. Within Spanish natural resources and chemistry scientists, no significant differences in productivity were found between genders within professional categories, but the outliers with the highest production were for the most part male [6]. In nano science and technology, female researchers are scarce in number, but perform equally in terms of scientific production and impact [31]. A comprehensive study involving the DBLP database of computer science publications ranging from 1936 to 2010 also indicates a low percentage of women in this field, albeit a steadily rising one [7]. The authors observed that men publish more than women, but attributed this to the fact that the average research life of men is longer.

Studies of gender differences in scientific productivity also produce varying results in different countries. In Croatia [29], within the studied young research population females are somewhat less productive than males which is in line with the observations by Xie and Shauman [34] discussed earlier. In Italy [1], there is also evidence of higher overall male productivity, but with difference smaller than reported in a large part of the literature, confirming an ongoing tendency towards decline. Russia [28], on the other hand, still exhibits strong gender disparity, which can also be said for Turkish social sciences [27].

The above constitutes only a small representative sample of studies dealing with gender differences in scientific production and teaching. A comprehensive meta-study of scientific literature on women in science and higher education, considering almost 1500 articles, shows continued growing interest in the topic, featuring more than 3000 authors, 67 countries, and 86 research areas [9].

2.2   CRIS UNS

The starting point in developing CRIS UNS was creating a well-structured and comprehensive metadata set for describing scientific results, as well as researchers and institutions. Paper [19] proposed the metadata model based on the MARC 21 library standard and compatible with CERIF (Common European Research Information Format). The CERIF data model provides a very rich and well-structured set of metadata. The core of CERIF are three basic entities Person, Project and OrganisationUnit, and three result entities ResultPatent, ResultPublication and ResultProduct [13]. The structure of CERIF enabled the development of the information system in which authors are uniquely identified and connected to their results, institutions and projects. The metadata set for some entities was further enriched by introducing the MARC 21 format of bibliographic data for presenting publications and the MARC 21 format of authority data for presenting authors [32]. The described model was the basis for developing the information system CRIS UNS for tracking research activity at the University of Novi Sad [25].

Speaking of research activity, one of the main purposes for developing the CRIS UNS system was providing automated evaluation of scientific results, researchers and institutions, which has become extremely important. Paper [20] proposed an extension of CERIF by data for evaluation of published scientific results. The extension is based on the CERIF semantic layer that enables classification of entities and their relationships by different classification schemas. The rules for evaluation proposed by the academic regulatory bodies were implemented within CRIS UNS and exposed as a service for evaluation of scientific results.

The architecture of CRIS UNS with its rich matadata model and module for evaluation of scientific results provided the environment for developing various techniques and tools for business analysis and gathering important information used by institutional management. These tools included a module for creating periodical reports on research activity and different analyses.

3   Preparing Data for Gender Analysis

Generally speaking, there were two options for preparing data for gender analysis: the first one was exporting all relevant data to a format suitable for analysis tools, and the second one was providing the interface for retrieving relevant data directly from the CRIS UNS database. In this paper we opted for the first option, and discuss the second option in Sect. 6.

The architecture of the CRIS UNS and adoption of international standards for presenting research data provided an appropriate environment for interoperability with other systems [18] including ontology-based integration [10].

We used the existing interoperability architecture of CRIS UNS for developing a module for exporting publications and authors to XML documents. Exporting publications and researchers consisted of several steps:

1. selecting researchers for the given institution,
2. for each researcher, select all her/his publications,
3. if the result is not already processed, i.e. stored in the resulting XML file, store the result metadata depending on its type (journal paper, conference paper, monograph, paper monograph, etc.),
4. for each publication included in the previous step, select all authors,
5. store each author to the authors XML file if she/he is not already there.

4   GERBER Tool

GERBER is a standalone tool implemented in Java that performs gender-based analysis of data exported from the CRIS UNS system. The tool consists of three modules: Data Loader, Author Metric and Gender Analyzer. The architecture of GERBER is shown in Fig. 1.

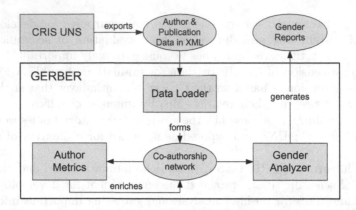

Fig. 1. The architecture of GERBER.

4.1 Data Loader

The Data Loader (DL) module parses two XML files that contain the data exported from the CRIS UNS information system and forms the co-authorship network of researchers appearing in the data. The first XML file contains demographic information about all UNS-PMF researchers and their direct external collaborators (researchers not affiliated to UNS-PMF). Each author is described by an XML element which includes unique author identifier, author name, date of birth, institution to which the author is affiliated, organizational unit within the institution, academic rank, and gender. The second XML file contains the data about publications which are authored by UNS-PMF researchers. Each publication is described by an XML element which consists of the following information: unique publication identifier, the complete list of author identifiers, publication year, title, publication type (journal, conference, monograph, etc.), information about publication venue and the categorization of the publication according to the rule book prescribed by the Serbian Ministry of Education, Science and Technological Development.

Co-authorship networks are undirected graphs showing collaboration between researchers [30]. The nodes of a co-authorship networks represent different researchers, and two researchers are connected by a undirected link if they co-authored at least one publication together. A co-authorship network can be viewed as an undirected, weighted and attributed graph $G = (V, E)$ where V is a set of attributed nodes and E is a set of weighted links. Namely, nodes have attributes that describe different demographic characteristics of authors. Also, author metrics are stored as node attributes. The strength of collaboration between two researchers is commonly quantified by one of three different weighting schema: the normal weighting scheme (the number of joint publications) [3], Newman's weighting scheme [26] which takes into account the number of authors per publication, and Salton's weighting scheme [23] which is a normalized variant of the normal scheme.

The extraction of a co-authorship network from CRIS-based data is a straightforward task since each author has an unique identifier which is used in publication records, and consequently there are no name disambiguation problems. The DL module forms the co-authorship network in three stages:

1. In the first stage the set of nodes is formed. The DL module iterates through the list of author XML elements and for each element creates one attributed node in the network.
2. The second stage forms the set of links and a decentralized inverted index which maps authors to their publications. Namely, each node in the network contains the list of publications written by the corresponding author. The DL module iterates through the list of publication XML elements and performs the following:
   - Connects each two authors of publication p by an undirected link.
   - For each author a of publication p, adds p in the list of publications a authored.
3. The third stage determines weights of links according to the three previously mentioned weighting schemes. Each link in the network is visited and for authors connected by the link weights are computed considering their lists of publications.

Table 1. The list of author metrics computed by the AM module.

Metric	Abbreviation	Metric category
Productivity, normal count	PRO-N	Productivity
Productivity, fractional count	PRO-F	Productivity
Productivity, straight count	PRO-S	Productivity
Serbian research competency index	CI	Productivity
Degree centrality	DEG	Collaborativity
Local degree centrality	LDEG	Collaborativity
External degree centrality	EDEG	Collaborativity
Betweenness centrality	BET	Social importance
Closeness centrality	CLO	Social importance
Clustering coefficient	CC	Cohesiveness
Co-author gender disbalance	CGD	Gender diversity

4.2   Author Metrics

The Author Metrics (AM) module enriches nodes of the co-authorship network formed by the Data Loader module with metrics that reflect author productivity, collaborativity, social importance and characteristics of ego networks. Table 1 shows the complete list of metrics computed by the AM module.

The AM module implements three commonly used schemes to evaluate the productivity of researchers which are known as normal counting, fractional (adjusted) counting, and straight counting [22]. Let p be a publication written by n researchers. In the normal counting scheme all authors of p receive equal credit for p, exactly one point. The straight counting scheme gives all the credit (one point) only to the first author of p. The fractional counting procedure assigns credit equal to $1/n$ to each of n authors of p. The AM module also computes the Serbian research competency index according to the categorizations prescribed by the rule book of the Serbian Ministry of Education, Science and Technological Development.

The collaborativity of a researcher can be quantified by its degree centrality in the co-authorship network. The degree centrality of author a is equal to the number of links incident to a. Each author in CRIS-exported data can be classified either as local or external. Namely, local authors are researchers affiliated to institution(s) covered by CRIS. In our case, local authors are researchers employed at UNS-PMF, while external authors are their collaborators from other institutions. Consequently, we can derive two other local centrality measures: local degree centrality (the number of local co-authors) and external degree centrality (the number of external co-authors).

The AM module also implements global metrics of social importance suitable for undirected graphs: betweenness centrality [16], and closeness centrality [4]. The betweenness centrality of node (author) a is the extent to which a is located on the shortest paths connecting two arbitrary selected nodes in the network. If a large fraction of shortest paths contain a, then a can be viewed as an important node of the network in sense that it has a vital role to the overall connectivity of the network. If the network has a clustered or community organization, then nodes with high betweenness centrality tend to be located at the intersections of communities, which means that they connect together different cohesive, homophilic social groups. The closeness centrality of node a is inversely proportional to the cumulative distance between a to other nodes in the network. Nodes with high closeness centrality can be considered as socially important since they are in proximity to a large number of other nodes.

The last category of author metrics computed by the AM module are metrics related to characteristics of ego-networks. The ego network of node a in undirected graph G, denoted by $Ego(a)$, is a sub-graph of G induced by i and its nearest neighbors. The cohesiveness of ego-networks can be quantified by the clustering coefficient [33]. The clustering coefficient of node a, denoted by $CC(a)$, is the probability that two randomly selected neighbors of a are directly connected. If $CC(a) = 1$ then neighbors of a forms the most cohesive ego-network – clique. The lowest value of $CC(a)$ is equal to 0 and happens when co-authors of a have never collaborated among themselves. The last metric computed by the AM module quantifies the gender structure of ego-networks. Let $M(a)$ and $F(a)$ denote the fraction of male and female collaborators of author a. Then, the co-author gender imbalance of a is defined as $CGD(a) = |M(a) - F(a)|$. If $CGD(a) = 1$ then all collaborators of a have the same gender, while $CGD(a) = 0$

implies that a equally collaborates with male and female researchers. It is important to emphasize that metrics of social importance and metrics related to ego-networks are computed on the reduced co-authorship network that encompasses only local researchers as nodes in order to have a clear institutional boundary when interpreting those metrics.

4.3   Gender Analyzer

The Gender Analyzer (GA) module performs statistical comparison of male and female researchers considering author metrics computed by the AM module. This module performs two non-parametric statistical tests which compare metric characteristics of male and female researchers. Implemented tests are the Mann-Whitney U (MWU) test [24] and the two independent samples Kolmogorov-Smirnov (KS) test [14].

Let M be an arbitrarily selected author metric. The MWU test is used to check the null hypothesis that concrete values of M for male researchers do not tend to be systematically higher or lower than concrete values of M for female researchers. The null hypothesis is rejected if obtained p-value is smaller than 0.05 and in such cases we can conclude that there is a statistically significant difference between male and female researchers regarding the aspect quantified by M. To quantify the effect size of the difference we use two probabilities of superiority [11]:

1. PS_m – the probability that for a randomly selected male researcher the value of M is strictly higher than the value of M for a randomly selected female researcher.
2. PS_f – which is the opposite probability of superiority, i.e. the probability that for a randomly selected female researcher the value of M is strictly higher than the value of M for a randomly selected male researcher.

The KS test checks the null hypothesis that cumulative distributions of M for male and female researchers are not significantly different. The test relies on the maximal vertical distance between two empirically observed distributions (the D statistic). The null hypothesis is rejected if the obtained p-value is smaller than 0.05.

As its final output the GA module makes three types of reports:

– basic gender statistics considering organizational units covered by the CRIS system (different departments at our faculty),
– results of non-parametric statistical tests, and
– tables that contain values of the Spearman correlation coefficient between different author metrics considering male and female researchers separately.

5   Gender-Based Evaluation of UNS-PMF Researchers

To demonstrate the applicability of GERBER in a real-world scenario we performed gender-based evaluation of researchers affiliated to our institution (UNS-PMF) using real data exported from our official CRIS UNS information system. The exported data covers 423 researchers employed at UNS-PMF and their

15097 publications written in collaboration with 5267 researchers not affiliated to UNS-PMF. The co-authorship network extracted from the exported data contains 34111 links, where 2859 links (8.38 %) represent collaborations between UNS-PMF researchers.

Table 2 shows basic gender statistics per organizational units (departments) of UNS-PMF. A majority of UNS-PMF researchers are female (60.76 % of the total number). Female researchers are in a strong majority at the Department of Biology and Ecology and the Department of Chemistry. The smallest gender gap can be observed at the Department of Mathematics and Informatics where male and female researchers are almost equally represented.

Table 2. Basic gender statistics of UNS-PMF researchers. R denotes the absolute number of researchers, while M and F are percentages of male and female researchers, respectively.

Department	R	M[%]	F[%]
Mathematics and Informatics	87	49.43	50.57
Geography	66	57.58	42.42
Biology and Ecology	118	25.42	74.58
Physics	57	56.14	43.86
Chemistry	95	24.21	75.79
Total	423	39.24	60.76

The results of statistical tests performed by the GA module of GERBER are summarized in Table 3. Although UNS-PMF male researchers on average have slightly higher values of all productivity metrics compared to UNS-PMF female researchers, application of non-parametric statistical tests revealed that there are no statistically significant gender differences regarding scientific productivity. Also, we noticed that there are strong positive Spearman correlations between different productivity metrics for both genders – the lowest value of Spearman correlations for a randomly selected pair of productivity metrics is 0.83.

Regarding social aspects of scientific collaboration, it can be observed that UNS-PMF male researchers do not tend to have more total/local/external collaborators than UNS-PMF female researchers, and vice versa. Centrality metrics also exhibit strong Spearman correlations to productivity metrics (see Table 4). Moreover, the external degree centrality stronger correlates to productivity metrics compared to the local degree centrality which means that external collaborations have a stronger impact to productivity of both UNS-PMF male and female researchers.

From the data presented in Table 3 it can be observed that the null hypothesis of both non-parametric statistical tests were rejected for the betweenness centrality metric, but not for the closeness centrality metric. This means

Table 3. The results of statistical comparison of UNS-PMF male and female researchers. $\langle M \rangle$ and $\langle F \rangle$ denote the average values of corresponding metric for male and female researchers, respectively. U is the value of the Mann-Whitney test statistic, MWU-p denotes the p-value of the MWU test, PS_m and PS_f are male and female probabilities of superiority, respectively. D is the value of the Kolmogorov-Smirnov test statistic and KS-p denotes the p-value of the KS test. Bold p values indicate that the null hypothesis of the test is rejected.

Metric	$\langle M \rangle$	$\langle F \rangle$	U	MWU-p	PS_m	PS_f	D	KS-p
PRO-N	82.72	65.40	20741	0.63	0.51	0.48	0.07	0.71
PRO-F	25.52	17.85	19975.5	0.27	0.53	0.47	0.10	0.29
PRO-S	25.83	19.33	20754	0.64	0.50	0.47	0.09	0.40
CI	132.05	101.40	20056	0.30	0.53	0.47	0.10	0.23
DEG	51.24	44.98	20440	0.47	0.52	0.47	0.06	0.78
LDEG	13.91	13.26	21194	0.91	0.49	0.48	0.05	0.95
EDEG	37.33	31.72	20301.5	0.40	0.52	0.47	0.07	0.66
BET	579.38	389.05	18564.5	**0.02**	0.55	0.42	0.14	**0.04**
CLO	0.30	0.31	18666	0.23	0.46	0.53	0.12	0.10
CC	0.49	0.55	18545	**0.02**	0.42	0.55	0.13	**0.04**
CGD	0.39	0.41	19004	0.35	0.45	0.51	0.12	0.10

Table 4. The values of the Spearman correlation coefficients between collaborativity and productivity metrics.

	Male researchers		Female researchers	
	PRO-N	CI	PRO-N	CI
DEG	0.86	0.79	0.87	0.82
LDEG	0.66	0.59	0.7	0.64
EDEG	0.88	0.82	0.88	0.82

that there are statistically significant differences between UNS-PMF male and female researchers considering their social importance. Namely, UNS-PMF male researchers do not tend to be dominant in the core of the co-authorship network, but they more frequently appear as bridges that connect different, highly cohesive research groups. Statistically significant gender differences can be also observed for the clustering coefficient: ego-networks of UNS-PMF female researchers tend to be slightly more cohesive than ego-networks of UNS-PMF male researchers. This suggests that UNS-PMF female researchers tend to stimulate their unconnected collaborators to work together more often compared to UNS-PMF male researchers. Having in mind that UNS-PMF male researchers tend to have higher betweenness centrality we can conclude the following:

- UNS-PMF male researchers tend to be more important for the cohesion of our institution at the macro scale – more often they connect different research groups, but
- UNS-PMF female researchers tend to be more important for the cohesion of our institution at the micro scale – more often they connect researchers from the same research group which previously have not collaborated.

6   Integration of Analytical Tools into CRIS

The main subject in the future work in this area is integration of GERBER and similar analytical tools with CRIS UNS. This can be done by applying a service oriented architecture in which CRIS UNS exposes services to the analytical tools. These services will include operations for obtaining relevant data that are inputs for analysis.

Instead of dividing the analysis in two independent stages, (1) export of all relevant data to XML documents and (2) loading data from these documents, the better solution is to load data directly from the CRIS UNS database through appropriate services. Some benefits of the proposed approach are:

- retrieving the updated states of the entities (as CRIS UNS is in constant use by authors who enter their publications, the latest state can be obtained only by real-time access),
- obtaining only data that are relevant for the analysis, and omitting redundant elements that will influence memory usage,
- exposing the complete CRIS UNS metadata set for analysis, including the attributes that are not recognised as relevant in time of export in the current solution.

As for the concrete technology and implementation of the services there are basically two solutions: implementing the web service with WSDL and SOAP and exchanging XML documents, or using the REST architectural style and exchanging either XML documents or JSON objects. Although there are some advantages of SOAP-based services in terms of tools support and type safety, REST services become very popular these days mostly due to ease of implementation based on the HTTP protocol.

The suggested architecture is shown in Fig. 2. GERBER (or some other analytical tool) accesses CRIS UNS data through the REST API. The complete set of operations remains to be determined but some of the operations are shown in the figure. These are the following operations: (1) retrieve all researchers for the given institution, (2) retrieve all publications for the given researcher, and (3) retrieve all publications entered after the given date. The third operation will improve the efficiency of an analytical tool such as GERBER because instead of loading all publications, we can load only those entered after the date of last access.

The architecture presented in Fig. 2 with a precisely defined set of operations is applicable for any analytical tool and any research information system. In other

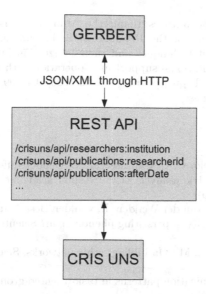

Fig. 2. GEBER and CRIS UNS integration through the REST API.

words, if we define the complete set of operations for the REST API, and extend GERBER to load data through that API, any other research information system that implements the API can use GERBER for gender analysis.

7   Conclusions and Future Work

As the main contribution of the paper we described the methodology and accompanying tool (GERBER) for gender-based evaluation of researchers. Using GERBER we analyzed gender differences for researchers employed at our faculty (UNS-PMF) relying on data exported from our official CRIS UNS system. The analysis showed that there are no statistically significant gender differences considering productivity and collaborativity of UNS-PMF researchers. On the other hand, gender differences can be observed with respect to the role of researchers in the process of improvement of institutional cohesion.

In future work we plan to improve GERBER in two ways: (1) by adding a new class of author metrics that consider weights of links in co-authorship networks, and (2) by including other culture-sensitive attributes such as age and academic rank in gender-based evaluation of researchers.

Finally, we plan to fully integrate GERBER into CRIS UNS as an analytic service. Full integration of GERBER into CRIS UNS will enable continuous gender-based evaluation of researchers employed at the University of Novi Sad. On the basis of the previously mentioned integration we will be in the position to propose general methodological and technical guidelines (APIs) for culture-sensitive extensions of CRISs.

344   M. Savić et al.

Acknowledgments. The authors thank the Ministry of Education, Science and Technological Development of the Republic of Serbia for support through project no. OI174023, "Intelligent techniques and their integration into wide-spectrum decision support," and for additional support in cooperation with the Slovenian Research Agency through bilateral project no. 451-03-3095/2014-09/43, "Culture-sensitive aspects in data technologies."

References

1. Abramo, G., D'Angelo, C.A., Caprasecca, A.: Gender differences in research productivity: a bibliometric analysis of the Italian academic system. Scientometrics **79**(3), 517–539 (2009)
2. van Arensbergen, P., van der Weijden, I., van den Besselaar, P.: Gender differences in scientific productivity: a persisting phenomenon? Scientometrics **93**(3), 857–868 (2012)
3. Batagelj, V., Cerinšek, M.: On bibliographic networks. Scientometrics **96**(3), 845–864 (2013)
4. Bavelas, A.: Communication patterns in task-oriented groups. J. Acoust. Soc. Am. **22**(6), 725–730 (1950)
5. Bayer, A.E.: Teaching faculty in academe: 1972–73. ACE Research Reports 8. American Council on Education, Washington, DC, USA (1973)
6. Bordons, M., Morillo, F., Fernández, M.T., Gómez, I.: One step further in the production of bibliometric indicators at the micro level: differences by gender and professional category of scientists. Scientometrics **57**(2), 159–173 (2003)
7. Cavero, J.M., Vela, B., Cáceres, P., Cuesta, C., Sierra-Alonso, A.: The evolution of female authorship in computing research. Scientometrics **103**(1), 85–100 (2015)
8. Cole, J.R.: Fair Science: Women in the Scientific Community. The Free Press, New York (1979)
9. Dehdarirad, T., Villarroya, A., Barrios, M.: Research on women in science and higher education: a bibliometric analysis. Scientometrics **103**(3), 795–812 (2015)
10. Dimić Surla, B., Segedinac, M., Ivanović, D.: A BIBO ontology extension for evaluation of scientific research results. In: Proceedings of the Fifth Balkan Conference in Informatics, pp. 275–278. ACM (2012)
11. Erceg-Hurn, D.M., Mirosevich, V.M.: Modern robust statistical methods: an easy way to maximize the accuracy and power of your research. Am. Psychol. **63**(7), 591–601 (2008)
12. euroCRIS: euroCRIS Current Resesarch Information Systems. http://www.eurocris.org/
13. euroCRIS: CERIF 1.3 Full Data Model (FDM) Introduction and Specification (2012). http://eurocris.org/Uploads/Web%20pages/CERIF-1.3/Specifications/CERIF1.3_FDM.pdf
14. Feller, W.: On the Kolmogorov-Smirnov limit theorems for empirical distributions. Ann. Math. Stat. **19**(2), 177–189 (1948)
15. Fong, C.J., Yoo, J.H., Jones, S.J., Torres, L.G., Decker, M.L.: Trends in female authorships, editorial board memberships, and editorships in educational psychology journals from 2003 to 2008. Educ. Psychol. Rev. **21**(3), 267–277 (2009)
16. Freeman, L.C.: A set of measures of centrality based on betweenness. Sociometry **40**, 35–41 (1977)
17. Gander, J.P.: Faculty gender effects on academic research and teaching. Res. High. Educ. **40**(2), 171–184 (1999)

18. Ivanović, D., Ivanović, L., Dimić Surla, B.: Multi-interoperable CRIS repository. Procedia Computer Science **33**, 86–91 (2014)
19. Ivanovic, D., Surla, D., Konjovic, Z.: CERIF compatible data model based on MARC 21 format. Electron. Libr. **29**(1), 52–70 (2011)
20. Ivanović, D., Surla, D., Racković, M.: Journal evaluation based on bibliometric indicators and the CERIF data model. Comput. Sci. Inf. Syst. **9**(2), 791–811 (2012)
21. König, C.J., Fell, C.B., Kellnhofer, L., Schui, G.: Are there gender differences among researchers from industrial/organizational psychology? Scientometrics **105**(3), 1931–1952 (2015)
22. Lindsey, D.: Production and citation measures in the sociology of science: the problem of multiple authorship. Soc. Stud. Sci. **10**(2), 145–162 (1980)
23. Lu, H., Feng, Y.: A measure of authors centrality in co-authorship networks based on the distribution of collaborative relationships. Scientometrics **81**(2), 499–511 (2009)
24. Mann, H.B., Whitney, D.R.: On a test of whether one of two random variables is stochastically larger than the other. Ann. Math. Stat. **18**(1), 50–60 (1947)
25. Milosavljevic, G., Ivanovic, D., Surla, D., Milosavljevic, B.: Automated construction of the user interface for a CERIF-compliant research management system. Electron. Libr. **29**(5), 565–588 (2011)
26. Newman, M.E.J.: Who is the best connected scientist? a study of scientific coauthorship networks. In: Ben-Naim, E., Frauenfelder, H., Toroczkai, Z. (eds.) Complex Networks. Lecture Notes in Physics, vol. 650, pp. 337–370. Springer, Heidelberg (2004)
27. Ozel, B., Kretschmer, H., Kretschmer, T.: Co-authorship pair distribution patterns by gender. Scientometrics **98**(1), 703–723 (2014)
28. Paul-Hus, A., Bouvier, R.L., Ni, C., Sugimoto, C.R., Pislyakov, V., Larivière, V.: Forty years of gender disparities in Russian science: a historical bibliometric analysis. Scientometrics **102**(2), 1541–1553 (2015)
29. Prpić, K.: Gender and productivity differentials in science. Scientometrics **55**(1), 27–58 (2002)
30. Savić, M., Ivanović, M., Radovanović, M., Ognjanović, Z., Pejović, A., Krüger, T.J.: The structure and evolution of scientific collaboration in Serbian mathematical journals. Scientometrics **101**(3), 1805–1830 (2014)
31. Sotudeh, H., Khoshian, N.: Gender differences in science: the case of scientific productivity in nano science & technology during 2005–2007. Scientometrics **98**(1), 457–472 (2014)
32. The Library of Congress: MARC Standards. http://www.loc.gov/marc/
33. Watts, D.J., Strogatz, S.H.: Collective dynamics of "small-world" networks. Nature **393**, 440–442 (1998)
34. Xie, Y., Shauman, K.A.: Sex differences in research productivity: new evidence about an old puzzle. Am. Sociol. Rev. **63**, 847–870 (1998)

Word Similarity Based on Domain Graph

Fumito Konaka$^{(\boxtimes)}$ and Takao Miura

Department of Advanced Sciences, Hosei University,
3-7-2 KajinoCho, Koganei, Tokyo 184–8584, Japan
`fumito.konaka.2t@stu.hosei.ac.jp`, `miurat@hosei.ac.jp`

Abstract. In this work we propose a new formalization for word similarity. Assuming that each word corresponds to unit of semantics, called *synset*, with categorical features, called *domain*, we construct a *domain graph* of a synset which is all the hypernyms which belong to the domain of the synset. Here we take an advantage of domain graphs to reflect semantic aspect of words. In experiments we show how well the domain graph approach goes well with word similarity. Then we extend sentence similarity (or Semantic Textual Similarity) independent of *Bag-of-Words*.

Keywords: Domain graph · Synsets · Similarity

1 Introduction

Nowadays we have huge amount of digital information such as Web. Typical examples are Social Network Service (SNS), such as twitter and BLOGs, which allows people to share their activities, interests and backgrounds. Text in SNS are generally composed of short sentences with semantic ambiguity (synonymous/homonymous words and jargons) and spelling inconsistency (or, *orthographic variants* of words) such as never/nevr. There can be no systematic formulation and we need computer-assisted approach to tackle with these problems.

A typical application is information retrieval and text mining by which we may get to the heart of interests in large datasets. In information retrieval, each document is described by a multiset over words, called *Bag-of-Words* (BOW). Here we construct a vector to each multiset where the column contains Term Frequency or the one multiplied by Inverse Document Frequency. The approach is called *Vector Space Model* (VSM). BOW approach assumes that a multiset describes *stable* and *frequent* meaning. For example, a multiset {John, Dog, Bite} means "a Dog Bites John" but not "John Bites a Dog". All these mean, for example, that we can give document similarity and ranking using vector calculation.

However, VSM is not useful to short documents, since individual words may carry a variety of semantics and context by word-order. That's why VSM doesn't always go well with synonymous/homonymous situation and we hardly overcome Word Sense Disambiguity issues.

One of the difficulties is how to define similarity between sentences independent of VSM. We like to give sentence similarity not based on syntactic aspects

© Springer International Publishing Switzerland 2016
L. Bellatreche et al. (Eds.): MEDI 2016, LNCS 9893, pp. 346–357, 2016.
DOI: 10.1007/978-3-319-45547-1_27

but on semantic ones so that we examine more powerful retrieval on both long and short documents, including SNS texts [9].

This work contributes to the following points: First, we propose a new similarity between two words to reflect semantic aspects and to give indexing. Second, we improve query efficiency with the much simpler indices to words. Finally, we show the effectiveness of new similarity over SNS sentences.

The rest of the paper is organized as follows. In Sect. 2 we introduce several concepts and discuss why it is hard to achieve the definition of semantic similarity. In Sect. 3 we propose our approach and show some experimental results in Sect. 4 to see how effective our approach works. In Sect. 5 we conclude this work.

2 Word Similarity

To describe word similarity, there are two kinds of approaches, *knowledge-based* and *corpus-based*. Knowledge-based similarity means that, using semantic structures such as ontology, words are defined similar by evaluating the structure.

Usually *knowledge-base* consists of many *entry words*, each of which contains several units (*synsets*) of semantics, explanation sentences to each synset and relations (*links*) to other synsets. The links describe several semantic ties, called *ontology*, such as *hypernyms, synonyms, homonyms, antonyms* and so on. A synonym means several words share identical synset and a homonym means a single word carries multiple synsets. One of the typical examples is WordNet [11], an ontology dictionary containing 155,287 words which are divided into 117,659 synsets, each of them corresponds to a synonymous group of words. Very often we see several links to other synsets of hypernyms (broader level) which have strong relationship of semantic similarity. For example, two words `Corgi` and `Bulldog` are similar because both are dogs where the synsets `corgi`, `bulldog` are defined in advance and they have links to a synset `dog`. In a same way, they are similar because both are mammals and because both are animals. However `Siamese` and `Bulldog` are not similar because both are not dog, but similar because both are mammals and because both are animals. We could even go so far as to say everything is similar because it is an object.

There have been several kinds of similarities proposed so far using WordNet, putting attention on the links and some of them are available and open in WordNet::Similarity or NLTK[1]. Some of the similarity definitions are provided as *Path, Lch, WuPalmer, Res, Jcn* and *Lin* as follows.

$$Path = \max_{s_i,s_j \in w_1,w_2} - \log pathlen(s_i, s_j) \tag{1}$$

$$Lch = \max_{s_i,s_j} - \log \frac{pathlen(s_i, s_j)}{2 \times D} \tag{2}$$

$$WuPalmer = \max_{s_i,s_j} \frac{2 \times depth(LCS(s_i, s_j))}{depth(s_i) + depth(s_j)} \tag{3}$$

---

[1] http://wn-similarity.sourceforge.net/, http://www.nltk.org/.

$$Res = \max_{s_i,s_j} - \log P(LCS(s_i, s_j)) \tag{4}$$

$$Jcn = \max_{s_i,s_j} \frac{1}{2 \times \log P(LCS(s_i, s_j)) - (\log P(s_i) + \log P(s_j))} \tag{5}$$

$$Lin = \max_{s_i,s_j} \frac{2 \times \log P(LCS(s_i, s_j))}{\log P(s_i) + \log P(s_j)} \tag{6}$$

In the definitions, w_1, w_2 mean words and s_i, s_j synsets belonged to words.

While *Path*, *Lch* and *WuPalmer* are defined based on minimum path length, all of *Res*, *Jcn*, *Lin* are based on entropy. Both *WuPalmer* and *Jcn* assume synsets become similar when they locate at deep level.

There exist cyclic structures among *verb* relationship in WordNet 3.0 as in a Fig. 1 [13]. Remember a *cycle* means a path (a sequence of arcs) such that there exist arcs $a_1, a_2, a_2, .., a_n$ and $a_1 = a_n$. We say a *loop* if $n = 1$. Then a graph is called *cyclic*. Otherwise *acyclic*. Also a *multiple path* means there are multiple distinct paths from a to b, or a node b has multiple parents[2]. Acyclic graphs may have multiple paths. Note that similarity based on minimum path length cannot be well-defined in a case of multiple paths as in the right of a Fig. 1.

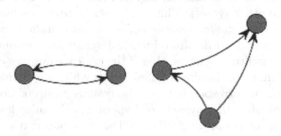

Fig. 1. Cycle and multiple path

As for corpus-based similarity, we take analytical information and apply characteristic features for similarity. One of the approach take advantages of Latent Semantic Analysis Here we build up a document matrix D over words and documents and decompose D into $D = U \Sigma V^T$ by Singular Value Decomposition. The technique is based on Principal Component Analysis and the *latent semantics* can be defined using co-occurrence of words and documents. Similarity corresponds to the one between two vectors of words over latent semantics.

3   Domain Graph and Similarity

Let us introduce a new similarity between words based on knowledge-base to capture their own semantic aspects. As we said previously, VSM means that we interpret words and sentences in a "common" way, i.e., we have frequent

---

[2] Sometimes this is called a *ring*.

interpretation to all the sentences and words even if we like to do that differently. The new similarity allows us to reflect role and relationship of the words.

Generally each word may correspond to a (non-empty) set of synsets with several features such as an ontological structure (considered as a directed graph) among synsets. To introduce similarity between two words, we discuss *Domain Graph* by which we take knowledge-base similarity into consideration, which mean we put our stress on relationship among words defined by knowledge-base. Generally word similarity can be defined with the one of synsets and ontology relationship among synsets: the stronger similarity means the closer relationship in a sense of path length or far apart distance. When two words are not similar, their synsets should be far apart with each other, the common synset has higher level in the ontology. Our discussion could have same motivation as *WuPalmar* and *Jcn*, but the similarity can be simple and efficient since we give the similarity in terms of graph structures.

Given a word, we assume there happen several synsets and each synset has *domain* feature as well as the explanation and links. A problem to decide which synset we think about, is called *Word Sense Disambiguation* (WSD) [12] and here we don't discuss WSD any more. Each synset belongs to several domains. For example, in WordNet, *Lexicographer File Names* (or *domains*) are defined as a Table 1[3]. Note that every domain is complementary to ontology, i.e., a collection of short-cuts over paths, apart from levels.

The idea of *Domain Graph* comes from hypernym relationship consisting of nodes (synsets) and arcs (hypernym relationship) between synsets. We may consider domains as a new feature of a synset (a node). Given a word w with the synset s_w, a *Domain Graph* of w means all the hypernyms (ancestors) in such a way that every path belongs to one of the domains of s_w. In Domain Graph, it is assumed that every pair of synsets at shallow level may not be similar. This means a notion of domains allows us to ignore high levels of abstraction (such as **object**) and to overlap several parts in the ontology structure.

The graph can be described by *sub-graph* (nodes and arcs) in the directed graph. To examine how similar two words are, let us define similarity of graphs. Considered P, Q as two sets of nodes, the most common similarity is *Jaccard* coefficient, denoted by $Jacc(P, Q) = \frac{|P \cap Q|}{|P \cup Q|}$, where $| P |$ means the number of nodes in P. Note it may take time to obtain the co-efficient to large P, Q.

Let us define the *Domain Graph similarity* of two words w_1, w_2. Let s_1, s_2 be synsets corresponded to w_1, w_2 respectively. The DG similarity is defined to be the Jaccard similarity of $G(s_1)$ and $G(s_2)$ where $G(s)$ means all the nodes in the sub-graph of s in the domain graph of interests.

$$DGsimilarity(w_1, w_2) = Jacc(G(s_1), G(s_2))$$

---

[3] There are 45 *Lexicographer Files* based on syntactic category and logical groupings. They contain synsets during WordNet development. There is another approach *WordNet Domains* which is a lexical resource created in a semi-automatic way by augmenting WordNet with domain labels. To each synset, there exists at least one semantic domain label annotated by hands from 200 labels [1].

Minimum Hash (MinHash) function h provides us with efficient computation [3] for Jaccard coefficients. In fact, we can estimate the coefficient $Jacc(p, q)$ which is equal to the probability of min $h(p)$ = min $h(q)$. Given k MinHash functions and n function values to p, q that are matched, $Jacc(p, q)$ should be simply n/k, i.e., $\hat{J} = n/k$. Since we can obtain k hash values immediately, we can estimate Jaccard coefficients very quickly without any structural information such as indices.

Table 1. Excerpt from domains over synsets

ID	Domain	Description
00	adj.all	All adjective clusters
01	adj.pert	Relational adjectives (pertainyms)
02	adv.all	All adverbs
03	noun.Tops	Unique beginner for nouns
04	noun.act	Nouns denoting acts or actions
05	noun.animal	Nouns denoting animals
29	verb.body	Verbs of grooming, dressing and bodily care
30	verb.change	Verbs of size, temperature change, intensifying, etc.
31	verb.cognition	Verbs of thinking, judging, analyzing, doubting
44	adj.ppl	Participial adjectives

Let us discuss how to construct Domain Graph. Among others, we need WSD process to specify which synset we have to a word w. Figure 2 shows algorithms for "`makeDomainGraph`".

To select single synset to w, we do WSD process (*doWSD* in step 1) based on Lesk Algorithm [12] as shown in an algorithm for "`scanDict`" Here we examine how many relevant words we have with respect to a query, and choose the synset of the biggest ratio. In the algorithm for "`makeDomainGraph`", we select a synset s_w defined as below:

$$s_w = argmax_{s \in Synsets} \frac{|T \cap (gloss(s) \cup synonyms(s))|}{|gloss(s) \cup synonyms(s)|}$$

In the definition, given a word w in the algorithm for "`makeDomainGraph`", *Synsets* means all the synsets the word w has, T all the words appeared in a query, $gloss(s)$ all the words appear in the explanation (in WordNet) of a synset s and $synonyms(s)$ all the words containing s as its synset.

Let $D(s_w)$ be a domain (through WSD) which a synset s_w of a word w belongs to. Let c be a hypernym of s_w, then we follow the link to c as long as c belongs to $D(s_w)$. In short, a *Domain Graph* of w means all the hypernyms (ancestors) of the domain $D(s_w)$.

Let us show areas in a Fig. 3. Let an area surrounded by solid lines be baseline synsets given by *Path* (formula 1), and an area by dotted lines be synsets in a

---

Algorithm 1 makeDomainGraph(Sentence T, Word $w \in T$)

Output: The Set of Subgraphs *DomainGraph(w)*

1: Synset $s_w \leftarrow doWSD(w,T)$, Domain $D(s_w)$
2: *DomainGraph(w)* ← *null*
3: *scanDict(s_w, $D(s_w)$, DomainGraph(w))*

Algorithm 2 scanDict(Synset s, Domain D, *DomainGraph*)

Output: *DomainGraph*

1: *DomainGraph.add(subgraphs)*
2: The List of Hypernyms *HList* ← *getHypernyms(s)*
3: **for each** hypernym h in *HList* **do**
4:     CurrentSynest $c \leftarrow h$, CurrentDomain $D(c)$
5:     **if** $D(c) = D$ **then**
6:         *scanDict(c, D, DomainGraph)*
7:     **end if**
8: **end for**

Fig. 2. Proposed algorithms

domain graph. We examine the similarity of synsets A and B in the left of the Fig. 3, and the one of A and A' in the right of the Fig. 3. Since a node A' has an arc to D but A doesn't, A' is more similar to B compared to A. In fact, in the baseline area, there are 2 arcs (AC and BC; A'C and BC) of the shortest path in a Fig. 3 so that we have same similarity of AB and A'B. On the other hand, in the area by domain graph, we have different situation. We don't have same similarity AB and A'B because there are 3 arcs ACD and BD on left and 2 arcs A'D and BD on right.

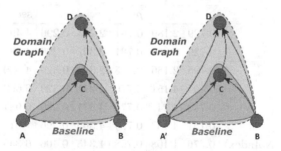

Fig. 3. Area by baseline and domain graphs

4   Experiments

In this section let us discuss experimental results to examine the proposed approach. First, we examine the effectiveness of domain graph by comparing several similarities among words through our approach with and without the domain graphs. Second we extend our approach to sentence similarity. We discuss Domain Graph Approach of words to sentences.

In these experiments, we assume WordNet 3.0 and its domains. We also assume $k = 10$ for a MinHash function *murmurhash3* (which is obtained by small experiments) through experimental Java libraries [7].

4.1   Similarity Among Words

Here we examine 4 corpus sets each of which has score values to each pair of words by hands: Li30 [10] RG65 [14] WS353 [6] and VP130 [16]. Once we obtain our similarity values, we compare them with the scores within by looking at Spearman order-correlations. In this case, we examine all the synsets of word pairs to obtain the maximum similarity, same as formulas (1)–(6).

We give similarity between two words with domain graph and without. As the baseline similarity values, we examine $Path, Lch, WuPalmer, Res, Jcn$ and Lin (formulas (1)–(6)) in Natural Language Took Kit (NLTK). Also, as the ontology in WordNet, we apply WS4J[4] as baseline Paths.

We show the results in a Table 2 which contains correlation values (ρ) and execution time (sec). The tables shows that ρ results with domain graph are the best ones except VP130, slightly superior to the one without: +0.045(Li30), +0.004(RG65), +0.12(WS353) and +0.032(VP130). The half of the execution shows the best ones too.

Table 2. Word similarity and efficiency

	Corpus							
	Li30		RG65		WS353		VP130	
	ρ	sec	ρ	sec	ρ	sec	ρ	sec
Path	0.729	2.189	0.781	2.243	0.296	4.495	0.725	2.817
Lch	0.729	2.219	0.781	2.302	0.296	4.58	0.725	2.776
WuPalmer	0.705	2.186	0.755	2.3	0.329	4.699	0.728	2.839
Res	0.704	4.151	0.776	4.271	0.329	6.608	0.661	4.717
Jcn	0.742	4.24	0.775	4.331	0.280	6.981	0.695	4.878
Lin	0.761	4.168	0.784	4.369	0.296	7.01	0.689	4.859
DomianGraph (NoIndex)	0.776	1.108	0.798	1.345	0.406	6.343	0.693	3.863
(Index)		0.127		0.208		0.778		0.721
No Domain	0.731	1.462	0.794	1.92	0.286	10.491	0.661	4.107

As seen easily, the domain graph approach in most of the corpus has better correlation values to others (ρ). Note we don't discuss WSD issue about s_w

---

[4] https://code.google.com/archive/p/ws4j/.

to construct domain graphs. There is no sharp distinction with and without domain graph in our approach, because the domain graphs contain few multiple paths (say, only 8 nodes have multiple parent nodes within whole relations in WordNet 3.0 [13]) so that the results by our approach become the best but no big difference. As for execution efficiency, our graph approach is superior to others in LI30 and RG65, and equal in VP130. Indexed one means all the hash values are prepared in advance and no CPU overhead arises.

4.2 Sentence Similarity

Let us examine how well the proposed approach goes with short sentences. Here we examine PIT2015 corpus, i.e., we examine PIT-2015 Twitter Paraphrase Corpus[5] [15] as a test corpus. Each pair has scored by Amazon Mechanical turk in terms of 0 (not similar) to 5 (most similar). Also morphological and proper noun information have been attached to each word.

Table 3. Sentence pairs in PIT2015

Similarity	Sentence 1	Sentence 2
0	What the hell is Brandon bass thinking	Brandon Bass is shutting Carmelo down
1	EJ Manuel Is the 1st qb taken huh	1st QB off of the board
2	Aaron dobson is a smart pick	They pluck Aaron Dobson from the Herd
3	Please give the Avs a win	Come on avs be somebody
4	Barry Sanders really won the Madden cover	So Barry Sanders is on the cover
5	I liked that video body party	I like that body party joint from Ciara

Let us show some pair of PIT2015 corpus in a Table 3. We apply preprocessing (lowercase conversion and making original form by TreeTagger[6]) to the corpus and provide the feature information as well as the one by the corpus.

Here we add *character bigram, trigram* for characteristic words and *word unigram, bigram* for word sequences to every sentence in a form of Jaccard coefficients as the feature values. Then we examine sentence similarity by Support Vector Regression (SVR) by using the features above. Given a sentence $n = 1, .., N$, let x_n be a feature vector of 5-dimension for the n-th sentence: x_n^1, x_n^2 for character bigram, character trigram respectively, x_n^3, x_n^4 for word unigram, word bigram respectively and x_n^5 for domain graph. Then $y(x_n)$ means the regression value to the 5 features of x_n through SVR. Using LIBSVM [2], we apply ε-SVR

---

[5] It includes many short sentences extracted at more than 500 Twitter sites from April 24, 2013 to May 3, 2013. The corpus contain 17,790 pairs of sentences divided into 13,063 pairs for training and 4,727 pairs for development. And there are 972 pairs included for test. We examine these 13,063 pairs for training and the 972 pairs for test.

[6] http://www.cis.uni-muenchen.de/~schmid/tools/TreeTagger/.

with default parameters by minimizing V targeted for better fitting as below:

$$V = C \sum_{n=1}^{N} (\xi_n + \hat{\xi}_n) + Z$$

$$\xi_n = \begin{cases} 0 \ if \ (t_n \leq y(x_n) + \varepsilon) \\ \xi_n \ if \ (t_n > y(x_n) + \varepsilon) \end{cases}, \quad \hat{\xi}_n = \begin{cases} 0 \ if \ (t_n \geq y(x_n) + \varepsilon) \\ \hat{\xi}_n \ if \ (t_n < y(x_n) + \varepsilon) \end{cases}$$

In the definition of V, the first term shows a penalty to data beyond an allowable error ε for regression while the second term Z means its normalization. We put the similarity values to each pair by SVR and compare them with the one in the corpus and we evaluate the result by Pearson correlations.

As the baseline, we discuss ASOBEK [5] proposed by Eyecioglu which is based on SVR with character bigram (x_n^1) and word unigram (x_n^3), Logistic Regression (LR) based on word n-gram (x_n^3, x_n^4) by Das [4], and Weighted Textual Matrix Factorization (WTMF) by Guo [8]. We apply DomainGraph approach to all the features $(x_n^1, .., x_n^5)$, the one except character bigram/trigram $(x_n^3, .., x_n^5)$ and the one with only domain graph (x_n^5) feature.

Let us show the result in a Table 4. Our approach with all the features scored the best because of domain graph feature (x_n^5). Compared to ASOBEK character 2-gram and (word 1-gram) and LR (word n-gram), this approach is at least 9.9 % better but comparable. So is true for our domain graph approach without character n-gram (14.9 % better). On the other hand, only one feature in word 1-gram and domain graph doesn't work well.

Table 4. Sentence similarity results (PIT2015)

	Model	Features	Correlation	Improvement
(1)	ASOBEK	x_n^1, x_n^3	0.504	0.90
(2)		x_n^3	0.071	0.13
(3)	LR	x_n^3, x_n^4	0.511	0.91
(4)	WTMF		0.35	0.62
(5)	Our Approach	$x_n^1, ..., x_n^5$	0.561	1.00
(6)		x_n^3, x_n^4, x_n^5	0.488	0.87
(7)		x_n^5	0.071	0.13

First of all, let us discuss why WTMF doesn't work well. As shown in the Table 3, WTMF works poor (62 %), because the approach comes from word co-occurrence in documents and the situation can be hardly detected in short sentences. It seems hard to solve the problem by Matrix Factorization.

In ASOBEK, two sentences in a Table 5 (1) and (2) look similar to (2). Note (1') and (2') contain words/morphemes and look alike. The corpus gives the similarity 4 while the correlation is 0.727 by our approach. The major difference of two ASOBEK comes from character bigram (x_n^1). Looking into the detail, we have Jaccard coefficients of character bigram 0.5714, character trigram 0.5294, word unigram 0.4375, and word bigram 0.3125 and domain graph 0.7241. ASOBEK (1) takes x_n^1, x_n^3 into consideration and the x_n^1 is bigger than x_n^3, so ASOBEK (2) goes worse. On the other hand, our approach (5) is 14.9 % better than (6) since x_n^5 is dominant.

Table 5. Similar sentences

(1) MHP wishes you a safe and happy Memorial Day weekend
(2) We hope that everyone has a very safe and happy Memorial Day Weekend
(1') wish#verb, memorial#noun, day#noun, weekend#noun
(2') hope#verb, have#verb, memorial#noun, day#noun, weekend#noun

Our approach (7) works poor because every sentence contains many words and word unigram and bigram should be considered. It is said that *character n-gram* may work well for spelling inconsistency. Some examples in PIT2015 are the following: "The **ungeekedeliteschicago** Daily is out", "Lydia is a **GROOOOOOOWN** woman", "I will **brin** them Taco Bell chipotle soo they let me stay".

Let us go into the detail of spelling inconsistency issue. We examine another corpus SemEval2012 MSRpar, MSRvid and SMTeuroparl for short sentences with training data, because they contain no spelling inconsistency. In a Table 6 we show the comparison results with and without character n-gram features (x_n^1, x_n^2). As seen easily, there happen no difference and we can say *character n-gram* maynot be useful for spelling inconsistency issue by our approach.

Table 6. Sentence similarity results (SemEval2012)

Model	Feature1 x_n^3, x_n^4, x_n^5	Feature 2 $x_n^1, x_n^2, x_n^3, x_n^4, x_n^5$	Improvement
MSRpar	0.409	0.610	1.49
MSRvid	0.684	0.811	1.19
SMTeuroparl	0.501	0.552	1.10
PIT2015	0.488	0.561	1.15

5   Conclusion

In this work, we have proposed a new similarity among words using domain graph. The similarity provides us with ontological aspects on similarity without trivial knowledge often appearing at shallow level. Also we have discussed semantic properties of the similarity based on domain graph independent of BOW aspects. We have shown how to obtain features of domain graph by minimum hash techniques so that the approach can be useful for information retrieval.

We have shown the effectiveness of our approach by experiments. The experiments show that the results by our approach become the best (but no big difference because of WordNet ontology) while the execution efficiencies are comparable. By extending the approach for sentence similarity, we have also shown domain graph approach works best, say, at least improved 9.9 %, (because of domain graph feature) than other baseline. All these show our approach is promising for query to short sentences.

Some problems remain unsolved. Often spelling inconsistency makes the similarity worse or incorrect, but no sharp solution is proposed until now. Character n-grams or any other techniques are not enough to improve queries, but domain graph with word normalization could help the situation better.

References

1. Bentivogli, L., Forner, P., Magnini, B., Pianta, E.: Revising WordNet domains hierarchy: semantics, coverage, and balancing. In: COLING 2004 Workshop on "Multilingual Linguistic Resources", pp. 101–108 (2004)
2. Chang, C.C., Lin, C.-J.: LIBSVM: a library for support vector machines. ACM Trans. Intell. Syst. Technol. (TIST) $\mathbf{2}$(3), 27 (2011)
3. Cohen, E., et al.: Finding interesting associations without support pruning. IEEE Trans. Knowl. Data Eng. $\mathbf{13}$(1), 64–78 (2001)
4. Das, D., Smith, N.A.: Paraphrase identification as probabilistic quasi-synchronous recognition. In: Proceedings of the Joint Conference of the 47th Annual Meeting of the ACL and the 4th International Joint Conference on Natural Language Processing of the AFNLP, vol. 1. Association for Computational Linguistics, pp. 468–476 (2009)
5. Eyecioglu, A., Keller, B.: ASOBEK: twitter paraphrase identification with simple overlap features and SVMs. In: Proceedings of SemEval (2015)
6. Finkeltsein, L., et al.: Placing search in context: the concept revisited. In: Proceedings of the 10th International Conference on World Wide Web. ACM, pp. 406–414 (2001)
7. Finlayson, M.A.: Java libraries for accessing the Princeton WordNet: comparison and evaluation. In: Proceedings of the 7th Global Wordnet Conference, Tartu, Estonia (2014)
8. Guo, W., Diab, M.: Modeling sentences in the latent space. In: Proceedings of the 50th Annual Meeting of the Association for Computational Linguistics: Long Papers, vol. 1. Association for Computational Linguistics, pp. 864–872 (2012)
9. Konaka, F., Miura, T.: Textual similarity for word sequences. In: Amato, G., Connor, R., Falchi, F., Gennaro, C. (eds.) SISAP 2015. LNCS, vol. 9371, pp. 244–249. Springer, Heidelberg (2015). doi:10.1007/978-3-319-25087-8_23
10. Li, Y., et al.: Sentence similarity based on semantic nets and corpus statistics. IEEE Trans. Knowl. Data Eng. $\mathbf{18}$(8), 1138–1150 (2006)
11. Miller, G.A.: WordNet: a lexical database for English. Commun. ACM $\mathbf{38}$(11), 39–41 (1995)

12. Navigli, R.: Word sense disambiguation: a survey. ACM Comput. Surv. (CSUR) **41**(2), 10 (2009)
13. Richens, T.: Anomalies in the WordNet verb hierarchy. In: Proceedings of the 22nd International Conference on Computational Linguistics, vol. 1. Association for Computational Linguistics, pp. 729–736 (2008)
14. Rubenstein, H., Goodenough, J.B.: Contextual correlates of synonymy. Commun. ACM **8**(10), 627–633 (1965)
15. Xu, W., Callison-Burch, C., Dolan, W.B.: SemEval-2015 task 1: paraphrase and semantic similarity in Twitter (PIT). In: Proceedings of the 9th International Workshop on Semantic Evaluation (SemEval) (2015)
16. Yang, D., Powers, D.M.W.: Verb similarity on the taxonomy of WordNet. Masaryk University (2006)

Author Index

Printed in the United States
By Bookmasters